Becoming a Courageous Manager:
Overcoming Career Problems of New Managers

Ross Arkell Webber

Prentice Hall, Englewood Cliffs, NJ 07632

Webber, Ross A.
    Becoming a courageous manager : overcoming the career problems of
new managers / Ross Arkell Webber.
       p.   cm.
    Includes bibliographical references.
    ISBN 0-13-086372-6 : $13.25
    1. Executives--Time management--Case studies. 2. Management--Case
studies. 3. Organizational effectiveness--Case studies. 4. Career
development--Case studies.   I. Title.
HD69.T54W43   1991
6584.4'093--dc20
                                                            90-42463
                                                                CIP

Editorial/production supervision
  and interior design: Sophie Papanikolaou
Cover design: Bruce Kenselaar
Manufacturing buyers: Kelly Behr and Sue Brunke

To

Andrew Ronald DePietro
Jillian Clair Foradora Bannister
Meghan Jane Stevens Bannister

May They Grow Up To Be As Courageous as Their Parents

© 1991 by Prentice-Hall, Inc.
A division of Simon & Schuster
Englewood Cliffs, New Jersey 07632

For information about our audio products, write us at:
Newbridge Book Clubs, 3000 Cindel Drive, Delran, NJ 08370

The publisher offers discounts on this book when ordered
in bulk quantities. For more information, write:

> Special Sales/College Marketing
> Prentice-Hall, Inc.
> College Technical and Reference Division
> Englewood Cliffs, NJ 07632

Printed in the United States of America

10 9 8 7 6 5 4 3 2 1

ISBN   0-13-086372-6

Prentice-Hall International (UK) Limited, *London*
Prentice-Hall of Australia Pty. Limited, *Sydney*
Prentice-Hall Canada Inc., *Toronto*
Prentice-Hall Hispanoamericana, S.A., *Mexico*
Prentice-Hall of India Private Limited, *New Delhi*
Prentice-Hall of Japan Inc., *Tokyo*
Prentice-Hall of Southeast Asia Pte. Ltd., *Singapore*
Editora Prentice-Hall do Brasil, Ltda *Rio de Janeiro*

Contents

Preface

This book is designed to assist present and future managers in developing the skills needed to balance their personal needs and ambitions with the legitimate demands of the organizations for which they work. It is structured around common problems young graduates confront in their careers as they move from entry-level professional roles into middle management and (hopefully) senior executive ranks. The major problems discussed in the chapters are:

- The transition from school to career and personal maturation on the job.
- Dealing with the frustration and disillusionment that so frequently accompany the early postschool years.
- Tactics for dealing with role overload and personal stress, particularly those affecting dual career families.
- Approaches to managing short-term daily and weekly time.
- Strategies for managing longer-term time.
- Techniques for provoking clarity of a superior's ambiguous delegation.
- Advice on staff-line relations and effective ways to give advice.
- Guidance on being a protégé to an older mentor.
- Understanding of the different forms of loyalty and suggestions on more and less dangerous ways to blow the whistle.
- Insight into how "being different" in gender or race can affect organizational status.
- Suggestions for how a manager can lead change in spite of possessing only ambiguous authority.
- Warnings about what happens when you become middle-aged as a manager and how you can prepare for this period.

Each chapter proceeds through five major parts:

1. An opening case describing a situation confronted by a real (but disguised) individual.
2. A section highlighting the issues raised in the case.
3. Several sections on theory and practice in the major issue areas.

4. A return to the opening case for application of theory and analysis of what actually occurred.

5. A final section summarizing advice for handling the major problems raised in the chapter.

In addition to research literature and the popular press, I draw heavily on my own experience as naval officer, engineer, consultant, professor, corporate director, and university executive. All the cases, for example, come from my consulting work or from former students and executive program participants. Many examples from political leadership are also given because such leaders provide particularly familiar illustrations of the problems with which we're concerned.

Of central focus in all chapters is courageously balancing one's commitment to the organization with one's self-obligation for growth, integrity, and health. The book's subtitle might well be: "how to survive and succeed in the organization with your sanity and integrity (more or less) intact."

I am indebted to the many former clients and students whose experiences are depicted in the cases that open each chapter. Of necessity I cannot cite their names because the cases are all disguised to protect the guilty and innocent (any similarity of names to living persons in analogous situations is purely coincidental). I can identify and thank, however, the following colleagues and friends who have contributed ideas sprinkled throughout this book: Donna Dick, Joseph Harder, Paul Rixon, Rosemary Rixon, Mary Joan Robertson, Sherwood Robertson, Patricia Schneider, William Schneider, Charles Summer, David Thomas, Carole Waraas, Ronald Waraas, and Jennifer Webber. Amanda McGibney has been invaluable in obtaining permissions and Sophie Papanikolaou indefatigable in striving for quality. I am grateful to both. Marcy Pleu, Alison Reeves, and John Willig all expressed early enthusiasm which helped me to push ahead on the project. Finally, my thanks to my son Stephen and my wife Mary Lou for whose help on the manuscript I am most grateful.

Ross Arkell Webber
The Wharton School
University of Pennsylvania
Philadelphia

Introduction:
On Heroes, Optimism,
and Cynicism

One must think like a hero to behave like a merely decent human being. (May Sarton, 1973)

Let's do this backwards by beginning rather than ending with a test. It is a simple test, anonymous, and there are no correct answers anyway (that's the new wave in academia). The test has ten questions. Please proceed in order; don't look ahead and don't look back to earlier answers even if the questions look similar.

1. Give me the name of a contemporary person (alive or deceased, but at least overlapping with your lifetime who *for you* best symbolizes the concept of heroine or hero.

_____

2. Cite three attributes that you associate with your hero or heroine that cause you to cite him or her (I'm not looking for a biography, just three nouns or adjectives).

_____

_____

Indicate the degree of your agreement or disagreement with each of the following two questions:

3. "Sound ethics are good business in the long run."

strongly agree   agree somewhat   neutral   disagree somewhat   strongly disagree

_____   _____   _____   _____   _____

4. "Competition today is stiffer and more unfair than ever. As a result many businesspeople find themselves forced to resort to practices which formerly were considered shady but which now appear necessary to survive."

strongly agree   agree somewhat   neutral   disagree somewhat   strongly disagree

_____   _____   _____   _____   _____

Please indicate what you think the *average manager* would do in each of the following three situations.

5. At a board of directors meeting, a director learns of an impending merger with a smaller company which has had an unprofitable year and whose stock is selling at very low price—a price which might well rise when news of the merger becomes public knowledge. What would the average director do?

    a. buy some in his or her own name _____
    b. have a friend or relative buy some _____
    c. do nothing _____

6. A manager earning $45,000 per year has been padding his expense account by $2,500 a year. What would the average manager think of this?

    a. acceptable if other company managers are doing the same thing _____
    b. acceptable if the manager's superior knows about it and says nothing _____
    c. unacceptable regardless of the circumstances _____

7. John Smith is a sales manager for a firm doing substantial business with the Doe Company. The purchasing manager of the Doe Company comes to town on a buying trip and asks John to arrange for him to have a prostitute that evening in his hotel room. What would the average sales manager do?

    a. refuse to make the arrangement _____
    b. wouldn't make the arrangement until a second request is made _____
    c. make the necessary arrangement _____

Please indicate what *you* would do in each of the following three situations:

8. At a board of directors meeting, you learn of an impending merger with a smaller company which has had an unprofitable year and whose stock is selling at very low price—a price which might well rise when news of the merger becomes public knowledge. What would you do?

    a. buy some in your own name _____
    b. have a friend or relative buy some _____
    c. do nothing _____

9. You earn $45,000 per year, but have an opportunity to pad your expense account by $2,500 a year. What do you think of this?

a. acceptable if other managers of the company are doing the same thing _____
b. acceptable if the manager's superior knows about it and says nothing _____
c. unacceptable regardless of the circumstances _____

10. You are a sales manager for a firm doing substantial business with the Doe Company. The purchasing manager of the Doe Company comes to town on a buying trip and asks you to arrange for him to have a prostitute that evening in his hotel room. What would you do?

a. refuse to make the arrangement _____
b. wouldn't make the arrangement until a second request is made _____
c. make the necessary arrangement _____

OPTIMISM AND CYNICISM

People vary widely in their optimism or pessimism about life. Questions 3 and 4 can suggest an index of optimism about the business environment.[1] You would be more optimistic to the extent that you *strongly agree* that "Sound ethics are good business in the long run" or *strongly disagree* that "Competition today is stiffer and more unfair than ever." Indices of optimism are summarized in Exhibit I–1 for a number of groups that have responded to these questions. Although the groups were targets of opportunity and not scientifically drawn samples, their numbers are sizable and the results do suggest a relation between age or organizational status and optimism: the younger and less experienced the respondents, *the more pessimistic they are about the general business environment and ethical trends.* In converse, older managers appear more optimistic about current and future conditions.

Those in an older generation have long liked to think that youth is naively overoptimistic about what life holds, but that *experience* would knock the idealism out of them so that they would eventually join the ranks of more realistic adults. But today's reality seems reversed. The younger appear to be less idealistic and more pessimistic. But who is more realistic? All of us have been inundated with media disclosures of new management chicanery, particularly in the financial and commodity markets in New York and Chicago. Reaching a pessimistic conclusion would certainly be understandable. Maybe older executives have reached

Optimism and Cynicism

EXHIBIT I–1: MEASURES OF OPTIMISM AND CYNICISM

Group	Mean Age	Optimism Index	Cynicism Index
Business Owner/Managers	>60	55	1.1
Corporate Executives	44	59	1.4
Middle Managers	34	41	1.4
MBA Students	25	30	1.8
Undergraduate Business Students	20	23	2.2

*Optimism Index is average of percentage of responses to Question 3 "strongly agree" and on question 4 "strongly disagree."
*Cynicism Index is Claims for Self Divided by Attributions to Others.

a level where they are insulated from messy marketplace realities or they deny them in order to justify their careers which are nearing an end.

Nonetheless, being over fifty years old myself, I tend to side with the older respondents—and with a recent survey of senior executives, deans of business schools, and members of Congress which indicates that 63 percent believe that "a business enterprise actually strengthens its competitive position by maintaining high ethical standards."[2] I think younger students and graduates are overly pessimistic about the state of business ethics and the pressures on them to behave unethically.[3] From the longer perspective of history, business behavior is *not* worse today than ever before. It is indisputably better, particularly in the most profitable firms. Good performance apparently allows greater freedom to behave ethically, rather than the other way around.[4] But of course some unethical firms are very profitable and further improvement is desirable.

Pessimism or optimism is related to one's cynicism about how others would behave in problematic situations compared with your own behavior. Questions 5 to 7 and 8 to 10 pose identical problems but are worded for how you believe the *average other* person would behave versus what *you* would do. Notice in Exhibit I–1 that all groups believe that others are a bit less ethical than they are (the Cynicism Index would be 1.0 if you attributed to others exactly the same behavior claimed for self.) Again, we find a relation to age, with the younger expressing greater cynicism about others' behavior. Forty-five-year-old business executives think approximately 30 percent of all other executives behave more unethically than they do. Young middle managers (average age thirty-three) think approximately 40 percent of others would be more unethical. Graduate MBA students think 70 percent would be more unethical. And nineteen-year-old undergraduate business students think *almost 100 percent of others would behave more unethically than they would!*

Whether this cynicism reflects the time in one's life or the times in which we are living is unknown.[5] If people become less cynical as they become older and see that everyone is not as unethical as they thought, today's young people might become less pessimistic as they climb their organizational ladders. More dangerous, however, is the self-fulfilling prophecy that cynicism promotes unethical behavior because "I'd be a fool not to if everyone else is." Nearly a quarter of 671 managers in one survey believe that *high ethics can impede a successful career—and that more than half of the executives they know would bend the rules to get ahead.*[6]

It is more likely, however, that if you believe everyone "does it" you will discover that they do not. Hence, "doing it" may lead to a ruined career, not to mention illnesses such as heart disease to which cynical, angry people are more prone.[7]

HEROIC ATTRIBUTES

Exhibit I–2 summarizes the heroic attributes admired by a variety of groups (I have not shown the names of heroes and heroines because the identities are not as important as the attributes seen in them). The groups are displayed by age and/or career level. With the exception of high school students, all the respondents are basically on a managerial career path from studying business administration in college to currently serving as senior executives.

Note that courage and leadership are the two most widely cited attributes. All groups mention one or both of these virtues, so they are virtually synonymous with the concept of hero. We admire the courageous leader. In comparing the various groups' responses, we can eliminate

EXHIBIT I–2: ATTRIBUTES OF HEROES AND HEROINES

Group	Mean Age	Three Most Cited Attributes
Senior Executives	45	vision, courage/leadership (tie) decisiveness
Older Middle Managers	53	leadership, courage, decisiveness
Younger Middle Managers	34	leadership, integrity, commitment
MBA Students	25	commitment, knowledge, leadership
Undergraduate Business Students	20	leadership, individuality, independence/concern (tie)
Suburban High School Students	16	courage, independence, concern
Urban Junior High School Students	12	concern, courage, strength

these two attributes and see how the remaining attributes differ. (Obviously, we are not deleting courage and leadership because they are unimportant; they are certainly the *most important* attributes in our respondents' eyes, but the differences are instructive.)

The respondents in each group seem to attribute to their hero or heroine those characteristics that are of great concern to them in their particular life stage. Thus, twelve-year-old junior high school students in Spanish Harlem see concern and love in their heroic figures, such as Mr. Gonzales, the janitor, who allows them to hang out smoking in his basement "office"; or Mr. Goldberg, the neighborhood pharmacist, who jokes with them and never chases them away from his soda fountain. In their life situation, they crave affiliation and acceptance and their hero embodies this.

The suburban high school students are a bit older sample from much more affluent families, but many of them also see love and concern in their heroes. The more important attribute for them, however, is independence. This is what it's all about at sixteen to seventeen in middle-class America—declaring your independence from Mom and Dad, and showing the world that you are your own person. Indeed, these students told me that they also admire classmates who have escaped from excessive peer group pressure by defining themselves as independent persons doing what make sense to *them,* not necessarily what their group defines as "cool," or "awesome." (The terms, of course, change as rapidly as the admired clothes, hair styles, or activities.)

The undergraduate college sample was from a large state university at which I was a guest lecturer in a regular meeting of a required management course. The auditorium was tiered, with me in the pit at the front and the upper ten rows seeming to disappear into the haze of altitude. Two banks of television monitors were arrayed along the walls so that the students could see the distant figure at the podium. When I collected their papers citing their heroes, words like "individuality," "personality," "unique," and "style" jumped off the sheets. Given the undifferentiated, masslike state in which they find themselves, unknown to their professors and identified by social security numbers, they admire people who have transcended the homogeneity by defining themselves as unique and individual, often by an exaggerated style of dress or behavior.

The MBA students are Wharton graduate students who have generally worked two to three years after completing college. Note the value they attach to commitment and intelligence. MBA students are the only respondents who see "intelligence," "brains," or "knowledge" as very relevant to their heroes—which seems to suggest some rationalization. Since they have on average left jobs paying nearly $40,000 per year, they want to believe that their income sacrifice and growing debt will be repaid by the knowledge gained from the program! The admiration for "commitment" also reflects this concern for whether they're doing the right thing. Their heroes seem to be people who are confident and certain that they are in the right place at the right time.

Younger middle managers in their mid-thirties are just a bit older than MBA students, but certainty about commitment also ranks high with them. At this age, if you listen in the middle of the night, you can hear the sound of closing doors—doors to the adolesent dreams of attending medical school, becoming a race car driver, or writing the great American novel. It is not that they become impossibilities, but career and family commitments sharply reduce the probability. And it is not that these thirty-five-year-olds dislike their families or careers. Indeed, most of them are in the happiest decade of their lives in terms of personal growth and satisfaction. Nonetheless, they still want reassurance that their commitments are the right ones and that they are not sacrificing their personal integrity for the goodies they are getting from job and family. Therefore, they see integrity and commitment in their hero figures because they want them so much.[8] John F. Kennedy is the most cited hero by this generation which readily suggests the ink-blot nature of attributes seen in heroes. It is not clear that the admired men and women actually possess any of the virtues attributed to them. To his critics, to see integrity and commitment in John Kennedy is a contradiction in terms.

Older middle managers in their forties and fifties particularly admire decisiveness, an attribute almost never mentioned by anyone under thirty. President Harry Truman is frequently cited for his decisiveness by these respondents in his ability to confront a problem, make a decision, and *move on,* not looking back with doubt and worry about past decisions. And indeed, overcoming regret may be *the* basis of courageously confronting future challenges.[9] His long-time Secretary of State Dean Acheson called Truman "the most decisive president in American history." And in his memoirs Truman claimed that all the time he was president, on no night did it take him longer than ten minutes to fall asleep (which suggests either decisiveness or an empty brain depending on one's politics)![10]

In their admiration of decisiveness, it is not clear whether these older middle managers are responding to the pressure on them to make decisions, or to their frustration with indecisiveness from their own top executive superiors.

The senior executive sample listed in Exhibit I-2 constitutes a group of stars just below the chief executive level. They are participants in the Wharton Advanced Management program whom their firms have identified as being prepared for the top. Somewhat younger than older middle managers, as a group they have better promotion opportunities. They also admire decisiveness in their heroes, but most frequently cite "vision," "mission," or "seeing the big picture." What they are most concerned about is transcending the technical and functional specialties that most of them came from in order to understand and communicate an overall purpose for their firms. They admire empire builders whom one biographer of successful entrepreneurs describes as living "in the grip of a vision. Work and career take on the quality of a mission, a pursuit of some Holy Grail. And because they are talented and convinced that they can change the world, they often do."[11]

The point of this ink-blot exercise on heroes is to show how central concerns change as you move through life and upward in an organization. As we discuss various common problems you may confront in your career, we return to the heroic attributes cited and show how they pertain to each stage. You may not change the identity of your hero as you mature, but the attributes projected onto him or her will vary. For example, my very first response to this hero question was Franklin D. Roosevelt (just as Ronald Reagan has cited FDR as his hero). At ten years old when I first became aware of President Roosevelt, it was to admire his knack for transcending his status and communicating a sense of love and affection to the American people. In later years as I read all the Roosevelt biographies, I recognized that he was not such a loving person (and indeed was quite Machiavellian), but by then I came to admire other traits. By the time I reached senior university management as a vice president responsible for public relations, alumni relations, and fundraising, the attributes I admired in my boyhood hero had shifted to his incredible optimism, the buoyant spirit that regardless of job pressure he seemed always to convey to his government colleagues and to the general public. He just never seemed to be *down*—a skill particularly relevant to my role as chief sales executive for a university.

THE PURPOSE OF THIS BOOK

Like this extended ink-blot exercise of the heroes, every book itself is a similar projective test revealing an author's concern. So this book reflects my own ambivalence about organizations—belief in their necessity and social benefit, but skepticism about their impact on members. Such skepticism is an old trait in the United States. That American midwestern commentator *par excellence*, Garrison Keillor recently wrote:[12]

Organizations have no inherent virtues: no conscience, no esthetic taste, no sense of humor, no sense of justice. This is true of the Immigration and Naturalization Service, a hell hole of bureaucratic nincompoopery and know-nothingism, but it is also true of the Campfire

Girls, the Sierra Club, Ben and Jerry's and the Order of St. Francis. Virtue can only be said to be possessed by individuals. God's grace is not dispensed at group rates.

Any portrayal of corporations or institutions as friendly or humane or virtuous is pure mythology. Therefore, we individuals have a moral obligation to look at them with a sharp eye and be prepared to yell at them, and to give aid and comfort to individuals who battle them. In the American democracy, in the battle between giants and individuals, the good citizen knows whom to give the benefit of the doubt to.

When I began to teach management in the late 1960s, antibusiness, antiorganizational views among young people were at their height. The "best and brightest" wanted no part of business and laments eminated from corporate and academic America decrying the loss of leaders and warning of the "coming shortage of managers."[13] Thankfully, the economic slowdown in the mid–1970s led to a dramatic resurgence of positive views toward business and management. Business won the battle for the minds if not the hearts of college students so that today business administration is the largest undergraduate major in the United States.

And these students are among the best and brightest of today's youth. Nonetheless, however similar in appearance and ambition students and young professionals today may seem like their 1950s parents, they are different. The passive, trusting, and loyal views of the 1950s "organization man" and the 1960s "company man" are mostly gone.[14] Instead we have what are described as "self-developers" who reject passive acceptance of organizational decisions and endeavor personally to structure the ambiguity that is a modern career.[15]

This book is designed to assist you as a future "self-developer" manager in strengthening the skills needed to balance your relationships with the organizations in which you will work. The traumatic downsizings and mergers of recent years amply demonstrate the dangers of personal passivity and excessive trust. But if a certain skepticism is helpful today, cynicism about organizations and management is doubly dangerous. Cynicism can prevent people from making the commitment necessary for significant achievement.[16] It is well to remember Dwight Waldo's warning back in the 1960s when antiauthority views were at their peak:[17]

> To most of our essayists, critics, philosophers—the intelligentsia as an establishment: organization is evil. As the literary men, they suffer with K and refresh their souls at Walden Pond; but they live by choice in Manhattan, Princeton, or Connecticut. Of course, organization is an evil—gray, brutal, obscene as charged. It thwarts, deforms, destroys human beings. It is also a good; it sends royalty checks and honoraria

to its critics, provides them with food, clothing, shelter, transportation, education, recreation, protects them against many forms of loss and violence, care in sickness, and on request, sacraments and solace.

Making commitment to a vocation, institution, or organization is often turbulent.[18] But it is still necessary. Indeed, with a slowdown in promotion rates and the elimination of managerial levels so common today, commitment to what one *does* (as opposed to your position or status) is increasingly important. Unfortunately, making commitments may be *the* major problem of today's young students, professionals, and managers.[19]

Most of our situations are not in the heroic mold of slaying the dragon and saving the medieval town. Involved are quieter challenges of organizational life when communicating truth to a superior or making decisions based on ambiguous power. But all these situations require you to "screw your courage to the sticking place" as Shakespeare put it—in short, the courage *to be* and *to act.*[20]

Fear of the unknown will test the souls of all of us. But perhaps this book can buck up readers' courage by lifting the veil from some unknowns so that when challenging situations occur they may at least be expected, if not welcomed. And knowledge forewarned can be courage armed. Your dragon may be a bit less frightening if you've seen his relative.

Finally, I emphasize the point that *you* are responsible for the ethical and social implications of your actions. However much an organization may pressure you, and however much popular psychology and social science jargon may argue that social forces and organizational conditions lead to improper individual actions (and they can make it tough for you), the bottom line is your individual responsibility.[21]

Nothing in your career will be more important than your personal reputation for credibility. And nothing is more crucial to your ability to sustain leadership over a lifetime than your personal integrity—that your behavior is consistent with your beliefs.[22] Perhaps this book can help you not to throw away your credibility and integrity inadvertently. More importantly, I hope what you read will help you to stand up for what you believe when given the opportunity.

1

Growing Up at Work

"I'm looking for an honest man, not an honest kid!"

Early one cold and drizzly October morning, Edward M. Kennedy was at a Massachusetts factory gate to greet arriving workers and seek their vote for the United States Senate. As one elderly, worn-down employee approached the entrance, the candidate introduced himself and made his pitch. Skeptically eyeing Kennedy, the worker replied, "I understand you've never worked a day in your life." Undoubtedly, the Senator would have liked to explain that he had always worked for the people, that he was working then, and that he would continue to work for a better world, and so on. However, he never had a chance to reply because the worker quickly added, "Well, let me tell you, you haven't missed a damn thing!"[1]

Differing views on work and careers are longstanding. The novelist Aldous Huxley once wrote, "Like every man of sense and good feeling, I abominate work." But another writer, George Sand, observed, "Work is not man's punishment. It is his reward and his strength, his glory and his pleasure." There will be tough days in your life when you will side with Huxley and better others when you understand Sand's words. Personal maturation and career commitment will help the better days outnumber the bad.

In this chapter we examine maturation and career development, particularly the "growing up" that most of us still must do after we graduate from college and begin our first jobs. Let's begin with a story of three young men and women whose childhood experiences are exerting a strong influence on their present work behavior.

EDWIN, MARIA, AND CYNTHIA

Edwin Mesko. Ed was the seventh and youngest child of Gertrude and Peter Mesko. He was born and grew up in a small western Pennsylvania mining town whose residents primarily worked in the region's coal mines. The town was deteriorating badly and had been since the end of World War II and decline in demand for coal. Peter Mesko had managed to work off and on, but it was a hard life.

Mesko distrusted both the mine owners and the union organizers so he tried to work nonunion mines. Peter was very cynical about business managers and union officials who wore ties and jackets while sitting around drinking coffee and exchanging money under the table (or so he suspected).

The pay and conditions have dramatically improved in recent years, but Peter was too old really to benefit and by then Ed had long since left home to join the Navy.

Although he had never seen an ocean-going ship, at age seventeen Ed left home to join the Navy as a seaman apprentice. A bit frightened to leave home, he nonetheless enjoyed his basic training at the Great Lakes Naval Training Station. He even found the discipline looser than at home. Ed liked his petty officer, but did receive some demerits for making derogatory remarks under his breath about the lieutenant in charge of his division.

Ed did surprisingly well on the mathematics aptitude test so he was assigned to a gunnery specialty as a fire controlman (as in gunfire and rocket aiming, not fighting fires). He was eventually assigned to a warship where his job was to maintain and operate a radar system that controlled a bank of antiaircraft missiles. Ed took great pride in his ability to keep his equipment operating and he enjoyed the comradeship of his fellow seamen. Because of his hard work and competence, Ed's superiors generally left him alone, even overlooking his usually sloppy appearance and occasional excessive drinking while on liberty off the ship. At age twenty-seven, Ed found himself one of the youngest of senior enlisted personnel in the Navy.

Ed even received a letter of commendation from the ship's commanding officer for an act of extraordinary coolness and courage. While the ship was engaged in a highline transfer at sea exchanging personnel with another ship, an unexpected wave forced the two ships apart. Unfortunately, this pulled the line taut between the two ships while it was wrapped around a sailor's hand. The hand was almost entirely pulled off right in front of the officers on the bridge. One fainted and even the captain vomited in horror. While others were frozen in shock, Ed instantly climbed up to the screaming sailor and cut him loose.

Impressed with Mesko's technical skill and personal courage, the commanding officer directed the gunnery officer to approach Ed about attending Officer Candidate School where in three months he could earn his commission as an ensign. The gunnery officer, Lieutenant Henderson, was a graduate of the United States Naval Academy and highly committed to his career as an officer. In talking to Ed, Henderson emphasized the honor that the commanding officer had done Ed in advancing the opportunity and praised the social prestige and potential power to command that goes with being a commissioned officer (along with more money, nicer uniforms, and more private living quarters). Henderson was surprised when Ed didn't immediately accept the offer, pleading that he wasn't sure and would have to think about it.

Maria Lopez. Maria has always admired her parents. Of course she argued with them from time to time, but she loved to be home to cook and sew, and to help with her younger brothers and sisters. To her parents, Maria was a model child. She did only average work in school, but never received a "D" or an "F" either. School social life was simply more important than studies to Maria. She was always at the center. Although she dated frequently, most of the boys seemed a bit immature to her.

Maria never planned to go to college. She had figured she would get married fairly soon, but at seventeen this seemed a ways off. So she began to look for a job as the summer after graduation wore on. Many of her friends left the neighborhood; some of the boys joined the Army and a few went to college. Maria missed the excitement of high school's crowded halls and lively conversations. Finally, in October she found a clerical job in the regional office of a large insurance company.

From the beginning, Maria fit right in. She did what she was told, was polite and willing. She thought the work was fine and she really enjoyed the beautiful new office. Even more, she liked the friends she made, the fun of chatting and planning bridal showers. Maria took an active role in running these affairs just as she had done in school.

Quite early in her employment, Maria had dropped a note into the office suggestion box. The clerical area was arranged in long straight rows and columns, all rather forbidding looking. Maria suggested that the setup be modified to several semicircles. This would facilitate communicating with the group leader located in the middle. She thought it would also create a sense of belonging. Management subsequently introduced the arrangement to almost everyone's approval.

As time passed Maria just never met anyone she wanted to marry, so she continued working. She perfected her computer skill, and telephone style so much that she received several merit raises. She was even given a post as office claims agent, becoming the first woman in her firm to handle routine policyholder claims. She was flattered by the promotion, but the job did make it more difficult to keep up with her friends in the office. However, the younger women still sought her advice on job and personal matters. And Maria enjoyed talking with policyholders and auto repair shops—and they liked to deal with her.

Shortly after Maria's twenty-sixth birthday last year, her mother passed away. At first, Maria wanted to quit her job to take care of the family, but her father said it wasn't necessary and she had her own life to live.

Last week, the regional vice president called Maria into his office, praised her and offered her a promotion to assistant officer manager in charge of hiring and training of all clerical employees. The position includes a private office, her own secretary and a higher salary (that in fact she knew exceeded her father's). Maria is now very confused because she just can't see herself in the new position. She doesn't know what to do.

Cynthia Wyeth. Cynthia joined the international division of the Gibraltar Bank after earning her MBA at Walton University. She was one of the first woman analysts at the bank and was a hard worker and fast learner. These attributes had characterized her from childhood when as an only child she had helped her father with the bookkeeping in his dental practice. They had spent many evenings discussing sports and investments rather than dental medicine, so Cynthia more naturally gravitated to business rather than health care. One of her proudest moments had come in college when her father gave her $5,000 to invest (but not spend) in any way she desired. She still has that initial capital, which has grown considerably.

Her MBA program was tough but not overwhelming, so Cynthia was very active in extracurricular activities at Walton serving as Vice President of the MBA Association, President of the Women at Walton club, and a member of the joint faculty-student curriculum committee. Cynthia was a very visible person and received several attractive job offers upon graduation.

Cynthia joined the Gibraltar Bank because it was a prestigious institution which she well knew because a former president had been her father's patient and friend. Cynthia had always called him "Uncle Ned." Mr. Frederick Adams was now retired but he was still a member of Gibraltar's board of directors. Cynthia's first position had been as junior and then senior analyst, which she found sometimes interesting, sometimes boring. She enjoyed the banking content but resented the repetitive telephone quotes, library research, and near-clerical work in serving the senior officers. She did, however, establish an enviable reputation for reliability and competence.

Four years ago she was asked to become administrative manager for the international department where she did a marvelous job improving clerical services, reducing secretarial turnover, and initiating formal training. She was named an assistant vice president. In time, however, Cynthia became a bit dissatisfied. Although her pay and title were not bad, she felt that she was not progressing in *banking*. Accordingly, she spoke to Sean Riley, the international department executive vice president, about a promotion to country manager. Months went by, however, and nothing happened.

EXHIBIT 1-1: PARTIAL ORGANIZATION OF GIBRALTER BANK

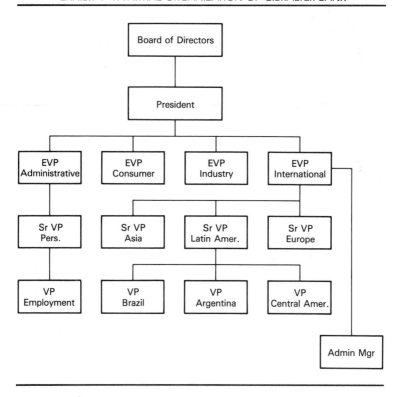

Three weeks ago, Cynthia mentioned her frustration to Uncle Ned while at her younger sister's wedding at the Union League Club. Two weeks later, Cynthia was offered the position as Gibraltar's employment manager. The position carries a vice presidency and a nice salary increase. When she talked about it to Sean Riley, he countered with an offer of country manager in charge of Central America. The area is the smallest in terms of business (and indeed has been declining in recent years), but the position carries full authority for loans and investments, substantial autonomy, and great opportunity to travel and deal with clients.

Cynthia is wondering which position to accept.

WHAT IS BOTHERING EDWIN, MARIA, AND CYNTHIA?

Most readers of this book will find it odd that Edwin and Maria experienced such difficulty accepting the promotions offered for their good performance. You probably more easily identify with Cynthia and her managerial ambition. Yet, the reality is that most people are closer to Ed and Maria than to Cynthia—at least to the extent that most people don't have careers at all. Rather they have a series of jobs. The difference is a matter of time perspective and planned direction.

Both Edwin and Maria seem to be looking backward, or at best at preserving the present, rather than to the future. Each seems to worry that they will lose too much of what they presently enjoy if they should accept the promotions offered. Attitudes and values they learned as children are limiting their choices for the future. Perhaps they are correct in not accepting the proffered promotions, but remaining in their present positions without examining their long-range ambitions would clearly be a mistake because it could lead to stagnation and bitterness.

Influenced by his father's skeptical views about management, Edwin fears that becoming a commissioned officer would compromise his integrity and be a sell-out. He worries that he would become like the (probably nonexistent) stuffed-shirt, parasitic mining officials of his childhood imagination. At present, he has a good deal. He takes great satisfaction in his technical competence and the Navy grants him enormous autonomy because his special skills are so prized. He is not held to normal military appearance and behavior standards that he would certainly be expected to manifest as an officer.

Maria Lopez also enjoys her present position, but seems to fear the consequences of accepting a promotion to assistant office manager, that somehow it would signify to the world that she is a "career woman" (and perhaps that she may never marry). This is an old-fashioned view to be sure, but one still held by many young women (and men) from traditional families. My mother-in-law was a young widow with two children at age thirty when in 1940 she began what became a very successful administrative career in a printing company. Yet in thirty-five years she never thought of herself as a career woman and disliked others to see her as such. The illusion that she would give it up when she remarried was so strong. Similarly, Maria has taken each job as it came, holding a short-timer's attitude that she wouldn't be doing it very long. Yet, because of her conscientiousness, she always did a good job, not because she craved long-run promotions, but because she wanted to please others. A management position to her is synonymous with an aggressive exercise of power which she feels would be incompatible with her personality.

In making the promotion offers to Ed and Maria, the naval officer and insurance manager emphasized rewards important to the offerers: money, power, prestige. They probably never entertained the idea that these goodies wouldn't be similarly valued by their lucky subordinates.

Cynthia Wyeth is clearly a different kind of person. From childhood she has pursued excellence and opportunities to distinguish herself. Selection of courses and summer jobs were oriented toward a career offering achievement, promotions, prestige, and power. She has been frustrated by exclusion from such opportunity in the international division of Gibralter Bank. Although she enjoyed her responsibilities as department administrative manager, she wanted to return to real banking activity—making loan decisions, facilitating international trade, and negotiating deals.

By her astute handling of a personal contact, Cynthia provoked an offer as vice president and employment manager for the bank. She now must choose between this and a belated counteroffer from the international department to assume responsibility for the Central American region. She must judge which position would provide the greater career opportunity she has been seeking.

Before describing how others feel about our young heroes, let us examine some central issues in personal maturation and career development. You will be more successful and satisfied if you take a career perspective toward your future—if you understand your own needs, strengths and weaknesses, and have a rough idea of the kinds of contributions you want to make and the rewards hoped for. These ideas are not to be engraved in stone, but are subject to modification with maturity and experience.

VIEWS OF MATURATION

A recent *Fortune* poll of business executives about MBA programs and students produced a litany of complaints that students are: too self-centered, too narrow in their interests, unwilling to commit themselves, ignorant of business realities, and ill-mannered and impolite! As one chief executive put it:[2]

> They (MBA's) have excellent technical qualifications, but the majority are virtually uneducated in what goes on in the real business world. (I am) fed up with young MBA's who wander into 9 o'clock meetings at 9:15 or 9:30, or who take two days to return a phone call. (I remember) a newly hired MBA (I) took to a meeting with the head of Twentieth Century Fox in Beverly Hills. As the kid walked in, he peeled off his jacket and threw it on the couch. (I am adamant about) teaching students kindness, courtesy, punctuality, cleanliness, proper dress, as well as academic subjects such as ethics and communications.

Whether especially true or not for today's students, such complaints have historically been voiced by an older generation toward those younger. Most of us have often been told to "grow up!" The command usually came from someone who disapproved of our behavior. And indeed, most of us from time to time have disliked our own behavior and wished that we could be more mature. We all traverse our own individual rocky road to whatever maturation is. We can consider the process from several complementary perspectives.

Behaving Like an Adult What most older people mean when they accuse young people of being immature is that they don't behave the way that the complaining generation expects. The executives surveyed by *Fortune* cited unreturned telephone calls, invitations never responded to, missing thank-you notes, gauche table manners, tardiness, and unreliable attendance—all criticisms familiar to most of us since kindergarten. Superficial as they may be, they *are* real and you will be handicapped if you have not learned basic courtesies by the time you start work.

Particularly disturbing to older managers is a junior's cavalier attitude about attendance. As Woody Allen is purported to have observed, "Eighty percent of life is just showing up." But reliably "showing up" at work after college means a dramatic shift in one's time perspective. Most of us experience difficulty in adapting to the changed time horizon that accompanies the transition from school to work. College accustomed us to almost immediate gratification and to short time spans—this semester, next academic year, a few years to graduation. Time's passage is clearly signaled by status changes punctuated by frequent vacations (in addition to winter and summer vacations, my school now gives fall and spring "breaks" in order to relieve the pressure on students). A permanent job is different. The time horizon is much longer, fewer events mark time's passage and a full year must be endured before a short two-week vacation! Not surprisingly, some young employees attempt to perpetuate the school perspective by changing jobs frequently, calling in "sick" on Fridays and Mondays, and taking time off for unofficial (and unpaid) vacations. However understandable this behavior, older colleagues perceive it as immature.

Extension of Motivating Needs. From infancy to adulthood, we gradually extend the needs that motivate our behavior.[3] Infants are dominated by physiological drives for safety and security. They are tyrannical and self-centered in their demands that these needs be satisfied, but they are helpless in doing anything for themselves. They must come to see the world as contributing to the satisfaction of their basic needs. When they do so, the world becomes less threatening and uncertain.

Then new needs emerge. Children discover the enjoyment of affiliation and love with their parents. Soon they acquire playmates and the joy of being *included*. As time passes, social needs for affiliation and esteem become more powerful. We tend to define ourselves in terms of others' response to us. The child wants to be like others, not out of step—as one might if you gave into your mother's demand that you wear rubbers over your shoes when no one else in the fourth grade does. Children and adolescents fear being different because they are so unsure of themselves. They are afraid that being different will mean exclusion, and exclusion will mean being nothing. In this period of life, most of us are quite "other-directed."[4]

Other-directed people are dominated by their social needs. They act in anticipation of how others will react afterwards: "What will others think of me? Will I still be part of the 'in' crowd? Will I be liked more—or less? Will I have more or less prestige?" Sometime in our late teens, however, most of us begin to realize that we don't have to be just like others, but can have wants and standards that are different from our companions. Most people are a little threatened by this realization because identifying oneself is a lonely and difficult process. Yet growth demands that the challenge be met and we become "inner directed."

Inner-directed people are motivated by needs for autonomy, competence, and achievement. They act in anticipation of what they will think of themselves: "Will I have a sense of freedom? Will I feel competent and proficient? Will I experience the exultation of achievement and creativity? Will I think more of myself, even if the world doesn't agree?"

Whether or not we move with maturation from being other directed to inner directed depends mainly on our experience. Childhood frustration of needs for safety, security, affiliation, and prestige (and in tragic cases, even physiological necessities) might mean that the future behavior of such a youth would focus on these needs with much less motivation from needs for self-esteem, competence, and achievement.[5] Thus, one might never have enough money to guarantee security or enough affection to satisfy a desire for love. Of course, even the most mature individuals never entirely give up their concerns about other people's responses to them. We are not *either* other directed or inner directed. We are all potentially both at various stages in life—but from time to time, depending on the situation such as losing a job, we may move back to an earlier other-directed stage.

Stages of Growth. Whether or not we are blessed with a fortuitous beginning, we all have our share of maturation challenges. These challenges present specific problems to be resolved at each growth stage.[6] Whether handled well or poorly, however, life impels us on to the next problem as the stages unfold.

Infancy—trust versus mistrust. Depending on the reliability of adult responses (mainly parents), the small child locates himself or herself somewhere on a range from "the world is a hostile or random place in which I can place no trust" at one end to the other extreme of "total faith in the behavior of adults." Most of us, however, come down someplace in between.

Young childhood—autonomy versus shame and initiative versus guilt. Again from and through parents (mainly in the conflict over toilet training and freedom to explore the home), we may or may not learn that we are autonomous persons who can exercise independence without guilt. The archtypical event here is not so much a spanking for "messing your pants," but what happens when the infant crawls into the kitchen and pulls out the pots and pans from the lower drawer. If parents respond with anger and punishment, we conclude that it is dangerous to exercise initiative in exploration. If, however, they had made the kitchen "child safe" so that they applaud our initiative, we incorporate the joy of autonomy. Of course, a single occasion doesn't settle this, but the pattern is critical.

Childhood and adolescence—industry versus inferiority. The development of one's need for achievement depends on the resolution of this issue through the proportion of early successes and failures. If we experience relative success in mastering self-maintenance tasks like tying shoelaces and walking home from school alone, we are more likely later to develop a significant achievement need and sufficient self-confidence to tackle tough problems. Thus, in adulthood, lower-rated managers tend to see their own personal inadequacies as their greatest hindrance to success while better performers see this challenge as external, primarily the task itself.[7]

Our parents' expectations of self-mastery affect this resolution, however.[8] Too early or too tardy expectations are detrimental to developing an industrious outlook. If parents expect too much too early, our failures are too frequent and we may feel overwhelmed; if parental confidence comes too late, the optimal period for discovering achievement's thrill has passed.

The level of our parents' performance standards also affects how we resolve this issue of industry versus inferiority. If parents expect little or think *everything* the child does is wonderful, achievement need development is hampered. Similarly, excessive parental dominance is perhaps *the* most destructive force hindering achievement need. Parents of a child with a sense of industry and high achievement need tend to: (1) expect and encourage high performance; (2) not give detailed instructions, but within broad guidelines allow the child many decisions; (3) reward good effort and performance with hugs and kisses (not money or gifts which is more characteristic of parents with less achievement-oriented children);

and (4) to withhold affection and parental esteem if the child doesn't strive for good performance.

The dynamic is the same for both sons and daughters, but many parents expect less from the girl and dominate her more, thus hindering achievement need development. My son and daughter, then ten years old and eight years old, and myself were subjects of an experiment in which a researcher observed my interaction separately with each while they were performing a task (piling up blocks). I couldn't touch them or the blocks, but I could talk. In 80 percent of the families sampled, the father expressed lower performance expectations and exercised more dominance over his daughter in directing her: "Mary, don't use the blue block, put the red and yellow one on next." (Thankfully, I was in the minority 20 percent that treated their son and daughter the same!) Many successful career women report being treated as "sons" rather than as daughters—that is, parental expectations were high, dominance low, and affectional rewards given for good performance (and probably withheld for poor effort).[9]

Adolescence—identity versus confusion. One of the cliches of American life is adolescence *angst,* but it is especially real in our culture because of the vast array of life styles we encounter as we move from grammar school to junior high and high school. Our task is to define ourselves by trial and error, to find out what actually works for us as opposed to what parents, teachers and even friends tell us. When my son was a sophomore in high school, he asked me what was so good about getting As; why did so many parents, teachers and even his classmates prize them? Never having seen many As on his report cards, I asked him why he thought he could get straight As. His reply was quick, "Because dumber kids than me get all As." His confidence was high that he could do it. His question, however, was "why bother?" I explained that good grades would help him get into a higher-quality college and this might assist in entry into one of the prestigious professions like medicine or law where the careers would be challenging and rewarding, and so on.

My parental reply was obviously valid and wise, but Greg's eyes began to glaze over with impatience and he finally said, "Dad, I'll grant that As are neat things to get in the long run, but what do they do for me now?" Perhaps he was fishing for a promised reward like a car, but more fundamentally, he was asking what he would have to give up in order to get As. My answer had dealt with a distant future and he was concerned about the present in which he had become a school and town celebrity by his athletic success. Introduced from the stage to over 2,000 schoolmates, pretty girls whom he didn't even know would greet him by name as they passed in the hall—heady stuff for a fifteen-year-old (heady stuff for a fifty-year-old too!). His concern was that studying to improve his grades would hinder his athletic and social success which was more important to him then. I tried with only limited success to explain that grades and athletics were not mutually exclusive because athletes tend to manage their time better. The straight As, however, never materialized.

We all must make these trade-offs during this period of identity versus confusion so that repeated decisions clarify who we are to ourselves and to others.

Young adulthood—intimacy versus isolation. Clarity about self should facilitate entering into close relationships through commitment to family, vocation, organization, or cause. Yet, it can be extremely difficult to give up some freedom after fighting for independence from parents and adult authority figures. Our views on authority evolve as we grow.[10] As infants and young children we are *dependent* on others, so we generally conform to what adults want. But we soon feel rebellious stirrings and become more *counterdependent* as we intentionally oppose authority's desires. We strive to nonconform. Note that the dependent person always conforms, while the counterdependent person is always nonconforming—but in effect his or her behavior is as much determined by others as for the dependent person. Such adolescent nonconformists may rationalize their behavior in fancy rhetoric about individuality and freedom, but they protest too much. They are every bit as much victims of pressure as is the conformist. Of course, this is not a one-way shift; we are often buffeted by periods of pride and shame about our behavior.[11]

Defining a clear identity means becoming *independent* by choosing behavior you think will bring you the greatest satisfaction regardless of whether or not your parents like it. This means that sometimes independents will behave just like their parents which may appear as conformity. When my two older daughters were in junior high school the fad was to go barefoot. Since I was hyper about wearing shoes (because as a boy I had almost lost a leg to blood poisoning from stepping on a rusty nail), to appease me, my daughters would leave the house wearing shoes but then deposit them under a thick evergreen tree at the corner of our block and go off gloriously shoeless for the day. In time, however, they independently discovered through various accidents that shoes are one of the great inventions of human history. They began to wear shoes, not because they were conforming, but because it came to make sense to them.

Independence, however, is not the final stage in maturation. The central issue of young adulthood is embracing *interdependence* by making commitments. After fighting so hard for independence, one then seems voluntarily to relinquish it by taking others into account when deciding how to behave. You consider the impact on those you love and to whom you have extended yourself in intimacy. I remember one former student telling me that she and her "significant other" were moving in together right after graduation. (Being a bit traditional on such matters, this disturbed me.) About a year later I saw Carole and asked how Stan was. She replied that they had recently separated because they had found themselves becoming too "dependent" on each other. I repressed my temptation to say, "What's the point of moving in with someone and sharing a bed unless you are going to be dependent on each other?" Of course, what I really meant was "interdependent," but a still immature person may experience interdependence not as growth but as a return to dependence.

Full independence from parents and interdependence with others occurs quite late in American society. Before our mid-twenties, most of us are not ready to appreciate parents as separate individuals, as having needs, strengths and weaknesses in their own right, separate from being our parents.[12] Even after leaving home physically, the less mature of us not only tend to rely on our parents to help with decisions, but are also sometimes overwhelmed by intense feelings of rage and dependency. At its worst, these feelings can lead us to lash out at our parents even when they are trying to be helpful.

By contrast, more mature young adults have strong confidence in their ability to make decisions on their own and feel in control of their emotions toward parents. They see themselves, rather than their parents, as the best judges of their own worth and so can risk disapproval by expressing values that may clash with those of parents. But in spite of the clashes, they are closer to their parents than the less mature—especially better able to understand the complexities of their parents' lives. So the best of us (but seldom before our late twenties) become more independent *and* interdependent with our parents.

Young people desperately seeking independence and fearful of interdependence often avoid the responsibilities of power. Among male college students, the desire for power declined during the 1960s and early 1970s.[13] It then stabilized until the early 1980s, but at a substantially lower level than in 1960 (we don't know what happened in the 1980s). This avoidance of power of course reflects skepticism about the national political leaders of the period, but it also suggests an increased intention to avoid having to hurt anyone through exercising power. It is an effort to remain *innocent.* But it is a vain intention. It is true that it is impossible to lead without someone being hurt in the process (some British were hurt as Gandhi led India to freedom; some employees were hurt as Iacocca saved the ailing Chrysler Corporation). But remaining aloof when power must be exercised for the common good is not innocence—it is another form of guilt.[14] Accepting interdependence means accepting power and the potential guilt that comes with it.

Middle age—generativity versus stagnation. With maturity and success we face the problem of maintaining effort and interest. We discuss this in depth in the concluding chapter.

Old age—ego integrity versus despair. With declining physical and mental states, we struggle to maintain a sense of self-worth and optimism (topics for another book you can read later in life).

Jobs and careers take on concrete meaning as we move through these various growth stages and mold our personalities. Especially as we reach young adulthood, our concerns focus more on the meaning of a career.

CAREER PERSPECTIVES AND CONCERNS

The term *career* is derived originally from the Latin *carraria* meaning "by road or carriage way." Drawing on this figurative imagery and later usage, career is defined as, "A person's course or progress through life— especially professional life or employment which affords opportunity for advancement."[15] Thus, our focus is on you as an individual in your career, not on the firm performing "career planning."[16]

Careers versus Jobs. Most people, however, do not have "careers," nor do they expect to. They simply anticipate "jobs."[17] In most countries, careers are thought to be open only to the upper and professional classes.[18] In the United States, the difference between a job and career orientation is a matter of time perspective and planned direction.[19] For example, future physicians tend to conceive of their careers early, during their early teens.[20] They select high school science courses and college majors linked to medical careers ten to fifteen years in the future. In contrast, most restaurant workers never plan for their positions, but merely take whatever work is available. Young physicians will probably pursue the practice of medicine until they die; busboys or waitresses will probably go on to other jobs. Even if they eventually become headwaiters, chefs, or owners, most did not start out envisioning such a path.

Of course exceptions to this distinction exist. Some students go to medical school mainly because their ambitious parents expect it; and some waiters and waitresses take great pride in their professionalism and aspire to operate their own restaurants in the future. The point is that career-oriented people have longer time perspectives and sense of direction.[21]

Many (perhaps most) high school students don't actually follow their career aspirations. In time, most of us lower our goals to be more realis-

15

tic.[22] Those that too slavishly follow their high school career direction may discover too late that they prematurely sought closure instead of trying to stay flexible. Consider the following two comments from a law student and a physician.[23]

> I was pushed by my parents into a pre-law program and now I'm in law school. . . . You can't possibly imagine the kinds of people I meet daily in law school—people who aren't aware that there's anything worthwhile in life, except law, getting into a good firm, making partner, making lots of money. It's all they talk about and, presumably, it's all they think about . . . I wish to God I could get out without disappointing my parents.

> I'm a physician not because that's what I want, but because my father and grandfather were physicians. I'm countinuing the noble family tradition. . . . What a joke. I'm miserable, even though last year I made more than $300,000. What a joke.

Now, most lawyers and physicians aren't miserable, but what of business managers? Are they career or job oriented? How many of you planned on a managerial career since your teens? Or are you just looking for a way to earn a living? Most business managers have probably held views somewhere between future physicians and busboys. They had faith that studying and going to college would pay off, but had little understanding of what managers actually do. Most current managers developed a commitment to their careers only after beginning work.[24] Grasping the visible opportunity seems to be the rule.

Encouragement of young girls to strive for wider career choice has not yet had a major impact on most. Female college students are markedly higher in artistic and social interests than their male classmates who are higher in investigative and enterprising interests. The women studied, however, still prefer occupations that are stereotypically feminine—perhaps because they still do not believe they have real choice.[25] Remember, however, many individual exceptions exist to these traditional orientations. Female enrollment in undergraduate engineering, for example, has jumped from less than 2 percent to over 10 percent in little more than a decade.[26] Nothing is as powerful in eliciting female commitment to a career (whether traditional or nontraditional) as perceived opportunity for promotions.[27] A real chance for a higher position is a strong career inducement.

Career Phases. As we move through our careers, most of us confront similar problems along the way. These career phases have been termed: pulling up roots, provisional adulthood, transition to commitment, settling down, potential mid-life crisis, and reestablishing and flowering.[28]

Pulling up Roots—Ages 16–22. We've seen that a major early concern is breaking away and establishing independence. We crave emotional and financial autonomy, but most college students must accept their continued economic dependence on their parents (most do it gratefully, of course, but some deeply resent this remaining blockage to independence and adulthood—some even "flunk out" to force their independence).

Once on a "real" full-time, year-round job, we are concerned with proving to ourselves that we are competent to make our own way. Jobs tend to be perceived as immediate vehicles for income and self-support, rather than as introduction to careers.

Getting established—ages 22–29. Making commitments to others through family, profession, cause, or organization sets the stage for developing the knowledge and behavioral skills necessary to become valuable to an employer. Career success becomes more important to most of us. Awareness of the inadequacies of one's earlier education leads some to attend graduate school in the hope that it will provide entry to a ladder closed to those without appropriate education. Most entering MBA students, for example, have worked for two or three years after college, in contrast to most medical and law students who go right from senior year into a new freshman experience.

Many organizations today put enormous pressures on new college graduates to prove their commitment to their careers by working enormously long hours and sacrificing personal recreation to their employers' needs. We talk about this more in Chapter 2, "Dealing with Early Disappointment."

Transition questions—ages 29–32. Uneasiness about progress tends to be common at this stage. Many of us worry about whether we are in the right place, or if we are headed in the desired direction fast enough. Shifting jobs and organizations is common at this age because we are already becoming aware that personal options will begin to decline in the not-so-distant future.[29] Past thirty, it becomes less reasonable to hold on to the myth that one could still start over and go to medical or law school, or change from engineering to English literature and become a college professor. (The mean age of earning a Ph.D. is thirty-one, ten years after college graduation—a fact reassuring to me because that was just the age at which I became an assistant professor.)

For those young business managers on the fast track, by their early thirties they may well have reached positions of significant and satisfying authority, but they are surprised by self-directed questions about the value of what they're doing. As one young branch manager put it to me,

"I'm a success, I earn over $70,000 per year and get a big kick from seeing the climbing sales chart, but sometimes I wonder if getting 'Colonel Zoom' cereal on every breakfast table is really worth devoting my life to" (especially since it was being attacked by nutritional experts as having little food value because it was mainly sugar-coated air).

This questioning can be difficult for a young manager to understand. After years of apprenticeship, he or she is beginning to reap the rewards of effort: autonomy, discretionary authority, and opportunity to achieve. Job morale is high. But for some this is not enough. They wonder: "Am I really selling out to the organization? Have I forgotten to ask the important questions of whether I'm growing as a person? Or am I contributing to society?"

As we've seen, the central issue of young adulthood is commitment versus isolation. But commitment is both admired and feared. A sense of certainty about career is desired because it simplifies one's life and stills the restlessness about whether you are in the right place. Nonetheless, one may also fear commitment because it means closing doors and giving up the pleasant illusion of unlimited choice. Maturity means facing reality and deepening interests. Therefore, a central facet of all careers becomes balancing commitment to performance with personal independence.[30] Pure rebellion, which rejects all organizational values, can end only in departure; pure conformity which accepts everything means loss of self. Creative individualism accepts pivotal norms but searches for ways to have individual impact.

Many young professionals who move into management are surprised by feelings of dependence on their new subordinates. Maturity demands a declaration of psychological independence from home and parental authority while identifying oneself as an individual. Dependence (or more precisely, interdependence) on others can be difficult to handle. But, independence is impossible as a manager. Superiors are dependent on subordinates' performance, subordinates are dependent on their superior's judgment, and middle managers are dependent in both directions.

This mutual dependence can provoke anxiety. Many junior military officers have suffered from stress-induced illness (especially severely inflamed gums, formerly called trench mouth) because they bear responsibility for their unit's safety and performance even though they don't have the experience or technical knowledge of their senior enlisted subordinates. Young officers cannot solve this problem by denying their downward dependence, but they can reduce it by learning the technical details of subordinates' duties. In the long run, however, young supervisors must recognize interdependence and strive to facilitate subordinate performance while representing their interests upward.

Settling down—ages 32–39. For ambitious, career-oriented people, this period is characterized by marked concentration on work, creativity, and advancement. For many people it is the greatest growth period in their lives, the era of greatest challenge and actualization of their potential—that is, if they have found a vocation or organization worth committing to. As a consequence of career demands, however, friendships and socializing are often curtailed compared with earlier periods. For many, career and family activities leave little additional time for other relationships.

Most young adults are aware of their aversion to being dependent on others, but they are usually surprised by their anxiety about having others dependent on them.[31] As we acquire spouse, children, job status, and community position, we receive increased demands to give financial, temporal, and emotional support to more and more people. This sense of others' dependency can be gratifying, but one's time and energy are limited. Independent and self-reliant managers are sometimes disturbed to discover they feel dominated by the very people dependent on them.[32] If and when the burden becomes too great, we must establish life priorities that balance the demands of employer, community, and family in a way that may fully satisfy none but allows relations to continue with all. We discuss this topic in greater depth in Chapter 3, "Overcoming Overload and Stress."

Now let's return to the three protagonists in our opening case and see how these ideas might apply.

WHAT OTHERS THINK ABOUT EDWIN, MARIA, AND CYNTHIA

Most people are more optimistic about Maria Lopez's decision in the insurance company than Edwin Mesko's in the Navy. Seventy-five percent of students and executives sampled recommend that Maria accept the promotion to assistant office manager because it would offer her opportunities to train, guide, and nurture young women in a manner consistent with her personality and values. To be sure, the regional vice president emphasized the wrong factors (status, power, and money) in his offer to Maria, but most feel that Maria would find the position's intrinsic activities satisfying. To do this, however, she needs to let go of the past and recognize that working in a professional capacity is not a deterrent to possible marriage (and indeed, it might offer increased opportunity to meet men more equal to her in maturity and competence).

Staying in her present role and trying to remain friends with all the support staff is not really a viable long-term option. The clock is ticking and Maria is already five to six years older than the average secretary. They will increasingly come to see her as an "older sister" and even "mother," a role which she seems to be already moving into gracefully. This could be formalized in the position of assistant office manager where she might make a valuable contribution to the firm by increasing staff concern for policyholders, which she did so well in her work in claims adjustment.

The 25 percent who feel that Maria should not accept the promotion are worried about her "softness." They fear that she would be unable to exercise discipline when necessary and would not protect the firm's interests while trying to keep everyone happy. Therefore, the company would have lost an excellent claims adjuster while creating (and eventually also losing) an ineffective office manager.

Toward Ed Mesko, my students and executives are more divided: 53 percent think he should refuse the offer to attend Officer Candidate School; 33 percent think he should go; and 14 percent think he should resign from the Navy and attend a university engineering school. The majority feel that his antipathy to authority and managers is just too deep-seated for him ever to be happy in that role. They feel he would just hate himself for "selling out" and that the stress of adhering to military standards and accepting responsibility for subordinates would exacerbate his drinking problem. In this view, his desire for independence is so strong that he would never be effective in an interdependent capacity.

Those who recommend that he resign from the Navy and attend engineering school agree with this assessment of Edwin, but feel that simply staying where he is will not work in the long run because he has a significant achievement need which would demand new learning experiences and challenges that could be satisfied only with greater education. Perhaps he could find an autonomous position in private industry that would allow substantially the same freedom that he presently enjoys in the Navy.

The minority 33 percent who say he should attend OCS are optimistic that Ed is now of an age where he can escape from his childhood memories and act on the intelligence, conscientiousness, and personal courage which he possesses. Indeed, with his understanding of life in the enlisted ranks, he might become an especially effective officer. Persuading him to do so would require a different emphasis than the prestige and power pushed by his Naval Academy division officer, but Ed might respond to challenge, personal growth, opportunity to serve, and patriotism.

With regard to Cynthia Wyeth at Gibraltar Bank, there is near unanimous agreement that she should accept the position as vice president and country manager for Central America. Eighty-eight percent believe that this position is most congruent with her desire to exercise power in a central banking function. The employment manager position would offer substantial power, but it is a staff function carrying less prestige and promotion potential than a line position in international banking.

A minority (12 percent), however, are worried about the Central American position. The manner of its being offered to Cynthia (as an apparently hurried response to her other offer) suggests to some skeptics that it could be a "no-win" post. Business in the area has been declining, perhaps because of political chaos and military action that are destroying the business climate. If so, significant improvement in the area's performance might simply be impossible so that Cynthia at best would be in a frustrating holding pattern or at worst might be blamed for the collapse of the bank's business there. Cynthia might be able to protect herself by analyzing the situation before she accepts the offer and attempting to define performance measurements in advance, but it still could be risky.

I once discussed Cynthia's situation with a group of professional women in a group called The Women's Personnel Manager's Association. They were more divided than most male respondents. About half the group agreed that the country manager vice presidency was more desirable as a role model for young professional women because Cynthia would be a pioneer at Gibraltar in what is clearly a power-axis function. The other half, however, argued for her taking the employment manager vice presidency on two grounds: (1) that her chances of personal failure would be less because it is a function where as a woman she would be less of a trail blazer; and (2) as the bank's employment manager she would have greater opportunity to fight discrimination and improve opportunities for women in all parts of the firm. These viewpoints were so disparate that substantial debate was provoked.

Now, let's summarize the practical advice implicit in the theory and cases we've described.

ADVICE ON GROWING UP AND STARTING A CAREER

- Recognize the difference between counterdependence and independence by understanding that a mature person sometimes behaves as if he or she were conforming to parental or authority figure desires even though the behavior is independently chosen.
- Don't be afraid to conform on superficial customs like dress and manners if this will give you more freedom to nonconform on more fundamental issues. Superficial as they may seem, promptly returning telephone calls, answering invitations (and keeping your word), sending thank-you notes, and practicing proper table manners *are* important. Practicing such courtesies may not get you promoted faster, but impoliteness will almost certainly hurt you.

- Don't avoid your commitments by "calling in sick" on Fridays or Mondays just because you'd rather be in the mountains or at the beach. Occasionally taking a midweek afternoon off when nothing is pressing to go to a museum or play tennis is more responsible than spontaneously stretching weekends.
- Understand that independent autonomy is not a viable long-term option for most people, that making commitments and accepting interdependence are essential for a successful organizational or managerial career.
- Accept that maturation is not always unidirectional: sometimes you will mature from being primarily other directed toward being inner directed, but financial or social anxiety can provoke a renewed (but hopefully temporary) dominance by security and social needs.
- Balance your awareness of how your life philosophies have been shaped by your parents' behavior and your childhood experiences with recognition that you are not enslaved by the past; that however valid your parents' admonitions might have been in their time, conditions change and life's successive new challenges are yours to deal with in the here and now.
- Accept that anxiety is endemic in human affairs. It stems from our fundamental nature that in contrast to all other creatures we are aware of our possibility for creative action, not mere slaves to genetically coded instructions. Potentially, we can stand outside of ourselves and be attracted by dreams. But anxiety often results from this consideration and its possibilities. To move on to higher needs for power, achievement, and creativity involves danger and the risk of failure in facing the unknown. To be sure, we mature from such confrontations, but facing successful challenges means repeated separations, giving up old and comfortable ways and embracing new ones. If we do not respond to our beckoning needs, we may stagnate and be permanently chained to lower drives, becoming frustrated and embittered. "To venture," wrote Soren Kierkegaard, "is to face anxiety, but not to venture is to lose oneself."[33]

2

Dealing with Early Disappointment

A recent popular book aimed at newly graduating college students is entitled *Real Life 101.*[1] The book purports to offer all the advice necessary to make the transition from the artificial world of school to the tougher world of life and work. Such advice is needed. American residential colleges and universities offer one of the most extraordinarily privileged, but insulated, experiences in the world. The best schools have striven to offer young people a safe environment in which to experiment on defining their values and aspirations. The lucky students who spend four years on such a campus are allowed the period from ages eighteen to twenty-one as one of minimal responsibility to others in order to focus on themselves. Never again will most have this luxury.

Although I pale sometimes at the self-centeredness that such a college experience encourages, I believe the benefits from intellectual, psychological, and even moral growth far outweigh the unpleasant selfishness that often is expressed. Nonetheless, the elevated judgment of one's self-worth and the high aspirations that school encourages do contribute to some disappointment with work and life in the first years after school. In this chapter, we explore some of the causes of this disillusionment and how you might counter them. First let's look at one ambitious young woman's unhappy experience.

THE DISILLUSIONING OF KIM WEBSTER

Kimberly Webster had it all—brains, beauty, and athletic talent. When she was twelve, her father had begun coaching her community girl's softball team and he took great joy in throwing the ball to Kim as hard as he could, while she was able to return it even harder. One of his most cherished momentos of Kim's athletic career is the summary of her eighth grade season in junior high school when she batted .850!

Kim's athletic success continued in high school; she was all-county in both field hockey and lacrosse, attracting the attention of numerous college coaches. She loved the feeling of just tipping an opponent's stick as they were about to shoot—and herself powering through an attempted block to score for her team. The agony of running and the weightlifting were all justified by those moments of pure joy. In addition, Kim was an exceptionally talented writer who delighted in writing outlandish stories and humorous critiques of her numerous male and female friends. She accepted a scholarship to the esteemed Kane School of Journalism at Midwestern State University. Perhaps her most outstanding attribute was her impressive organization and self-discipline. She knew what she wanted to do and was able to structure her time and energy to accomplish her athletic, social, and academic goals.

College was a continuation of her success story. She majored in journalism while also taking management and marketing courses in the business school. She received eight varsity letters, was named all-league in field hockey and lacrosse, serving as captain of the latter team (she even received one vote for All-American). She was elected to the senior honor society for all-around contributions to the school.

As senior year progressed, Kim interviewed several advertising and public relations firms. While in college she had worked in alumni relations and athletic fundraising so she had good experience in dealing with the public through correspondence and telephone. In addition, because of her athletic visibility, she had valuable alumni contacts in in the industry, so she got interviews at several firms. She finally joined the advertising department of Hayfield's, a large multiple outlet regional department store chain.

Although not considered as prestigious as the prominent advertising firms, Hayfield's seemed to promise greater opportunity to quickly learn the fundamentals of catalog promotion and newspaper and electronic media advertising. The advertising department vice president Dexter Moore, happy to land a rare graduate of the university, assured Kimberly that she would have a private office, would be shifted between different sections, and would receive a salary review after six months. Susan Corman, the long-term Hayfield's employee who was her initial supervisor in catalog traffic control, promised that she would be sent to a computer training program, would have her own PC and would soon be able to work directly with the printer on galley and color separation approvals. Kim began work with great anticipation that in spite of Hayfield's rather shabby offices, she would be doing real work that would allow her to learn. She moved into a nice apartment with two friends and bought a new Volkswagen GTI.

Unfortunately, Kim was soon disillusioned. It bothered her that after three months she still had not received her own work station or computer, but had to borrow the desk of whomever was out of the office. Although she enjoyed the challenge of teaching herself how to use the computer, she couldn't understand why she was never sent to the training program on page design and desktop printing. What bugged her even more, however, was the routine and repetitive space calculation and manufacturer billing she had to do for the catalogs. It primarily involved arithmetic calculations (and Kim had avoided all mathematics courses in college). Hayfield's would prepare periodic catalogs and special promotional flyers that would be mailed to customers in various area codes. The manufacturers whose products appeared in each catalog would reimburse Hayfield's for printing and mailing costs depending on economic potential of the different customer areas and their products' share of the total catalog space. It was Kim's job to make these calculations, which she did basically sitting alone in the office. She rarely got to deal with the page designers, copywriters, product manufacturers, or printers.

Kim's supervisor Susan checked her work very closely and literally would peek over her shoulder at least ten times a day, yet would say little about what was being planned next. On a rare occasion when Susan asked Kim to substitute for her at a printer meeting, Sue neglected to tell Kim about special requirements on that particular catalog with the result that two pages featuring Estée Lauder and Adrienne Vittadini products were printed with the wrong colors. Since these two firms are *extremely* concerned about image, they refused to pay for their portion of the catalogs. Susan was very upset with Kimberly and yelled at her in front of the vice president. Kim kept her cool, but it took all her self-discipline to refrain from echoing Johnny Paycheck's song "Take this Job and Shove it" while quitting to go to the ski slopes which she so badly missed (along with her friends) since graduating.

After seven months when the half-year point for her promised salary review had passed with no action, Kim went to Mary Pinelli, the human resources manager, to whom she had talked when she was hired. Mary told her, however, that human resources could not compel the advertising department to change her salary and that perhaps Kim should wait until she had been there a year.

Still unhappy after eight months, Kim asked for an appointment with Dexter Moore, the vice president, to discuss the situation. After a three-week delay due to his traveling, Kim finally voiced her complaints about the absent performance review, salary reassessment, personal work station and computer and, most of all, Susan's overbearing supervision and inadequate sharing of information.

Dexter Moore assured Kim that he had heard nothing but good reports on her performance and that he had been impressed with her work on several occasions (what "occasions" they were, Kim couldn't imagine). The only complaints he had received had been when Kim had taken unexpected vacation or sick days on some Fridays and Mondays. Moore said that the advertising office needed a complete physical overhaul before they could fit in additional private work stations, but that he was hoping to have the funds for this in next year's budget. He also said that the human resources department had cancelled Hayfield's training agreement with a computer service firm so no courses had been offered for the last six months. He added, however, that Susan had told him she was impressed with Kim's self-developed computer skills. With regard to a salary adjustment, he said that a 5 percent increase was the most that human resources would approve at this time. Finally, Moore suggested that Kim be more patient with Susan Corman, a very loyal and valued Hayfield employee who cared deeply about advertising and about getting things right.

Kimberly tried to accept Moore's advice but began to be more assertive in making suggestions on catalog design. On several occasions she corrected some copywriter errors and even rewrote copy to make it more "playful" just before Susan would take it to the printer. Usually, however, the printed page came out closer to the original copy. In one instance Kim prepared a series of dummy newspaper ads that were very modernistic—over 90 percent was blank white space in contrast to the telephone directory appearance of most Hayfield ads. Her ideas were rejected with a comment that they were "pretty," but that Hayfield's traditional customers wanted more factual information.

When complaining to her parents about her unhappy experience at the department store, she said she was considering interviewing for another job that she had heard about at a recent meeting of the metropolitan public relations professional association in which she was active. She then asked, "Why did all those people make so many promises and then not keep them? Promises about an office, a computer, training, job rotation, and salary increase? Why did they say they wanted my creative ideas and then reject them all? Why do they all lie?"

WHY WAS KIM UNHAPPY?

Kim, like all of us, takes a self-centered view of her job search and first position at Hayfield's. In her eyes, Hayfield's "lied" to her about what they would do for her. If is not that her perception of things is wrong (factually she is probably correct), but that others saw Kim as less unique than she considered herself and were taking a longer-term view by testing whether she really wanted to be in advertising or at Hayfield's. But, Kim understandably was in a hurry.

All her life, Kim had found that hard work and supreme effort would bring success—stardom in athletics and good academic performance. Shots blocked, goals scored, and test grades were all concrete measures of what she had accomplished. Her need for achievement was strongly stimulated and satisfied by such feedback, not to mention recognition and attention from others. She thought the repetitive calculations at Hayfield's to be beneath her. Worst of all, any extra effort (such as correcting writer errors, rewriting copy, and proposing new styles) were systematically rejected.

In one sense she was correct: Kim's abilities are well above and beyond these particular tasks. But she is also a bit of a snob in denigrating the importance and difficulty of doing even simple tasks correctly. And the bad experience with the Lauder and Vittadini pages in the Hayfield catalog, although perhaps not her fault, illustrates the importance of getting details right. Still, Hayfield's presented a particularly frustrating situation for an ambitious person—repetitive and nonchallenging work, overly close supervision, no autonomy, and mainly negative feedback. No wonder she quit after little more than a year.

Kim asked her parents why her superiors at Hayfield's "lied" to her about the personal work station, computer, training, rotation, and salary review. Truth and falsehood of course are sometimes hard to tie down; but a generous interpretation of Dexter Moore and Susan Corman is that they were not "lying" so much as administratively disorganized and excessively concerned with landing Kim as an employee. No previous graduate of Kane School of Journalism had ever come to work at Hayfield's and so during recruiting and hiring they tended to say yes to whatever Kim wanted. Either Dexter or Susan didn't have the resources to deliver on their promises or they were so disorganized that they never recorded what they had promised. By not following through, however, they irredeemably lost Kim's trust.

Hayfield's would probably argue that everything would have come Kim's way if only she had been more patient. The nondelivered promises were delayed because of short-run budgetary problems and longer-run renovation and reorganization plans. They were pleased with her performance (except for her unanticipated absences, usually when she went skiing!) and even happy with her rebuffed creative initiatives, but they wanted to be sure she understood Hayfield's conservative customers and tradition before giving her more responsibility and autonomy. Most of all they wanted to see if she was really committed to Hayfield's, as were Moore and Corman who were referred to as "lifers."

But Moore and Corman were of a different generation and background than Kim. Coming from their more limited and modest situations, Hayfield's represented security, predictability, and community prestige along with moderately challenging and rewarding work. For Kim, however, economic security and social prestige were not goals; they were just assumed because she had always had them. And Hayfield's came to represent sacrificing her dreams for a challenging and successful career—and of course individual stardom.

Kim is unique, but her dissatisfaction with her first job and the first years after college is a common complaint. As General Motors' director of personnel development puts it: "The very best students tend to be more willing to leave an employer if that employer isn't providing them with opportunities to fulfill themselves."[2] Let's examine some of the reasons that the best and brightest often become frustrated and unhappy in this period.

CAUSES OF EARLY JOB DISSATISFACTION

The transition from college to the "real world" can be very difficult. Even the most ambitious (and perhaps especially the most ambitious) often become unhappy. The causes are several: time and money reality shock, conflicting individual and organizational expectations, possible overeducation, inadequate first supervisor, rejection of supervisory style, insensitivity to political environment, personal passivity, ignorance of real evaluative criteria, and tensions with older managers.

Time and Money Reality Shock. Graduating from school, becoming self-supporting, and starting a career is one of life's most exciting transitions. But it is also one of the most difficult because the reality is often quite different than what one hoped for.

The rhythms of time in one's life change dramatically from school to work. Time in class was seldom more than 15 to 18 hours a week. And supposedly, over half of all college students take a nap every day![3] That immediately disappears when you start work (unless you can catch some winks right at your desk, which of course is not unknown). While in school, time horizons are relatively short—six weeks to spring break, or a month to winter vacation, or only three months to a four-month summer vacation. Of course, most of you worked summers, but it was a different experience. In general, young adult males express the least future orientation and are more hedonistic and concerned with the present than *any* other age, group, or gender.[4] After graduation, however, time seems to stretch out endlessly. It can seem an eternity until you are eligible for a two-week vacation. The United States appears to have fewer vacation days than almost any other country: on average 14 days compared with a world-wide average of 21.3 days (in Holland, the average is 34.7 days!).[5] Even vacations for American senior executives in recent years have declined from 16 to 14 days per year.[6] And at twenty-one years of age the idea of a forty-year career is incomprehensible.

If time seems endless, money seems to evaporate as quickly as it is earned. Even a business school curriculum doesn't prepare people for dealing with the world of taxes, insurance, and budgets. You may have heard your parents complain about taxes, but that doesn't toughen you for the emotional shock of how much even a modest income is consumed by federal withholding, social security, state income, and local wage taxes. Starting salaries sound high to parents who remember their own pre–1970/1980s inflation income and even high to new graduates in comparison with their summer and part-time jobs. But unfortunately, while every other age group in the United States has over the past fifteen years experienced an increase in their real average incomes (for example, they can buy more than those who were their present age fifteen years ago), employees under the age of thirty are earning *less* in purchasing power than their older brothers and sisters did at that age. In most firms, starting salaries have not climbed as rapidly as inflation so that the real wages for those eighteen to twenty-nine have dropped by 18 percent in the 1970s and 1980s.[7]

Many MBA graduates are able to leapfrog this stagnating salary picture with offers in the $40,000 to $60,000 range. But even here, many of them sharply overestimate their ability to make time payments so they buy or rent excessively expensive automobiles, apartments, and homes. The *Wall Street Journal* survey of buying habits documents how impulsive and imprudent younger buyers tend to be. As one respondent in his twenties put it, people of his generation "want things fast—they want it now. They are less concerned with quality. They want short-term pleasure. They are less frugal. Companies have to be more competitive—they need flashier products and flashier names."[8]

Conflicting Individual and Organizational Expectations. School acculturates us to frequent promotions. Something happens every year to mark our climb up the educational ladder. Most of us would like something similar at work. Through rotating training programs and creating new positions from rapid growth, some firms are able to emulate school's upward movement. Promotions every 18 to 24 months were not rare in the past. But increasingly, corporations have come to see such rapid promotions as costly. As growth slows, the firm finds itself with excessive managerial levels, and many firms are trying to sharply reduce their number of managerial levels in order to promote more flexibility and greater efficiency.

Even if growth continues, many fast-trackers are promoted too rapidly, beyond the level of their competency so that they fail. Rather like the hot shot high school baseball player who is prematurely brought up to the major leagues, striking out causes confidence to evaporate and a promising career is truncated. Many firms report their intention to slow down their promotion rates, thus reducing the number of promotions in most people's careers.[9] This may be desirable from management's perspective, but younger graduates may not understand why things are moving slower for them than they did in the past.

Business school graduates often are trained with case studies to think like executives by defining solutions to top-level problems. If they enjoy this perspective, they may expect real work to be similar and assume their actual authority will equal the synthetic power accorded in class exercises. But such authority takes years to achieve and the ambitious are impatient.

Firms contribute to this dissatisfaction when they don't provide young graduates with sufficient challenge.[10] Large employers too often treat newly hired professionals as identical and assign them repetitive tasks that could be performed by people with less education. Although perhaps not formal "training programs," these early positions can be a kind of quasi-training, socialization program—the firm testing to see whether you "fit in." In the absence of objective performance results, subjective factors like social behavior and dress can weigh heavily in the firm's deciding whether or not you are a potential star. Older managers may argue that your expectations are unrealistic and you must "prove" yourself before being assigned to more important jobs. But most of us detest being treated as "average" or merely a member of a category. We want to be considered unique, if not special. Management's attitudes and policies may promote the very "immature behavior" that is given as the reason for their establishment. Patience and understanding are needed on both sides.

In thinking about my first two postcollege jobs, I am struck by the contrast between the excitement and satisfaction I found as a junior officer in the U.S. Navy and the boredom of my later engineering work at Eastman Kodak. At Kodak (a marvelous company which has made great revitalization strides in recent years) I occupied a desk in an enormous room with only glass dividers between some 300 of us best and brightest. The size of our desks, file cabinets, and coat stands (along with a dress code) were all identical and prescribed. But that was true in the Navy also. What was different, however, was that at twenty-four in the Navy I had a *real* job: managing four officers and 85 enlisted personnel with additional responsibilities as operations officer and navigator for a destroyer. The lives of 320 men depended on my conning the ship at high speed when on darkened ship plane guard duty at sea. And I navigated the ship from Newport, Rhode Island to Beirut, Lebanon and back. It was heady stuff. How different was my next job at Kodak when I had no authority, no subordinates, and shared a secretary with ten others. I had no responsibility other than trying to persuade middle-aged line managers to follow my advice (which they often thought hopelessly theoretical if not naively idealistic).

Life on a small warship like a destroyer is more like working for a small business than a large corporation. Beginning professional and managerial positions in small firms appear to be more challenging and satisfying than similar posts in the large.[11] Small companies cannot afford to train graduates on marginal tasks, so they put them to work on necessary activities immediately. Such operating responsibilities are more easily measured than large corporate staff jobs so young managers can demonstrate their ability objectively, which in turn gives them greater freedom from conformity to marginal behavior and appearance pressures.

Overeducation of Managers? Managers are increasingly well educated. At least they are going to school longer than did their predecessors. Today, over 90 percent of the executives at the top of American corporations have attended college.[12] As Exhibit 2–1 illustrates, thirty years ago this would have been less than 50 percent; eighty years ago, less than 40 percent.[13] Even more dramatic has been the increase in executives with graduate degrees. In 1986, 63 percent of chief executive officers had continued studies after getting a bachelor's degree with 22 percent possessing an MBA. By the mid–1990s, perhaps 50 percent of top executives will possess graduate degrees and 10 percent doctorates. The composite of recent attendees at the Wharton Advanced Management Program (average age forty-five and identified by their firms as their brightest coming stars) is 100 percent with bachelor's degrees, 29 percent with master's degrees, and 25 percent with Ph.D. degrees.

EXHIBIT 2–1: EDUCATION OF EXECUTIVES

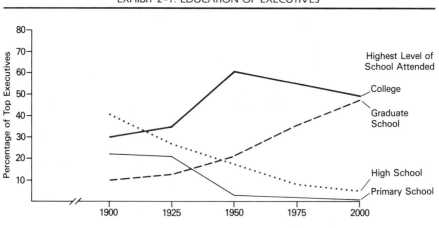

Causes of Early Job Dissatisfaction

Of the college-educated managers who climbed to the chief executive officer level, up until the early 1960s the most common main field of study was liberal arts. In the mid–1960s undergraduate engineering became the most common collegiate field. But by the mid–1980s undergraduate business had emerged as the most represented college major. As a management professor, I can hardly complain about the preeminence of business education as a source of chief executives, but others are voicing deep concern about declining interest among young Americans to study engineering (now under 10 percent), physical sciences (under 3 percent), mathematics (under 1 percent!).[14] Exhibit 2–2 summarizes undergraduate and graduate major fields of corporate chiefs as described by a *Fortune* survey.[15]

EXHIBIT 2–2: MAIN FIELDS OF SCHOOL STUDY FOR UNITED STATES CORPORATE CHIEF EXECUTIVE OFFICERS

UNDERGRADUATE		GRADUATE	
business	(33.3%)	business	(56.3%)
engineering	(24.0%)	law	(21.4%)
economics	(17.5%)	engineering	(10.8%)
humanities	(15.3%)	economics	(4.6%)
physical science	(5.8%)	physical science	(3.1%)
social science	(5.6%)	social science	(1.5%)
other	(5.4%)	humanities	(0.9%)
		other	(2.8%)

This emphasis on managers' educational credentials has transformed the organizational shape from a single pyramid to a small pyramid sitting atop a truncated larger one. The Horatio Alger myth was that a young man with no special education could enter at the bottom and through years of diligent effort work his way to the top on merit (women, of course, were not included in this early dream). This upward climb is virtually impossible today. A college degree or more is needed just to gain entry to the bottom rung of the managerial ladder in the wings of the upper pyramid.[16] In larger firms, these wing positions are more staff than managerial. Only as graduates establish and sell themselves do they move laterally or diagonally into line management. Unfortunately, this emphasis on higher education has made it increasingly difficult for the bright noncollege worker to jump from the lower pyramid to the upper. Unless he or she obtains the necessary educational credentials (perhaps by attending school at night), the barrier from lower to upper has become more impenetrable.

EXHIBIT 2–3: CONTEMPORARY CORPORATIONS

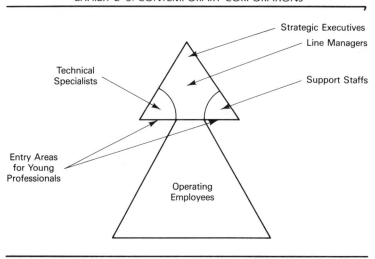

No one can knock the desirability of better-educated employees and managers. They offer great opportunity for more creative and productive firms. Nonetheless, the immediate impact appears less sanguine. Boredom and resentment can fester if the skills of the better educated are not utilized. At all organizational levels, employees with more education tend to have lower morale and to perform no better than those with less education working at the same level.[17] Thus, high school graduates working alongside college grads tend to be happier. Whether this also applies to those holding only bachelor's degrees working at the same level as MBAs is unknown.

Education increases (some say, inflates) expectations of intrinsic job challenge and satisfaction. So when jobs do not draw on the skills people think they possess, or when they believe they are being used below their status, employees become angry and withhold their commitment (and weld Coke bottles in the doors of luxury cars as has happened at some automobile firms).

These results do not argue for abolishing college (after all, college may be helpful in living a better life, even if it doesn't get you a better job). Rather, the situation suggests that companies should eliminate arbitrary educational requirements in favor of evaluating individual ability. All custodians don't need to be high school graduates, as some blue-chip corporations require. Similarly, all department heads need not be college graduates, nor need all vice presidents be holders of master's degrees. Finally, we need to recognize that greater education cannot carry an automatic guarantee of a more interesting and rewarding job.

Inadequate First Supervisor. Your first boss plays an especially important role in your career. The example he or she sets can dramatically affect the way you think about yourself, your employer, and your career for good or ill.[18] Supervisors who think poorly of young subordinates and fail to challenge them generally elicit weak performance in a kind of self-fulfilling prophecy.[19] Even worse, uncaring supervisors who present themselves as negative role models by not setting high standards for themselves cause everyone's performance to deteriorate. Other managers do not want alumni of such groups, so if you work for such a supervisor your guilt by association can mire you in a dead end.

Ambitious young specialists and managers want visibility and exposure—opportunities to show senior executives how well they can perform and to learn to understand corporate-wide objectives. Today, such access to the top appears to be even more important than predictable promotions. As an AT&T executive puts it:[20] "They don't want to know how they can go up the corporate ladder; they want to know about the environment they'll be working in. They don't want to know the pecking order as much as if they'll have access to the top."

Earlier generations were more mindful of their lowly status: "I revered the people at the top," says a 50-year-old G.E. manager. "I thought the person who ran the plant was a god. I had no contact with him at all. There was a tremendous caste system. You didn't go to him for anything without going up his chain of command."

A fearful intermediate supervisor can block such opportunity by relaying all communications himself or herself and not allowing subordinates to see higher levels. Handing a report to your immediate boss with no opportunity to argue in its favor and never hearing what happens to it can be very irritating (especially if you later discover that your name on the cover was replaced by your superior's!). Feeling no control over your job may be *the* strongest predictor of dissatisfaction and poor performance.[21]

The best firms institute policies to ensure that young professionals enjoy opportunities to communicate with and be evaluated by several higher executives, not just their immediate supervisors. One of Kodak's practices that I came to appreciate was its insistence that the staffer who drafted a proposal be present at each higher-level meeting on the issue. Thus, I would go all the way to the vice president's office (accompanied by my more immediate superiors) if that was to be the ultimate decision level. This gave me an opportunity to understand the vice president's objectives and to show how I could be valuable to the company.

When blocked from on-the-job opportunity to demonstrate your competence to high-level management, you can look for off-job possibilities through community volunteer activities.[22] Whether in Boy Scouts, Junior Chamber of Commerce, or volunteer rescue squads or fire departments, your commitment and good performance can come to the attention of various corporate officials who may then keep a special eye on you at work. One of my key opportunities at Kodak was serving as chairman of the engineering department annual clambake. Planning, coordinating, and executing this big function gave me direct access to the departmental vice president long before anything in my daily job would have (although it was a matter of courage when he insisted I eat raw clams with him—something I had never done before!).

Such outside work participation can be implicitly expected by companies, particularly in smaller cities and rural locales. Indeed, the demands can be so explicit that one can resent them as intrusions on personal time. Nonetheless, they offer opportunities to gain visibility earlier than might otherwise occur at work.

Traditional manufacturing firms often assigned young graduates to older supervisors who had lost out in the competition for promotions. Sometimes they took special interest in their young charges, but all too often the old-timers were perceived as "losers" and they behaved accordingly, thus providing poor models for the newcomers. Just as bad, however, can be initially reporting to stars and "winners." The complaints of young graduates entering prestigious investment banking houses and major management consulting firms are legion. Excited at obtaining a coveted position at a blue-chip firm, ambitious professionals often are disappointed to find that their intensely achievement-oriented superiors just don't have the time (or patience) to talk to them—or at least with nothing more than curt demands.

Craftsmanlike people who are primarily motivated by their own achievement needs are often very good as independent staff professionals and technical specialists. They are driven to get the job done. Unfortunately, they often run into difficulty as they move into management positions requiring stronger interpersonal skills.[23] They often see other people as tools or obstacles, not as fellow human beings. All too often such managers emphasize short-term results heedless of longer-term consequences—so much so they have been called "*destructive achievers.*"[24]

Not that intensely achievement-oriented supervisors dislike others; liking is simply irrelevant. What counts for such people is getting others to behave in the interest of their personal achievement. Understandably, most of us dislike such impersonal and manipulative behavior—behavior that often is labeled Machiavellian after the Italian sixteenth-century philosopher, Niccolo Machiavelli. And indeed, high achievement need seems associated with a test measuring one's index of Machiavellianism.[25] As a result, poor interpersonal skills represent the single largest reason for early and mid-career managerial failure.[26] The *Wall Street Journal* article on an intensely achievement-oriented Washington, DC Treasury Department star illustrates this human insensitivity:[27]

> In a city where comity and cooperation get things done, and where egos are easily bruised, Mr. Mulford's manner sometimes undercuts his best intentions. That was certainly the case earlier this year when Manual Johnson, vice chairman of the Federal Reserve Bank, traveled across town to visit Mr. Mulford. Mr. Johnson had scheduled the meeting to smooth over some policy differences. Mr. Mulford, however, kept him waiting in his outer office for more than 30 minutes—a first degree insult by sensitive Washington standards. Usually a patient man, Mr. Johnson finally left without seeing Mr. Mulford—and without getting an explanation until months later . . .
>
> Mr. Mulford defends his policy initiatives, but doesn't entirely dismiss the criticism of his style . . . "As I look back over my past experiences . . . I was always on my own. Without meaning to, that develops characteristics which are sometimes not as sensitive to coordination as it might otherwise be."

As one executive expressed his concern about current MBAs: "Something has happened. These young people seem intent on destroying each other to get to the top."[28] A former automobile company executive described what he saw as Motown's Machiavellis.[29]

> We almost never said publicly what we actually thought about the merits of an issue. Instead, we concocted positions we hoped would help us rig relationships with customers, suppliers or competitors in our favor. I hated this approach which was contrary to my beliefs and harmful—I felt—to (the company's) business . . . It took me a while to put the pieces together. But soon I understood that by working at (the company) I was witnessing people betraying themselves and their neighbors in pursuit of personal advancement and corporate advantage.

This Detroit complainer felt that such machiavellianism brought personal success at the firm's expense so he quit. Actually, I think it is more likely that in time such manipulating managers are rejected by their colleagues because of the havoc they create. And my subjective feeling is that since the evaporation of the Wall Street myth of young wealth in the crash of October 1987, current MBAs are becoming less arrogant in their attitudes toward prospective employers and colleagues.

Surprisingly, managers who are primarily concerned about people also are usually inadequate as first supervisors. Managers who are driven by their affiliation needs often express great commitment and loyalty to the firm and to their subordinates. At first, they appear to young professionals as being desirable supervisors, but in time their faults emerge. Affiliative-oriented managers are dominated by a short-run concern for pleasing people and being liked. When talking with a subordinate, such a supervisor is mainly concerned with the here and now. He or she is extremely sensitive to whether you are happy with what you are hearing. So you leave the meeting with the words you wanted to hear. But later you discuss your boss's promises with your colleagues John and Mary and discover that they have different (and perhaps better) deals. Or in time you become disenchanted when your supervisor is unable to deliver on the promises made.

The problem here is less the affiliative-oriented manager's "lies" than a short-range perspective in which unique deals are made heedless of the precedents they may set or even of the manager's ability to deliver on the promises. Uncoordinated deals are struck with individual subordinates who later are angry with perceived inequities. Because of their inconsistency, such managers are accused of "playing favorites." Some strongly affiliative-oriented managers are so submerged in the moment's emotions that they don't even make notes on what they've promised their subordinates—and *nothing* will more surely guarantee a manager's loss of credibility.

Managers who desperately want to please their subordinates can make disastrous mistakes in budget management. Particularly right after assuming office, some immediately transfer department discretionary funds to subordinate managers' control. Thus, subordinates are happy to have what appears to be "new" money, but the appreciation-craving superiors have eliminated their marginal control and flexibility. They become victims of an inflexible budget growing out of their own desire to please. To be an effective manager requires transcending the immediate event to see it in the long run. You shouldn't make decisions just to satisfy the present moment without anticipating how the decision will affect others in the future.

Rejection of Supervisory Style. When I was serving full time in university administration, I did very little teaching. I was totally out of the classroom for five years and didn't teach any undergraduates for eight years. Upon announcing my intention to return to the teaching faculty, I consulted several of my junior colleagues for guidance on what teaching techniques worked among young students. I was told that old-style, one-way lectures were anathema. In the absence of compulsory attendance, students wouldn't even show up because they so disliked such a unidirectional, authoritarian style. This didn't surprise me because this rejection began twenty years ago.

I was surprised to hear, however, that my junior colleagues felt that students also didn't particularly like a Socratic style with the teacher posing questions and guiding the students to uncover the relevant issues by answering their questions with more questions. Students preferred this to lectures but felt (according to my junior faculty advisers) that the teacher was manipulating the class.

In growing alarm, I asked what techniques did work well with today's undergraduates. My colleagues responded, "experiential exercises." In their opinion, what students like the most are exercises in which the faculty role is minimized. After structuring the exercise, the professor steps aside and the students *behave*. Records are kept, notes taken, and results tabulated which are then discussed. But it is the exercise itself and the ensuing discussion that elicits learning, not the teacher. Students construct the meaning of what they've done from the experience, not from the teacher's knowledge or expertise being handed to them or used to influence their answers.

Of course, the professor is not as passive in this process as the students may think, but my young faculty colleagues' observations are entirely consistent with what has been termed the "self-developing" motivation of today's best and brightest students, young professionals, and junior managers.[30] They are supposedly characterized by the following attributes:

Skepticism about authority. It is less that they reject authority than they don't believe its experience and expertise are relevant to the situation they confront. As managers themselves, this means they feel uncomfortable telling their subordinates what to do, preferring joint decisions and participation. This contributes to their long work weeks, many over sixty hours per week.[31]

Lack of faith in the firm or in loyalty. They have learned (validly) that the "organization man" route of upward success through loyalty is dead, so they don't believe the firm has the right to make decisions about their careers without their involvement. Indeed, many believe their primary obligation is to their own career so that all opportunities must be listened to, even if not solicited.

Rejection of passivity. Skepticism about the knowledge or intentions of the firm forces young self-developers to conclude that they must be active in structuring their learning environments. They don't want to be told what to do by a wise or expert superior, but would rather learn through trial, error, and success.

A "playful" attitude. They desire a blurring of the boundary between work and play, so that work is "fun" and "fun" occurs on the job. Superficially, this takes the form of practical jokes, company ski lodges, and Silicon Valley-like afternoon beer parties. More fundamentally, it means discretionary resources to "play" with in exploring new ideas without having to account for immediate results as closely as with regular duties.

These attitudes are a distillation of values found among today's best and brightest so they are not a description of any single person. Nor do they purport to describe the majority of young people, many of whom express more traditional views. Self-developers are clearly a socioeconomic and educational elite. Nonetheless, most of my graduate students feel comfortable describing themselves along these lines and feel no need to apologize. Many older executives, however, disagree because to them these attributes are devoid of a sense of commitment and responsibility— and are just plain selfish.

Whatever one's value judgment about the attractiveness or unattractiveness of this self-developer motivational profile, such people are uncomfortable with superiors whose leadership styles are bureaucratic ("obey because the organization chart says I'm the boss"), authoritarian ("obey because I have the power to hurt or help you"), and even persuasive ("do it this way because my expertise and experience indicate it's the best choice"). Rather, they are best motivated by a superior who creates a kind of game, allowing room for their autonomy and innovation. By giving them resources to play with, allowing them time and freedom to do so, and promising a share in the rewards from their innovation, such a leader draws out their best energy and effort.

I recently spoke to all senior managers at a large state university. I tried to explain why after the countercultural movement of the late 1960s and early 1970s, business won the battle for the minds (if not the hearts) of America's best students. Most of my audience were children of the 1950s and 1960s and could only attribute current student interest in business careers as greed. I said it was equally a desire for autonomy and action. At General Electric, for example, the chief executive officer, Jack Welch, has instituted a kind of "playpen" system. In this organization, if you head one of the twelve major businesses each year, you are given $25 million dollars to allocate among your managers for play. Of course it can't go to buy cigarette boats or BMWs, but the money can be used to try out new ideas without need to account for expenditures or justify any immediate results. It is "play" that reflects deadly serious investment in the future.

On describing this concept to my university audience, they just groaned; not so much at the amount of money, but at the unhappy fact that they must prepare and account for every dollar in their budgets up to eighteen months in advance. *No* slack or flexibility exists. They can't "play" with any money and *this year* is the longest time horizon their system allows. And it is boring and frustrating.

Government and not-for-profit institutions particularly suffer from a shortage of resources and overly restrictive bureaucratic controls, but of course many businesses do also. In general, however, today's most innovative firms provide internal environments more attractive to self-developer types.

Insensitivity to Political Environment.

All human organizations are political. For a business to be effective, its managers must engage in the politics by which power is directed to problems and solutions implemented. Unfortunately, many young managers are insensitive to or resentful of "office politics." This hurts them personally because they become passive about their careers and it hurts the firm because it hinders the power coalition development necessary for effective performance.

Managers who rapidly climb hierarchies tend to be protégés of successful higher executives.[32] We discuss mentors in greater detail in Chapter 8, but in general, sponsor-protégé linkages move together because their members come to respect and trust each other. They personalize organizational life and make it more predictable. A manager who has a problem prefers to consult a friend, not just an anonymous incumbent of a bureaucratic position. Unfortunately, the criteria for inclusion in the group are often arbitrary and undemocratically devoted to old school ties and "proper" religion, race or gender, but they are still important.

The importance of political relationships to the corporation is that they form the power coalitions necessary to implement decisions. Very few firms are autocratically ruled by an omnipotent chief executive; even fewer are pure democracies in which the majority dominates. Most require a skillful minority coalition able to lead the majority through competent argument and common action. Without strong coalitions, power remains fractionated, actions are divisive, and the firm drifts willy-nilly.

Older pragmatic executives sometimes complain that recent business school graduates overemphasize rational analytical tools to the detriment of human understanding.[33] Like the primarily achievement need-oriented managers described in the preceding section, many young grads treat others as manipulable objects. And indeed, business school students appear to be even higher in their indices of machiavelianism than practicing managers.[34] With experience, successful managers learn that they generally must treat people with respect and honesty or retaliation will render them ineffective. Unfortunately, some bright and ambitious young professionals learn too slowly. One senior corporate executive told me that half of the MBAs he hired failed and were asked to leave after three or four years because they still hadn't learned that "people are human beings and not merely entries in some analytical equation."

Personal Passivity. Young professionals who are insensitive to their political environments frequently are also characterized by personal passivity and inadequate probing of the world around them.[35] Overly confident people may assume that their virtue guarantees reward and that their good intentions are enough to make everyone think they are doing a fine job. The less confident may feel helpless because organizations seem to have so many confining rules and traditions that one can't risk being different. To behave differently might be dangerous because "one simply doesn't do that." Of course, corporations demand substantial conformity, but many binding chains are of our own forging because we are afraid to test ourselves or lack faith that the firm would reward our initiatives.

Drifting with the times in the hope that things will work out for the best is tempting but not a recipe for managerial success. The paradox is that it may be the most promising young staff specialists who find it easiest to drift. To be in demand connotes status, and being busy gives a feeling of importance. Talented young people sometimes allow themselves to be dominated by others' desires, to become captives of narrow specialties, and to remain in staff positions too long. If you think of the firm as a cone, as in Exhibit 2–4, staff tends to be on the outer surface whereas line management is closer to a central power axis. A thirty-year-old staffer fairly high on the surface of the cone might erroneously denigrate a lower line position physically farther away from the top but closer to the power axis with a more direct route upward.

EXHIBIT 2–4: THE CORPORATE POWER AXIS

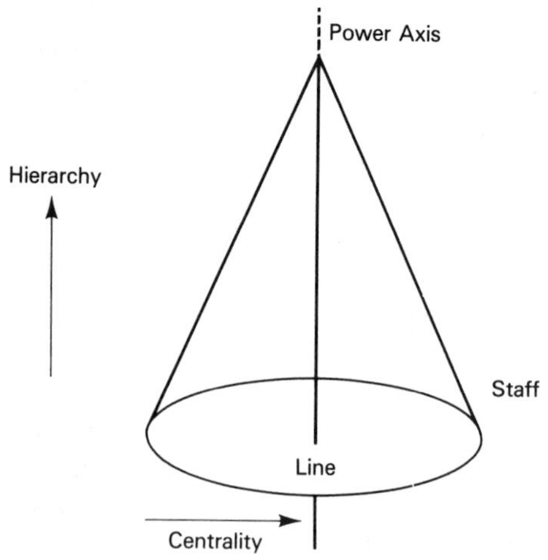

A firm's various functions and departments don't carry little red flags identifying their centrality and firms vary according to their industry, products, and services. Nonetheless, one overall measure suggestive of proximity to the power axis is the primary functional experience of the chief executive officer. A *Fortune* survey of large firms indicated the backgrounds of CEOs as:[36]

sales/marketing (31.6%)
finance (27.0%)
production/operations (19.5%)
legal (9.2%)
engineering/research/development (9.0%)
personnel/human resource management (0.2%)

Concern about declining manufacturing competitiveness in the United States has led to a call for more emphasis being placed on manufacturing and operations management. With the stock market crash in October 1987, the MBA classes of 1988 and 1989 did appear to somewhat shift their interests from finance to production management. Whether this was a temporary or more lasting reorientation is not yet known. Clearly (and unfortunately given its importance in solving today's management problems), personnel or human resource management experience has not been particularly relevant to becoming a firm's chief executive officer.

Tension with Older Managers. Tension between different aged professionals is very common. It may be greater or lesser depending on personalities, but basically the tension stems from differences in life and career stages. Recent graduates understandably rely on what they know best—academic knowledge from school. Statistics, finance, psychology, and economics learning, of course, can all be very valuable, but they can also hinder working relationships with older colleagues. Armed with an arsenal of analytical techniques, you look for problems to which they can be applied. But frequently the problems the textbooks have solved are not the important ones in your firm. Worse yet, talking to seniors in the arcane vocabulary of *stochastic variables, portfolio theory, breakeven points,* and *self-actualizing opportunities* can be threatening to them. Older managers to whom such terms are unfamiliar may believe they are being manipulated.

In some cultures older persons are automatically respected for age and assumed wisdom, but in the United States the young often respond to older people's skepticism with thinly veiled contempt. Because an older manager does not know the latest techniques, the young professional erroneously infers that the manager is incompetent or impotent. This can be a career-crippling mistake, because political influence has little to do with technical knowledge. An offended older executive can scuttle the offending younger manager's advancement.

You need to recognize that some older managers may see you as a threat (although they will deny it even to themselves). The threat is not to their job, but to their obsolescence. You are a reminder of human mortality—and this is so even when your boss personally likes you.[37] The best younger managers know how to project themselves into the shoes of their boss and anticipate what his or her needs and anxieties are, recognizing that they must give as well as receive.[38]

WHAT DID KIMBERLY WEBSTER DO?

After fifteen months, Kimberly resigned from Hayfield's. Everyone expressed disappointment with her departure, but from the grapevine she later learned that Susan Corman and several other supervisors were pleased to see her leave because in their opinion Kim was just "too unreliable, impatient, and aggressive to fit in" at Hayfield's.

Kim accepted a position she had heard about at her professional society meeting: promoting travel and tourism for the state government (with a 50 percent increase in salary). Although the department has its share of bureaucratic red tape and political log-rolling, she was immediately given much more authority and autonomy than she had ever achieved at Hayfield's—partly because her boss is a political appointee looking for a new job since the governor was in the last year of his second term and couldn't succeed himself. Within her first year, Kim became the publisher, editor, and writer of the statewide newsletter for travel agents and primary liasion with all of the travel-related industries in the state's lake resort area, its primary tourist attraction. She gives numerous talks to business organizations and even represented the state on a promotional tour of western Europe to drum up foreign tourists. The midwestern tourist agents professional association featured her in a photograph and first-page interview about this trip in their newspaper. (To Kim it felt a little like her college newspaper's coverage of her game-winning goal against Northwestern.)

Although burdened by the demands on her time, she takes great pride in various groups explicitly asking the state to designate her as their liaison (not to mention the unsolicited job offers which she receives). She spends approximately half of her time out of the office and enjoys great discretionary control over how she allocates her time. The two-hour automobile drives for luncheon with executives of a major tourist attraction are a bit of a pain, but she enjoys the luxury of working late when she needs to and taking an afternoon off when no pressing duties or meetings are calling.

Kim's ultimate dream is to open her own business because she doesn't want to have to report to *anyone!*

Kim clearly craves autonomy in her daily work life with an eventual target of being her own boss. She is not frightened by having to structure her environment and rather enjoys unpredictability in her work. She is not entirely a loner, however, because she still wants to be a star whose performance is seen and praised by others. Perhaps in time she will not be so dependent on others to ratify her competence, but it is important to her now.

ADVICE ON COUNTERING EARLY DISSATISFACTION

- In taking a job, don't be seduced by a firm's "glamour" or the luxury of its offices. What counts is whether your duties are "real" in that the firm will depend, however modestly, on your performance.
- In considering a job, ask senior managers and junior professionals what policies the firm has for ensuring that you will have opportunities to learn about top corporate concerns and to demonstrate your abilities to higher levels.
- From the beginning, balance your work and personal life. Don't allow your first job to so dominate your time that quitting becomes the only means of escaping the pressure.
- Clarify in advance what criteria are used to evaluate your performance. Aim to work in a job where your results are measurable. Insist on frequent informal performance feedback rather than allowing your supervisor to save it all up for an annual merit review.
- Minimize your time in quasi-training staff positions where subjective factors dominate your performance evaluation.
- Strive to move toward the firm's power-axis functions. If offered a move toward the center, never quibble about title, pay, or prerequisites. A lateral move toward centrality is a promotion even without more money.
- If you have been unable to earn the higher educational credentials so valued by many firms, strive to work for a less structured, probably smaller, entrepreneurial business where degrees are less critical than experience and performance.
- If unhappy with your first supervisor, don't denigrate him or her but attempt to please while simultaneously seeking opportunities to im-

press other managers and executives. Off-job professional, church, service, and political activities can sometimes provide chances to make contacts and demonstrate your abilities.

- Fight for the right to go with your project analyses and proposals to whatever level at which they are discussed. Be prepared to talk about your ideas when chance opportunities occur.
- After conversations with your supervisor, write a memo summarizing your understanding of what was said. You might then share it with him or her in the manner of, "Here's what I understood you to say at our meeting. Is my interpretation correct? Anything I missed?" And, "I really appreciate your taking the time to talk to me."
- Recognize that your intellectual knowledge and analytical skill are to be admired but will seldom be sufficient for you to be successful. Accept that less technically knowledgeable employees and managers are also valuable and are to be respected. Be careful to avoid embarrassing them by using arcane vocabulary with which they are unfamiliar.
- Accept that your very youth can be a little threatening to middle-aged colleagues and superiors. Don't respond by avoiding them. Rather, reach out to build the vertical coalitions so helpful to both older and younger managers.
- All other things being equal, try to work for a manager who is like you in personal style, values, and philosophy. He or she will be a bit more likely to value your contributions highly.
- Look for opportunities to do what is right for the firm even if corporate policies (but not society's laws) would be violated. Almost all human groups, from families to nations, bend the rules for those deemed most valuable. This mild hypocrisy allows exceptional individuals to depart from accepted policy and initiate new ideas. Avoiding punishment, however, depends on successful contribution to the organization. Failure usually brings rejection.

3

Overcoming Overload and Stress

To paraphrase William Shakespeare, all the world's a stage and we men and women are players attempting to fulfill the requirements of our various roles to the cheers or jeers of our multiple audiences. Students may also be sons or daughters, boyfriends or girlfriends, athletes, reporters, church members, and citizens. Professors may be teachers, researchers, consultants, wives or husbands, mothers or fathers, community volunteers, or home mechanics. A business executive may also be trustee of a local hospital, area chair for college alumni, deacon at church, finance committee member at the country club, and candidate for election to the township board of commissioners. Some of these roles are more enjoyable than others, but virtually all generate stresses and strains.

In this chapter we examine the concept of role demands and desires and the ways in which we become overloaded by competition among the various expectations others have of us. We describe several helpful tactics for handling (if not eliminating) the stress we feel including flight (seldom desirable), selective ignorance (easier for some than others), responding to power (a favorite of office politicians), responding to legitimacy (the bureaucrat's salvation), compartmentalizing responses (the time manager's favorite), modifying demands (the courageous hero's approach), and changing your desires (the advice of many religious seers).

To provide concrete examples of role overload and life stress, let's first look at two young, dual-career couples whose success appears to be creating new problems.

LOVE IN THE AIR

Robert Goldman and Sylvia Garfein. Sylvia was the only daughter of a successful New York physician. Her mother was a mathematics teacher in a Manhattan high school. Sylvia was pushed to excel; she did; and she enjoyed it. After attending the prestigious Bronx High School of Science, she entered M.I.T. where she majored in chemistry, graduating *magna cum laude*. Her focus was medicine from the beginning, so she worked part time and summers in a Boston hospital. Her parents missed her but supported her independence and ambition. All this drive left her little time for social life, platonic or romantic. The family was disappointed when Sylvia was rejected for admission to Harvard Medical School, but she persevered by working full time for a year in a research laboratory (earning an M.S. in biochemistry along the way). She so enjoyed the process of experimental research that she considered going on for a Ph.D. However, on her second round of applications, she was accepted to Columbia College of Physicians and Surgeons at Columbia University in New York City. During her fourth year in medical school, she met Robert Goldman.

Goldman was somewhat older than his fellow students at Columbia's Graduate School of Business. He had also grown up in New York, but his parents had operated a grocery store in Queens. He had attended City University of New York, majoring in accounting because it seemed to offer the best promise of secure employment. It did, but he hated it. He felt that the firm treated him like a child with its rules and procedures that drained the auditors of any discretion. After three years, he left to start his own wholesale food business. He loved being his own boss and even enjoyed the early morning hours. But his ambitions seemed to outreach his business knowledge, so Goldman decided to study for an MBA (while still running his business). During his second year he met Sylvia.

It was not love at first sight, but a kind of instant old friendship that sometimes springs up between two mature people who have had little time in the past for such a relationship. Although their childhoods in New York had been different, they shared the city and the commonality exceeded the difference. Both Robert and Sylvia were a bit surprised when they decided to get married before living together. At ages thirty-one and twenty-seven, respectively, they felt quaintly old-fashioned.

Careers and marriage went well for the first two years. Sylvia interned at Mount Sinai Hospital and Robert built his wholesale business along with other New York ventures. Last year, however, Sylvia was offered an opportunity as senior resident at Peter Bent Brigham Hospital in Boston with an instructorship at Harvard Medical School. It was a once-in-a-lifetime opportunity that both Sylvia and Robert reluctantly agreed she should take. They vowed to visit whenever possible and they have, although somewhat less than anticipated. About one weekend in three Sylvia gets to New York or Robert to Boston. Unfortunately, the sometimes long and unpredictable hours in their careers make planning difficult.

Sylvia comments on the situation:

> "I love my work and I still get a thrill walking into the Harvard Medical School building. In the beginning I was having panic attacks because I didn't know what to do. My lab director just left me alone so I had to figure out what I was to explore. For a while I suffered a kind of writer's block; I just couldn't get started after all those years of jumping through the hoops that others held up for me. But gradually I was able to focus on my own

coherent project involving sensitive gene splicing. Did I tell you, I've been made an assistant professor? And Dr. Stromberg, he won the Nobel Prize three years ago remember, he's asked me to join his research team. I will be operating on the frontier of genetic theory. There's no limit to where it can lead—the people who can be helped, the parental grief prevented. It's great, but I do wish my husband would move up here. I love Boston. It's so much more civilized than New York. We could get an apartment in Cambridge near the river. We could certainly afford it. We must be making well over $100,000 per year between us. So far, he refuses even to discuss the possibility. Even my parents are angry at me."

Robert comments:

"I can't leave New York. I'm a *New Yorker*. Sylvia can operate in Cambridge, but I can't. She has a thing about Harvard and M.I.T. They make her feel like Abigail Adams or something. I feel like a foreigner. And, sometimes I think Sylvia's associates snicker at my accent. I'm treated like Mr. Garfein. Besides, my businesses are here; they can't just be moved. And I won't allow someone else to run them. That's how companies get ruined and owners robbed. Someday I'll have the biggest food brokerage firm in the city. I know it. I've backed Sylvia; I've cooked the meals; I've cleaned the apartment—or I did when she lived here. Now I eat out mainly and the place is a mess. I'm going to be thirty-five years old soon. I'm too old to be living as a bachelor. I'm in no hurry to have children, but we can't wait forever. And Sylvia's parents are getting older. They need her too."

Louise O'Brien and Mark Grazia.

Louise and Mark have been married since senior year at the University of Illinois. Both worked for a year in Chicago after graduation. Mark was disappointed in his work in a bank, however, and decided to get an MBA. Louise more or less decided to apply also, although she wasn't really sure that she was committed to a serious career. Since they were both good students with valuable work experience, they were both accepted to the Kellogg School at Northwestern University. Between part-time work, family support, and loans, they survived. Louise had to take a semester off to have an unplanned child, but Mark became an adept father, able to split chores. One or the other appearing at school with the baby in a backpack was not unknown.

After graduation, Louise accepted a position with the Chicago-based national account office of a major consulting firm. Mark had already started with a large accounting firm as a tax specialist. Once again, the sharing and parental help assisted them in bearing the burden of child-rearing and business travel. They set up a system whereby if they weren't both home, each weekend Louise would fly to wherever Mark was or vice versa. The one coming from Chicago would bring their son. Unfortunately, the travel has proved to be more than either anticipated.

Mark comments on the situation:

"I'm getting tired! And my mother worries that I'm too thin. All this flying around with Kevin is ridiculous. He's almost four now and will have to go to school soon. Besides, we must spend $20,000 a year on airplane tickets just to be together. I know it would mean a big income loss, but I think Louise should get a local job where she can stay put and we can begin a normal life. To tell you the truth, I could do better in my job if I had more support from Louise. I've heard that you can tell a dual-career marriage by looking in the refrigerator. It's empty while the freezer is full. That certainly describes our home! Anyway, we'd save on the airline fares."

Louise comments:

"Mark wants me to quit my job. I guess I will. Life at work has really been a pain lately. Oh, everyone thinks highly of me, but that's part of the problem. All sorts of senior and junior partners want me to work on their projects and I usually say yes because many of them are exciting. But sometimes they bump into each other. For the last six months my major assignment has been analyzing regional competition and customer attitudes for a large food company. Frank Contaldo is the partner in charge and he is a real star, a bit compulsive in his work demands and singlemindedness, but I've never had any trouble with him—at least not until two weeks ago when I wasn't around when he needed someone to fill in for him at a meeting in New York. I was in Los Angeles participating in a sales pitch on a new project that Aubrey Bedford (the consulting firm's managing partner) was trying to sell. Aub has been kind of an informal mentor for me and I just couldn't disappoint him because he has grown comfortable with me assisting on these presentations. Then last week, out of the blue, one of the largest computer manufacturers called the office and asked for me personally to come out and talk about a possible project the next day. They had heard about me from a recently acquired small software firm for whom I had done some work a year ago. It was really flattering, but I had to ask for a two-week postponement of the meeting because I was just so tied up with Frank's work. I must have set a company record for billable hours this month!

In all of this Mark has been a real support, but now he wants me to quit this job because Kevin must enter kindergarten next year. I worry that I'll be bored at home or that I'll settle for some lousy job just to fill up my time. It would be a waste of my MBA and I really worry that years from now I'll blame Mark for my not making partner (at the consulting firm). Still, it would be nice to wake up in the same bed every morning!"

HOW MUCH CAN PEOPLE DO?

Our fledgling "thirtysomething" foursome are deeply enmeshed in the complexity of modern, dual-career life. By dint of great commitment and hard work, they are apparently achieving all of the goals which they set for themselves: valuable academic education and degrees, challenging work with prestigious firms, and attractive remuneration. But the burdens of "having it all" are becoming excessive and both couples are experiencing great strain. Clearly they have shared family burdens to a greater extent than in traditional families, but however modern they feel themselves to be, they (the men especially) are beginning to long for a more "normal" life style—which shapes up as having the wife sacrifice something in her career to give priority to family.

Louise is particularly tempted by an opportunity to simplify her life because of the role stress built into her job. Because of her past good performance, she receives multiple, uncoordinated offers from various partners to become involved in their projects. The assignments are interesting and because she wants to impress her seniors, Louise finds herself overburdened with competing demands—and runs the risk of committing the most heinous of crimes in consulting: missing a promised deadline or barely making it with shoddy work. However attractive the possibility of getting out of the rat race, Louise fears that dropping out will make it impossible to ever return to the fast track with its possibility of making partner.

Sylvia Garfein, however, loves virtually everything about her job. The prestige of association is great, the money adequate, the environment pleasing and, most important, the work offers enormous potential for aiding people. To her, medicine is a real calling—and pressed deeply, she might well feel that what she is doing for mankind is more important than what her husband Robert Goldman is doing with his several entrepreneurial ventures.

Our four careerists are not alone in feeling the pressures of work and their own aspirations.[1] A 1987 Harris poll illustrated the decline in leisure time in the United States (for example, hours per week available for leisure-time activities not including sleep, household chores, and work):

1973—26.2 hrs/wk
1975—24.3
1980—19.2
1984—18.1
1987—16.6

The consistency of this fall reflects the entry of women into the workplace, the expansion of dual-career couples, the increase in single-parent households and a general increase in the work year for Americans because of intensified foreign competition and staff reductions. Among the major industrialized nations, the United States appears to be second only to Japan in an employee's hours worked per year (well ahead of the United Kingdom, France, and Germany). And the United States is the *only* one of these countries where the work year has increased since 1970.[2] From 1973 to 1989, the average work week in the United States increased from 40.6 to 48.8 hours per week. And on average, professional people and those with incomes over $50,000 per year work over 52 hours per week.[3]

No miracles exist to eliminate the stress felt by our four brave souls, but tactics are available for managing role and life stress which we consider after presenting some role theory.

THE CONCEPT OF ROLE

Every person in an organization is expected by his or her superiors, peers, subordinates, and others to behave in certain ways called role demands. These demands are made by various people with whom we work and live—those role partners who collectively comprise one's role set.[4] These expectations often are not identical to what we perceive or desire the role to be. Our actual behavior or role performance reflects a reconciliation of our desires and others' demands. To all those in our role set, our effectiveness depends on how closely our behavior meets their demands. Our role satisfaction, however, depends on how closely behavior fits our role desire. Exhibit 3-1 summarizes these elements.

EXHIBIT 3-1: ROLE DIMENSIONS

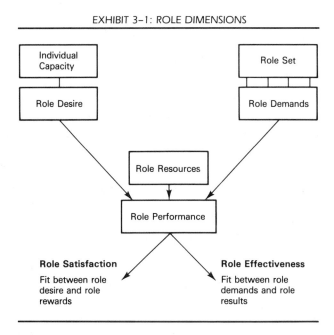

Individual Capacity	Role Set
Role Desire	Role Demands

Role Resources

Role Performance

Role Satisfaction
Fit between role desire and role rewards

Role Effectiveness
Fit between role demands and role results

Conflict Between Desire and Demands. If a person's characteristics are largely unsuited to role demands, he or she is likely to experience frustration leading to dissatisfaction, reduced commitment, and eventually poorer performance.[5] Hence, a quiet, passive, contemplative person may heartily dislike the pace and initiative required in sales. Or the achievement-oriented, hard driver may have difficulty teaching when student progress is so slow and ambiguous that little performance feedback is received.

Most people are unhappy when they are misassigned so that position demands are mostly outside his or her capacity. An example is the mythical misassignment of military personnel: the civilian truck driver is assigned to the mess hall as cook; the former restaurant chef is ordered to become a radio operator; the former television repairer is sent to the motor pool as a driver, and so on (actually, the modern Army generally strives to match people and positions).

Insufficient Resources. Wanting to meet the demands upon you and feeling confident that you have the personal capacity to do so can be particularly frustrated by insufficient resources, inadequate power, and persistent failure.[6] In telemarketing, for example, those unwelcome calls that always seem to interrupt your dinner are rejected perhaps 85 percent of the time with a "no," "don't call again," and unprintable oaths. It can be rough on the callers (assuming they are real humans and not a computer), especially when they feel the same way about being interrupted.[7] Not surprisingly, turnover is extremely high.

Lack of time, money, material, or people are all well-known causes of frustration. Of increasing importance in personal feelings of stress and hopelessness is the inability to get the information needed to act.[8] Not being able to access the required files or get meetings with appropriate people tends to breed feelings of powerlessness and anger which often find outlet in "bossism" toward those people unfortunate enough to have you as a superior.

Inadequate Demand. When a position's demands are small compared with your capacity, you become bored rather quickly. This is the familiar stereotype of the narrowly defined and programmed blue-collar production job (which many college students take as summer jobs and find excruciatingly boring). As we saw in Chapter 2, many young college graduates also find their first professional positions unchallenging. For example, some firms have graduate engineers performing tasks that don't draw on their analytical skills and could be performed by lesser-educated technicians (if they were available).[9]

Demand Overload. Even the best of us can find ourselves in a situation where the demands exceed our capacity to respond. You may feel that you have already been there because in 1988 21.5 percent of all college freshmen reported feeling overwhelmed by all they had to do—the highest recorded in the twenty-three years of the survey.[10] The popular Peter Principle suggests that everyone eventually suffers this fate by rising to the level of our incompetence—that is, based on good performance that meets demands we are promoted up the ladder until we reach a post where we can't meet the demands so we are no longer promotable.[11] There we plateau. The popularity of the concept suggests that it has some validity, but most of us probably use the "principle" to explain our superior's problems, not our own. Besides, we can grow when confronted by excessive demands. Harry S. Truman perhaps rose to the level of his incompetence, but to the surprise of most critics he then developed into a competent (perhaps even outstanding) president.[12] Somewhere there is a job that is bigger than almost all of us, but it is not necessarily in our hierarchy, and we do not necessarily reach it.

Contradictory Demands from One Source. The dual role of Dr. Jekyll and Mr. Hyde in Robert Louis Stevenson's tale is an actor's dream. It is a challenge to portray the dual facets of a person's character, but in the horror story the facets are displayed sequentially, not simultaneously. Unfortunately, sometimes we are under simultaneous conflicting demands. The demands may call for behaviors that are impossible to combine. Mother expects little David to keep clean, straighten his room, study his homework, practice the piano, play with his friends, and take out the garbage—all between 4:00 and 5:00 PM.

Colleges frequently hire senior students as dormitory advisers expected to live with underclassmen, be friends and advisers to them, act as social leaders, be communication links to the administration, and enforcers of university regulations outlawing, say, underage drinking. However, it is virtually impossible to be both friend and police officer. Being too conscientious in the latter role can destroy the former. Similarly, in industry, some industrial engineers are expected to be advisers to line managers at the same time they monitor production performance and set standards and budgets.[13] But advising and monitoring are tough to combine because people are unlikely to discuss their inadequacies with anyone who evaluates them. The managers may not necessarily lie, but they sometimes hide the truth (just as teen-agers do not always confide in their parents, seeking instead the counsel of friends or even friends' parents because they don't want to destroy the ideal image they want their own parents to hold of them).

Conflicting Demands from Different People. All members of your role set (especially your boss) depend in some way on your performance; perhaps they require it in order to perform their own tasks. Because they have a stake in your effectiveness, they make demands. Unfortunately, these several demands often are conflicting so you are compelled to contradictory behavior. For example, university professors are expected to teach (and pressure is increasing from students and administrators to do a better job of it). They are also expected to perform research and publish articles in prestigious journals; their colleagues expect them to be good citizens in serving on the endless committees that characterize academia (not to mention community expectations and family needs for additional income).

Managers occupying boundary-spanning positions, such as sales managers who have extensive contacts with outsiders, work under role conflict.[14] Their customers' expectations on delivery time, product quality, and credit terms may be inconsistent with company policies to stretch out delivery, reduce product cost, and minimize accounts payable.[15] Nonetheless, corporate executives still expect the manager to compete.

Division general managers in large corporations occupy rewarding but stressful positions.[16] They must maintain three-way relationships: upward to corporate staff, lateral to other divisions, and downward to subordinates. Responding to one of these can undermine another. A middle manager who obediently follows orders from headquarters may thereby weaken his or her authority over subordinates who perceive the manager as a flunky for top management. Pushing the subordinates' interests too strongly, however, may lead superiors to conclude that the manager has no overall perspective, or even worse, is disloyal to the chain of command. Adding to the stress is the reality that responsibility frequently exceeds authority. The middle manager is responsible for division performance, but sometimes corporate staff sets policies that hinder achievement of objectives.

Conflicting Roles and Demands from Multiple People. In the complex theater of modern life, most of us play not to one audience but to several, and we play multiple roles almost at the same time. Unfortunately, one role's expectations can conflict with those of another. Married men and women often suffer from competing demands about their several roles: their spouse's expectations of devotion to family and employer's demands for job commitment. The working parent may want to be both an attentive father or mother *and* an ambitious, mobile employee, but there is neither time nor energy fully to live up to both competing desires. Career women with high self-esteem and sense of competence especially are prone to role overload.[17] As one researcher on working parents put it:[18] "It was an extraordinary experience for me, going to those homes and talking to those women who had great circles under their eyes. These were women who talked about sleep the way a starving person would talk about food."

After doing interviews with exhausted working mothers, she would worry about the "naive" young women in the classes she teaches at the University of California at Berkeley: "These kids have no idea what is coming. They all expect to have careers and to have children. I really wonder if these kids are going to walk off a cliff in a short five or six years later without knowing what they are "getting into."

American managers may also experience conflict between competing ideologies of success and equality.[19] Success is often associated with attainment of higher status. But equality is also a strong American value, so managers strive to differentiate themselves from peers and subordinates while still considering them as equals. One result is the strange (to most foreigners) custom of American superiors and subordinates calling each other by their first names. Another is a disappearance of executive perquisites such as reserved parking spaces and special catering and food services, in the name of equality and setting an example for lower employees.[20]

Learning the subtle expectations of various demanders can be particularly wearing on managers who climb upward from modest socioeconomic backgrounds. Moving up the ladder usually means moving physically and psychologically away from old neighborhoods and companions into a more affluent social set that expects different behavior (for example, no white socks, less public swearing, perhaps less smoking and drinking, more emotional control, and so on). To a remarkable degree in post-World War II America, white males from modest backgrounds have made this climb, but the stress of letting go of the old and learning the new demands appears to weigh heavier on those from working class families than on those reared in a professional or managerial, upper-middle-class home. And as we see in Chapter 10, it can be particularly tough on upwardly striving females and African-Americans.

RESPONSE TO ROLE STRESS

Paradoxically, the most debilitating response to role stress is to be passive—and in this regard, no difference exists between men and women.[21] We could respond by simply sleeping and playing less while working harder to meet everyone's expectations. We may even welcome the demands in order to justify being a workaholic.[22] Working mothers especially are pressed to meet traditional homemaking expectations while working outside the home full time. In general, such women do twice as much around the house as men—ten hours more a week (although it drops to only a difference of five hours when both are college-educated professionals).[23] One loss from this extra duty is sleep: working mothers average almost one hour per night less sleep than their husbands. Unfair, but put in historical context, twenty years ago women did six times as much at home as their husbands.[24]

Some of us succeed with this doing-everything approach for a long time. Many medical school students, for example, have been so ambitious, so conscientious, and so bright that up until age twenty-three or so they have literally met all multiple role demands—been the A student, the model citizen, and the good son or daughter. But suddenly in medical school for the first time they confront overload where they simply can't meet all demands. This can be particularly trying if one has never experienced failure before (see how lucky you've been to have been spared a record of unbroken success up until this point in your life).

Burnout. A few great men and women may be all things to all people, but most of us cannot. Trying to meet all demands can simply make us sick, particularly when you have few friends or relatives to lend support.[25] Descriptions of the so-called "Type E" woman, for example, highlight the socialization that some girls receive to sacrifice self in service to assorted others without concern for one's own ambitions.[26] However attractive such a saintly image may be (especially to those benefitting from the saint's sacrifice), it is not a viable tactic for most of us. In extreme cases, responding to all demands can lead to a burnout in which life turns dull and all activity seems meaningless.[27] Becoming inert becomes protection from others' demands for people who in response to others' requests just don't know how to say "no."

Medical experts don't know exactly what constitutes burnout, but warning signs include:[28]

- periods of sustained lethargy or lack of consistent productivity
- preoccupation with nonwork-related issues
- feeling that changing one's job and living arrangement may improve one's happiness on the job
- changing jobs frequently without evidence of increased responsibility or upward mobility
- indication that the person is a loner but that isolation causes acute discomfort
- failure to analyze future directions by claiming that no direction is the best direction
- a deep, if superficially considered, concern about the meaning of one's life

Flight. Running away from life, abandoning your family, or quitting your job and becoming a ski bum in Colorado all reflect flight as a way of alleviating stress. It can be tempting because it appears so easy to drop out of school, divorce your spouse, or tell your boss to go to hell. And of course some or all of these dramatic actions may be justified in certain circumstances, especially when you feel burned out.[29] Nonetheless, their simplicity is misleading because short of suicide or total insanity, no one can flee entirely; you cannot live in a vacuum. And living with too narrow a set of roles can actually hurt you. People involved in many different groups and activities appear to live longer than more narrowly focused people.[30]

Besides, people who habitually run from stress have a way of repeatedly finding themselves in similar stressful situations because they cut themselves off from the real world, retreating to illusions.[31] So people who divorce once are more likely to experience a second divorce than those who have not. And men who desert their families when under emotional or economic pressure seldom later make lasting commitments (one of the sad aspects of increased career opportunities for women has been an increase in the rate of their family desertion, although it is still much less common than among men). Married working women under extreme pressure are simply more likely to quit their jobs and focus on family. The rate of turnover in management positions is two and a half times higher among top-performing women than it is among men.[32]

Partial flight into alcohol or drugs unhappily is a path that some stressed-out people pursue. Too often such a "partial" flight has a way of turning into total as the habit overwhelms the addict. A survey of personnel administrators indicates that drugs and alcohol are *the* leading causes of career derailment.[33] Another unfortunate byproduct of the fortunate expansion of women's career opportunities has been the increase in drinking by career women. Whether as an escape from job stress or merely trying to keep up with one's male colleagues at the bar after work, drinking an equal amount of alcohol tends to have more serious physical impact on women simply because of their lighter average weight.

Certainly, resignation from a job is sometimes a valid step for courageous people, which we talk about in Chapter 9 "Loyalty and Whistle Blowing," but generally only when other stress-handling tactics will not work.

Partial Withdrawal. Rather than fleeing from everything, you could selectively ignore certain demands, in effect withdrawing from (or postponing) certain life dimensions. For example, ambitious young graduates frequently postpone marriage and family in order to simplify their lives while they focus on building a career. The age of first marriage and first parenthood is the oldest in United States history. Senior female executives have particularly difficult ladders to climb and they are much less likely to marry and have children than their male colleagues (44 percent of women vice presidents at *Fortune* 1000 companies are unmarried compared with but 7.5 percent of men at similar levels).[34]

Ambitious family men, however, often ignore all requests from their communities to become involved in volunteer activities like coaching Little League baseball, serving as a Boy Scout leader, or running for the school board. In older traditional families, they would simply abdicate all community relations to their homemaker spouse. Now with over 50 percent of married women working outside the home, meeting community expectations and needs has declined even further. Bedroom suburban volunteer rescue squads and fire departments are facing this crisis all over America because people don't feel they have the time or energy to respond to these demands.

When faced with dangerous role overload, of course, it is certainly legitimate to examine what demanders can be ignored. One needs to be aware, however, that there are consequences.

Selective Ignorance. Rather than ignoring a whole set of demanders like one's neighbors, you could instead accept some of their demands and reject others.[35] Most students quickly size up a teacher to determine whether he or she *really* expects them to do all the reading as well as keep good class notes. Prior tests may suggest whether class or reading might be ignored. The dormitory adviser mentioned earlier might minimize communications with school administrators and quietly not enforce anti-drinking regulations while trying to remain an older sister and social leader with her residents. The university professor might simplify his situation by teaching as little as possible and hiding from students while focusing on his research and writing.

Like partial withdrawal, the aim of selective ignorance is to reduce and simplify role demands, perhaps by responding only to exceptionally important demands. The dormitory adviser might take action only against *major* rule violations and ignore the more numerous minor ones (for example, ignoring underage drinking, but reporting illegal drugs). A newly promoted business supervisor might apply pressure on his former working buddies only when a crisis arises or when senior management is present. Otherwise, the supervisor adheres to the group's informal code.

Key in selective ignorance is accurate assessment of the political environment: just whose demands are more important or what expectations are less valid. Analyzing power and authority may be useful.

Respond to Power. The most pragmatic response to conflicting demands from various people is to minimize potential pain by giving priority to the person who can punish (or reward) you.[36] Working parents, for example, tend to give priority to job demands at the expense of children and spouse. Only 6 percent of women and 7 percent of men say they slight their job to satisfy family demands, but 30 percent of women and 33 percent of men feel that children's demands are given lower priority when there is a conflict between a working parent's job and home.[37] Children simply are deemed to have less power than employers.

But ignored children often get an unintended revenge. The number one cause of guilt feelings among executives is not making a bad decision on the job; it is guilt about not paying enough attention to their children.[38] And they are right to feel guilty and afraid because unhappy adolescent children can impose an enormous burden on executives precisely at the time that their job responsibilities are expanding most rapidly. As one stress counselor put it:[39]

> Just about everyone dealing with (executives who crack up) comments on the ubiquity of problems with adolescent children. Don't underestimate the damage that parental heartache can do; the president of one *FORTUNE* 500 company, distracted by the emotional problems of his daughter, ended up acting so strangely that he was forced to forfeit both his job and his status as heir apparent to the chairman.

At work, the political question is who has the most power to satisfy or frustrate your needs. This is likely to be a hierarchical superior. Unfortunately, it is not always easy to determine who has the most power. And even if you know this, responding only to that person can still hurt you because ignored others may possess sufficient power to retaliate—and your preferred one may not want to expend political capital to defend you.

Even your boss may not be happy if giving him or her priority means your role is not performed well. Lower-rated managers seem to conform the most to direct superiors, while higher-rated managers ignore demands that interfere with performance. They get the job done and most superiors value results over blind obedience.

Respond to Legitimacy. Rather than raw power, you could give priority to the demands judged most legitimate. The questions are: "Who has the most right to the results of my performance?" Or, "What behavior on my part will contribute most to the organization's mission?" Power and legitimacy may reside in the same superior, but not always. A powerful vice president might bypass your department head to direct you to concentrate on "Project Baker," while your direct superior wants "Project

Able" completed first. The most legitimate demand is probably the department head's, but the vice president has more power.

Conflict between power and legitimacy can be particularly acute where powerful figures want you to exploit others or to violate the law. The most influential pressure for unethical behavior is the example of senior executives. Some unfortunate managers see their careers blocked unless an undeserving subordinate is wrongfully dismissed, a competitor illegally spied upon, or an antipollution statute broken. You as an ethically sensitive person may know what is right in such (I hope) rare circumstances, but the choice will be unpleasant either way.

Compartmentalize Demands. Under stress you can define arbitrary personal rules that separate demand responses.[40] Usually this means changing priorities depending on where in the daily, weekly, monthly, or yearly calendar the demand occurs. For example, a professor might sequence demand response by devoting Tuesdays and Thursdays wholly to classes and students; Mondays to paperwork, committees, and administrative chores; Wednesdays to earning extra income through consulting; and Fridays and weekends to research and writing. Note that the intent of such arbitrary rules is to simplify the professor's life. She does not have to decide what to do with each demand; she just fits it into a category (so if a student knocks at her office door on a Friday when she is writing, the knock is ignored—not "fair" and not pretty, but effective).

Although business managers seldom enjoy the discretionary control over their time that professors do, an executive might allot three nights a week to his family regardless of job demands, but on other nights unexpected job demands have priority regardless of his daughter's field hockey game or his wife's need for assistance with the laundry. The advantage of such impersonal rules is that you don't have to analyze the specific situation before applying the prescription. You don't have to reinvent the wheel repeatedly.

Increasingly this approach is being applied to one's life and career. Many young people are simply postponing family demands early in their careers in order to give priority to job demands. They hope that early success will give them political strength and financial resources later to withdraw partially from the job and then better balance work and personal demands. For some women, this takes the form of temporary partial withdrawal after an early fast start in order to give more time to family for a while before reassuming a larger commitment to career. Such approaches can be wise, but they are not guaranteed to be successful given the vagaries of humankind's biological clocks, the work and fun of being a full-time parent, and a firm's uncertainty about the true commitment of someone who partially withdraws for a time.

Calls for dual-career tracks for women, the so-called "career" versus "mommy" tracks, flexitime (allowing employees flexibility on when they put in their weekly forty hours), four-day work weeks, parental leaves of absence, and longer vacations all reflect employee desire to have more control over how they compartmentalize the various demands in their lives.[41]

Even elimination of compulsory retirement reflects older workers' desire to determine when they change their role behavior. The reality is that actual retirement age has been decreasing, presently at approximately sixty-two (the age at which partial social security payments can begin). Some unhappy executives are able to hang on in stressful work situations because of their dream of retiring at fifty-nine-and-a-half when they can begin drawing on their individual retirement accounts without a tax penalty. A short-timer's attitude can be helpful in handling stress because it becomes a psychological withdrawal—you perform the tasks but don't worry about the results. Too many such people, of course, can hurt the organization.

Modify Demands. The healthiest and most courageous response to role stress is to modify the demands on you by confronting your role set. The misassigned individual could apply for a transfer; the underchallenged could request more interesting work (or just find it and *do it*); the overwhelmed could demand less pressure; one under role conflict could inform his or her superiors that they should coordinate their demands. The college dormitory adviser could ask to be relieved of her police duties; the professor could request evaluation as a teacher *or* researcher, but not both; the supervisor could ask for a transfer to a department where he is not supervising old friends; the division general manager could ask central corporate staff to rescind undesired policies; and spouses could agree to change their mutual expectations.

All of these initiatives involve small acts of courage because the people imposing demands may be unwilling to modify them. Whether their reasons for refusal are valid or not is quite irrelevant if they believe in their legitimacy. A wife who talks with her spouse about changing the ground rules over respective duties can deeply offend the other party. A boss might become angry with a star-performing woman who requests a reduction in her responsibilities for a period of time so she can care for her young children. And if the subordinate becomes too insistent, the boss may threaten retaliation.

A sense of proportion is critical. An astute manager will fight to change role demands, but not always. A division general manager, for example, should oppose the most crippling central policies, but continual fighting can exhaust his or her upward influence and destroy credibility. Like an army general, battle only on the most favorable grounds.

Change Desires. Role stress invariably forces you to reexamine what you really want.[42] You may desire security, but also want love. The latter, however, means exposing yourself to another who then can hurt you. Or you desire social prestige and self-esteem, but in some situations the former may require sacrifice of the latter. Well known is the dissonance of the ambitious person who seeks fame, finds it, and then bemoans the lack of privacy.

Most of us desire fulfillment *and* consistency.[43] We want to satisfy multiple needs simultaneously while maintaining consistency in our behavior. Critical of hypocrites who say one thing and do another, we want other's perceptions and judgments about ourselves to be consistent with our own. If a professor who believes he is a good teacher hears that his students consider him a bore, to restore equilibrium he will either: (1) reorganize and upgrade his notes and seek guidance to improve his teaching; or (2) reject the validity of the students' assessment by pointing out their immaturity and lack of knowledge. Either approach might succeed in eliminating his dissonance and restoring his sense of well-being.

When caught in incompatible desires and demands, you might respond by changing your desires. You might conclude that autonomy is not *that* important to you, or that you *really* didn't want a promotion anyway. For example, "I wouldn't want that guy's job for all the money in the world. How does he stand it?" Or, "I'm glad I didn't get the promotion I requested; I sure would've missed all my pals in this department."

Such redefinition of desires may be either a mature decision that clarifies one's personal identity or a game to fool oneself out of frustration.[44] An ambitious manager whose route upward is blocked may tell himself that, after all, leisure and family are more important. Whether he really means it will depend on later actual satisfaction. If the ambition still drives him, he may even resent his family because they symbolize his lost opportunity.

Mature reexamination of one's desires can be particularly difficult for ambitious managerial types who have prided themselves on their fortitude, self-discipline, and rationality. Expressing emotion, particularly discouragement and anxiety (or worse, panic), is deemed unacceptable by many executives and corporations. Consequently, the stress is bottled up, thus cutting off sensitivity to their real desires. Consider the words of one very successful thirty-four-year-old woman:[45]

> I've been married for ten years and this looks as if it will be the last year. I've put everything I had into my career—and I've done very well. My friends ask, "How could *you* have problems?" If they only knew.
>
> I have two problems really. One is that I've concluded that the climb toward the top in business isn't worth the effort. You get high

enough up to look out and see the scenery, and you realize how much you've missed by keeping the nose to the grindstone. . . . Life has passed me by. I don't know how to do anything but work and make money and get promotions.

The other problem, of course, is with the marriage. My husband has done well, too, but we've gone off in opposite directions. He's as unhappy with himself as I am with me and as a result, we're unhappy—and often uncivilized—with each other. . . . We've started therapy, but I'm afraid it's too late . . . I wish I had a soapbox to stand on and an audience to preach to. I'd talk about priorities.

Now, let's return to our two increasingly unhappy career couples.

LOVE ON THE GROUND

Robert Goldman, Sylvia Garfein, Louise O'Brien, and Mark Grazia unfortunately are facing many of the role conflict situations described. In her consulting work, Louise suffers particularly from the ambiguity of the partnership's management hierarchy, so she receives uncoordinated simultaneous demands from partners whose power to help or hurt her is uncertain. She tries to satisfy all job demands while trying to balance being a wife and mother. Her husband Mark has been generally helpful and sharing, but he now wants Louise to give priority to his and their son's needs because he believes they are the most legitimate. Louise is considering flight from the job, at least for some time, but she worries that she would never be able to get back on the track that leads to partnership—and that this would remain an unfulfilled dream for which she would blame her family.

Sylvia's work situation seems happier, but she did comment on her task ambiguity when she first started in full-time research. In medical school, and even during internship and residency, tasks were rather clearly defined by a professor or the patient's illness. Research, however, was so much more ambiguous. Her mentor wouldn't tell her what to do; those kinds of clearly defined tasks are handled by laboratory assistants. Sylvia's challenge was much less structured and this created anxiety until she gained a fuller understanding of what the role demanded.

Sylvia appears to expect her husband Robert to change his desires and move to Boston to accommodate her ambitions. She probably feels that Robert's sacrifice would be less than her own if she acquiesed to his wish for her to come home to New York and practice medicine on a part-time basis. In this respect, Sylvia and Mark Grazia are similar. He seems to feel that his career desires are more legitimate than his wife Louise's so that she should reduce her career aspirations and get a "local" nontraveling job that would facilitate better balance and compartmentalization of her life.

At stake in these two situations is more than work, of course. The stability of their marriages will be affected by the tactics exercised. In surveying how married couples handle these problems, four observed strategies can be arrayed along a stability continuum.[46]

Most Stable: Mutual Partial Withdrawal from Career. Among dual-career families, the most stable marriage relationship seems to exist when both parties lower their career aspirations and give central priority to their family relationships. One marriage therapist argues:[47]

> What I see with two careers is more planning of leisure time together and a heightened concern about what can happen to the marriage if there's too much work and not enough play. In a single-career marriage, there seems to be a greater tendency for the husband to get all wrapped up in his career and to deny family responsibilities. This can lead to all kinds of trouble.

This tactic seems most relevant in dual-professional couples (sometimes even in the same field) who work quite independently of organizational hierarchy—for example, two professors or two physicians. They both try to limit their work to a "normal" 40 hours, reject overtime or travel demands, and define their career success by the quality and enjoyment of their work rather than by promotions or income increases. A study of married psychologists indicated virtually identical work weeks for husbands and wives—41.5 hours per week for the men versus 41.3 for the women (although in addition, the wives put in 23 hours per week on household work versus only 18 hours for their husbands).[48]

Compare these working hours with the 60 hours per week reported in a *Fortune* survey of fast-track corporate executives (most of the men having noncareer wives and many of the women being unmarried).[49]

Even this mutually balanced strategy involves some risk, however. We may underestimate the effort needed to maintain job competence, or in time become bored because we didn't take enough risks in accepting moves and promotions. Or the husband and wife may not be entirely honest with themselves. As the years pass and they see more career-committed colleagues surpassing them in renown or income, one or the other of the married couple (more likely the male) may come to blame the other for not being "supportive" enough, thus blocking the success they might have had.

Relative Stability: The Wife Changes Desires and Withdraws from Career. Even the most modern of couples tend to feel that if some-

one should sacrifice career aspirations, temporarily or permanently, it should be the wife. In the 1980s, employment in part-time jobs rose almost twice as fast as full-time employment. And the vast majority (73 percent) of those working part time are women who claim to prefer the arrangement.[50] Hence, Mark Grazia's belief that his wife should come home, take care of their son for a couple of years, and then if she desires get a "job" that is more easily controllable than a high-powered career. And because the pressures on a working wife/mother *are* in fact higher than on most husbands (a recent survey indicated that 77 percent of working mothers still handle cooking and 64 percent dishwashing *without assistance!*),[51] she is likely to be under greater stress, which makes this option more attractive to her than to her husband.

Her sense of loss, however, may well be tempered, if not nullified, by an often unexpected enjoyment of maintaining a home and being a full-time parent—joys that many highly educated women have been surprised to discover.

Like the first strategy of mutual withdrawal, focusing aspiration change and career withdrawal on the wife carries a danger of subsequent resentment when she finds it impossible to pick up the threads of her career if she desires later to reenter the fast lane. Even worse, by in effect becoming a "corporate wife," the woman may lose a sense of personal identity as her role becomes an adjunct of her husband's (which is what Robert Goldman fears).[52]

This tradeoff of husband focussing on career and wife on family is of course the modern version of the "traditional family." Although much is said about it being a dying model, a *Fortune* survey of the most successful of the baby boomers in their late thirties revealed that only 25 percent of the males had wives who were pursuing careers. Most of the others in these over $100,000 a year households didn't work at all outside the home.[53] Apparently, high income makes the traditional pattern possible or attractive—or reduces the incentive for the wife to work because of the additional taxes that would be paid.

Relative Instability: Husband Changes Desires and Partially Withdraws from Career. Given the persistence of the traditional image of the husband as breadwinner (and the reality of higher salaries for males), having the man lower his career sights to accommodate his wife's ambitions is rarer than the opposite. Most couples, but especially the husband, would be more uncomfortable with this approach—particularly if the man became known as "Mr. Garfein" or a "househusband" like Robert Goldman fears. Nonetheless, this accommodation is not unknown, particularly on a limited time basis as when a wife is finishing school or starting a new career. One of my closest professional colleagues was an incredibly talented woman who moved up a ladder of increasingly prestigious academic and government administrative positions including being a member of the governor's cabinet and senior vice president of a major university. She even had five sons along the way. But she had a husband who accommodated (and limited) his entrepreneurial activity to her achievements apparently without resentment or loss of self-esteem. The test of this strategy's rarity and difficulty, however, is measured by the general perception that he was indeed a "saint." My guess is that Sylvia Garfein would admire my colleague's husband more than Bob Goldman would.

Most Unstable: Both Put Career First. Putting one's career first and sacrificing family activities is a time-honored strategy among men, of course, but rarer among married couples. And except among exceptional independent people, this approach appears to contain the seeds of its own dissolution. If careers are so central to both parties, it is just not likely that their relationship would be so unique as to survive its peripheralness. One review of a book on working parents observed:[54]

> In general, the upper-income professionals in Ms. Hochschild's sample tend to be the worst hypocrites. (They) seemed to capitulate to a workaholism *a deux*, each spouse equitably granting the other the right to work long hours, and reconciling themselves to a drastically reduced conception of the emotional needs of a family. Such couples almost totally parceled out the role of mother into purchased services."

It doesn't appear that either of our traveling loving couples could really make this approach work.

No one can predict how our two couples will end up. In terms of family stability, I guess I would put my money on Louise O'Brien and Mark Grazia because they are heading toward a more traditional relationship, but just as there is more to life than a career, there is more to life than a marriage. Therefore, who will maximize life satisfaction is unknown. What is known, however, is that all approaches to handling role stress require trade-offs. In no other area is the old economic proverb "there ain't no free lunch" more valid. The key is making your decisions and staying committed to them without continually looking over your shoulder and wondering "what if?" As the poet put it, "Of all the words of mice and men, the saddest are it might have been."

ADVICE ON HANDLING ROLE STRESS

Your greatest enemy in handling role stress is passivity. Responding to everyone's demands is not a long-term viable strategy. It is a recipe for burnout.

- Total flight from an unhappy situation can be valid under extreme circumstances, but only as a last resort. Fleeing can become a habit and a strategy for avoiding commitment.
- If you decide to stay, don't keep looking for other opportunities. The strongest defense against stress is commitment to what you are presently doing.[55]
- Experiment with your environment to determine what demands you can ignore at acceptable cost and what aspirations you can compromise with minimal guilt. Self-flexibility, indeed delight in varying your behavior, is key to being effective in complex roles.[56]
- Under short-term pressure, it is acceptable to give practical priority to demands from the most powerful, but it is seldom a satisfying long-term strategy because other people whose demands may be more legitimate may still be able to hurt you.
- Recognize that demands from your immediate superior are usually more legitimate than those from higher-level mentors who cannot be counted on to defend you from your boss's anger if his or her legitimate demands are unmet.
- Most organizations don't expect perfect conformity to all policies and procedures if doing so undermines your performance. Performance is generally valued and rewarded, even if it requires some policy violations (and is not illegal). However, if your results are unsatisfactory, you may well be punished for not following rules.
- Be courageous in confronting people who make demands on you when necessary to negotiate new terms.
- Periodically examine your values and life desires to ensure that your necessary compromises are mature decisions and not rationalizations.

4

Managing Short-Term Time

Long ago, François Rabelais, a French poet-statesman, asked, "How shall I be able to rule over others if I have not full power and command over myself?" Well, no person can enjoy "full" self-control, but effective professionals and managers seem to be better than others at managing their time, for time is your most precious resource. This chapter examines several approaches to managing time including lists, activity analysis, diaries, and time inventories, as well as tactics for using discretionary time and fighting procrastination. (I know the last topic doesn't apply to *you*, but you might enjoy reading about *other* people's problems.)

In the following case, we follow a management consultant as he works with a marketing vice president and a promotions manager as they deal with time management problems.

LIFE AT HIGH LIFE SPORTING COMPANY

High Life Sporting Company, Inc. is a medium-sized manufacturer, distributor, and marketer of sports equipment. Its customers are various independent and chain sports specialty retail outlets. Top management is striving to broaden its product line and bring more sales stability to its predominantly winter-oriented catalog.

Scene 1: "To Go or Not to Go?" Office of the Vice President of Marketing. Present are the vice president, Sandor Alexander, and Clark Gilman, a management consultant.

Alexander:	Hi, Clark; have a seat. I've just been handed an assignment that creates a real challenge for my time management. A few minutes ago I had a call from the boss telling me that negotiations just went through for acquiring a new line of skis to add to our offerings. He got the deal together much earlier than I thought, which means that I'll have to start the promotion campaign right away. But I'm scheduled to go to Europe next week. I don't see how I can do both. I just may have to cancel the trip.
Gilman:	Sandy, I know how pressured you must feel, but before you make a decision to cancel your trip, I hope you take some time to review the issue.

71

Managing Short-Term Time

Alexander:	But the decision is obvious to me, Clark. If I start up the campaign right away, I can make a bunch of trade shows and advertising deadlines I'd have to forego if I'm traveling.
Gilman:	I'm not disagreeing with you, Sandy. I just see you ready to jump into action, changing well-laid plans all because something unexpected came up. To me, that kind of behavior is a red flag for thinking about time management. When you react to a crisis, you're putting off something else you had decided to do which might be more important. The crisis feels urgent, but you don't really know whether you're making the best use of your time until you really look at all the issues carefully.
Alexander:	Well, that still sounds like straight decision making to me. I thought time management was finding ways to organize your desk or, you know, using time-saving tricks so you won't have to stay at work late every night.
Gilman:	It's that too. But it's much more—especially for a senior manager like you, Sandy. As an executive, your decisions have long-term effects, not only what you do and how you use your time, but also for the people who work with you. Whenever you have to make a decision about what to do and when, you should first ask if the projects are important in furthering the firm's long-term goals.
Alexander:	Well, that sounds good in theory, but to apply it in practice. . . .
Gilman:	OK, Sandy. The major choice you are faced with is the trip versus the campaign, and how those two fit in with all the other responsibilities you have. Tell me the specifics of each.
Alexander:	All right, I'll start with the trip. I started planning for it a few months ago. It's to Europe to explore new products we might add to our line next year and after. As I'm sure you know, we're looking to add products to balance our strong winter lines such as skis—something to balance the other half of the year.
Gilman:	And when are you scheduled to go?
Alexander:	In ten days. Everything's set—tickets, itinerary, meetings and conventions, the works.
Gilman:	Well, what are the details on the promotion project?
Alexander:	We were going to start the promotion campaign on the new ski line we've been negotiating to acquire when I got back. We didn't expect the deal to come through so quickly, but now that it has we should begin right away. The head start would mean a big boost to sales this year because we can now make some important U.S. trade shows and advertising deadlines that will pass by the time I return from Europe. The campaign is obviously more important. It's money in the bank *this* year. And given everything else I have to do, the trip belongs on a back burner.
Gilman:	Well, I think we need more information before I can agree with you about that. How do these projects relate to your long-term goals?
Alexander:	The specific result the president wants from the campaign is to increase sales by 15 percent by the end of the year. So if I catch

these trade shows and advertising deadlines, I'd improve my chances of achieving the income goal for the year.

And for the trip, our goal is to have five new, nonwinter products in our line three years from now. It's the first step in diversifying our product line called for in our five-year plan. We expect that it will take us to the $50 million sales level.

Gilman: Is there anyone else who could take over either the trip or the campaign?

Alexander: I don't think so. The boss could do the trip, I suppose, but he's much too busy. Besides, it's my job and I want to make the contacts. Diane Switzer is my new marketing promotions director, but she's just joined us. She doesn't have the experience to run a whole campaign by herself. I've just got to decide to go, or not to go.

ʍ·ʍ·ʍ·ʍ

Scene 2: "Who Should Do It?" Office of the Vice President of Marketing. Present are the Vice President, Sandor Alexander, Diane Switzer, newly appointed Marketing Promotions Director, and management consultant, Clark Gilman.

Alexander: (On the telephone). That's right, Megan. I need the 9:00 AM flight to New York in order to catch the plane to Paris. And you've got my hotel and car in London? . . . Great. Now get me Sam Ranor at the graphics house. Let me know when he's on the line (hangs up telephone). OK, Diane, what do you have?

Switzer: Here are the photos we've got, Sandy. What do you think?

Alexander: I like this one, Diane. But I think if we had it cropped like (telephone rings) . . . excuse me, Diane . . . (into telephone) Yes, Megan . . . OK, I'll talk now . . . Hello, Sam. Listen, we're gonna go down to the wire on this one. . . . I understand, Sam, but I want you to know that this campaign is very important to us and . . . that's great, Sam. I'll call you later when I have all the details. And thanks a lot.

Switzer: Now, how do you want the pictures?

Alexander: (Examining paper stock) Leave these samples with me and I'll let you know.

Switzer: OK, but one of us needs to get back to Sam with the decision.

Alexander: Good enough, Diane. I'll call Sam and speak to you later. (Switzer leaves)

Gilman: It looks like the campaign is moving along pretty well.

Alexander: Yes, it really is. Diane now has a sense of what needs to be done. She's learning fast and I'm getting a chance to supervise her quite a bit before I leave.

Gilman: Glad to hear it, Sandy—though judging from the last few minutes, it sounds like you're handling quite a lot of the details yourself.

Alexander: Well, I called Sam Ranor because we've worked together a long time. And paper stock is something that I know a lot about. Besides, my standards are very high. There are many small details that take less time for me to do than to wait for Diane, correct her mistakes, and then give her another try.

ა·ა·ა·ა

Scene 3: "Interruptions! Interruptions." Office of Marketing Promotions Director, Diane Switzer. Present are Switzer, her secretary Sheila Armstrong, and management consultant, Clark Gilman.

Switzer: I don't believe this! First they ship us 2,000 fewer pairs of ski boots than we ordered and now the poles are going to arrive a week late!

Armstrong: That's what Jarvis said on the phone.

Switzer: All right. We better get a memo off to all sales reps immediately. In the meantime, we're gonna be swamped with phone calls.

Armstrong: It's started already. Bob and Paul are coming in today to meet with you, and Sarah Barstow from Zenith Stores wants to see you this afternoon. (she leaves)

Gilman: It sounds like you're losing control of the day, Diane.

Switzer: It's really tough when you get so many unexpected interruptions.

Gilman: So, what's going on?

Switzer: Well, on top of this marketing campaign that I'm working on for Sandy, and all the other things that I had planned to do, this supplier problem has caused more demands on my time than I anticipated.

Gilman: And even though you did schedule time to be responsive to just these kinds of demands, you feel pressured.

Switzer: And out of control. How am I going to get everything done?

Gilman: Well, first Diane, keep in mind that you can't control other people and the demands they make on you. But you can control your responses to those demands—which is what managing interruptions is all about.

Switzer: I know, Clark. But so many interruptions just seem to slip into the flow of things. I'll be concentrating on a letter and Sheila, or Sandy, or one of the salespeople will just look in and ask me a question on something—and I'll respond without thinking about it.

Alexander: (Walking in) Hello Diane, Clark. Please excuse the interruption, but Diane I won't be able to see Sidney Perlman from the Mountainside Sports chain today and I'd like you to keep my appointment.

Switzer: When is he coming in?

Alexander: At three. I'll have Megan bring him over. Tell him we want nothing less than twelve feet of wall space in every store next fall.

Switzer: OK, Sandy.

Alexander: Thanks, Diane. See you later.

Switzer: (Adding appointment to her calendar). I guess it's hard to anticipate when interruptions will come in a new job. That meeting
with Perlman will really screw up this afternoon. It'll be 8:00 PM
before I'll get out of here!

Gilman: Tell me about your interruptions yesterday.

Switzer: Well . . . I had the usual number of phone calls and visitors with
appointments. Some mail. . . . a staff meeting. You know, all the
routine demands you need to respond to. Then there were several unexpected ones too. Word must be out on the new ski because several reps called to ask when we'll be ready to add it to
our catalog. Then we had a problem with a shipment to a trade
show, an important client dropped by so I had to make time for
him, and my boss wanted to see me about a few things late in
the afternoon . . . I have to admit that I am surprised at the frequency of interruptions in this job.

HOW ARE SANDOR AND DIANE HANDLING TIME?

Sandor Alexander and Diane Switzer are clearly confronting major
issues of time management: too many visitors, too many telephone calls
with rambling conversations, involvement in excessive detail, inability to
delegate, and emphasis on urgency rather than what is important. The
vice president of marketing is inclined to simply cancel his product development trip to Europe in order to personally direct the promotional campaign on their new line of ski equipment. Obviously, both of these activities are important to High Life Sporting Company, but the trip has
possible long-term benefits that could be lost. And even when Alexander
tries to delegate the new ski promotion, he makes too many decisions
because he knows he can do it faster than Switzer.

As the newly appointed marketing promotions director, Diane
Switzer has energetically addressed the campaign and other responsibilities, but unpredicted difficulties threaten to overwhelm the time she has
available. She is spending so much time responding to telephone calls
and visitors that pushing ahead on her most important project is hin-
dered—a condition she contributes to because of her unwillingness to
limit social conversation.

Before offering advice to Alexander and Switzer, let's look at possible time management tactics.

TIME MANAGEMENT TACTICS

Like death and taxes in life, making lists will always be part of time
management. As we will see, however, lists alone are never sufficient for

personal effectiveness. Therefore, after examining the strength and weakness of list making, we describe activity and diary analysis.

To-Do Lists. One of the oldest schemes in time management literature is a management consultant's sixty-year-old advice to the chairman of Bethlehem Steel Company.[1] The tale is that consultant Ivy Lee was having dinner with Chairman Charles Schwab who complained of the many things he had to do and wished that Lee would give him good advice on time management. The resourceful Lee wrote out the following on the back of the menu:

Every evening . . .
> *write down your six most important tasks*
> *for tomorrow in order of priority.*

Every morning . . .
> *start working on item 1, and continue until*
> *you finish it; then start on item 2; and so on.*

At end of day . . .
> *tear up list—and start over!*

Upon being handed the list, Schwab supposedly asked how much Lee wanted for this advice. Lee replied that Schwab should use it for several weeks and send him a check for whatever Schwab felt it was worth. Several weeks later Lee received a check for $25,000 (more like $200,000 in today's values!).

The advice appears to be simplicity itself. Especially attractive is the idea of tearing up last night's list at day's end whether or not you have completed it. Drawing up a new list for tomorrow demands that you reexamine your tasks and priorities in terms of the present situation. In addition, most people are much more likely to remember and perform tasks if they write them down than if they carry around lists in their heads. (Remember your parents trying to get you to write down your homework assignments in a small spiral-bound notebook?) And most of us feel less nagging tension if we have at least listed what we intend to do.

Unfortunately, simple lists like Ivy Lee's suffer from a glaring weakness that renders them of limited usefulness. Working in order from item 1 to item 6 implies that the list maker controls all of his or her time. No equipment breakdowns, uncertain subordinates, insistent customers, or rapacious competitors would seem to interfere with the manager sitting alone in a private office as he or she serenely moves down the list.

This is an unrealistic assumption about an unreasonable world. No manager can control all of his or her time. No executive can singlemindedly proceed down a list of tasks. Former Secretary of State Henry Kissinger once compared his life as a Harvard professor with government service.[2] He said that as a professor he could make a list of papers to grade, class notes to prepare, articles to outline, and so on and work through them in sequence. He tried to do this in President Nixon's White House, but after starting on his list at 7:00 AM there would be a revolution on some Caribbean island and the rest of the day would be shot to hell!

Perhaps only independent professionals like college professors, dentists, or lawyers can truly work on sequential lists. Virtually all managers and organizational professionals, in contrast, are subject to routine interruptions and unforeseen emergencies. You cannot entirely escape them, nor should you necessarily try if responding to them is a central aspect of your job.

Thus, making lists is necessary but not sufficient. We will see such lists embedded in other time management approaches.

Utilizing Discretionary Time. We need to distinguish between two kinds of time.[3] On the one hand, there is the time that is not under a manager's control, variously termed *uncontrollable time, job-imposed time, required time, fixed time,* and *response time.* The last term is most appropriate because this is the time consumed in responding to events and people with their requests, demands, and problems. On the other hand, there is the time that a manager can control, called *controllable time, self-imposed time, disposable time,* and *discretionary time.* Again, the last term is the most appropriate.

Probably no more than 25 percent of a manager's time is under his or her control.[4] Regardless of what the precise percentage is, most would like discretionary time to be greater, especially because it is so chopped up that it is virtually unusable. Since on the average events occur every five to ten minutes, managers may underestimate how much discretionary time they potentially possess or may find it impossible to start anything substantial for fear of being interrupted.

Effective use of discretionary time and progress on discretionary projects are possible only if discretionary time periods are long enough for concentration. The minimum usable time span required for most people to really focus on a complex issue is in the ninety-minute range. Anything less requires too many transitions. Several techniques exist for getting usable discretionary time: insulation, isolation, and reserving blocks of time.

1. *Insulation.* Insulation consists of buffering oneself from incoming demands for limited periods. The most common tactic is to scan and sort incoming communications. For example, by executive order in 1939,

Franklin D. Roosevelt created the Executive Office of the President "to protect the President's time" by "excluding any matter that can be settled elsewhere."[5] This mechanism evolved into a group of assistants and counselors who stand between the president and almost all incoming communications. They decide: (a) what (matters to be brought to the president's attention), (b) who (by the originator or by a White House aide), (c) how (by letter or oral communications), and (d) when.

Of course, most of us will not have such elaborate staffs. To gain similar benefits from an insulating buffer, we will have to depend on an assistant or a secretary (who does more than type and answer the telephone, however). A competent buffer should have sufficient discretion to redirect about half of a manager's incoming messages to more appropriate people. On matters that should reach the manager, an astute subordinate can anticipate his or her needs and save time by gathering relevant data and preparing preliminary suggestions. The intent of such activity is to ensure that the manager reads each incoming communication only once before a reply is drafted.

Using a buffer to limit access and interruptions is widespread, but it does cause problems. Assistants may insulate their chief from information which they consider trivial to their less experienced eyes, but which the executive, for example, might recognize as critical. What reaches the senior executive may be so filtered that he or she is out of touch with reality. Hubert Humphrey commented that he never perceived the magnitude of anti-Vietnam War feeling until he left his position as Vice President of the United States. And President Johnson's White House Press Secretary argued that the chief executive was so enveloped in "a velvet cocoon" that keeping touch with reality was so difficult as to pose a danger to the country's future.[6] Clark Clifford, a former adviser to President Kennedy and Secretary of Defense in Lyndon Johnson's cabinet, remembers being told by an Eisenhower aide that Ike was spared night work because his staff boiled 150-page memoranda down to two pages. Clifford replied, "There is only one trouble. If I could be the fellow who prepares the two-page memos, I'd be president instead of Ike!"[7]

Similarly, if less dramatically, every executive runs some risk of being isolated from his or her organization by excessive insulation. But to run *no* such risk is to be swamped in trivia.

2. *Isolation.* Insulation's most extreme form is physical isolation from one's normal workplace. Across the street from the White House in the Executive Office Building, President Richard Nixon had a small private den in which he could work alone.[8] All recent presidents have found it essential to make use of secluded retreats such as Hyde Park, Key West, Key Biscayne, Camp David and Kennebunkport. Business executives may similarly maintain two offices (an entrepreneur in Connecticut erected an office building near the Stamford train station that was specifically in-

tended to provide second offices for Manhattan executives residing in Connecticut), but more common practices are to close your office door and refuse all calls, or to work at home periodically.

When I served as a university vice president, I found it essential to spend three full days at home alone working on my annual budget proposal. For me the process required spreading out on my dining room table all of my subordinate's investment desires for the new year. I could then walk around the table and steep myself in the various arguments looking for a strategy to fit their dreams to available resources. This simply could not be done at work in even ninety minute bites. I once described this tactic to a group of senior executives at the Du Pont Company when the chief executive officer exclaimed that he did something similar. He would collect all his tough thinking-type projects in a special briefcase and every three weeks take them with him to work uninterrupted out on the veranda overlooking the ocean at his home in Bermuda. (I guess, if you got it, flaunt it!)

Note that isolation is not postponing routine or boring tasks to the evening. Sometimes, of course, we must take such work home, but putting things off until the evening is more often procrastination than time management since it allows us to avoid organizing our time during the day.

Any withdrawal may create animosity. The subordinate who calls with a problem that is important to him or her may be offended if denied access to you. And courage may be required to withdraw from a superior's reach, who may simply expect you to be on tap always. A professor colleague of mine worked for the President's Council of Economic Advisers during the later stage of the Johnson and early period of the Nixon presidencies. He said Nixon was a pleasure to work for because he respected a subordinate's need for isolated time, whereas Johnson interpreted lack of instant availability to him as disloyalty.

Even in business, a manager may be afraid to close his door because a closed door may suggest that secret changes are being plotted, or because of misplaced pride that "my door is always open," or maybe even because the boss may think that he or she is asleep. And unfortunately, contemporary office design frequently eliminates doors and private offices by open-landscape layouts utilizing shoulder-high modular furniture. Everyone can enjoy the windows and potted palms, but find it difficult to get sufficient privacy to think. In some firms, jockeying for real offices with closable opaque doors is rampant.

3. *Concentration during reserved blocks of time.* Carving time chunks out of most weeks is tough. You will really have to fight to schedule them and then to preserve them from interruption. Techniques like insulation and isolation will help. More fundamental, however, is an awareness of the need to plan on a weekly basis for those periods when

you will escape from present demands and focus on longer-run discretionary concerns.

During blocks of discretionary time you should focus on relatively few discretionary projects. Don't expect to move ahead on ten different projects during a ninety-minute period. To attempt to do so will only fractionate your attention just as occurs during response time. Your transitions from topic to topic will probably be inefficient and your thinking murky.

A variant of the $25,000 advice list described earlier might be helpful in handling discretionary projects.[9]

- Each evening draw up your "to do" list of ten desirable discretionary activities—those activities which you will probably not get to under the press of tomorrow's demands unless you fight for time.
- Schedule at least one ninety-minute block of time for the two highest-priority activities on the list.
- Perform the two activities in the scheduled time. If you complete them and discretionary time is still available, move on to the other activities on last night's list, but if you only progress on the two you still will have been effective.

This approach is a little more modest than the original list. You shouldn't feel defeated if you are unable to complete all of the items on a current list. Eighty percent of the importance in a ten-item list may be contained in only two items. Hence, completing two activities out of a discretionary list of ten may accomplish 80 percent of what was truly important.

Fighting Procrastination. For all too many of us too, frequently the chief enemy is procrastination. When you were a child, did you eat your spinach first or last? It could have been cauliflower or broccoli, but almost all of us had a vegetable that we hated to eat. Many of us also had parents who simply enforced a rule of no dessert until *all* of the main course was eaten, including the dreaded vegetable.

If you really wanted that sweet reward at dinner's end, your two polar choices were to eat the spinach first and then be home free or to save it until just before the ice cream. No data exist on what percentage opts for either course, but effective time managers seem to consume the spinach of their jobs first. Procrastinators, in contrast, put off the spinach in the hope that the demanding parents will relax their guard and forget to enforce the rule. Such delay works sometimes, but probably rarely. Procrastination stems from complex causes that may well require Freudian analysis to unravel. We can't provide that here, but we can describe tactics for combatting procrastination.

1. *Set starting times.* This can appear to be an excuse for delaying rather than starting immediately. But not every task can be started immediately, so starting times are appropriate. Of course, you can lead yourself to water, but you must also force yourself to drink.

2. *Generate momentum.* Some people have trouble starting any task (especially in the morning or after lunch). A tough, ambiguous, postponable task can be extremely discouraging. Momentum can be developed, however, by beginning with some easy matters, such as straightening your desk, routine correspondence, and bureaucratic detail. But set a time limit on how long you will do this, and stick to it. A desk alarm set for thirty minutes will signal you to stop the easy and start the difficult. Don't be sucked in by the sense of achievement you may feel from completing the routine tasks. Give them up after a half hour and confront the ambiguous.

3. *Reward yourself for progress.* All big complex projects have smaller parts whose accomplishment can be celebrated. Small self-rewards such as a coffee break or even an afternoon off to play golf *are* justified if they mark significant progress on a lengthy project. Just be scrupulously honest with yourself and see that the rewards follow rather than precede the actual work.

4. *Include others in the rewards.* One of the sad aspects of modern work is that it is divorced from family life. Other family members may not even know when a spouse or parent has accomplished something significant on the job. Perhaps you could invite them to join you in a small dinner-time ritual. Have a little ceremony; tell them about your progress and your ultimate goal; give yourself a small gift that can be shared with them; and thank them for their implicit support of your work. After a while, they may share more with you and the exchange of small rewards will become mutual.

5. *Discount in advance.* No one is *perfectly honest* with himself. Even the healthiest of us utilize certain games to deal with difficulty. Discounting is one of the mose useful devices (and basically "healthy" if not excessive).[10] Discounting is projecting yourself into the future to an imagined completion of the task and dealing with inevitable disappointment in advance. Then, when the job is actually completed, you will have already worked through the letdown that comes because the result is not exactly as you wished.

6. *Set early deadlines.* The moral of the spinach tale is that effective time management usually includes courage to confront the difficult and unpleasant sooner rather than later. In high school, those who ate their spinach first may have started Saturday's chores on Friday afternoon,

thus gaining flexibility if something interesting turned up on Saturday morning. In college, they probably tried to get in a solid hour of afternoon study before dinner (worth probably two hours of late night time).

Effective time managers seldom accept other people's deadlines, but create closer, artificial deadlines. Although this would seem to increase the pressure on them, paradoxically such self-set deadlines have an opposite effect. They create the illusion of being a little more in control of time. Nonprocrastinators know they have a little leeway beyond the artificial deadline, but they almost never use it. One of my college roommates was one of the best time managers I've ever seen. He simply refused to engage in mad typing of a paper all night before the morning class at which it was due. And he never studied a particular subject the night before the examination. He set his deadlines twenty-four hours in advance and, if necessary, might pull "an all-nighter" to meet them. But when others were trying to cover everything at the last minute, he had a serenity that helped him fit ideas together in creative ways, while others of us could only regurgitate the facts hurriedly memorized.

In short, effective time managers try to act upon time instead of passively letting it just happen *to* them.[11] No one is entirely successful at this, but the effort seems to give a feeling of self-control which makes the battle easier.

Activity Analysis. Activity analysis involves making several lists, but not on a daily basis. Rather, this approach is a strategic analysis of your job activities so that critical decisions can be made about urgency, importance, and delegation.[12] It might be done beneficially once a year. Activity analysis begins with a single list which is then divided and analyzed in three ways.

1. *Activities list.* List all of the recurring "activities" that characterize your job. These might include answering mail inquiries, checking product quantity and quality, counseling subordinates, tracking down lost parts, planning the budget, and so on. Don't list them in order of priority, merely according to some scheme that ensures that your list is comprehensive. Include both routine matters and predictable types of emergencies. The list should fit on one sheet of paper and should require approximately thirty minutes to complete. Make three copies of the list. Exhibit 4–1 illustrates the process with the activities list for my former position as a university vice president for development and university relations, a position which directed 120 professional and support staff in fundraising, alumni relations, public relations, and publications.

2. *Analysis for intrinsic importance.* Take a second sheet of paper and construct four columns: (a) very important—must be done; (b) impor-

tant—should be done; (c) not so important—may not be necessary; and (d) unimportant—can be eliminated.

EXHIBIT 4-1: ACTIVITY ANALYSIS—LIST OF ACTIVITIES FOR VICE PRESIDENT FOR DEVELOPMENT AND UNIVERSITY RELATIONS

* propose/advise president on his personal cultivation and solicitations
* participate in president's mangement group meetings
* support president/attend university-wide events
* prepare, argue for, and negotiate about annual departmental budget
* call on/develop new individual alumni relationships
* solicit gifts from (a) alumni, (b) friends, (c) corporations, and (d) foundations
* respond to individual alumni calls/complaints about admissions, gifts
* initiate letters to alumni about their public accomplishments
* monitor gift receipts and acknowledgment letters
* maintain relations with Deans of Schools
* solve personnel and gift-situation problems with Deans
* recruit and hire senior development and public relations staff
* deal with university Human Resources office on salary and job classification situations
* plan strategy and design organization structure for (a) development, (b) university relations, and (c) alumni relations
* meet with senior departmental staff as individuals and in group
* respond to senior departmental staff requests and inquiries
* conduct annual performance reviews with senior staff
* review and make salary decisions on all professional staff
* serve as cheerleader/maintain morale for staff through visits and entertainment
* meet with/advise alumni job seekers
* attend professional association meeting
* maintain relations with other university department senior managers
* serve as liaison to Trustee Development and University Relations Committee
* prepare agenda and make reports to two Trustee Committees
* maintain relations with chairpersons and members
* maintain relations with Alumni Regional Development Committees

Now take a copy (you will need three copies) of your activities list, cut the items apart and parcel them out across the four columns analyzing them for intrinsic importance (and don't put them all in column a). Intrinsic importance is a subjective concept which might reflect several questions. In my own analysis I asked myself:

- What activities have the most moral legitimacy given the mission of my institution?

- What activities, if done well, could lead to my being rewarded and honored by the institution? (My predecessor had a building named after him.)
- What activities, if done poorly, would likely result in my being asked to resign my position (or get me fired in a less polite organization)?
- What activities if not performed would not be missed by anyone who could hurt (or help) me?

Exhibit 4–2 indicates my own activity analysis for intrinsic importance. I had plenty of items for the first three columns, but unfortunately couldn't find anything to allocate to the category of "unimportant—can be eliminated" (a difficulty I'm sure that most readers will share).

3. *Activity analysis for urgency.* On a third sheet of paper, make four columns headed: (a) very urgent—must be done immediately; (b) urgent—should be done soon; (c) not urgent—long range; and (d) time not a factor. These categories reflect how quickly after a "cue," such as a telephone call or a meeting, the activity must be performed. For example, if you are sitting at your desk and analyzing last week's production figures and you hear a loud crash and scream from the manufacturing area, you

---

EXHIBIT 4–2: ACTIVITY ANALYSIS OF INTRINSIC IMPORTANCE FOR VICE PRESIDENT FOR DEVELOPMENT AND UNIVERSITY RELATIONS

Very Important—must be done

* propose/advise president on his personal cultivation and solicitations
* prepare, argue for, and negotiate annual departmental budget
* call on/develop new individual alumni relationships
* solicit gifts from (a) alumni, (b) friends, (c) corporations, and (d) individuals
* make decisions on alumni children applications to support
* solve personnel and gift-situation problems with Deans
* recruit and hire senior development and public relations staff
* deal with university Human Resources office on salary and job classification situations
* plan strategy and design organization structure for (a) development, (b) university relations, and (c) alumni relations
* review and make salary decisions on all professional staff
* serve as liaison to Trustee Development and University Relations Committee
* prepare agenda and make reports to two Trustee Committees

Important—should be done

* participate in president's management group meetings
* respond to individual alumni calls/complaints about admissions, gifts
* maintain relationships with Deans of Schools
* meet with senior departmental staff as individuals and in group

EXHIBIT 4–2: CONTINUED

* respond to senior departmental staff requests and inquiries
* serve as cheerleader/maintain morale for staff though visits and entertainment
* maintain relations with chairpersons and members
* explore ways in fundraising, public relations, and alumni communications to emphasize the central and the whole
* propose means of generating development investment funds beyond the president's budget allocation
* find ways of providing performance-based rewards such as bonuses for outstanding individual or unit performance

Not So Important—not necessary, but useful

* support president/attend university-wide events
* attend regional alumni relations meetings
* initiate letters to alumni about their public accomplishments
* monitor gift receipts and acknowledgment letters
* support schools/attend overseer meetings and events
* conduct annual performance reviews with senior staff
* meet with/advise alumni job seekers
* attend professional association meetings
* maintain relations with other university department senior managers
* maintain relations with Alumni Regional Development Committes

Unimportant—can be eliminated

* nothing!

would immediately put aside your computer printouts and investigate the emergency.

Take another copy of your activity list, scissor each entry apart and allocate them across the four columns of urgency analysis. Exhibit 4–3 illustrates my own distribution. Note that "very urgent" activities include attendance at meetings that the president or trustees schedule at their convenience (rather than mine). I must attend at the time appointed on the calendar or miss the meeting. My urgent list is somewhat longer than very urgent because I felt that on these matters I generally had anywhere from three to eight hours to deal with the issue or get back to the person involved by the end of the work day.

The third column, labeled "not urgent" is comprised mainly of activities and projects that I envisioned being dealt with during a four-month semester. On most of these, I enjoyed discretionary control over when I performed the activities. The very short list under "time is not a factor" reflects the major discretionary projects which I hoped to accomplish over several years. I'm afraid the paucity of this list illustrates my tendency to be submerged in the short-run.

4. *Activity analysis for delegation.* Put your "intrinsic importance" analysis next to your "urgency" analysis. There should be few activities in the left-hand columns of both analyses. That is, few activities will be "very important" and "very urgent." For the most part, important activities will not be urgent because they don't have to be performed immediately.

President Dwight Eisenhower reportedly conducted such an analysis early in his first term when he felt overloaded by staff pressures to make decisions more rapidly.[13] He concluded that most of the matters his staff considered urgent were of minor importance. In his opinion, the really big issues tended to have substantial time for analysis. Similarly, in Robert Kennedy's analysis of his brother John's decision making, President Kennedy learned to slow down his decision making after his early Bay of Pigs fiasco.[14]

This comparison of importance and urgency sets the stage for delegation analysis. This fourth sheet of paper should have a column for yourself ("Must be done by me") and separate columns for each of the immediate subordinates to whom you might delegate activities. Each of the scissored activities should be parceled out among the columns.

- Assign the relatively few "very important" *and* "very urgent" activities to yourself.
- Also assign the "very important" but not urgent activities to yourself.
- Delegate the urgent but not so important activities to your subordinates.

Activities analysis attempts to free you from the dominance of urgent but less important demands. This should allow you time for longer-range but fundamentally more important matters. The key assumption is that urgency and importance do not generally march together: that few managers will be overloaded with "important *and* urgent" matters. To the extent that this assumption is not valid for your job, this approach loses its value. And obviously, if you are not a manager with subordinates, you will have no one to whom you can delegate anything. Nonetheless, even if you have no subordinates, distinguishing between urgency and importance may help you to decide what activities you should give priority to and what you might be a bit less conscientious about.

Analyzing Your Diary.
Effective time managers tend to be assertive toward their environment. They do not passively accept all demands that

EXHIBIT 4–3: ACTIVITY ANALYSIS OF URGENCY FOR VICE PRESIDENT
FOR DEVELOPMENT AND UNIVERSITY RELATIONS

Very urgent —must be done immediately after or at scheduled time

* propose/advise president on his personal cultivation and solicitations
* participate in president's senior management group meetings
* participate in president's management group meetings
* support president/attend university-wide events
* support schools,/attend overseer meetings and events
* serve as liaison to Trustee Development and University Relations Committee

Urgent—should be done within hours after cue

* monitor gift receipts and acknowledge
* solve personnel and gift-situation problems with Deans
* recruit and hire senior development and public relations staff
* deal with university Human Resources office on salary and job classification
  situations
* meet with senior departmental staff as individuals and in group
* respond to senior departmental staff requests and inquiries
* conduct annual performance reviews with senior staff
* review and make salary decisions on all professional staff
* serve as cheerleader/maintain morale for staff through visits and entertain-
  ments
* meet with/advise alumni job seekers
* attend professional association meetings
* maintain relations with other university department senior managers
* prepare agenda and make reports to two Trustee Committees

Not Urgent—can be done during the four-month semester

* prepare, argue for, and negotiate annual departmental budget
* call on/develop new individual alumni relationships
* attend regional alumni relations meetings
* solicit gifts from (a) alumni, (b) friends, (c) corporations, and (d) individuals
* respond to individual alumni calls/complaints about admissions, gifts
* make decisions on alumni children applications to support
* initiate letters to alumni about their public accomplishments
* maintain relationships with Deans of Schools
* plan strategy and design organization structure for (a) development, (b) university relations, and (c) alumni relations
* maintain relations with chairpersons and members
* maintain relations with Alumni Regional Development Committee

Not Urgent—long range

* explore ways in fundraising, public relations, and alumni communications, to
  emphasize the central and the whole
* propose means of generating development investment funds beyond the president's budget allocation
* find ways of providing performance-based rewards such as bonuses for outstanding individual or unit performance

impinge upon them. Selectively ignoring certain cues is one of the tactics they use.[15] Your list of activities and precipitating cues can be analyzed for what could be ignored the next time it occurs. Even more helpful in generating cues to be ignored would be to maintain a diary for a couple of weeks to a month. This is not going to be permanent record keeping, but will generate basic working data which you will analyze.

The diary's format is not important, but the entries should be frequent, perhaps every fifteen minutes or so. Don't wait until lunchtime to write down what you did in the morning. You won't remember. If feasible, a parallel record of your activities kept by a secretary would be valuable. This short motion picture of your work life is to be subjected to three questions: (1) what does not have to be done?, (2) what must be done by me?, and (3) what could be done by someone else?

1. *What does not have to be done?* Examine each diary entry initially to see whether the activity could have been eliminated. That is, when the cue presented itself or when the thought occurred to you, could it have been ignored without cost to you or the organization? Such judgments are not easy of course, but ability to make such decisions is at the core of being an effective manager—a person able to transcend the flow of current events, to imaginatively project self above the present and visualize the past and the future. From this perspective, one can distinguish the important from the unimportant, the fundamental from the trivial. Using such an admittedly intuitive analysis, the effective manager may be able to detect those activities which could be eliminated and those cues which could be ignored at acceptable cost.

Consider my experience when working as an industrial engineer at Eastman Kodak Company, certainly one of the world's best-managed firms. Since silver is the most expensive raw material in photographic film, it pays to reprocess old film to recover the precious metal used in the light-sensitive emulsion that is coated on the plastic film base. Production waste, outdated film from camera shop shelves, and worn out motion picture reels are purchased from distributors to be sorted, chopped, and chemically treated to recover the silver.

Monthly, the motion picture film processing group reported to plant headquarters on the count and physical condition of the film: the pounds sorted, the pounds unsorted in inventory, and a subjective description of how powdery and brittle the film was. When asked if he used the report data in managing the department, the department head said no. The pounds sorted were measured automatically because the sorters were paid on a production incentive basis. The inventory could simply be eyeballed to judge backlog, and the state of the film seemed irrelevant.

An inquiry at plant headquarters resulted in my being shown the files of several year's reports, but the clerk indicated that no one ever looked at them. What was going on?

Some historical digging revealed that the report originated in the 1920s when motion picture film was on a nitrate base. Such material was and is extremely dangerous. It deteriorates with age, temperature, and low humidity, becoming near explosive in the presence of a spark or flame. Thus, in the early days, the older and more dangerous reels were sorted first and a close watch was kept on the film's condition.

But by the 1960s when management was still making the report, the nitrate base had long since been discontinued. In 1938 Kodak had invented an acetate base ("safety film") which was much more stable (the firm won a belated Academy Award for this in 1979). Yet the report on nitrate film was still being made twenty-five years after it was replaced and perhaps ten years after the last nitrate reel had passed through the department!

Note that the department had become quite efficient in collecting the information for the report; it didn't consume a lot of time. But it was useless activity. What the department head might have done is simply not make the report to headquarters on the next due date. And wait. Wait until someone complained about the missing report. And even then, not automatically respond but judge who is complaining. Is it someone with power to hurt the manager or authority to direct compliance? If not, if it is just the clerk, ignore him or her. And even if the department head's direct superior finally gets involved, use that as an opportunity to argue for eliminating the report. This is the kind of assertive experimenting with their environment that characterizes effective time managers.

2. *What must be done by me?* A manager has an obligation to optimize the performance of the unit he or she directs. You should not allow your work time to be consumed by the activities you most enjoy, or even those you do best. Rather, you should focus on those activities in which you enjoy the greatest differential advantage over those to whom it might be delegated.

You should compare your own performance on your major tasks with that of each available subordinate. The easiest situation to visualize is when you are truly superior. You can do every task in your unit better than any one of your subordinates. You have the training, expertise, and experience to be literally the best person for everything! But you can't do everything yourself (and live very long). You must delegate.

More realistically, as Exhibit 4–4 illustrates, on some tasks you will enjoy a large advantage; on others it will be small or even negative. Task A is something the analyzing manager does very well; he enjoys the sense of accomplishment, as it feeds his need for achievement. But Amy can perform the task almost as well so the manager's advantage is small. Task B is something the manager doesn't do as well as A (and perhaps doesn't enjoy as much). Unfortunately, the only possible delegates are Frank and Bob, and their performance is markedly below the manager's. The man-

EXHIBIT 4–4: ANALYSIS OF DIFFERENTIAL ADVANTAGE

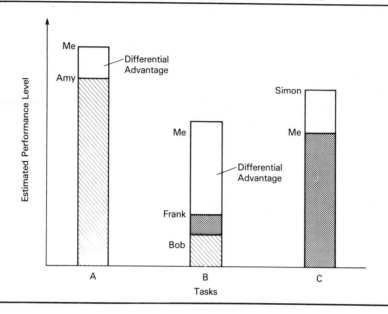

ager here should keep the activities in which he enjoys the greatest differential advantage (up to his time and energy capacity) and delegate the activities on which he possesses the least advantage.

One of the criticisms of Jimmy Carter as President of the United States was his apparent immersion in details to the detriment of communicating the big picture to the American public—and particularly to Congress. Extremely bright and more technologically literate than any prior President (except perhaps Herbert Hoover), he focused a major portion of his time on analyzing problems and formulating detailed legislation to be proposed to Capitol Hill. However, he delegated the actual lobbying for those bills to junior aides who shared his skepticism about senators and representatives. Standing on the White House balcony recently, long-time Democratic party leader Robert Strauss recalled his 1977 advice to Carter:[16] "I told him to invite (Senators) Russell Long and Bob Dole up here and have a drink out on this wonderful balcony and then go and have dinner. . . . When it's all over, sometime during the evening, Russell Long will tell you how to get your tax bill done."

Unfortunately, President Carter didn't take the advice. Because he had run for president as an outsider and because he simply didn't enjoy smoozing with legislators, he never developed the personal relationships essential to getting his proposals implemented. There is an old saying in Washington, DC that "no one gives a damn about having breakfast with the vice president." This is not a comment on any particular vice president; it simply reflects the fact that the president's differential advantage over the vice president or any White House staffer is so great that his time must be focused on those activities where he (or she someday) can make the biggest difference.

Ronald Reagan understood this, especially early in his administration. The day after his November 1980 election, he visited on Capitol Hill. Four times before his first inauguration, he held meetings with Congressional leaders in their offices. In his first six months as president, he held over 100 one-on-one meetings with senators and representatives—a multiple of what Carter did in four years. All of this contributed to President Reagan's greater success in seeing his proposals implemented into law (whatever one may feel about the substance of some of that legislation).

Focusing according to any criterion entails risk. It means being less knowledgeable on activities that you are not doing personally (and all presidents, but especially Reagan, have suffered for this). But this is one of the burdens of being a manager that must be borne if one is to have effective opportunity to make good things happen through your personal attention.

Now let us apply these concepts of selective ignorance and differential advantage to the delegation questions posed by our importance and urgency analysis.

3. *What can be delegated?* In analyzing my own activities as Vice President for Development and University Relations, I developed three categories: (a) must be done and by me; (b) must be done by me, but relax; and (c) can be delegated.

Going back to another copy of my original list of activities, I once again scissored them apart and distributed them among my three delegation categories. The result is illustrated in Exhibit 4–5. The first category reflects my judgment of importance and differential advantage. These are the activities which simply must be done if the department is to succeed (and I was to survive). And these are the activities where either because of my personal attributes or the clout of my office, my differential advantage was greatest.

"Must be done by me, but relax" is a don't-be-so-conscientious category. The activities can't be delegated entirely, but some proportion of the cues could be ignored and the activities not always performed. My analysis in Exhibit 4–5 in this category contains mostly standing meetings and ritualistic events.

The remaining activities on the delegation analysis in Exhibit 4–5 are those which I concluded could be delegated most if not all of the time. In general, these are activities in which I enjoyed little differential advantage, and some where certain subordinates could do a markedly superior job to me.

EXHIBIT 4–5: ACTIVITY ANALYSIS OF DELEGATION FOR VICE PRESIDENT
FOR DEVELOPMENT AND UNIVERSITY RELATIONS

Must Be Done By Me

* prepare, argue for, and negotiate annual departmental budget
* call on/develop new individual alumni relationships
* solicit gifts from (a) alumni, (b) friends
* make decisions on alumni children applications to support
* maintain relationships with Deans of Schools (major schools only)
* solve personnel and gift-situation problems with Deans
* recruit and hire senior development and public relations staff
* deal with university Human Resources office on salary and job classification situations
* plan strategy and design organization structure for (a) development, (b) university relations, and (c) alumni relations
* meet with senior departmental staff as individuals and in group
* respond to senior departmental staff requests and inquiries
* review and make salary decisions on all professional staff
* serve as cheerleader/maintain morale for staff through visits and entertainment
* propose means of generating development investment funds beyond the president's budget allocation
* find ways of providing performance-based rewards such as bonuses for outstanding individual or unit performance

Must Be Done by Me, but Relax (don't be so conscientious)

* propose/advise president on his personal cultivation and solicitations
* participate in president's senior management group meetings
* support president/attend university-wide events
* attend regional alumni relations meetings
* support schools/attend overseer meetings and events
* conduct annual performance reviews with senior staff
* attend professional association meetings
* maintain relations with other university department senior managers

Can Be Delegated

* solicit gifts from (c) corporations and (d) foundations
* respond to individual alumni calls/complaints about admissions, gifts
* initiate letters to alumni about their public accomplishments
* monitor gift receipts and acknowledgment letters
* maintain relations with Deans (minor schools)
* meet with/advise alumni job seekers
* serve as liaison to Trustee Development and University Relations Committees
* prepare agenda and make reports to two Trustee Committees
* maintain relations with chairpersons and members
* maintain relations with Alumni Regional Development Committees
* explore ways in fundraising, public relations, and alumni communications to emphasize the central and the whole

ADVICE AT HIGH LIFE SPORTING COMPANY, INC.

Since Vice President of Marketing, Sandor Alexander, and Marketing Promotions Director, Diane Switzer, both had management consultant Clark Gilman present and available as they faced several time management dilemmas, we can listen in on the advice he offered.

Scene 1 continued: To Go or Not to Go? Alexander is trying to decide whether to cancel his product development trip to Europe in order to direct personally a promotional campaign for a new line of ski equipment.

Gilman:	So, it's pretty clear that both your projects are important and they fit in with your long-term goals.
Alexander:	Well, of course they do, Clark! I wouldn't be doing these things to begin with if I didn't believe in their value.
Gilman:	That may seem clear to you, Sandy, but it's still an important question to ask. You may discover that one of your goals is not as important as you thought and that you need to redefine it, or reevaluate how much time you're spending on activities related to that goal.
Alexander:	Well, I'm clear that these are important goals. In fact, to tell you the truth, Clark, I'm beginning to suspect that this trip is *very* important to the long-term goals of High Life. I guess I shouldn't be so impulsive about cancelling it.
Gilman:	That's why I wanted you to take this time so you could reevaluate your decision.
Alexander:	Before our discussion I was convinced that I had to postpone the trip and concentrate on the campaign. I have pretty well made my decision that the trip is important, but I'm still faced with my problem! My new promotions director is not ready to handle introduction of a new product on her own. She couldn't handle the campaign.
Gilman:	Sandy, if you break down the campaign into its individual tasks you may discover that Diane can do some or all of those tasks. You could still provide her with guidance. You want to be able to anticipate any obstacles which might prevent her from completing the project and be prepared for them with contingency plans.
Alexander:	Well, I guess that Diane could handle more of the individual tasks than I had originally thought. But she's just beginning. She's never had any experience doing a big campaign like this one. I would still like to be here to supervise.
Gilman:	So what are your alternatives?
Alexander:	All right then, I would say the basic choices are (1) to start the campaign early and cancel the trip so I can supervise Diane; (2) to start the campaign early and still go on the trip as planned, which means I won't supervise her as closely as I'd like to; (3) go on the trip and start the campaign when I get back, which was

93

	the original plan. That way I could supervise Diane and take care of many tasks myself. And (4), I suppose I could consider asking someone else—the boss or even Diane—to go on the trip while I run the campaign. But that's not very practical.
Gilman:	So, what's your decision?
Alexander:	After thinking about it, I realize that there really are certain meetings in Europe that the company can't afford to miss. Therefore, I'm going on the trip and delegating much of the campaign to Diane. It'll be a good opportunity for her to show her stuff. I've cancelled all of my metings for next Monday and Tuesday so Diane and I can discuss the project before I leave. Then, I was able to shuffle some European commitments to leave two afternoons open to hold conference telephone calls with Diane and the people here while I'm away. And I've given her my schedule so she can call me if it is essential. At least I'll be able to give advice on the toughest problems Diane might encounter. Believe me, I've got some stomach butterflies about being away during the campaign, but I think this is the best use of my time.
Gilman:	Congratulations, Sandy—and good luck!

◌◌◌◌

Scene 2 continued: Who Should Do It? Sandor Alexander, Vice President of Marketing, has just given his marketing promotions director, Diane Switzer, instructions on the campaign prior to his departure for Europe.

Gilman:	I'm trying to get a sense of how much of this campaign you're actually *doing*, Sandy, rather than *managing*. And from what I've just seen and heard, I'm not sure that you're using your time and Diane's as effectively as you possibly can.
Alexander:	How's that?
Gilman:	Well, phrases like, "It's easier to solve these problems myself," or "It takes me less time to do it than to wait for her to do it"— to me, those are red flags for delegation problems that waste time. All those minutes you spend doing things "because it is easier" soon add up to hours. You need to be consciously aware of the best use of your time, where you can make the biggest difference.
Alexander:	And you don't think I'm doing that already?
Gilman:	Well, let's find out by reviewing the decisions you're making about delegating, seeing if we can discover how to use delegation to manage your time more effectively.
Alexander:	OK, Clark, but if this doesn't work you may have to drive me to the airport next Wednesday.
Gilman:	All right, Sandy, you're on. Now the first three sets in delegating effectively are: (1) distinguishing between *managing* and *doing;* (2) identifying specifically the activities *you* are doing rather than managing; and (3) deciding which activities *you* need to do and which you should delegate.

ADVICE ON MANAGING SHORT-TERM TIME

- Maintain to-do lists but remember that you will rarely be able to accomplish everything on such daily lists—and that you are not a failure if you don't.
- Organize daily and weekly to-do lists in priority order and fight to reserve interrupted time blocks to focus on the highest (say, 20 percent) of the listed items.
- Periodically insulate or isolate yourself to allow concentration on more complex, more ambiguous, and important projects. Closing your door, finding a second hide-away space, or working at home are possibilities.
- Once a year or so, analyze your job activities for urgency and importance or maintain and examine your job diary for cues and activities that might be selectively ignored.
- Analyze your activities for delegation potential. Try to delegate the urgent but less important ones as well as those to which you offer little differential advantage.
- On your especially disliked tasks, set early starting times and artificial deadlines. Generate momentum with easier tasks but shift to the difficult at the predetermined time.
- Reward yourself for progress on the tough jobs and include others in your mini-celebrations.
- Remember that few projects will turn out quite as well as you originally envisioned so anticipate some disappointment even as you enjoy the process of accomplishment.

5

Managing Longer-Term Time

Alexander:	By *managing*, you mean . . .
Gilman:	All the things you do to get results through others—like planning the campaign, motivating sales staff, controlling the budget. And by *doing* I mean anything you perform which could be done by someone else regardless of whether or not you actually have someone else to do it.
Alexander:	Like calling the printer, or looking at paper stocks.
Gilman:	Like I said before, Sandy, you obviously know the difference. And as a vice president, I'm sure you know that you're being paid to manage, not perform activities.
Alexander:	Of course, that's clear. But there are some things I really have to do—like taking this trip. There's no one else in a position to do that right now, even though in theory it is something someone else could do.
Gilman:	Managers should perform certain tasks, Sandy. But the trick to being an effective manager and of making the best use of your time is to know which tasks you should perform and which ones you should delegate. Basically you want to focus on those things where you would make the greatest contribution to the firm, where your performance would be so superior to anyone else's. And this might not even be the task you most enjoy and do best. That might well be delegated if you can do only a little better than someone to whom you could assign it.
Alexander:	Well then, I'd better take a closer look at this campaign to make sure that I'm managing and not doing activities that should be delegated to Diane.
Gilman:	Good idea, Sandy. Since this is Diane's first campaign, there are clearly a lot of activities you have to and should perform. But you're walking a fine line. When you're supervising persons who have never done a job before, it's often easier to *do* their job for them than to train and supervise them so they learn how to handle it alone.
Alexander:	I see what you mean. I've got to analyze exactly how much I need to be doing on this campaign and make some decisions. Like just this morning, I could have simply approved Diane's choice of paper stock. But instead I kept her waiting while I tried to reach a decision myself in between finalizing the plans for my trip. Her work ground to a halt because I wouldn't let her make a decision that she was perfectly capable of making.
Gilman:	And if you had even greater faith in Diane, you could have just defined your promotion philosophy to her allowing her greater

discretion—that, perhaps, you want this program to convey a "class" look so don't cut corners on paper or printing, and that you want something that looks expensive.

Alexander: And Diane could choose within those guidelines.

ௐௐௐௐ

Scene 3 continued: Interruptions! Interruptions! Marketing Promotions Director, Diane Switzer, is becoming frustrated because of the volume of unexpected interruptions in her new job.

Switzer: Sometimes I feel like a puppet. I hardly have time to light a cigarette.

Gilman: Keep in mind that interruptions happen on the average of about every eight minutes for a typical manager. The key to managing them is to anticipate, as much as possible, the ones you will experience on a given day like phone calls, visitors, and mail. Then you can plan to schedule time to respond to these routine interruptions and develop techniques for responding to them.

Switzer: Well, I see how I can plan for the time I'll respond to incoming mail, but some of the demands that come my way are pretty unexpected, like this sky delivery delay.

Gilman: I agree. But when a problem like that does come up, then you can anticipate interruptions which might follow it such as complaints from the field. You can anticipate additional phone calls and schedule time for them. I think you'll learn more about what you can anticipate in this job as time goes on. By identifying the kinds of interruptions you experience on a given day, you can distinguish between those you can anticipate and those that you can't . . . The most immediate problem seems to be the supplier delivery delay. What are you doing about that?

Switzer: Eight retailers have already been called. And a memo is out, but all the sales people won't have it until Monday. I've told my secretary to handle all my calls on this. So if any sales reps call, she can let them know that the memo is on the way. And if customers call, apologize to them and tell them that we're moving to correct the problem and that they'll hear from their sales rep on Monday.

Gilman: Diane, you handled that problem very well. Now Sheila is equipped with enough information to head off some interruptions before they reach you. You might also make a memo to yourself that at a later time you should look into the whole issue of notifying sales staff and customers more rapidly on these matters. Perhaps, prewritten telegrams, telephone calls, electronic mail, or by fax. When things are a bit slower, you could initiate a project that might reduce interruptions on some matters before they occur.

ௐௐௐௐ

When your home is burning, you rightly don't stop to figure out how the fire started or how the next one might be prevented. You focus on the present, deciding whether to fight or flee the flames. "The only reality is the present" goes an old Indian proverb. And it is true. Yet, if executives pay attention only to the present, they will be out of control and their firms' resources will be expended willy-nilly. The greatest risk for achievement-driven professionals and managers is being submerged in the short run, oblivious to the adverse long-range impact of immediate decisions—this criticism is often voiced by Japanese about the United States as a whole.[1]

Of all people, managers especially should manage longer-term time. In this chapter, we examine the factors that tyrannize managers in the short run and then consider how long-range planning can be integrated into personal time management. First, however, let's compare four successful executives who are contending for the presidency of a company. Each of them expresses a philosophy of management in general and time management in particular. See whom you think would make the best chief executive officer.

A NEW PRESIDENT FOR PYRAMID

Pyramid Electric Company is seeking a new president to replace the current chief executive officer, Russell Erheart, who will retire a year from now. Four senior executives at Pyramid are being considered: Robert Findley, Vice President of Manufacturing; John Andrews, Vice President of Sales and Marketing; David Williamson, Vice President of Engineering and Research; and Samuel Scott, Vice President of Finance.

Pyramid is an old family firm that turned to professional management ten years ago. No family members are currently active in management although the two sides of the founder's family are represented on the board of directors. The family controls approximately 35 percent of the outstanding shares of stock and the rest are widely owned. The chairman of the board is a retired bank president who is not employed by Pyramid.

Pyramid has moved from fairly simple electrical components into sophisticated electronics products utilized by computer manufacturers and various users of integrated circuitry including automobile companies. Sales last year totaled $253,000,000.

Following are excerpts from interviews with each of the four presidential candidates followed by comments of the incumbent president.

Robert Findley, Vice President of Manufacturing. Findley is forty-two years of age and holds a B.S. in engineering and an M.S. in industrial administration.

Question:	What would you consider your greatest accomplishment during the time that you've been here?
Findley:	I suppose the most important thing I've tried to do is to make production more quality *and* cost conscious. The two never seemed to go together in the past. We now are producing the best-made product in our business and I think at less cost than many of our competitors.
Question:	From your own personal point of view, what do you regard as your greatest asset for the company?
Findley:	Know-how. I've made it my business to learn everything I could about this industry. I believe I know as much about cutting edge electronics manufacturing as anyone.
Question:	And what would you say is your greatest weakness?
Findley:	My main interest is in *doing* the job, not talking about it. I don't like a lot of smoozing with employees.
Question:	Now, what are your general views on how you manage your time?
Findley:	Time is everything—our most precious resource. And it is more than Ben Franklin suggested. It is more than money; it is the stuff of life. I don't want to be chained to my job and I don't have to because I am able to plan and control my time fairly closely. I allocate certain hours and days for specific activities and try to stick by it. Every so often I work at home in order to have uninterrupted time to think and plan, and I've trained my people to respect my closed door here in the plant. It is systematic habit and control that is the key.
Question:	Now, let me ask you what you consider to be the most important aspect of the president's job?
Findley:	It is to make the firm *run*—not with a lot of bells and whistles, but like a beautiful clock. This means a well-defined organizational structure with clear lines of authority so that everyone clearly understands his responsibilities. You can't manage a growing firm like this from your hip pocket, so clear policies and procedures are imperative.
Question:	Who would be a possible successor to head manufacturing if you moved up to president?
Findley:	That would require some consideration, but I think I have two department heads who would be strong candidates and good performers, as long as I clearly expressed my expectations of them. But, I would like to compare them to outside candidates before making a decision.

John Andrews, Vice President of Marketing and Sales. John is fifty-three years old and has a B.A. in history and Spanish.

Question:	What do you think has been your greatest accomplishment since you became vice president?
Andrews:	Corporate visibility! I've really made the company well known

through our advertising, public relations promotions, and political activity. Oh, we had a good business when I took over, but the public didn't know much about us. In my opinion, our higher profile has really helped our sales.

Question: And what do you think is your greatest asset as an executive?

Andrews: The people I know, those in business and government who will take my telephone calls. Especially here in Chicago I know everybody who is anybody, but I frequently visit New York, Washington, DC and the West Coast. Sam Scott uses my banking contacts from time to time and I helped get Dave Williamson appointed to that presidential commission on national innovation.

Question: And what would you say is your greatest weakness?

Andrews: Perhaps you should ask my two former wives! I was never home, perhaps because I do too much for others who then mistakenly assume I'm a soft touch. Not everyone appreciates what I do for them.

Question: Tell me Jack, how do you feel about the way you manage your time?

Andrews: Time is all we have and it's for enjoyment, my boy! I like to keep moving around and to keep contacts open. I don't worry much about planning every minute. And I hate a calendar cluttered with standing meetings a year in advance! People appreciate it when I drop by for a chat and a cup of coffee (fortunately, I have a cast iron stomach). Efficiency neurotics forget that people can't be slaves to their watches.

Question: Last question. What do you consider the most important job that the president has to do?

Andrews: Like the old real estate axiom on location, the three leadership keys are communication, communication, and communication! To retain interest and excitement, people have to understand each other. This is what I've tried to do at Pyramid—tell everyone what fine people we have here and what a good firm this is. Headquarters especially needs to hear from the people out on the firing lines in the field and I try to serve as a conduit. As I've said, I visit a lot of people and I write many letters, notes, and cards of congratulations and thanks. Management even inside the firm is mainly sales and we should never forget to encourage and praise good work. On my office wall, I have framed the saying, "Sales is not the most important function in this company, it is the *only* function." That includes selling employees on Pyramid.

Question: Jack, do you have anyone to take over for you if you moved up to president?

Andrews: Boy, do I! Almost any one of my regional sales executives could take over tomorrow.

David Williamson, Vice President of Engineering and Research.
Williamson's age is forty-eight and he holds a B.S. and M.S. in engineering.

Managing Longer-Term Time

Question: Dave, what would you consider your greatest accomplishment?

Williamson: I suppose you mean here at work, in engineering. My greatest concern has been incorporating more concern for the customer and the environment into our designs. Product reliability and efficiency have increased substantially. Our designs use less energy and pollute less. On top of this they are easier for customers to use and repair. All of this costs money, of course, and has probably reduced corporate profits a bit, but such innovation keeps a business alive.

Question: You may be right, Dave. Now let me ask what you think is your greatest asset to the company?

Williamson: That is difficult to say. I think encouraging innovation is absolutely critical so I try to keep an open mind to all possibilities. My job isn't to know all the answers, but to be able to really listen to others' ideas.

Question: And what would you consider your greatest weakness?

Williamson: Sometimes I so enjoy the debate and deliberation about new ideas that decisions get delayed. A closed mind is a great asset in making decisions rapidly, but I'd rather make better decisions—even if I appear to be, and sometimes am, indecisive.

Question: What are your general views on how you manage your time as a manager?

Williamson: I'm a lousy one to ask. I may be the worst time manager in the world. Most of the time I feel like my day is determined by my people. Seriously, I do think a manager should be available and approachable so his or her people will come with problems and ideas. But it is a dilemma because I also think a manager needs time alone to think about tomorrow. I try to fit this in by coming in early, but frankly this conflicts a little with the variety of activities I like to engage in during the evening. Burning the candle at both ends is not as easy as it used to be! The whole business is difficult.

Question: Now, what do you think is a president's principal job?

Williamson: Getting people's commitment is a major objective. In a firm like Pyramid with so many skilled people, real authority must flow upward. You just can't tell people what to do, so they must feel like they are real partners in the enterprise. And this means substantial participation in company decisions. Oh, I don't mean that senior management should just abdicate to employee desires, but all managers must consult and really listen if people are to feel part of our effort. A president should set such an example.

Question: Finally, if you were to become president of Pyramid, do you have someone who could take over your present position?

Williamson: I have several who might be happy to have me out of this office! And I do think two or three of them could do a good job. But before we did anything, I would like to get together with them to explore whether this position should be redefined. At present there is just too much in it and we might benefit from separating some of the functions.

A New President for Pyramid

Samuel Scott, Vice President of Finance. Scott is fifty-five years old and holds a B.S. in business administration, an M.B.A., and is a C.P.A.

Question: Sam, what do you think is your greatest accomplishment with Pyramid?

Scott: I've brought control and efficiency to our handling of funds. Our accounts receivable are the smallest in the industry and we are able to take maximum discounts on all our purchases. In addition, personal expense accounts have actually been reduced by better auditing procedures. Most of all, however, I've gotten the big banks interested in backing us so interest rates on our loans are the best available.

Question: Yes, I wish I could get those rates. Now, if you were president Sam, what would you consider your greatest asset?

Scott: Courage and decisiveness. I'm willing to have the buck stop at my desk. I accept responsibility. Too many people around here just try to postpone their decisions by keeping their so-called "options" open. What nonsense.

Question: And what do you think is your greatest liability?

Scott: I sometimes step on timid people's toes with my willingness to call a spade a spade—but to me, that's not a liability.

Question: Tell me, what are your general views on how you manage your time?

Scott: A boss should be involved. No sitting around drinking tea and playing golf. I am at the center of my department's decisions and I want them made correctly. I save time by being decisive and by making sure that people don't make mistakes. I make decisions quickly. When you've been in this business as long as I have, you get to know what's right without a lot of talk.

Question: Now Sam, what do you think is the most important job for the president of Pyramid?

Scott: To set targets and make sure the firm gets there. You've got to see that people do their jobs and that matters don't drift. The CEO has to bear that final responsibility—with the advice of the board of directors, but nonetheless, ultimately alone.

Question: If you were selected as the next president, do you have someone available to replace you as Vice President of Finance?

Scott: You mean, if I accept the position as president?

Interviewer: Yes.

Scott: I will have to find someone from the outside, although I don't think I will need to hurry on this. There is no one here now. Young people today are just so impatient that they don't stay around long enough to learn their jobs, so no one in the department now is experienced enough.

Russell Erheart, President of Pyramid. Following are excerpts from a conversation with the current president.

Managing Longer-Term Time

Question: Russ, you've known all four candidates longer than anyone else in the firm. What would you say about them as individuals?

Erheart: I'm glad to answer, but frankly I don't believe an outgoing chief executive should name his own successor. We would all be too tempted to name someone just like ourselves and there never would be necessary change in style or philosophy. I will, however, say something about each of the candidates because they are all outstanding people who have served me and the firm very well. The board doesn't have to go outside after Lee Iaccoca to get a new president!

Bob Findley is probably the most organized person I've ever met. He is so planned and in control that I've never understood why he is so overweight. He dresses well, but he always looks so rumpled!

Nonetheless, he is terrific and quite active in quality improvement professional circles such as the Deming movement. I know he is very close to his still growing family—he became a father for the fourth time last month. No one is more reliable in meeting his commitments with outstanding work. He just doesn't make mistakes.

Dave Williamson is a gem, maybe even a saint. He has cared for his sick wife for many years with never a complaint while still deeply involved in charitable activities as a contributor and volunteer. He even finds time to teach one course a year at Northwestern. I don't see him much socially because his friends lean more to the intellectual than mine, but I certainly like him. He does smoke virtually nonstop, however, and that worries me a little. He is very well known in the high tech research and development community and currently serves on a national presidential committee in this area.

Jack Andrews is my best friend and I, along with many others, love him. He is always good for a joke and a positive word. Many a day I've felt discouraged, but Jack would cheer me up. And of course he is an attractive man whom everyone seems to know—the only guy I know who still wears a fresh lapel flower every day! You'd never know from his demeanor that he's been divorced twice. He will joke about being married to Pyramid, but it's true that he's always pushing the firm wherever he is and whatever he's doing. And the results show it. My only problem is that sometimes I'm unable to find him when I need an answer to a question. He seems to disappear on the road sometimes. There are rumors about a drinking problem, but I've never noticed anything.

Sam Scott is a big and impressive person. As you may recall, he was an All-American tackle in college and even had a short fling in the pro's. He had a sense of the future, however, and he studied for his CPA and eventually earned his MBA while working for Pyramid and going to school at night. He stays in shape and still referees college football games. He has real perseverance. Since my background was in engineering, I've pretty much let him run the show in the financial area here and he has never let me down. Sometimes I flinch at his brutal candor though! He is the only other executive on the board of directors and they respect him greatly. I think they would worry about his leaving the company if he is not elected president.

സ്റ്റ

WHO SHOULD BE ELECTED PRESIDENT?

Incumbent President Russell Erheart is confident that a strong replacement can be found among the four candidates. However much you would like to dispute this and go after Lee Iaccoca, let's restrict ourselves to the four insiders.

Exhibit 5-1 summarizes the four interviews and the president's comments. Making such an important decision should involve comparison on several dimensions, but we focus primarily on their approaches to time management. Robert Findley, Manufacturing Vice President, appears to be the most effective practitioner of the short-run time management tactics discussed in the preceding chapter. He is systematic in making lists, in evaluating activity priorities, and in focusing on what is most important. He is probably an excellent delegator because of his ability to clearly define authority and responsibility. And he seems to be able to perform his job well while maintaining a balance between work and home life. There seems to be little danger of his burning out, although I would worry a bit about the impact of his weight on his health as he becomes older.

Dave Williamson, Engineering and Research Vice President, jokes about being a poor time manager because of the tension he feels about being available while also having time alone. It doesn't appear that he is as orderly as Findley in managing his daily activities, especially since he sometimes loses track of time when discussing new ideas. Because he fears premature decisions that might reject creative proposals, he likes to keep deliberation going long enough for possible proposal strengths to emerge. He feels that the responsibilities of his office might be too great for a single replacement, so as president he would consider dividing his current position.

John Andrews seems at the opposite extreme from Robert Findley. Andrews rejects overly planning his time because it might restrict his flexibility. He particularly dislikes being tied to his office by standing meetings scheduled weeks and months in advance. He prefers to "take" time to move around the firm maximizing opportunity for chance conversations. He invests time in communicating and doing favors for people, but wonders why some people don't appreciate what he does for them. His time commitment to Pyramid may be reflected in his two divorces—at least he jokes about this.

Finally, Samuel Scott, Finance Vice President, is a linear time manager who simply works through problems as they come, minimizing discussion and making decisions rapidly based on his deep experience. He doesn't appear to be overloaded in spite of his making most of the decisions in his department.

Before seeing how various students and executives have voted on the four candidates, let's examine some guidelines on managing longer-term time.

MANAGERIAL TIME WASTERS

When asked to describe what wastes their time, managers mention the following:[2]

misplaced material	incoming telephone calls
visitors	poor organization
interruptions	structure
commuting	coffee breaks
long letters	procrastination
waiting for people	preparing unread reports
failure to delegate	talks with subordinates
meetings on trivial	keeping up with former
matters	position
lack of preparation for	unclear job descriptions
meetings	interpersonal conflict
correspondence delays	inadequate performance
conflicting goals	feedback
obsolete policies and	approval delays
procedures	
unnecessary	
correspondence	

Such items are familiar to most managers. Nonetheless, most causes cited are superficial; they represent mainly symptoms. They also erroneously imply that anything that interferes with the way *you want* to spend your time is wasteful. But that is nonsense, because being a manager often means doing what others want you to do rather than what you want. We need to examine more fundamental time wasters: fractionated days, transition difficulties, short-run perspectives, and fear of ambiguity.

Fractionated Days. The reality of most managers' days is not like the time implied in most management textbooks, neatly divided into periods of planning, controlling, structuring, staffing, and directing.[3] Rather, it is a seeming chaos of a lot of time talking in many short conversations cov-

EXHIBIT 5–1: COMPARISON OF CANDIDATES AT PYRAMID

	Samuel Scott	John Andrews	Robert Findley	David Williamson
	Finance V.P. 55; BABA, CPA, MBA	Marketing and Sales V.P. 53; BA	Production V.P. 42; BSE, MSIA	Engineer V.P. 48; BSE, MSE
Accomplishment	▪ Control in funds accts. rec.; exp. accts.	▪ Made Co. well known ▪ Sales results	▪ Quality *and* cost cost conscious	▪ More concern for customers and environment ▪ Reliab., eff., less energy
Asset	▪ Willing to take responsibility	▪ Contacts	▪ Know-how ▪ Tech. knowledge	▪ Open minded
Liability	▪ Outspoken	▪ Do too much ▪ Not hardboiled	▪ Not a talker	▪ Sometimes indecisive
President's job	▪ To take resp. for results ▪ See that people do jobs	▪ Communication ▪ Understanding ▪ Excitement	▪ "Run" org. ▪ Clarify lines of auth./duties	▪ Gain commitment ▪ Generate participation
Time management	▪ Involved, work ▪ Don't waste ▪ Decisive	▪ Too valuable to be rigidly planned ▪ "Take time"	▪ Too valuable to be unplanned ▪ Plan, habit, and control	▪ Tension; wants to be available ▪ But needs time alone ▪ Tough problem
Replacement	▪ No insider ready ▪ Go outside	▪ Yes ▪ Regional mgrs.	▪ Perhaps ▪ Compare inside and outside	▪ Perhaps ▪ Reexamine position
Erheart's comments	▪ Big and impressive ▪ Perseverance ▪ On board ▪ Respected ▪ Would leave?	▪ Best friend ▪ Humor ▪ Divorced ▪ Successful ▪ Available?	▪ Organized ▪ Reliable ▪ Family ▪ Overweight	▪ A gem ▪ Teacher ▪ High-tech visibility ▪ Smoker

ering many different topics, broken by four to five scheduled meetings each day.[4] Exhibit 5-2 summarizes how time is spent by 54 managers whom I was able to shadow.[5] Observable time working per week was approximately 44 hours per week plus they self-reported another 10 hours a week working outside the office for a total of 54 hours per week. A study of chief executive officers reports similar hours:[6]

- 13 percent work less than 50 hours per week
- 31 percent work between 50 and 59 hours per week
- 39 percent work between 60 and 69 hours per week
- 16 percent work over 70 hours per week!

On an average day the average manager whom I've observed talks with more than 25 different people, which takes over 60 percent of his or her time (perhaps 13 hours per week on the telephone!).[7] Most of these talks are initiated by others who require response. And the day is very jumpy. The average incident, such as talking to someone, lasts about two minutes. The average interval of quiet time without interruption is only five minutes.

Under such conditions, a manager's average day is devoted mainly to responding to various telephone calls, visitors, voters, and colleagues. His or her life is dominated by the present and by fighting immediate fires. The future shrinks in apparent importance because there is no time to deal with it.

EXHIBIT 5-2: MANAGERS' TIME ALLOCATION (HOURS PER WEEK)

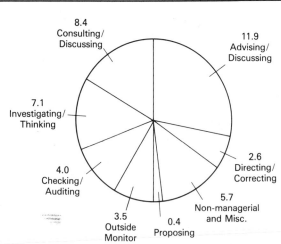

8.4 Consulting/Discussing

11.9 Advising/Discussing

7.1 Investigating/Thinking

2.6 Directing/Correcting

4.0 Checking/Auditing

5.7 Non-managerial and Misc.

3.5 Outside Monitor

0.4 Proposing

Transition Difficulty. Making transitions from short-run emergencies to longer-term problems is tough. Once while I was observing a United States Senator's executive assistant, there was a lull in the day's activities. Five minutes, six minutes passed without an incident. As the minutes passed, he began to get nervous, playing with his pencil, glancing at his watch, and shuffling papers. At about the tenth uninterrupted minute, he said to me that this was the most difficult part of the day. He pointed to a pile of papers and explained that they were nominations from the White House for positions in the State Department. Since his senator was a ranking member of the Senate Foreign Relations Committee, he was to draft letters for the senator to send to the president commenting on each of the nominees.

This was a ticklish assignment. Since the letters might well be leaked to the press, they had to be carefully crafted so as not to offend political friends. The harried manager indicated that he couldn't bring himself to begin the tough thinking and writing because he expected to be interrupted any minute. Finally, he chose to put the nominations into his briefcase for consideration later at home. Perhaps it was proper time management to take the creative work home, but the present often tyrannizes the future. Programmed and immediate tasks tend to be handled before more ambiguous longer-run matters. Such tyranny of the present is not confined to government, of course.

Five or ten minutes alone are helpful only for work on small, immediate issues. They are unsuitable for longer-range, less structured projects. Many executives do not believe that they spend up to ninety minutes alone during the day. All they know is that they scarcely have time to start a new task, drink a cup of coffee, or even take a deep breath before being interrupted by the arrival of a visitor or a ringing telephone.

Too Little Thinking. Continual dominance by immediate demands means inadequate time for reading and thinking. As a result, many managers tend to be narrow in their interests and concentrate on technical and economic reading. Worse, time-harried people take insufficient time for exploration. Dominated by response behavior for long periods, they can lose track of who they are and what they believe. Losing touch with their own values and aspirations, they find it impossible to initiate fundamental changes. The future is never confronted.

A United States Senator poignantly complained of the pressure of the present when he said to me, "This job gets you. You lose track of what is your basic political philosophy. You start voting to maintain your image rather than what you really believe."[8] This was from a senator who as a young Congressman had started out very liberal in his views. He continued to vote liberal as he moved into middle age, but felt increasingly uncomfortable with it. Only when he finally began to take time to examine bills in the light of his evolving beliefs did he begin to vote more as a conservative (to the consternation of his liberal staff and constituents). Perhaps Winston Churchill's famous repeat of an earlier British Prime Minister Benjamin Disraeli applies here, "Anyone who is not a socialist at age twenty has no heart, but anyone who is not a conservative at forty has no brains!"

Short-run Reward and Punishment. Politicians and government officials tend to concentrate on the short-run because of the threats in the near future: a bill's defeat, reduction of the annual appropriation, rejection by constituents. Long-range demographic, agricultural, and environmental problems will not hurt them *now* (although they may not be able to say this much longer). In this short-range view, small matters loom large.

Similarly, in business short-term performance standards encourage managers to concentrate on the now. They feel that they are rewarded or punished for *this* year based on annual measures of profits, costs, and growth. In the long run they will be dead—or transferred. A competitive business system encourages a short-time perspective of course; only a monopoly can ignore today. Yet, even given competition, management tends to measure performance over too limited a time span. Concentration on the present is usually rewarded, while sacrificing for the future is often ignored (or punished).

Corporate rotation and transfer policies also contribute to the dominance of a short-run orientation. General Electric has a justified reputation as a well-managed company. Yet back in its most decentralized period during the 1960s, operating managers would sometimes exploit equipment, employees, and even customers to get the best budget numbers. Equipment would not be maintained, employees would not be trained, and customer complaints not responded to in the hope that a department's results would look so good *this* year that the manager would be rewarded with a promotion. An unsuspecting replacement would have to pick up the pieces.

In some growing firms, supermobile managers average a position change every eighteen months; even average managers may move every two to three years.[9] Such transfers and short tenures do not reflect job mastery as much as they express impatience with progress up the hierarchy. Mobile managers tend to measure their success by how frequently they are promoted or transferred, not by how well they perform. One desirable result of the tough downsizings of corporate managerial and professional staffs in the 1980s appears to be a slowdown in promotions and longer tenures in positions, however hard it is for ambitious achievers to accept.

Fear of Ambiguity. Many managers focus on the present because the future is too ambiguous and threatening. Everyone has limited tolerance for ambiguity; we tend to prefer the known to the unknown. We opt for an act that has measurable results to the intangible or unmeasurable. This often leads us to concentrate on details about which then we can complain.

Every organization has an inexhaustible supply of detailed issues needing attention *now!* "I waste my time on trivia," managers complain. "If I could get rid of such nonsense, I would spend my time on important planning and evaluating" is their plea. Perhaps they mean it, but many really want the detailed activity. Managers are not forced to expend all their time on trivialities. The opposite may be true: the real challenges of managing are so difficult that they allow their days to be filled with detail and trivia. This protects them from having any time to contemplate what they are *not* doing. At least when they issue a detailed memorandum on office telephone calls, they "accomplish" something tangible and comforting. A former chairman of Inland Steel writes about the self-appointed martyr that is the poor, harried manager:[10]

> Pity the overworked executive! Behind his paperwork ramparts, he struggles bravely with a seemingly superhuman load of responsibilities. Burdened with impossible assignments, beset by constant emergencies, he never has a chance to get organized. Pity him but recognize him for the dangerous liability that he is.

This attention to familiar detail often leads newly promoted managers to hold onto their former positions through temporarily postponing announcing replacements or overly supervising them. This is partly because they lack trust in the new people, but mainly because they seek the comfort of the familiar tasks in which they have proven their competence. We tend to concentrate on what we know we do well. But such behavior emphasizes the present at the expense of the future, and the old to the detriment of the new.

The desire for control and certainty leads to strange inversions of managerial values. My uncle owned a small print shop in which walk-in customers were the life of the business. He had no sales staff. Mail orders were impossible, and telephone orders fairly limited. The person who opened the front door jingling a little bell *was* the business. Yet, my uncle would be clearly annoyed by their arrival. He perceived customers as interruptions to his completing job tickets, estimating costs, calculating bills, preparing the payroll, ordering paper, and so on—none of which could exist without the customers.

As much as we complain about paperwork, it is tangible and superficially controllable. We can start and stop as we please, take a drink of water when thirsty, speed up or slow down. In contrast, the customer is not under control; he or she initiates the conversation and tries to persuade the manager to do what he or she wants. Of course, to serve the customer is your main function, but unconsciously we may prefer the known, the concrete, and the self-controlled.

Fear of ambiguity and losing control also contributes to a crisis syndrome. Legitimate crises stemming from competition, technology, or environment can foster effective performance and high morale,[11] but many crises are artificial, like the "hurry up and wait" of military infamy. A high-level executive wonders about a certain open-ended issue and asks about it. The next level down assigns it to a subordinate along with a reasonable completion date. As the matter moves down the hierarchy, however, each subordinate manager wants to impress a superior so he or she advances the date a little. Thus, time pressure increases as the deadline moves downward, generating an arbitrary crisis that no one understands.

Fear of not being in control and of being adrift in ambiguity thus contributes to the long hours of some managers. An oil company president complains:[12] "I don't know why, but everyone around here works too hard . . . My executive group all work too much. I think that's a bit characteristic of business executives in the United States today. If anything, they spend too many hours at work."

INTEGRATING PLANNING AND LONGER-TERM TIME MANAGEMENT

Managers with high achievement needs desire feedback indicating that they have used their time efficiently, but they tend to be impatient.[13] They want results quickly, for that is the purpose of their effort and discipline. Unfortunately, excessive concern with rapid progress and feedback can hinder long-range effectiveness.

Effectiveness, however, is more important than efficiency. In time management, means and ends can become confused. The various lists, diaries, logs, and inventories can become ends in themselves if keeping track of time becomes more important than what is done with it. The purpose of the tactics is not to save time itself, but to allow time for accomplishing important tasks, and this means tying time to organizational objectives.

Perspectives on Planning and Objectives. The definitions of planning are numerous: thinking about what you want and how you are going to accomplish it; determining in advance what is to be done; preparing for the future by making decisions now.[14] Planning represents management's attempt to anticipate the future and guard against the threat of undesired change. It is humankind's effort to visualize "the future as history" by determining how we would want the future to appear if we could jump ahead in time and look backward.[15] "The purpose of planning," according to one executive, "is not to show how precisely we can predict the future, but rather to uncover the things we must do today in order to have a future."

Beautiful words, but tough to act upon! All managers have to face the nagging reality of their jobs—pressure to ignore the past, concentrate on the present, and let tomorrow take care of itself. Managers who are so taken in, however, are not exercising human leadership to its potential which is oriented toward the future by carving time out of the present in the service of tomorrow.

Business Objectives.

Tomorrow begins with formulation of management's continuing objectives.[16] These are the long-run, ongoing concerns that contain no time limits and no numbers. In an ultimate sense, the central business objective is profit or shareholder value, but no firm will survive unless it pays attention simultaneously to additional objectives. Here is Peter Drucker's list of multiple objectives:[17]

1. *Profitability:* Gross profit or net profits, perhaps as a percentage of invested funds
2. *Market standing:* The proportion of the market enjoyed compared with competitors
3. *Productivity:* Ratio of output of goods or services to input of resources such as labor, material and money
4. *State of resources:* Protection and maintenance of equipment, buildings, inventory, and financial assets
5. *Service:* Timely and appropriate quality response to customers' and clients' needs
6. *Innovation:* Development and delivery of new products or services
7. *Social contribution/public responsibility:* Improvement of environment and quality of life

Note that no single set of answers to these objectives is always the best. One could choose to be an innovator or a follower, emphasize service as a competitive tool or discount prices, hide from customers and merely replace products when pressed. One could aim for a full umbrella of products or narrowly specialize. What is important is that the definition of objectives is consistent with your firm's capabilities and the competitive realities of your industry.

Process Objectives.

The business objectives described above emphasize results, but we need also to recognize process objectives that apply to business and all other institutions.[18] An organization's success will be limited if time and attention are not allocated to these process objectives.

1. *Identification:* Clarity of purpose cannot be assumed. Attention must be devoted to achieving concensus and commitment to organizational objectives. Top managers should be internal salespeople selling the idea of the organization to its own people. During his long tenure as chief executive officer at General Motors, Alfred Sloan spent almost half his time from 1923 to 1963 traveling around the company articulating his conception of the company's strategy.[19] In more recent years, Jack Welch of General Electric and John Scully of Apple have been especially visible in articulating their firms' unique visions by investing much personal time in talking to groups of current junior managers in training programs and prospective managers in college.

2. *Integration:* No organization can exist unless its members perceive some overlap between their own personal objectives and the firm's. This may mean only exchanging their time and muscle for the institution's money, but it generally implies a feeling that at least some needs such as security, affiliation, and esteem are served by contributing to the organization. Some businesses, of course, go much farther. At the core of Thomas Watson's original vision of IBM was a more family-like atmosphere where managers and employees would all be treated equally and respectfully by being paid salaries rather than wages with every effort made to maintain employment without layoffs. At its best (as apparently is common in Japan), employees feel great overlap between their personal needs and the firm's objectives.

3. *Social influence:* To facilitate problem solving and goal achievement, all organizations must distribute power and authority. Traditionally, power flows down the hierarchy from the top. But this can no longer be assumed because of greater lower-level expectations, increased task complexity, and expanded burdens on the top. Therefore, power distribution should be as planned as other aspects of management.

4. *Collaboration:* No matter how well managed, all organizations composed of human beings will experience internal conflict. Rather than bemoaning this as a sign of management's failure or personal irrationality, management should see it as another area in which to set objectives. That is, management should institute means of managing conflict (such as grievance procedures, open-door policy, corporate ombudsmen, due process, and internal organizational development consultants).

5. *Adaptation:* All organizations confront time and environmental changes. Competitors introduce new technology, market tastes change, and new laws are passed which threaten the firm's viability. Accordingly, management needs to define processes for monitoring the external world and internally responding appropriately to threats and opportunities.

6. *Revitalization:* Even if no external threats or opportunities exist, management should strive to exercise the organization's ability to change. This is revitalization. How can we keep the firm light on its feet and able to move if it has to? Admittedly, this is the most subjective objective, but perhaps ultimately the most important.

In the short run, some objectives can be competitive. Simultaneously expanding profits and market share, for example, may be impossible because price cuts may be necessary to attract new customers. And improving productivity and curbing pollution may be mutually exclusive in the short run because pollution control equipment tends to increase costs. When management sets goals to be accomplished in a specific time period, it has to deal with this competition among objectives.[20]

A firm's multiple objectives can be arrayed along a continuum of "most dominant" to "most deferrable" based on the clarity of the cues precipitating activity on each objective and the time span until measurement for inadequate performance. For example, Exhibit 5-3 illustrates how the fifteen-person senior management team of Metropolis Electric (name disguised), a large public power utility, arrayed their objectives.

Most dominant are those that demand everyday attention, while deferrable objectives are those that have few explicit cues so that they can be safely ignored for some time. Clearly, the central purpose of this department is to design and construct reliable electrical generation and distribution facilities so that energy consumers in their geographical area

EXHIBIT 5-3: ELECTRICAL UTILITY COMPANY OBJECTIVES

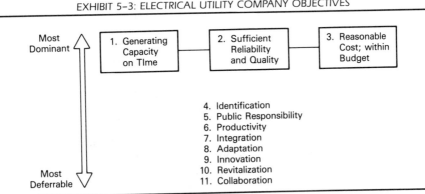

will have sufficient energy when needed. And the company must do this within the financial resources available. These are the dominant objectives.

Note, however, how high in importance the executives ranked identification. They put it immediately after their top three objectives. One might think that a stable business such as a power company would have long since settled its identification issue. Yet, the activities of this firm showed several glaring contradictions. On the first floor of their building was a retail store operated by the marketing department that sold electricity-consuming appliances such as ranges, refrigerators, air conditioners, and heating units. On the fifteenth floor, however, top management was worrying about how it could possibly meet the region's energy needs next summer if the temperature reached 95 degrees—or even next winter if everybody turned everything on at 6:00 PM when they got home from work. Marketing was trying to increase energy consumption while top executives were dealing with a growing need for conservation.

Public responsibility, ranked fifth, was of increasing concern because of criticism from an ever-expanding array of interest groups. Top management was trying to get engineers to incorporate into their designs increasing public demands such as prevention of river thermal pollution and more attractive transmission towers. The firm's management was genuinely surprised to pick up the local newspaper one morning and see a cover-page picture of the firm's country club along with an article sharply critical of the "sybaritic luxuries" that rate payers were funding. The company had no public relations argument to make because for them the country club, along with other attractive fringe benefits, had always been a way of integrating employees into an organization that paid relatively lower wages. Besides, the country club was totally democratic, open to everyone from the lowest janitor to the chairman.

Objectives like adaptation and revitalization were deemed deferrable. The executive team concensus was that these objectives could safely be postponed without immediate adverse impact on performance. Only a voice or two in the group asked whether the company had already delayed too long on these matters, whether in the past too little time had been allocated to these nonspecific objectives so that troubles loomed. Consider one incident. The company lagged in using computers in engineering design. A large mainframe handled payroll, billing, and cost accounting, but the design professionals still used desk calculators and manual drafting. No computer-aided design capability existed. In contrast, designers in advanced electronics firms had computer work stations at their desks. They could call out already designed components from a stored memory, move them around the display screen into a desired configuration, add custom circuitry, push a button, and produce a hard drawing.

To advance the design process, a department manager at the power company decided to hire a design systems expert from a cutting-edge electronics firm. He discovered, however, that to hire an experienced person he would have to pay a salary markedly higher than his own. And even if he were willing to pay a subordinate more than he made, the company's personnel polices would not have allowed it. Therefore, the manager hired a junior systems designer who failed because he didn't have sufficient experience, his salary was still higher than most senior engineers, and at the time he had long hair down to his shoulders when most of the middle-aged engineers had crew cuts.

That was a revitalization issue. The firm's policy arteries were so inflexible that they couldn't adapt to labor market realities. Its internal world was out of touch with its environment. The engineering managers' low ranking of revitalization on the most-dominant/most-deferrable continuum is both cause and effect of not carving time out of the present to deal with such long-range matters.

Metropolis Electric's troubles in recent years were almost predictable from the ignoring of more deferrable objectives. Accidents, operators sleeping on the job, alcohol and drug involvement, and assorted mishaps led in 1988 to the firm's being labeled by the Nuclear Regulatory Commission as a "disgrace to the industry" with subsequent dismissals of the chairman, president, and vice president of operations.

Incorporating the Long Run into Daily Schedules.

Effective time managers are adept at near-simultaneity, that is, pushing ahead on short-run and long-run issues on a daily and weekly basis. They are not perfect, of course, and sometimes daily routine and weekly emergencies totally dominate. But generally, the key is maintaining progress on longer-range, more deferrable matters while still handling the short run.

Exhibit 5–4 suggests a daily time management form designed to remind you of the multiple fronts on which you as a manager should be progressing simultaneously. Section 1 in the upper right is for entering scheduled meetings, whether long-term standing meetings or those of more exceptional variety. Standing meetings are commitments in advance to protect time for meeting with a specific individual or group, perhaps even a year in advance. I strongly advocate standing meetings because they have several advantages:

1. Standing meetings symbolically communicate the importance you place on meeting with the people involved. For example, I would not accept my university president's invitation for me to become vice president of development and university relations until he committed to a two-hour meeting with me every other week for a full year

in advance. I needed this as verification of the priority he would place on public relations and fundraising.

2. Standing meetings also can reduce interruptions by encouraging you and others to save your questions and comments, perhaps by simply depositing reminder notes into a folder marked with the other person's name. When the time for the standing meeting arrives, you virtually have an agenda in the notes collected in that person's folder. This does not mean, of course, that one can't call the other when necessary, but it can reduce interruptions.

3. Finally, standing meetings serve as self-discipline to communicate with certain people that you might rather avoid because you don't like them or you find the topics unpleasant. Standing meetings can

EXHIBIT 5-4: DAILY TIME SCHEDULE

Activities	Communications	
2. Most Dominant (must be done today)	1. Scheduled Meetings	
	Time	Name(s)
	8:00	
	8:30	
	9:00	
	9:30	
	10:00	
	10:30	
	11:00	
	11:30	
	12:00	
	12:30	
	1:00	
	1:30	
	2:00	
	2:30	
	3:00	
	3:30	
	4:00	
	4:30	
	5:00	
3. More deferrable (discretionary)	4. Other people to see/telephone	
6. Personal	5. People to write to	

be a pain because they clog your calendar and reduce personal flexibility. Nonetheless, in my view their advantages outweigh their disadvantages.

This upper-right section can also be used to block out those time periods when you want insulation and isolation for chunks of time to focus on more ambiguous and deferrable tasks.

The upper-left section 2, "Most Dominant Activities," is where you can write the regular daily to-do list for all those things that must be done today.

Section 3 for more deferrable activities is smaller, of course, because the most dominant by definition will usually consume most of the day. Nonetheless, this section is very important for it represents what you can do today to push ahead on long-range, more deferrable (but very important) objectives like innovation, revitalization, and collaboration. For example, in my position as university vice president, two continuing, long-range objectives were particularly important:

- Focus on the central and shared rather than the separate. Some large, complex, multischooled universities enjoy affluence in the professional and health school parts, but are poor in the core arts and sciences programs as well as in shared academic resources such as libraries. Corporate support is increasingly being restricted to specific programs deemed most important to the donor's interests. And alumni may identify more with the part of the university that they attended or with the program closest to their vocation. As a result, support for the core resources that bind such a university together can lag.

  To counter this trend, I felt it necessary repeatedly (ad nauseum to many I'm sure) to emphasize that the whole is more important than any single part; and that undergraduate alumni are first graduates of the university and not primarily of the particular school. We can't assume that the alumni will only be interested in their undergraduate school. We should communicate the mission of the whole institution to all potentially interested parties prior to their identifying a particular part as a special interest. And even if potential donors narrow their perspective, they should be gently and persistently reminded of the whole through words and images that emphasize the connectedness of the institution.

  In terms of the activity analysis in the preceding chapter, this is a "time not a factor" activity of which I should always be aware in order to repeat the message and take advantage of unplanned opportunities to present core possibilities. And this means that some activities that promote this objective must appear on my daily to-do list under the "more deferrable" heading.

- Generate development investment funds. My university's fundraising and public relations opportunities sharply exceeded my department's budgetary resources. Using our resources to maximum efficiency and strengthening our case for increased allocation from the president was critical. Nonetheless, I came to feel that running our operation solely on funds appropriated by the president would never supply enough resources. Perceived competition for limited dollars among all administrative departments, academic distrust of more funds for central administration, and a policy forbidding soliciting gifts directly for development use would always put us in an excessively restricted posture.

A continuing objective, then, became broadening the source of development's resources. What are the theoretical alternatives? How did other schools do it? What are the political advantages and disadvantages of different approaches? So here we have another "time not a factor" objective although deadlines can be set for specific steps to push along the objective (for example, canvas fellow vice presidents at other schools, call the Council for Advancement and Support of Education in Washington, DC to see if they have any information, and draft a think-piece for the president to consider).

The lower right-hand side of Exhibit 5–4, boxes 4 and 5, are to remind you of the need to invest time in building and maintaining long-term relationships. These are not the daily telephone calls or letters that would be on today's to-do list. Rather, these are investment communications. Effective time managers don't allow a week's routine or day's emergencies to totally determine with whom they communicate. Others may resent us for always expecting them to respond when we have invested little in building a relationship or in offering them opportunities to draw on our advice or service. Perhaps even more important, we are not likely to discover those people who share our values or vision of the institution—in short, those people who might be allies in an unknown future debate.

When Lyndon Johnson was a young Senator, he would leave his office several times a day to go to the lavatory.[21] Rather than using his own private facility adjacent to his office, he would walk around the senate office building. These rambles were not random. They precipitated meeting people "accidentally on purpose." Thus, he tried to frequently chat with senior members of the senate establishment like Richard Russell of Georgia or Robert Kerr of Oklahoma from whom he could gain informal advice on difficult situations—as well as paying the elder senator a compliment while drawing attention to himself. Upon returning to his desk, he would cross off their names on his daily to-do list.

A cynic might refer to this as "office politiking," "apple polishing," "brown nosing," but a more charitable perspective is to see it as investing short-run time in building long-term relationships (which in Johnson's case saw him elected the youngest senate majority leader in history). A report on the early career experiences of young MBA graduates suggests that this is one of the sharpest differences between those who are more successful and those who are not.[22] The less successful passively allow their current tasks to determine what they learn and with whom they communicate. In contrast, the more effective actively explore the organization by developing and maintaining relationships with a wider variety of people. And sometimes this means simply calling people when you are passing through town or stopping enroute to another city in order to lunch with an old college friend.[23] Basically it entails going out of your way to spend precious short-run time in the interest of the long run.

To gain greater control over such interpersonal relations, one can make a list of people with whom you should communicate.[24] As in the previous chapter's activity analysis, these names can then be spread across four columns: (1) people I should talk to every day, (2) people to talk to frequently, (3) people to talk to regularly, and (4) people to talk to infrequently. The precise meanings of "frequently," "regularly," and "infrequently" are up to you to specify.

Exhibit 5–5 illustrates my own application of this analysis (substituting position titles for names). For me, frequently means weekly, regularly means monthly and infrequently a vaguer something in this semester or academic year. In the positions listed, I've distinguished between subordinates, other university staff, and outsiders. Note how important I felt it was to maintain relationships with certain administrators that in the normal course of events I would see only infrequently. For example, I tried to chat with the president's executive director of the budget at least once a week. In terms of task, we were intensely involved with each other for only about a month during the annual budget process. But that process was likely to be more effective if we shared our concerns about the university away from the pressures of pie dividing. Similarly, I tried to "bump into" the deans of the most critical schools in order to provide opportunity to defuse issues that could fester if they had to await scheduling a formal meeting.

Many of the positions listed are of course people within my own department whom I would undoubtedly see whether or not I made such a specific analysis. Nonetheless, thinking about it did encourage me to set up the standing meetings discussed earlier and to ensure that I initiated some long-range investment communications every day.

Managing Longer-Term Time

The sixth and smallest section on the Daily Time Plan form in Exhibit 5–4 is for "personal" activities which will probably receive too little attention anyway, but get none unless you give them dignity equal to your job's demands.[25] When I accepted my position as university vice president, I immediately acquired a gym locker which I promised myself I would use three times a week in order to maintain my stamina and recharge my competitive juices. Unfortunately, in almost five years, I never used it once! May you be more successful.

EXHIBIT 5–5: EXAMPLE OF COMMUNICATIONS ANALYSIS

People to talk to every day
* Executive Secretary
* Assistant to the Vice President
* Director of Development
* Director of Development Systems
* Budget Administrator for Development and University Relations

People to talk to at least weekly
* President
* President's Executive Assistant
* President's Secretary
* Provost
* Executive Director of University Budget
* Director of University Relations
* Director of Alumni Relations
* Director of News Bureau
* Director of Major Gifts
* Associate Director of Major Gifts
* Director of Annual Giving
* University Director of Federal Relations
* Alumni and potential donors as recommended

People to talk to at least monthly
* Senior Vice President for Business Affairs
* Vice President for Human Resources
* University Director of Wage and Salary Administration
* Vice President for Operational Services
* Vice President for Finance
* Vice President for Medical Affairs
* University Treasurer
* Director of Publications
* Director of University Planning
* Dean of Admissions
* Deans of major schools
* Director of Recreation and Intercollegiate
* Major Schools Directors of Development
* Director of Planned Giving

EXHIBIT 5–5: CONTINUED

* Vice Provost for Research
* Vice Provost for University Life
* University Counsel
* Vice Provost for Computing Services
* Trustee Chair of Development Committee
* Trustee Chair of External Affairs Committee
* Chairperson of the Board of Trustees
* Chairpersons of the Faculty Senate
* Editor of the *Penn Paper*
* Editor of *The Faculty Almanac*
* Editor of *The Pennsylvania Gazette*

People to talk to during the semester or year (when necessary)
* List of 50 important past and potential individual donors
* Chairpersons (and as many members as feasible) of regional development committees
* All Trustees
* Deans of less major schools
* All professional staff in development and university relations
* Members of athletic advisory council
* Development Vice President's of the Ivy-MIT-Stanford Group
* Applicants for major positions in department
* Attendees at *Inside Pennsylvania* programs and monthly presidential dinners
* Chairperson of Undergraduate Student Government

Using such a daily form seems like a lot of work and time, but it is really not much more than most everyone's daily to-do lists and calendars consume. It just gets everything in one place. And this can be invaluable for providing data to periodically review in order to question what you've done as a well of guiding decisions on what you *shouldn't* do in the future. The chief executive of Pacific Telesis has developed the custom of reviewing on Sunday evenings everything he did during the previous week. Before laying aside the past week's agenda and looking over the coming week's, he asks himself: "Why did I do all these things?" The resulting answers often lead to changes in how he handles future time. As he says, "There is no point in trying to manage your time unless you're willing to change the way you spend it."[26]

THE NECESSITY FOR RESPONSIVENESS

Consider the mental patient who suffers from what psychiatrists call "the God complex."[27] *His* time is more valuable than others'; *his* time is correct; *he* alone is justified in not being punctual; and *his* prediction of future events alone will be fulfilled (not unlike some bosses whom I've had!). Such distortion can afflict most ambitious, achievement-oriented people like you and me. In striving to improve our time management, we must avoid becoming too self-centered in assuming that *our* time allocation is *the* critical issue.

A *Business Management* survey of 179 executives states, "The telephone does even more to prevent these top level executives from making the most effective use of their time . . . 87 percent spend an hour or more (a day) on the telephone and 40 percent a minimum of two hours."[28] An *Associated Press* survey of 200 corporate chief executive officers reports that 25 percent of the nearly 14 hours per week they spend on the telephone is "wasted."[29] But what nonsense to assume this telephone time is wasteful. Are no important deals arranged on the phone? Is no critical information tracked down? Is no gratitude conveyed to a distant associate? Of course, all these things are done and this is not wasted time just because it is on the telephone.

A *Wall Street Journal* article describes how business executives complain how much time they "waste" listening: "I get up in the morning and the phone rings and things go downhill from there," gripes one company president. Another says that 70 percent of his time is just spent listening and half of that time is "wasted on things you'd avoid if you had any way of appraising them in advance."[30] But to imply that time is wasted *just because it is consumed in an unplanned way* is a distortion of values, a misguided overconcern for time at the expense of the job. Behind this distortion lies the unspoken assumption that unless managers totally control their own behavior and do only what they intend to do, they are wasting time. This is absurd.

We *cannot* manage all of our time, nor should we try. We must be available and responsive to others, especially to subordinates seeking our opinions, judgments, and decisions. Therefore, at times we must feel as puppets dancing to their tugs on our strings of time. Shortly after the death of Winston Churchill, his long-time subordinate Anthony Eden was asked what he considered to be Churchill's outstanding leadership characteristic. Eden responded that the indefatigable former prime minister always seemed to be available, ready to listen without premature criticism of new ideas. He would focus on his visitor as if the lucky person was the most important person in Churchill's day (an observation also made by admirers of John F. Kennedy).[31] Thus, he wouldn't fidget in his chair, glance at his watch, shuffle papers on his desk—all the nonverbal ways that impatient people communicate their time harriedness.

Such openness and availability also characterize effective business executives. When I compared the detailed time allocation for a sample of fourteen senior managers, the results were striking. Those rated by their superiors, peers, and an external management consultant as "more effective" spend significantly more time advising and discussing issues with people *who called or came to them.*[32] In contrast, as Exhibit 5–6 summarizes, lower-rated executives spend more time on self-initiated talking. In short, more effective managers initiate less and respond more.

Even more striking is effective managers' emphasis on two-person conversations. Exhibit 5–6 also summarizes time distribution among (1) being alone, (2) with one other person, and (3) in a group. More effective managers emphasize one-on-one meetings. They seem to extend invitations to individuals to come to them personally rather than waiting for the next scheduled group meeting. This appears to be an untidy way to operate because two-person meetings consume a lot of time. It might be more time efficient to make group announcements. Yet executives derive benefits from a two-person style. It promotes more rapid feedback, facilitates frank expression of opinions, and builds subordinate loyalty. Mentally separating response and discretionary times can help you to maintain responsiveness to others. You could decide that certain periods are to be primarily response time. You might work on discretionary matters if no one contacts you, but you should not assume great progress. If you do, it would be an unexpected bonus. This sensitivity to responsiveness will help to overcome your natural irritation from having outside events interfere with self-determined plans. Such self-discipline is essential to create a climate of openness and responsiveness.

EXHIBIT 5–6: COMPARING MORE EFFECTIVE AND LESS EFFECTIVE EXECUTIVES

Activity	Less Effective	More Effective
	(mean hours per week)	
Responding: talking to others who started the conversation	9.5	16.0
Initiating: talking to others when the executive initiated the conversation	11.3	6.5
Monitoring: paperwork auditing and checking performance	15.8	11.7
Alone	12.7	9.9
Two-person Conversation (face-to-face and telephone)	12.6	21.2
Group Meetings (three or more people)	19.9	12.1

*All differences between more and less effective executives are significant at the 5 percent level.

You should strive to project an unrushed image, to avoid appearing preoccupied with your own concerns, and especially to give subordinates your undivided attention.[33] A manager needs to show that he values the other person's time. A subordinate's respect for himself and for his superior can be undermined without it. Such behavior takes more of your time in the short run but eventually will pay off.

Availability and openness to subordinates and associates are imperative for managers if they are not to lose touch with their organizations. You cannot possibly initiate enough interrogations to maintain control of a complex operation. Effective managers seem to maintain control by creating a climate where people voluntarily keep them informed by seeking information and guidance.

HOW PEOPLE RATE THE CANDIDATES AT PYRAMID COMPANY

Four candidates are vying for the presidency of Pyramid Electric Company. Several hundred students and executives have voted on their first choice for president and their cumulative results are as follows:

David Williamson, V.P. Research and Engineering 52%
Robert Findley, V.P. Manufacturing.. 27%
John Andrews, V.P. Sales and Marketing 16%
Samuel Scott, V.P. Finance... 5%

Agreement is strongest that Scott would be an undesirable appointment. In spite of his professed decisiveness and time-efficient style, the vast majority of respondents see him as very risky because his approach is so authoritarian that the firm's performance would depend so much on the quality of his decisions. If he makes the right decisions, such a centralized approach can be very effective and time saving (as it frequently is in the developmental years of an owner-manager-inventor-entrepreneurial startup). But in this case, if Scott became president he would be moving beyond his established finance expertise to oversee areas in which he has very limited experience. Most observers worry that he would not recognize the difference, that he would continue to make decisions without involving his senior subordinates (indeed, his domineering style seems to repel people as they gain experience, so he has no senior candidates to replace him in finance).

John Andrews, the vice president of sales and marketing, garners more support, but the majority feel that as president he would also entail substantial risk. To most he appears unstructured, even undisciplined. His unwillingness to commit to standing meetings and time schedules suggests potential sloppiness in his management of the enterprise—particularly timely addressing of tough decisions that might make him unpopular. Many fear that he would simply avoid sensitive issues to the firm's detriment.

Robert Findley is more highly regarded (and is most frequently cited for an executive vice presidency under either Andrews or Williamson when this possibility is raised). The risk to Pyramid is seen as substantially less than for Scott or Andrews because Findley is such an orderly person and systematic time manager. He clearly emphasizes rational analysis and judgment whereas most see Scott and Andrews operating more on emotion or intuition.

Findley, however, is not seen as the most desirable candidate. Reservations about him focus on what most see as a somewhat compulsive approach to time management. Respondants worry that he is too inflexible and that his time management tactics might hinder his ability to deal with the wider variety of less structured problems that he would confront as Pyramid's president. Particularly disturbing to many is the clock analogy he makes when he suggests that an organization with well-defined job descriptions, policies, and procedures would almost run itself. Would such a structuring person squeeze out the all spontaneity and ambiguity tolerance so important in dealing with a turbulent competitive environment?

The majority like David Williamson the most—in spite of his professed concern about how he manages his time. They feel he would strike the best balance between personal initiative and making himself available to people with ideas. With Williamson, creative proposals would be more likely to get a fair hearing than most think would be so with the other candidates.

To be sure, some critics worry that the talk would go on too long and that Williamson would be indecisive in blocking less desirable, resource-wasting ideas. But the majority of managers and students project themselves into the case sort of like an ink-blot exercise. They see themselves as working at Pyramid and they ask: "For whom would I prefer to work?" The majority answer Williamson because they can identify with his time management problems and they feel that their ideas would be taken seriously.

ADVICE ON LONGER-TERM TIME MANAGEMENT

- Fight the tendency for short-run routine and urgency to determine totally how your time is expended. In the long run, this can lead to personal obsolescence and even burnout.
- Ensure that time is invested in developing and maintaining personal relationships. Analyze the people with whom you relate and determine who you need to talk with daily, weekly, monthly, or less frequently. Allocate daily time to communicating with them.
- Define your organizational continuing objectives and analyze them

for dominance and deferrability. Ensure that some time is allocated in your daily plans to less structured and less explicitly cued objectives like identification, integration, adaptation, revitalization, and collaboration.

- Periodically monitor your daily time plans for preceding weeks and months to see if more deferrable activities are being performed and whether you are maintaining communications with people other than those required for daily tasks.

Strive to create an unharried climate of availability to subordinates and colleagues. Practice being mentally prepared during your response time to shift from desk work to openness to callers and visitors. Control fidgety body language which might repel visitors.

- Minimize group meeting announcements and emphasize one-on-one conversations, particularly with those subordinates whose loyalty and motivation are critical to your organization's success.

6

Clarifying Delegation

"*Now, now, Mr. Trombley, you <u>know</u> you don't have access!*"

No prediction is more certain than that you will confront ambiguous delegation in your first few years on the job.[1] Because of your credentials and potential, a superior will offer you an opportunity to attack a task that could provide you with visibility and honor if successfully handled. With encouraging words of "you run with the ball and score the touchdown," the boss will send you off charging with energy and excitement. Unfortunately, all too often, he or she will have neglected to define adequately your actual power or exactly how decisions are to be implemented. And you in the rush of ambition may well not be enough aware to ask. The result can be disaster. Indeed, having a boss who assigns a task, but who later undercuts your authority may be *the* most stressful situation you will ever encounter.[2]

After describing a case where a firm's young star drifted toward failure because of unwillingness to confront her boss for clarification of her authority, we examine delegation theory and the questions you might pose to define your responsibility more precisely.

JANE WILSON AT CUTTING EDGE

Cutting Edge Associates, Inc. is an aggressive engineering design and consulting firm. Geographically dispersed, it contains five divisional branches that operate quite autonomously in bidding for and conducting projects. Business has expanded tenfold in the past twenty years.

At a meeting of the board of directors two years ago, attention was directed to the noticeable rate of increase in divisional operating and overhead costs. E. P. Jefferson, the president, indicated that a study would be initiated to investigate these costs.

The Systems Committee. Shortly thereafter, Jefferson called in Jane Wilson, one of his two assistants, described the general problem of reducing costs and told her that the firm had reached the size where it needed a person to devote full time to operating methods and facilities. He said that he had talked this matter over with Frank Surface, the vice president of personnel, and that both of them had agreed "that you would be a fine person for this position. Surface and I feel that you might have an advisory committee made up of one representative from each branch, and that such a group could decide on ways to utilize our buildings, equipment, and people more effectively. Each of the division managers will appoint a person to meet with you regularly."

EXHIBIT 6-1: SIMPLIFIED ORGANIZATION OF CUTTING EDGE ASSOCIATION, INC.

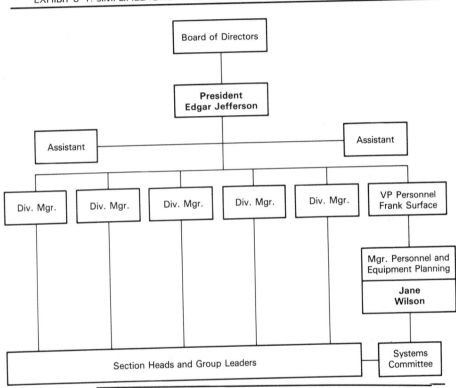

Within three months of the original reference to the subject at the directors' meeting, Wilson received the title of manager of personnel and equipment planning. All division managers had appointed, at Jefferson's request, a person to what became known as the "systems committee." At the present time, two years later, the committee appears to have taken its work seriously, as evidenced by: (1) a record of regular meetings held over an eighteen-month period, (2) transcripts of those meetings and exhibits which show that all six members entered the discussions, (3) seventeen recommendations in writing, supported by a total of 1,800 pages of research data and reasoning, (4) the fact that meetings often lasted four to five hours extending after working hours, and (5) the statements of all committee members that they enjoyed the project, felt that they were accomplishing something for the firm and had personally enjoyed being on the committee. All members also expressed their high regard for Jane Wilson and felt that she has done a good job.

The seventeen recommendations cover such matters as salary scales, a policy on days off for personal business, a policy on central purchasing of janitorial supplies, and a recommendation that certain models of personal computers, dictating machines, and copy machines be adopted uniformly in all branches.

About a year ago, Wilson had made an inspection trip to the branches and had come to the conclusion that there was much wasted space in the offices because administrative, professional, and clerical personnel had purchased equipment such as desks, computer stands, and tables that pleased them personally but that were too large and expensive for what the firm needed to keep up its public appearance. In addition, group leaders in some branches had succeeded in having the manager approve walls for private offices. A consultant had advised Wilson that the firm might save $40,000 a year if only division managers were to have private offices and if furniture were more modest and standardized. The committee, however, has not yet formulated recommendations on this matter.

Relations with Division Managers.
Managers have been kept informed of the committee's general work over the eighteen-month period. Most managers selected a section head or group leader to represent them. It appears that these members made a real effort to keep their managers informed. Sid August from the midwestern branch reports that he has spent at least an hour a month with his boss telling him what the committee is doing and asking for his ideas. Audrey Gambrino of the southeastern branch says that she has been able to confer briefly with her boss about once a month on the subjects the committee is working on. Other members report that they too have been able to see their superiors. Nonetheless, in all cases except for the midwest, they say that their managers quite naturally do not have the time to go into the details of committee recommendations and that the managers have not been enthusiastic about implementing any of the proposals.

The committee has talked about the best way to get its recommendations adopted. Sid August claims that his manager is ready to implement many of them and that it is up to each member to convince his or her own manager. All others argue that the president should issue the recommendations as directives over his signature. The reason given by

Gambrino is typical: "We're convinced that the recommendations are best for the firm but the managers just won't buy them. The only way to get the managers to carry them out is to have Mr. Jefferson lay them out as official, and let it be known that they are going to be put into effect. Of course, they should be acknowledged as being drawn up by the department of personnel and equipment with some advice from our committee."

Jane Wilson reported in her meeting last month with the president that it looked as if it is going to be "rather touchy" to get the division managers to accept the recommendations. Jefferson thereupon stated that his own knowledge of the committee proposals was rather sketchy (even though he had discussed them in part with Wilson periodically over the past year). Jefferson therefore decided to call a meeting of all division managers and committee members so that he and everyone concerned could be acquainted in detail with them.

The Meeting of the Committee and Division Managers. The meeting started at 2:00 PM and was scheduled to last until 5:00, but actually ran over until 6:00. The committee, division managers, Jefferson, and Wilson were present. Jefferson opened the meeting by stating that its purpose was to study the committee recommendations and, it was hoped, to arrive at a decision on whether they should be implemented.

The committee members had talked confidentially among themselves before the meeting and agreed that Jane Wilson must be the one to present the findings and, by and large, the one to defend them. This plan was carried out. After a reading of the seventeen recommendations, the entire meeting was taken up by a discussion of the first two which covered a standard salary scale for clerical and nonprofessional staff and a specification of the rules on employee personal days off (anything in excess of two days must be taken on vacation or without pay).

In the discussion, the division managers found some points on which they disagreed among themselves, and some on which they all agreed but disagreed with the committee—especially on how certain individual employees might be hurt by standard policies. After the meeting, the president remarked to Jane that "the combined thinking of the managers, with all their experience, made quite an impression on me. I have confidence in you, but I can't help but wonder if your committee really worked out the best recommendations for all on these issues. If you had, why couldn't you convince the managers instead of raising all this criticism?"

$\mathcal{D} \cdot \mathcal{D} \cdot \mathcal{D} \cdot \mathcal{D}$

WHAT WENT WRONG?

At Cutting Edge, Jefferson (and Wilson) seemed to assume that if the committee came up with "the best" recommendations that somehow they would be automatically implemented by division managers because of their brilliance or because the managers would have bought into the recommendations since they supposedly came from their "representatives" on the committee. But these were naive assumptions.

The so-called representatives on the committee were cast in a very difficult role—that of initiating changes that would reduce the autonomy of their direct superiors! Since the firm had a history of encouraging entrepreneurial independence in the field, strengthening central rules and standardization flew in the face of a decentralized tradition that the division managers felt was still working fine. Given the awkwardness of their position, it is not surprising that the committee members quickly decided not to be "representatives" but simply a task force concerned with overall problems. Thus, most of them avoided communicating anything too threatening to their branch managers while warning Wilson that few proposals would be implemented unless Jefferson issued directives.

Wilson never pressed this warning with Jefferson. Although Jane did see the president fairly frequently, Jefferson never really seemed to *listen*. Even after eighteen months, he was not familiar with the recommendations, probably because he didn't deem them pertinent to his own behavior. Given that Jefferson expected the changes to be made automatically without his involvement, he didn't connect Wilson's words with any action that he personally as president would have to initiate.

And Wilson, in her inexperience, let the president get away with his noninvolvement. Jane let the months drag by and the analysis pile up while she drifted like some classic Greek tragedy toward the disaster that is the situation at the end of the case.

To consider what Wilson might have done, let's first look at theory about delegation.

DELEGATION CLARITY

The purpose of delegation is to transfer legitimate power from a superior to a subordinate so the latter can accomplish a necessary task.[3] Unfortunately, so much delegation shares a general theme: begrudging assignment of tasks that managers would prefer to do themselves if only they had the time. And all time is not saved when a task is delegated. The superior must still supervise, monitor, and correct especially those inexperienced subordinates still learning their newly assigned tasks.

Delegation Clarity

Some managers think they can do the job faster themselves. In the short run, they are probably correct. In the long run, however, delegation will enable the subordinates to develop competence and free superiors to devote time to other perhaps more important and challenging matters. That is, they will be freer if they have delegated clearly enough so that subordinates know what to do and what is expected. Unfortunately, a too frequently recurring problem is that harried superiors do not take the time to define what they expect, and inexperienced or fearful subordinates do not ask the tough questions to clarify what is expected.[4]

Delegation Forms. Delegation is not an *either/or* matter; it is not either I do it, or you do it. Delegation lies on a continuum.[5] Both managers and subordinates should realize that multiple forms of delegation exist. And each group should know what form is intended between them, particularly what degree of initiative is expected of the subordinate. Consider the eight sets of instructions in Exhibit 6–2.

When delegating, a manager should be clear about which of these patterns is intended. Clarity of initial instruction will save both time and embarrassment. After the pattern is defined, the superior should adhere to it consistently to the completion of the delegated task. Without such clarification and consistency, many subordinates will tend to patterns 1, 2, and 3 because they fear taking actions for which they will be criticized. More ambitious subordinates, however, may assume form 8 because it maximizes their freedom.

Note that no form of delegation is inherently better than any other. Each has its advantages and disadvantages. Consider examples of United States Presidents. Dwight Eisenhower was said to prefer delegation types 3 and 4. He wanted his White House assistants to provide a detailed proposal which he could approve and implement with his signature.[6] This approach freed him from devoting time to detailed problem analysis and

---

EXHIBIT 6–2: DELEGATION FORMS: SUPERIOR'S INSTRUCTIONS

1. Look into this problem. Give me all the facts. I will decide what to do.
2. Let me know the alternatives available with the advantages and disadvantages of each. I will decide which to select.
3. Recommend a course of action for my approval and signature.
4. Let me know what you intend to do. Delay action until I approve it orally or with my initials.
5. Let me know what you intend to do. Do it unless I say no.
6. Take action. Let me know what you did and how it turns out.
7. Take action. Communicate with me only if you are unsuccessful.
8. Take action. No further communication with me on this matter is required.

alternative generation. But it was precisely this aloofness that the incoming Kennedy administration in 1961 sharply criticized. John Kennedy favored delegation forms 1 and 2; he wanted to be involved in early discussion where his own intelligence and creativity could be applied (particularly after the 1961 Bay of Pigs fiasco where he felt he delegated excessive power to his military advisers).[7] This may have worked for Kennedy (who was a speed reader) but it certainly consumes time and attention, which became especially evident in the stress that fell on President Jimmy Carter because of his apparent submergence in excessive detail.

Presidents Harry Truman and Ronald Reagan seemed to lean toward forms 7 and 8 which grant the greatest autonomy to subordinates and require minimal time demands on the delegator. Indeed, Harry Truman was widely beloved by his subordinates for the enormous faith he expressed in them. One cabinet member reported that he once tried to report to Truman on his activities, but the president cut him short, "John, you're doing a good job. You'll hear from me when you're not. Now, let's talk about the Civil War."[8] In similar fashion, President Reagan was praised by subordinates and others for his broad delegation. Giving autonomy and expressing faith in subordinates can be a powerful motivator.

The problem with delegating in forms 7 and 8 is that the superior runs the risk of being out of touch with what is going on. *Fortune* magazine did a cover article in the summer of 1986 praising President Reagan's ability to find good people, then to delegate tasks and leave them alone—just months before the Iran-Contra affair began to come to light.[9] And more profoundly, the organization's interest can be severely endangered by a subordinate out of control. Truman experienced this with the revered General Douglas MacArthur who, as supreme Allied commander in the Far East during the Korean War, threatened to invade China (and perhaps use nuclear tactical weapons) all without the authority of the president. Because he had such weak in-process control, Truman's options were reduced to only the exercise of his ultimate power to fire MacArthur from his job—at immense political cost to the president. Some would argue that Reagan confronted the same problem with his national security adviser John Poindexter and his assistant Oliver North.

The current perception is that George Bush is a much more involved executive than Reagan was, frequently asking questions and wanting clarification of details (at the risk, so his critics say, of not devoting sufficient attention to defining an overall vision).[10]

Where would President Richard Nixon fit in this analysis of delegation styles? Perhaps an additional form 9: "Do it, but under no circumstances should you tell me *how* you did it!"

Delegation Sufficiency. One of the most hallowed of traditional organization principles is that authority should equal responsibility. Perhaps no other principle makes as much intuitive sense to the typical subordinate who feels that one should have authority sufficient to perform the task for which he or she is held accountable. If the boss has assigned responsibility for keeping the office clean, the worker must have authority to enter and to obtain the necessary supplies. Meeting this responsibility is impossible with insufficient authority. Likewise, a manager charged with increasing widget sales in Texas will be frustrated if not given authority to set competitive prices, to hire and discipline salespeople, pay market wages and bonuses, and perhaps modify the product to local customer demands.

Managers could find themselves without sufficient authority because it was never delegated to them or if offered, they failed to accept it.

Lack of Delegation. Many owners, executives, and managers complain of how overworked they are but will not delegate enough to lighten their burdens. Fear deters them. The superior may be afraid that a subordinate will not be able to perform the activity as well as he or she can and therefore fears that his or her boss will be displeased with the results. Worse, an insecure manager may be afraid that his or her subordinates will do a better job, thus threatening the manager's future. More subtly, a manager may be anxious about not being continually on top of everything. Dependency downward on subordinates can be stressful for those adverse to risk. This anxiety can be especially great when the superior can't define precisely what is to be done and how results are to be measured.

One can sympathize with such concern, but a manager who cannot stand the anxiety of delegation is fleeing from the managerial role and ought to look for other work.

Failure to Accept Delegation. Inadequate delegation is not always the superior's fault. Some subordinates resist delegation because they want to avoid anxiety, dislike their superiors, or simply do not want to be bothered.[11] Others may resist because they lack the self-confidence to stand criticism. Finally, subordinates may not be offered sufficient incentive to accept more than the most narrow job task. ("It's not *my* job.") If forced to do more, they find it easier to ask the boss repeatedly for detailed instructions. The superior may well conclude that delegating the task is not worth the effort.

Pseudodelegation. Sometimes superiors intend to delegate and even think that they have done so, but the monkey of responsibility keeps jumping off their subordinate's shoulders and back onto their own.[12]

Clarifying Delegation

Pseudodelegation occurs when a subordinate manipulates a superior into relieving him or her of responsibility for taking the next step in a delegated task. In a kind of rubber-band effect, the intended delegation snaps back to the superior.

1. *"We've got a problem."* Manager A greets one of his subordinates, B, while late for a meeting. B says "Good morning. By the way, we've got a problem. The . . ." As B talks, superior A recognizes that he is not knowledgeable enough to make an immediate decision. To save time at that moment so he can get on to his meeting, A responds, "Glad you brought this up. I'm in a rush right now. Let me think about it and I'll let you know."

   In such an exchange, the subordinate has cleverly relieved herself of responsibility for the next step. She only has to wait until her superior gets back to her. Miraculously, the subordinate has transformed herself into the superior because manager A now has an obligation to do something and to report back to B. Subordinate B may even "supervise" her superior by later asking how things are coming along on the problem.

2. *"Send me a memo."* Suppose that, at the end of a conference with subordinate C, manager A concludes, "Fine, send me a memo on that." The responsibility temporarily remains with the subordinate, but only until he sends the requested note. Once the memo leaves C's desk, the action obligation jumps to manager A. Subordinate C will do nothing until he receives A's response to the memo (and may well grumble at A's slowness).

   To push the boss along, subordinate C may well write another memo to A indicating that he needs a response soon. Once again, manager A is time pressured and "supervised" by his own subordinate.

3. *"I've drawn up a discussion draft."* Consider the situation in which a new position has been created and subordinate D is appointed. Manager A has told her that they should get together soon to define the new job and that "I'll draw up an initial draft for our consideration." Once again, manager A has put himself into the position of making the next move. Subordinate D may spin her wheels until A produces the draft and calls for a meeting.

In each of these three incidents, the superior mistakenly assumes that the problems are "joint" when in fact they are primarily the subordinate's. Pretty soon he will be working on Saturdays while his subordinates are playing golf.

Keeping Delegated Jobs Delegated. Managers should not allow themselves to be manipulated into relieving their subordinates of responsibility for the next step. The initiative should remain with the subordinate who should then report to the superior. When talking to a subordinate about a problem, the manager's self-reminder should be, "At no time while I am helping you with this will your problem become my problem. When this meeting is over, the problem will leave this office exactly the way it came in—on your back."

With regard to the three incidents described previously where responsibility snapped back to the superior, perhaps manager A could have clearly directed the subordinates to take the next step.

1. When told by subordinate B, "We've got a problem," A could tell B to come to his office later with the possible alternatives and her recommendation. Thus, B must work until the decision is made, not A.
2. On "Send me a memo," if A understood C's problem, he might have made a decision right away. If not, he should have told C to proceed but to keep A informed.
3. On "I'll draw up a discussion draft," he shouldn't. The superior should have the subordinate draw up a proposal for consideration at a time set by the superior.

NONDELEGATABLE RESPONSIBILITY

The principle that a manager can delegate authority but not responsibility has taken on the mantle of moral truth, but it is extremely difficult to follow rigorously. If A assigns certain activities and necessary authority to B, B may in turn delegate the duties and authority to C (assuming he controls sufficient resources). However, if C fails to perform the activities satisfactorily, A still holds B accountable. A would hang B, not C. In short, B can delegate some authority and *create* responsibility for C, but B cannot delegate his responsibility or relieve himself of his accountability to A. Thus, every delegation act involves two sets of correlative and equal responsibilities: (1) the obligations which the delegatee owes to the delegator, and (2) the obligations for which the delegator is accountable to his or her superior.

We can distinguish between real and symbolic responsibility.

Real Responsibility. "Real" responsibility is the moral and practical responsibility for decisions and events. This was the essential guideline that the United States applied in the war crimes trials after World War II.[13] Prosecutors maintained that higher leaders were responsible for the atrocities committed by subordinates even if it could not be proved that they had ordered them. In the celebrated case of the Japanese General Yamashita, it was ruled that he should be executed because of his troops' ill treatment of American prisoners of war in the Philippines.[14] He was held responsible for prisoner welfare and could not relieve himself of the responsibility even though his defense established that he had issued orders for correct treatment. His lawyers argued that it was impossible for Yamashita to know what was going on in the camps. The military court didn't buy the argument.

A literal application of the rule of nondelegatable responsibility is attractive, but it creates problems. A manager who really believes he or she will be punished for every subordinate mistake will delegate little and will limit subordinate autonomy for fear they will fail. A group of state prison wardens were once informed by the governor that they would be held responsible for all transgressions by prison guards (ranging from smuggling in forbidden copies of *Playboy* magazine to assisting inmates to escape). The wardens felt that this was totally unfair because their hierarchies were too long and they didn't control the hiring and firing of guards (which was subject to civil service regulations). One warden lamented that he couldn't even tell the difference between the guards and the prisoners! To be held to a rigorous responsibility principle in their view would require them to hire a secret set of guards to be scattered among the civil service appointees with a personal obligation to report directly to the warden. Such centralization would be costly.

Some years ago several managers in large electrical equipment companies were convicted of violating federal law by meeting with competitors to fix prices and territories.[15] In one company the department marketing manager was convicted because he personally participated in the meetings. His boss the department manager and a division vice president were convicted because they knew of the meetings. The product group executive vice president was also convicted because circumstantial evidence suggested that his behavior reflected knowledge of the illegalities. The government prosecutor then went after the president with the argument that he was ultimately responsible, but the judge ruled against this because the prosecutor had no evidence that the president had known of the actions and it was considered unreasonable to expect the chief executive to know about everything in such a large corporation. In short, if an organization becomes large enough, top executives may be able to delegate responsibility and blame failure on subordinates. Counter to the Yamashita example, the United States tended to follow this more relaxed responsibility guideline in our investigations of alleged atrocities inflicted by American troops in the Vietnam War. Only the troops immediately present, as at Mai Lai, were blamed.

Symbolic Responsibility. Symbolic responsibility usually involves a senior executive assuming responsibility for failure even when most reasonable observers would conclude that he or she shouldn't personally be held guilty. So in Japan a bank president might resign when low-level teller fraud was uncovered, or the president of Fujitsu resigned when it was disclosed that his firm had violated laws by supplying sensitive computer equipment to the Soviet Union. In the United States, such symbolic acceptance of guilt seldom includes resignation, but it might involve a public *mea culpa* as in Lee Iaccoca's extraordinary apology to the American public for Chrysler's disconnecting odometers while its cars were being used as executive vehicles prior to public sale.[16]

Restoring morale is the primary purpose of such symbolic responsibility. When something goes wrong, the senior executive presiding over the mistake will "take responsibility" to lift the blame from his or her subordinates. This encourages a conscious mutual dependence between seniors and juniors. Those below know that those above will protect them, but they have a corresponding obligation not to embarrass their superiors. This was a tactic practiced brilliantly by President John Kennedy in accepting final responsibility for the Bay of Pigs fiasco in the Cuban invasion of 1961.

WHAT JANE WILSON MIGHT HAVE DONE

At the height of the Civil War, President Abraham Lincoln wrote to General U. S. Grant expressing:[17]

> . . . entire satisfaction with what you have done up to this time so far as I understand it. The particulars of your plans I neither know nor seek to know. You are vigilent and self-reliant, and pleased with this I wish not to obtrude any constraints or restraints upon you. . . . If there is anything wanting which is in my power to give, do not fail to let me know it. And now, with a brave army, and a just cause, may God sustain you.

Unfortunately, President Edgar Jefferson at Cutting Edge was no Lincoln so the easiest stone to cast in the case of Jane Wilson is of course at Jefferson. He simply didn't clarify what form of delegation he was using. If he intended form 1, "Gather the facts and I will decide," Wilson probably did an adequate job. But apparently Jefferson expected more, unclear as it is. Why Jefferson was so uninvolved in these events is unknown. Perhaps he was basically pleased with division performance in pursuing new business and didn't deem expense control as important as encouraging entrepreneurial zest. Or perhaps the changes would have been nice but not worth his personal investment of time or expenditure of his political capital. Or most cynically, perhaps the committee was just a bone thrown to the board of directors to placate their concerns.

Our primary interest here, however, is not with Jefferson, but with Jane Wilson's dilemma. Most ambitious young subordinates think that they would want very broad delegation like Lincoln's to Grant. But the risk is that your boss will not be available and supportive when needed. And when Jane needed support, she just couldn't or didn't try to get the president involved. What could she have done to provoke action?

Let's recast the delegation continuum as in Exhibit 6–3 in terms of questions the subordinate might ask a superior.

EXHIBIT 6–3: SUBORDINATE'S POSSIBLE QUESTIONS
TO SUPERIOR TO CLARIFY DELEGATION

---

1. After I look into the problem, should I give you all the facts so that you can decide?
2. Should I let you know the alternatives available with the advantages and disadvantages of each so you can decide which to select?
3. Should I recommend a course of action for you to implement over your name?
4. Should I propose for your approval a course of action to be implemented in my name?
5. Should I take action in my name, informing you in advance and of results?
6. Should I take action in my name, informing you after I've acted?
7. Should I take action in my name informing you only if I am unsuccessful?
8. Should I take action in my name without any communication of intentions or results?

In dealing with her dilemma, Jane Wilson might well have put some of these questions to the president, preferably different questions for different recommendations. Good political advice on her part might have divided the seventeen proposals into implementation modes. For example:

- "Proposals 13 to 18 I will simply implement over my own name. They only deal with minor issues like office supplies. But, if you get complaints from the divisions, I'd appreciate your support."
- "Proposals 8 to 12 are a little tougher and it would help me if you put your approval initials on my notices."
- "The first seven proposals are more fundamental and I think they must go out over your signature. In fact, the first three raise basic strategy issues so there will be strong field resistance. I would sug-

gest that you call all the division managers together and mount a major meeting to dramatize their importance."

Such recommendations would require a wise and politically astute Jane Wilson, but that is precisely what you should strive to be. To speak so candidly to the boss also requires courage. In effect, you would be saying, "Boss, you're wrong; your theory of how the decisions would be made and changes implemented just won't work. It won't happen automatically, you must get invoved. *I can't do it alone.*" Admitting your own weakness is tough, but Wilson exhibited even greater weakness in abdicating to the committee and in not pushing Jefferson (however politely) to action.

Initiation upward can be difficult when the boss seems uninterested or unreceptive. The athletic metaphor of "you score the touchdown" that your superior may profess is often misleading, however. In an effort to appear to be a "modern" manager able to pick good people and then not interfere, your superior may seem to not need to be kept informed. Often, it is just an act, however. While the boss doesn't want you repeatedly to seek permission, he or she does want to know what is going on. The head of a network-owned local television station was recently fired after only a year on the job even though market share, advertising revenue, and profits had all increased. Upon being queried by a reporter, the network chief complained that, "He just didn't tell me what he was doing; I kept waiting for shoes to drop without warning."

Remember that your superior has his or her own anxieties. His or her boss may expect him or her to be always current, but your boss doesn't want to be continually interrogating you. A sensitive subordinate finds subtle ways to keep the superior aware, perhaps by soliciting advice: "J.R., I feel I have a viable solution. Here's what I am going to do. Based on your experience, have I missed something?" Such an approach can be flattering to the superior as well as relieving his or her anxiety by giving an opportunity to head off an expensive error.

Undercommunicating upward is particularly common among ambitious, self-confident young people. Some years ago I told my wife that my superiors never seemed quite as pleased with my performance as objective results indicated they should be. My wife replied that I suffered from "a closed hand syndrome." She described canasta which is a rummy-type game in which you can meld or lay down your sets as you go or hold them until the end when you can declare "canasta!" and catch your opponents with penalty points. In her opinion I tended to do excellent work, but never told anyone about it until I could dazzle my audience with a brilliant surprise. Unfortunately, some of my superiors haven't appreciated the surprises.

Ambitious young women like Jane Wilson can experience a particular double bind. They want to demonstrate that they are self-reliant, that counter to chauvinist expectations, they don't need their "hand held" when engaging tough tasks. Therefore, they are reluctant to solicit advice from superiors for fear it will be perceived as a sign of weakness.[18] Unfortunately, they thereby miss out on some informal guidance while contributing to their superiors' anxieties.

ADVICE FOR HANDLING UNCLEAR DELEGATION

- Temper your excitement about a challenging high-visibility assignment with awareness of the need to clarify what degree of delegation is intended.
- Be willing to provoke delegation clarification through manufacturing incidents that require the superior to monitor, approve, or initiate directives.
- Remember that most senior managers have their own anxieties. They don't like surprises. So keep your superior informed of what you are doing, even if he or she professes not to require such communication.
- It is safer to err on the side of excessive upward communication. Above all, don't flee from potentially difficult conversations with the boss by avoiding him or her.
- Be courageous in confronting your superior with political information that suggests his or her strategy will not work. Offer an objective political analysis of what people and forces are with this strategy or against it. But focus political intelligence on the effect on performance, not its affect on your own standing with the boss.
- Accept the inevitable limitations of the principle that authority can be created, but responsibility cannot be delegated. Adherance to the rule is desirable in theory and worth striving for in most actual situations, but rigid application can be unfair to many individuals and lead to excessive centralization.
- Recognize that stomach butterflies usually will accompany your delegation to subordinates. Of course you could do the job better if you had time, but your job is to train your subordinates to surpass you.
- Don't allow your subordinates to escape responsibility for actions by pushing the next step back on your shoulders. End most conversations with a statement of the next action expected of them.

7

Giving Advice

My first job after engineering school and naval service was as an industrial engineer. My central function was to provide advice to production managers. Initially, my only means of influence was persuasion. I prepared elaborate presentations, even rehearsing with a colleague to anticipate questions. By data, argument, and the use of my golden tongue, I attempted to gain agreement from these much more experienced executives. After a year of this relationship with a certain production department head, one day I was ten minutes into a scheduled hour-long meeting when he explained, "Ross, the Yankees are playing on television and I want to watch it. I'll tell you what: *we'll do whatever you want to do.*"

That manager's *de facto* delegation of authority to the staff adviser (me) is every staff person's dream. Unfortunately, such faith comes only after a proven track record so in this chapter we examine staff-line relations and how advisers can improve their effectiveness. We begin with a young former Peace Corps member who, perhaps, became too dominant.

RICHARD'S ADVICE

Richard Rule was an only son of a minister and school teacher. In later years he used to joke that he would have had to really goof up if he failed given the advantages of that background with its expectations of moral and intellectual success. And Dick certainly did not disappoint his parents. He was outstanding in school and a deeply committed young man concerned about his obligation to those less blessed. In high school, he strove to be a student leader, serving as president of the National Honor Society chapter and captain of the cheerleaders as well as head of the youth group at his church. His striving for leadership and service continued in college where he particularly enjoyed being selected as student representative on the college governance board which met frequently with the president to discuss administrative plans and problems.

He worked in a variety of the usual summer jobs during college but two experiences were particularly influential. One summer at his father's suggestion he worked as a door-to-door evangelist distributing literature and attempting to kindle religious interest in suburbia. He absolutely hated the experience, particularly the blank stares and even slammed doors he would sometimes encounter. In contrast, he loved his last col-lege summer when he worked as an intern in the regional office of a well-known consulting firm. His job was to collect market data from shoppers in local malls and he found most of them very cooperative (and thankful for the product samples he would hand out in appreciation of their an-swers). His long-range plan after graduation was to go to either business school or law school, but first he decided to devote two years to the Peace Corps.

After orientation, Dick was sent to Cuenca, the third largest city in Ecuador with a population of approximately 80,000 people. Ecuador is a small country, larger only than Uruguay in South America, with a popula-tion of some five million. It is very poor, relying on agricultural exports for much of its income. The Andes Mountains run through the nation's center making trade and communications between areas very difficult, and particularly retarding the economic development of the inland region where Cuenca is situated.

Richard's main task was to assist in the formation of credit coopera-tives in Cuenca. A credit cooperative is known to people in the United States as a credit union or a savings and loan cooperative. Members place their savings in the cooperative, as they would in a bank, but loans are available only to members, at a lower interest rate than at commercial banks. Yearly, all profits are returned to the members based on the amount of savings they have in the cooperative.

A cooperative is usually governed by a board elected by and from the membership. It includes a president, vice president, treasurer, and the heads of the credit and supervisory committees. The credit committee approves all loans and the supervisory committee insures that the cooper-ative is being operated according to its by-laws. Professional managers can be hired by the cooperative, but this is only feasible when the cooper-ative is large. In most cases, all leadership comes from part-time, unpaid, volunteer members.

Credit cooperatives have been formed in many less developed areas because of the lack of credit resources available to small merchants and farmers at reasonable interest rates. Credit cooperatives can help in filling this gap. At the same time, they mobilize community capital by teaching members the importance of regular saving. Unfortunately, such cooperatives were unknown to most of Cuenca residents and those in existence had fared poorly.

When Dick arrived, three formally organized cooperatives had al-ready been founded, but one had failed and the other two were stagnat-ing. The strongest of the three was named "La Merced" after the patron saint of the neighborhood in which the cooperative was formed. The pres-ident Juan Caldera and the treasurer Carlos Marchan were familiar with the mechanics of operating a cooperative, but were not aggressive in promoting it. As a result, "La Merced" had only 100 members and $4,200 in capital. No new members had joined in the last six months. Most of the members were small shop, husband and wife merchants.

The other existing cooperative in Cuenca was headed by Felipe Mendosa who was tremendously proud of being the founder and president. He ran the entire show in the manner of a grand patrone, serving as president, treasurer, and chief loan approver (an illegal combination of functions). He did not delegate any authority and resented criticism from anyone. He restricted membership to his friends and boasted of his efforts to look out for their welfare, but limited their voice in the operation of the cooperative.

The third credit cooperative was made up of local carpenters, but it had failed because its political agenda dominated its loan mission. The membership did not seem to understand the specific purposes of a credit cooperative and how it was to operate (for example, the leadership would take members' savings and spend them on flyers and billboards for local elections). The carpenters' cooperative had not been officially disbanded, but only a complete recasting could save it.

After working with these cooperatives for six months, Dick Rule had made the most progress with the carpenters' group. They had accepted him as a member and had essentially turned over all operations to him. He was custodian of the funds which had grown to almost $8,000 and he restricted loans to legitimate member personal emergencies and work requirements such as the purchase of wood and tools. Dick felt deeply honored to be so trusted by the cooperative's members and he enjoyed being able to help them.

This experience was so positive that Dick concluded that more people should be involved in credit unions than just the two hundred then participating. He thought a single large cooperative for the entire city was desirable. Instead of independently improving the other two existing cooperatives, he thought it would be more sensible to merge all three into one. He hoped that this would produce a nucleus of trained personnel to manage itself and other cooperatives and a larger base of members from which to convince others that credit cooperatives could be a success.

Toward this merger objective, Dick met in turn with each of the three cooperative presidents. Listen to Dick's words describing what happened:

"I approached each of the cooperatives with my idea. Señor Mendosa strongly rejected the plan and dismissed me saying that the other cooperatives should be dissolved, with their members joining his organization. The other two cooperatives in turn rejected Mendosa's position, but did agree to discuss consolidation of their two groups.

When the meeting was held, I explained the purpose of the merger and carefully detailed how it could be accomplished. Each cooperative would officially withdraw from the national federation and a new one would immediately be established so that there would be no loss in services to present members. With the increased membership and more capital, the new cooperative would be able to make larger loans to its members with greater regularity. All present officers would resign and a new directorship would be elected from the combined membership.

At this point, the proposal began to encounter difficulties. The president of "La Merced," Señor Caldera, did not like the idea of disbanding his cooperative because it would lose its name. He felt that the name's religious significance was extremely important and should be retained. Señor Maldonado, the president of the carpenter's union, rejected "La Merced" name because it would seem like they were capitulating to the other cooperative—and besides his members wouldn't like the conservative religious association.

When the discussion dealt with election of officials, fear was expressed that if one cooperative outnumbered the other, their directors might be completely reelected leaving the other cooperative without representation. I suggested that the president could be from one cooperative, the vice president from the other, and so on, but each wanted the first president to be drawn from its ranks. Neither existing president was willing to accept the second position in favor of the other (and in theory, we shouldn't even have been discussing such office "deals" because the law clearly requires nominations from the members).

The meeting was finally adjourned with no progress toward consolidation, but with heightened suspicion between the two groups. Later when I met with individuals in each cooperative, I could see that they did not want to discuss the matter further. Future plans were dropped and the idea died. I continued to run the carpenters' cooperative with satisfying success, but of course had to leave when my Peace Corps tour was up. Unfortunately, I was unable to replace myself with someone equally objective in decisions so the carpenters' credit cooperative reverted to its former mix of political and personal purposes to the detriment of its real mission."

Upon returning from the Peace Corps, Dick earned an MBA while majoring in operations management and decision sciences. As always, he was an outstanding student and was much courted by prospective employers. He accepted a position as senior management consultant in the corporate headquarters of Passy Chemicals, a medium-sized, multiplant chemical company. Dick was given a modest but nice office with freedom to hang his favorite pictures and framed credentials on the walls. A memorandum went out from the senior vice president of administration to all sixteen plant managers announcing Dick's availability, "to consult on production and policy matters, especially for facilities in the Southwest and in Latin America because Dick speaks fluent Spanish and has extensive experience in the area." His biosketch and picture were published in the monthly company newspaper which circulated throughout the company.

After the initial flurry of introductions and meetings with plant managers, however, Dick grew quite bored. He just did not receive the telephone calls and invitations that he expected. Sometimes a day would pass without any request for his services. Given the press of moving into a new home and helping his wife with their new daughter, at first Dick was grateful for the relaxed work place. But he began to miss the action, to feel excluded from situations where he might be helpful, and even rejected by high-status executives whom he knew he could impress if given the opportunity.

Dick spoke with Scott Tatum, the firm's executive vice president, of his growing anxiety about his future at the firm. Tatum replied that things are often slow for a new staff person until line management gains confidence and trust in his or her ability and integrity. But he suggested that Dick be more active in reaching out to the field managers—and indeed, in "selling himself" to the field.

Since chemical operations were widely distributed, Dick had to travel quite a bit to develop relationships with plant managers. Sometimes he was angry about spending five hours on a plane only to discover the plant manager was "too busy" to see him or that he was "shuffled off to some local assistant" (Dick's words). At times he felt like he was being patronized.

During these plant visits (even the unpleasant ones), Dick began to notice things that he was certain he could improve, if only he could get the plant managers to listen to his ideas. But he needed good data to formulate his suggestions and in most cases he didn't know how to get them. While visiting a plant in Houston, Texas, however, Dick met Jesus Hernandez, an Ecuadorian who had emigrated to the United States. They would chat about the hard life in Ecuador. Hernandez had a position as assistant foreman in the local Passy Chemicals plant and from him Dick learned a great deal about its operations. Because Hernandez completed the production and quality reports for his shift, Dick learned what they contained and where they were filed. Hernandez would show him his shift's reports which suggested some problems to Dick, but he knew that he also needed historical records. Although refused access to the files by the plant director of administration, Dick learned where they were stored and by coming in on the evening shift when the office was usually empty, he was able to make surreptitious copies of the reports simply by removing them from an unlocked office file and photocopying them. It took him three night-time visits to copy the desired records. (On the last occasion the office door was locked, but Dick was so excited about finally having real data to work with that after only a few minutes of hesitation, he opened the simple lock with a plastic charge card.) Based on these data, he was able to propose a waste reduction program to the plant manager, but it was rejected out of hand.

Fortunately, his analysis was not entirely wasted because Dick knew that conditions were quite similar at a sister plant in Monterey, Mexico. And here he was in luck because a new plant manager, Andres Galapardo, had just been appointed. While still at headquarters, Galapardo had informally drawn on Dick's computer skills to install an office network. About a month after Galapardo's appointment, Dick spoke to him about his observations in the Houston plant and his feeling that significant improvement was possible in Monterey. After initial hesitation at rocking his plant boat so soon, Galapardo accepted the plan. Although the program only reduced waste by half of what Dick thought it could if better implemented (at one point, he almost resigned because he *knew* that he could do it better than the plant manager), Galapardo was pleased and praised Dick to other company executives. After fifteen months at Passy, this was his first significant success and it was replicated in other locations. Dick's reputation climbed and in time his telephone was ringing more than he had ever wanted!

Eventually Dick was appointed corporate director of production technology whose staff has full access to all of Passy's chemical plants and who indeed must be consulted by any plants proposing significant maintenance expenditures or production investments. The firm's chief executive officer is unlikely to approve any such plant request without concurrence from Dick's staff.

♫·♫·♫·♫·

WHAT DID DICK DO?

Richard Rule is clearly an ambitious, hard-working person with significant needs for esteem, power, and achievement. He wants respect for his competence and recognition for his accomplishments. All his life he believed that his brains and energy would bring him success, and for a long time he was correct.

In Ecuador, however, he experienced failure because the three cooperatives were unwilling to implement his merger solution to what he saw as their problem—too few members and too few deposits. Sr. Mendosa's refusal to even discuss the issue, Sr. Caldera's opposition to a name change, and the carpenters' rejection of association with a religious-oriented group all appeared to Rule to be irrational. A merged, single cooperative seemed to Dick to be so clearly the best alternative that he couldn't understand any rational reason for rejection. He was insensitive to the social and political purposes that most members wanted the credit cooperatives to pursue.

Later in his corporate staff position at Passy Chemicals, once again Dick faced failure, not so much from rejection as from being ignored.

Field managers just didn't draw on his abilities even though Dick was convinced he could improve production performance. After his initial period of passively waiting to be called, Dick sought counsel from the senior vice president of administration who suggested he visit field personnel so that he could sell them on his abilities. Although uncomfortable with the cavalier manner in which he was sometimes treated, (remember how he had disliked being rejected in his religious proselytising), in time Dick did gain sufficient access to the Houston plant to formulate a waste control plan. Although rejected initially in Texas, this plan was later adopted by the Mexico plant manager with success. In both Houston and Monterey, Dick was "lucky" in drawing on personal relationships that helped him get access to data and then managerial faith in him to try out his proposal. His drive to succeed led him to ethically suspect actions like surreptitious entry to plant files, secret copying, and even "picking" the door lock of the Houston plant office. These actions did not bother Dick. He justified them to himself as being in the best interests of the firm because his motivation was to reduce waste. And in the long run, he did just that.

Dick's long-time dilemma will be whether or not he will enjoy serving as a consultant. He seems inclined to want to make the decisions and implementations *himself* rather than being the adviser. Indeed, in his present role as corporate director of plant technology he appears to have accumulated joint authority with plant managers over issues of plant maintenance, innovation, and investment. Let's look at staff-line authority and the process of giving advice.

STAFF-LINE RELATIONS

The distinction between staff and line has its origins in the military: line officers were to exercise command in battle while staff were planners or advisers.[1] In business, a classical principle emerged that only line managers had the authority to make operational decisions; staff existed merely to give advice.[2] As we will see, modern firms have greatly elaborated the staff role, but let's start with that traditional advisory role.

Advisory Staff. Such professional staff are specialists hired to provide expertise to operating managers who feel they could benefit from their advice. As indicated in Exhibit 7–1, it assumed that a line manager will initiate a request to the appropriate staff person. A production supervisor having equipment trouble might call a mechanical engineer; or a department head experiencing repeated discipline problems with a particular employee would call a human resource specialist. In this communication flow, the staff possess no legitimate power and they appear quite passive, awaiting invitations to get involved.

In spite of the impressive framed credentials which they may hang on their office walls, however, newly hired staff specialists may find themselves a bit lonely with silent telephones. Operating managers are simply not familiar with them and skeptical of what they can contribute, even if their biosketchs have been published in the plant newsletter.

Older staff colleagues and superiors will instruct young advisers to "sell" themselves to line managers. Such selling as shown in Exhibit 7–2

EXHIBIT 7–1: ADVISORY STAFF

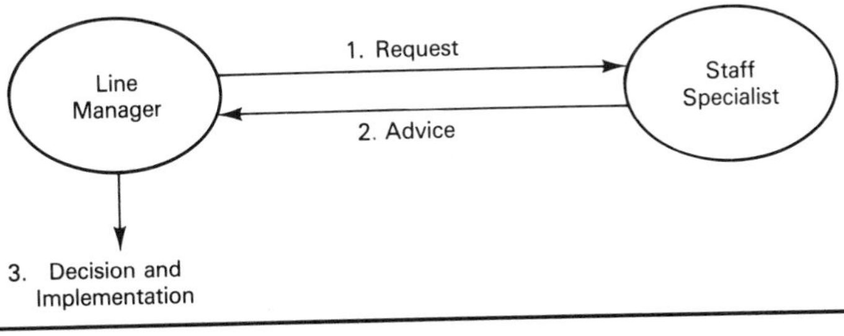

EXHIBIT 7–2: "SELLING" STAFF

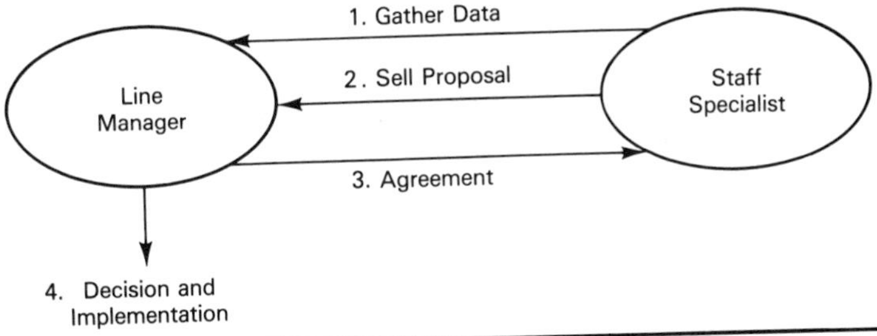

requires frequent and vigorous overtures to line management, a reverse of the behavior usually assumed of an adviser (that is, that managers initiate, advisers respond).

Surprisingly, staff specialists spend *less time responding and more time initiating than any managers.* Exhibit 7–3 summarizes the hours per week on self-initiated and response behavior for five management positions as well as staff specialists (a total of fifty-four persons were observed).[3]

Giving Advice

EXHIBIT 7-3: TIME ON RESPONSE AND SELF-INITIATED ACTIVITIES

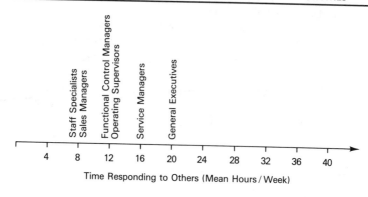

Time Responding to Others (Mean Hours / Week)

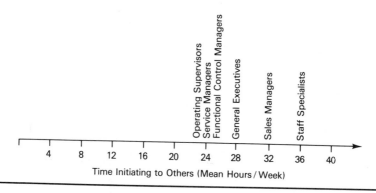

Time Initiating to Others (Mean Hours / Week)

Response time is the mean hours per week on activities that others initiate. It includes talking to other people who call or come to the specialist or manager, attending meetings scheduled by others, and reading, analyzing, and thinking about received written materials. Self-initiated time is devoted to activities that the manager or staffer initiates such as calling someone on the telephone, setting up a meeting, going to someone's office to talk, or drafting correspondence and reports on one's own initiative. Although my sample size of eleven is small, the staff specialists observed spend less time responding to others who have come to them for advice or service than any of the managerial positions. In contrast, they initiate more consultations and discussions and spend more time making proposals and initiating innovations.

Not surprisingly given the poor support services often provided staff specialists, they spend more time on clerical activities and paperwork than any of the managers sampled.

In order to have something to sell, a staff specialist must have greater familiarity with line's problems and possibilities than he or she would derive from passively waiting to be called. But to gather data necessary to frame proposals, staff must gain entry to operating departments. Unfortunately for the staff, right of access cannot be assumed. For legitimate security or paranoic defensiveness, operating managers may sharply limit physical access. When I worked as an industrial engineer at Eastman Kodak, I literally had to show my identity card through a peephole in the door because Kodak depends more on secrecy to protect its technological advantages than on public patents. Therefore, controlled personnel access was important.

Most staff advisers will not have such dramatic limitations on physical entry, but substantial exclusion from an operating department's data files is common. Departmental personnel may simply not trust the staff specialist, perhaps even seeing him or her as a spy from headquarters.

Thus, the best-intentioned advisory staffers are caught in a dilemma. They can't wait to be called; they must sell themselves and their ideas. To do this they must have new knowledge or proposals to sell, but to develop these proposals they need access to data. Several tactics are used to gain sufficient trust, information, and power.[4]

1. *Becoming familiar.* In uncovering problems, there is no substitute for immersion.[5] The would-be adviser can just "hang around" socializing, trying to make friends by doing favors and odd jobs when possible. In time, he or she hopes to become so familiar that defenses drop and problems become visible so he or she can analyze and propose solutions. This tactic demands that the aspiring adviser invest time and maintain patience—resources often in short supply for an ambitious, achievement-oriented person.

Investing sufficient time to gain access and trust may be especially difficult if the adviser is expected to maximize "billable" hours, that is, to justify his or her time by charging them to an existing account or project. Some companies charge line managers for advisory staff services. The intent is threefold: (a) to put pressure on staff to justify themselves by proving their worth to internal clients; (2) to counter operating managers' perceptions that "free" staff can't be valuable; and (c) to pressure management to work more effectively with staff since it is charged to the operating budget.

Such charges can be helpful, but they do hinder the development of a new relationship if staff personnel don't have someplace to charge risky developmental hours. Most staff time accounting forms do have an unassigned line for project development, but informal norms usually warn a staffer not to charge *too* many hours to this code. To do so would be an admission that you are not in demand!

2. *Hiding the hours.* To create time for new project development, staff sometimes hide the time in existing large projects. Thus, the hours for one project can be padded with extra hours that are invested in investi-

gating opportunities with another client. Since both "clients" are managers in the same corporation as the ambitious adviser, this practice is easy to justify because no one is really being cheated; it is all in the firm's overall interests, or so it is rationalized.

Although this subterfuge is clearly not as serious as an external consultant overbilling one client to invest in another (and certainly less unethical than overcharging one fat client like the Department of Defense in order to give a more competitive price to another), internal billing manipulation is lying and it can distort internal cost data important to management pricing and investment decisions. Nonetheless, the pressure on staff specialists to find time to develop new proposals is substantial.

3. "Stealing" data. To speed up proposal development, a staff specialist often is tempted to obtain data surreptitiously, perhaps by copying office files without permission. Such files are frequently not locked and access is a matter of sweet-talking a clerk into making the copies or the specialist hanging around until late in the evening and making copies after everyone has left. Again, such behavior is easy for the staffer to justify as being for the operating department's own good, even if they don't know what's best for themselves.

The most problematic situation is when the desired files are locked or protected by a computer security code. Very seldom will any staff superior direct you to break into the files. But (and this is a big but), successfully doing so without detection and selling a new project based on the data will be praised. And the staff department grapevine may even build up the offender's reputation so that he or she is perceived as a person "who gets things done" (perhaps the supreme accolade).

Again, rationalization is easy based on public glorification of those who are "creative" in gaining information for the greater public good (as with investigative reporters and secret government information a la President Nixon and *All the President's Men*). If you are caught in the process, however, it is very doubtful that any of your staff superiors will rush to your defense. I must admit that one of my breakthrough projects when I worked in industry grew out of data I was able to copy when the plant manager's office was empty on the midnight shift (thankfully for my conscience, the door and files were unlocked).

Conflict Between Generalists and Specialists. Given this cold war climate, some line managers may (rightly) fear that staff specialists will infringe on their jobs and diminish their power and status. The structural evolution of many organizations suggests expansion of staff influence, often at the expense of line authority and autonomy. Two of the most time-honored management principles are disappearing: (1) unity of command (one should have one and only one immediate superior) and (2) authority should equal responsibility. Unfortunately, growth in organizational complexity with its accompanying specialization has made it virtually impossible to adhere to these old principles. The aeronautical engineering group leader responsible for developing an airframe is dependent upon access to a wind tunnel controlled by a testing manager over whom the group leader has no authority. It would be much too expensive for the group leader to have a separate tunnel, nor does he have the necessary expertise to operate it. Similarly, a production manager is responsible for her department's productivity, but she is dependent upon planning specialists, industrial engineering, and human resource specialists over whom she has no authority. Although the manager presumably receives no orders from these staff people, she does receive "suggestions," "proposals," and sometimes even "schedules" and "procedures." Under these conditions, conflict is not rare.

For line managers, the proliferation of staff advisers and specialists means that they no longer have complete control over their own operations. They personally may not have the knowledge necessary to manage their departments, so a gap between knowledge and authority develops.[6] Generalists come to depend on specialists who appear to be lower on the hierarchy. As a result, over time their relationships become more stable.[7] Line managers may possess the formal authority to make decisions, but if all they can do is sign the proposals submitted by staff specialists, who is really in control? One of the special burdens of Lyndon B. Johnson's presidency (and indeed any presidency) is that he felt himself inadequate to judge who was correct among his various military advisers on Vietnam.[8] Some told him to put up an electronic wall between North and South Vietnam; others to retreat into fortified enclaves turning the rest of the country over to the Vietcong. He had the power to decide, but lacked the knowledge to judge which of many contradictory proposals was most valid. According to his brother Sam Houston Johnson, the president sometimes complained that his Texas state college education had not prepared him to judge between ideas from his Harvard and MIT advisers.[9] But of course, he was not "dumber" than these advisers. His expertise lay in domestic politics and social reform, not military and foreign affairs.

Line-staff tensions can be exascerbated by age and social differences. The younger, more educated and better dressed staff may be distrusted by older production managers who came up via what they perceive as a harder route.[10] To make matters worse, the ambitious specialist sometimes betrays condescension toward the generalist whom he or she sees as less able and less promotable. The younger college graduate specialist understandably relies on what he or she knows best—academic knowledge.[11] The specialist is at least somewhat familiar with statistics, computers, psychology, and economics (and they can be very valuable).

Unfortunately, these theories can also hinder working relationships with older managers. Armed with an arsenal of analytical techniques, the graduate looks for problems to which they can be applied.

Unfortunately, the problems solved in the textbooks are sometimes not the problems important to *this* manager. Worse, talking to older executives in the arcane vocabulary of *stochastic variables, multiple-channel processing, breakeven points,* and *self-actualizing opportunities* can be threatening to them. Older personnel to whom such terms are unfamiliar may believe they are being manipulated.

In some cultures, older persons are automatically respected for age and assumed wisdom, but in the United States the young often respond to older people's skepticism with thinly veiled contempt. Because an older manager does not know the new techniques, the young specialist erroneously infers that he or she is incompetent or unimportant. This can be a career-crippling mistake, because organizational contribution and influence at higher levels have little to do with technical knowledge. An offended elder can oppose the brilliant younger staffer's advancement.

Of course, some staffers are only putting on an act, attempting to appear more confident and influential than they really are. To support this image, they try to appear infallible, which backfires into undermining communications with possible clients. Insecurity about their status and contributions leads many specialists to feel greater anxiety than operating managers.[12] In general, staff professionals feel less job satisfaction and more conformity pressure than do operating line managers at the same hierarchical level. The greater ease of objectively measuring the line manager's value to the firm gives them somewhat greater independence than staffers whose performance evaluation is more subjective— and who then worry more about whether they are fitting in with the correct appearance and behavior.

Finally, staff and line sometimes perceive time and change differently.[13] The staff specialist is often anxious to establish his or her reputation by persuading an operating manager to make changes. But the manager may not feel there is a problem and besides he or she would prefer to keep things as they are. "If it ain't broke, don't fix it" is a practical person's aphorism. Of course, in the long run it is dangerously misguided by promoting stagnation. Nonetheless, organizational stability is a virtue and it is understandable that a busy manager would prefer to maintain stability. With uninvited change proposals, the ambitious staffer can be seen as a threat. The staff "adviser" often sees problems needing correction when the managing generalist sees none or different problems.

Why Staff Advice Is Often Poor. Even under the best conditions of trusting access, operating managers often deem staff advice as unsatisfactory. Line management feels that it can't use staff's advice, or the specialists complain that the managers don't know what they want. Each side has a different explanation.

1. *Line manager's view:* "Staff are so eager to sell a project that they make unrealistic promises. Their results are much more modest—and disappointing to me."
   * "Staff proposals are sometimes theoretically correct and I'm sure would have gotten them As from their business school professors, but their answers don't apply to my practical problems."
   * "Staff people tend to be overspecialized. They look at the world through their own particular telescopes. Their perspectives are too narrow and their recommendations not integrated. I must consider, however, how implementing their recommendations would affect the total performance of my organization."
2. *Staff adviser's view:* "Line managers blame us when projects don't work out. But they create many of the failures themselves. For example, a manager will sometimes toss a problem to me and expect an 'answer' without his involvement. If I try to get him to spend time with me analyzing the issues, he complains that he called me in to do that. In short, he tries to delegate the responsibility for the project to me without giving me either the authority to do it or his personal support."
   * "Line managers often want improvement in their unit's performance without any change in their own behavior. They want me to change other's behavior and performance while their behavior remains unchanged."
   * "Sometimes a line manager will tell me to give priority to a project. So I charge off and invest a lot of time in it. When I come back with recommendations, however, the line manager has lost interest. His priorities have changed, but I was never informed."

Given the differing perspectives of staff specialists and operating managers, to be an effective adviser requires substantial political competence as well as expertise.

Giving Staff More Authority. Top management may discover that hiring specialists and providing them with nice offices does not guarantee that line managers will utilize their services.[14] Therefore, the top executives may strive to strengthen staff's position by mandating right of entry, compulsory consultation, concurrent authority, or functional authority (Exhibit 7-4).

EXHIBIT 7–4: INCREASING STAFF INFLUENCE

| Availability | Right of Access | Compulsory Consultation | Concurrent Authority | Functional Authority |

To ensure that staff can obtain data necessary to analyze conditions in operating departments and prepare recommendations, senior management can inform line managers that the relevant staff personnel must be granted access to departmental data (Exhibit 7–5). Implied is that if staff specialists complain about lack of cooperation from operating managers, top management will side with staff. Such a hierarchical directive does of course greatly facilitate staff access to desired data, but it doesn't auto-

EXHIBIT 7–5: STAFF WITH RIGHT OF ACCESS

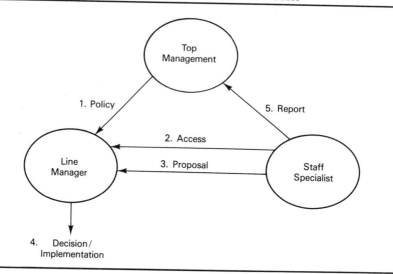

matically guarantee a trusting line-staff relationship. Operating managers may resent staff's intrusion and perceive a control link back to the top where none was intended. However, in many cases of right of entry, the top *does* intend such a monitoring role. In general, mandated right of access will in the short run improve opportunities for staff specialists, but in the long run it probably hinders those advisers who would be most effective in developing valuable client relationships.

An even stronger form of right of access is compulsory consultation (Exhibit 7–6). To ensure that operating line managers consult the relevant

EXHIBIT 7-6: COMPULSORY CONSULTATION STAFF

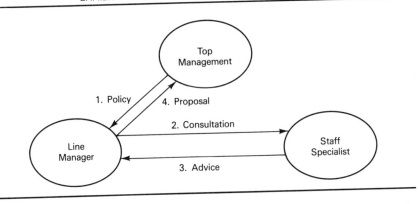

staff on specific matters, top management may refuse to discuss lower line proposals unless staff has been involved. Thus, a senior vice president may refuse to discuss a manufacturing department head's request to replace manufacturing equipment until the department manager has discussed this with a staff consultant in engineering. Perhaps the firm's president insists on this to ensure that the engineering specialists have the opportunity to influence manufacturing methods and prevent unproductive duplication or dead-end projects. In this situation, the staff specialist's potential influence has been sharply increased, but the consultant-client relationship is even more strained. The operating manager who "consults" the staff adviser may feel that he or she is doing so under duress with little receptivity to the proferred advice (which indeed, the manager may interpret as a veiled directive).

Even more extreme, top management may give staff concurrent authority so that operating managers must obtain staff agreement with their major proposals. In effect, this gives a staff specialist veto power over a line manager if the staffer disagrees with the proposal. For example, a company president might require manufacturing to obtain the concurrence of the industrial engineering department before scheduling employee overtime. Top management hopes that such divided responsibility would reduce poor planning and excessive labor expense.

Concurrent authority is common in government, primarily to limit individual corruption, but it can be helpful in keeping interdependent persons informed of what others are going (Exhibit 7-7). The built-in checks can prevent mistakes by ensuring that every relevant specialist has an opportunity to block potential errors. Unfortunately, in blocking mistakes a system of multiple concurrences can lead to overconservatism and rejection of promising innovation. Multiplying the number of people who can say "no" has the effect of reducing both errors and creative breakthroughs.

Giving Advice

EXHIBIT 7-7: CONCURRENT AUTHORITY STAFF

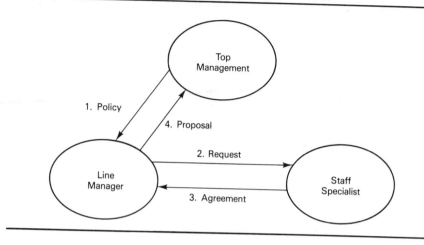

In terms of staff-line relations, requiring line to gain staff's agreement absolutely *reverses* the traditional pattern: Now the line manager has to sell his or her idea to the staff specialist! To be sure, the manager and staffer who get along well can transcend the quasi-authority staff position and maintain relations as adviser-client, but this is rare.

An organization can go so far in support of specialists that the distinction between line and staff is dissolved by functional authority.[15] Each functional unit is assigned authority to initiate, veto, and control policies and procedures in its area of expertise. Thus, the personnel vice president may be responsible for all employment and training; the engineering vice president for all product design; the director of industrial engineering for production methods and incentive standards; and the financial vice president for all cost control and accounting procedures. Each is supreme in an area as long as top management supports and validates the vice president's decisions.

Functional authority ideally ensures that persons with expertise have authority in their areas, independent of traditional boundaries between staff and line. Nonetheless, real problems remain.[16] Each function tends to see its responsibility as most important when in fact they are all dependent on one another. Coordination becomes difficult. Undermined is the principle of unity of command, especially for lower line managers. So many functional authorities can influence operating activities that a manager can receive contradictory directives from different specialists. As one refugee from Harold Geneen's ITT once put it, "ITT is the only firm where if a line manager and staff specialist get into a fight, the line manager is the one fired."

WHO ARE EFFECTIVE STAFF ADVISERS?

Not every bright, analytically competent person is suited to giving advice, especially as a long-time career role. Indeed, the very attributes of high-achievement need and personal ambition that impelled them to academic accomplishment and credentials necessary to gain a staff position can work against being an effective adviser. Thus, the classic personality profile associated with effective senior managers is high need for achievement, high need for power, and low need for affiliation.[17] Such people are motivated to define challenging objectives, enjoy influencing subordinates and associates to accomplish them, and are not dependent on whether they are liked by the people involved. This kind of person is often unhappy as a staff adviser, however, because he or she is impatient with less quick or less hardworking line managers. Therefore, they tend to push the line too hard, perhaps even striving to assume implementation power.[18] Listen to the lament of one experienced consultant:[19]

> Most consultants I know would secretly like, just for once, for the tables to be reversed—for the consultant to hold the power in the relationship and to dictate to the client what resources will be available, how the change process will occur, and what the client's role in the process will be.

A passive operating manager may give way, but more likely an overly aggressive staffer will simply be rejected. And even if such an achievement/power-oriented adviser masks impatience with the line manager, he or she will eventually become frustrated by an inability to actually direct others in implementing proposals.

Excessively passive staff specialists are also ineffective. If need for achievement and power are too low, high-affiliation need may motivate a potential adviser to be too submissive to line management's desires. Not being involved in meaningful projects might not bother such staffers sufficiently for them to exercise the data gathering and selling initiative necessary to gain sufficient access.

Effective advisers in personality are someplace between hyper-achievement/power and hyper-affiliation. They have significant but balanced needs for achievement, power, and affiliation. They have outgoing personalities responsive to others' needs, enjoy talking to people and derive satisfaction from solving challenging problems, but are happy to be a contributor to the solution and privy to the decision rather than the sole decider.[20] And they seem to take special satisaction in assisting high-status authority figures. Successful external management consultants often have demonstrated a lifelong pattern of moving from modest socioeconomic backgrounds and seeking association with prestigious people and institutions, including private colleges and service as officers in the United States Navy.[21] I once invited a friend of mine who was senior partner in a blue-chip management consulting firm to visit with my MBA class. He spent the first fifteen minutes boasting to the class about the famous government and business leaders with whom he had met in the past month. This association seemed more important even than the conversations' substance or the quality of solutions suggested. He was proud of himself and felt that nothing else would so establish his credibility with the students than his access to managerial celebrities. But of course it is not really that superficial. The quality of his recommendations had to be high to maintain his access, but one wondered what were means and what were ends.

Most long-time adviser-consultants are a bit more ambivalent on this issue of prestigious association. On the one hand, they enjoy it and measure their own career success by who telephones them and who accepts their calls and acts on their advice.[22] On the other hand, they don't want to perceive themselves as sycophants toadying to the powerful so they incessantly complain in private (especially to other consultants) about the intellectual and managerial inadequacies of their famous clients (to an outsider, the stories can sound truly amazing).

WILL DICK RULE BE HAPPY AS AN ADVISER?

Richard Rule's career has elements similar to those of successful and effective advisers, but in general he appears more power oriented. All his life he has striven to be outstanding and to be recognized by prestigious authority figures for his accomplishments. In high school and college, he wanted to be privy to principal and presidential decisions through his involvement in student government. Serving in the Peace Corps in Ecuador, he certainly wanted to help. But even more he wanted the cooperative members and leaders to implement *his solution* to their problems, whether or not they agreed with his definition of their problems. Whether it was cultural imperialism or personal ambition, Dick was insensitive to local conditions; he just assumed that bigger and more centralized was better. If necessary, as in the case of the carpenter's credit cooperative, he assumed complete leadership. Although successful in the short run, such an approach doesn't prepare the "client" to gain independence from the "adviser." Upon his departure, things were not better (and perhaps worse) for his having been there.

Dick's laudible ambition was continued at Passy Chemicals where he became impatient with noninvolvement and passivity. He exercised initiative in gathering data and developing a waste-reducing proposal. One could decry his too easy ethics in surreptitiously obtaining his data, but he sincerely was interested in helping the company while building his own record of success. But even here he fought his frustration that the plan wasn't implemented as well as he thought he could have if he were in charge.

By the end of the case, Dick has convinced top management to expand his authority by giving him virtual veto power over operating management's production technology decisions. The line must consult his staff in order to proceed. In a sense then, he is really no longer an adviser who must sell his ideas and repeatedly prove his credibility. Dick has almost obtained total functional authority. He has escaped from being a staff adviser.

ADVICE ON GIVING ADVICE

- Begin each assignment only when a line manager is ready. Don't "sell" so hard that the manager gives you a go-ahead only to get you off his or her back. Remember that your first task is to help the manager become aware of blocks to the unit's effectiveness of which he or she may be unaware. If you fail to develop this awareness, your advice is not likely to be accepted.
- Build on success. Key is to have the manager-client develop rational faith in your knowledge and in your commitment to his or her interest. Therefore, no project is too small to complete well so long as the manager considers it worthwhile.
- Don't do the whole job for management. You should share your knowledge with operating people so as to educate them, not replace them. As an adviser, you should insist that line management share control of the project by assigning a liaison person to work closely with you. Your responsibility is not so much to supply line with answers as to help them develop their own solutions. And implementation is likely to be more effective if line management feels that the recommendations represent its own best thinking, not yours.
- Try to submerge your own needs into the operating manager's goals. Acting on your achievement and power drives can undermine your effectiveness because you may push too hard to run your client's affairs.
- Don't over-identify with line management. Maintain some distance. On the one hand, you should not overly identify with line management because this will cause you to lose objectivity. On the other hand, you should not be seen as a spy from headquarters. Resist the temptation to acquire more power by having top management give you concurrent or functional authority.
- Resist being treated as an "expert." Communicate honestly; tell the

operating manager what higher management expects of you. Admit what you don't know, and don't tell the manager what he or she wants to hear if you believe his or her problem diagnosis to be incorrect.

- Remember that a major responsibility is to help the operating manager develop better diagnostic skills so that he or she becomes less dependent on you. A paradox seems to exist: You promote your success as a personal adviser by working to eliminate your own job through helping your client to become more self-sufficient.
- Recognize that older operating line managers may be less knowledgeable than you are regarding sophisticated analytical techniques, but this doesn't indicate that they are less intelligent or always resistant to change. Rather, your proposals must be expressed in their terms.
- Recognize your bias to perceive and define problems that can be treated with your analytical tools. As sophisticated as they may well be, these academic tools may not directly apply to the problems that line management is confronting.

8

Being a Protégé

"*You remind me of myself when I was a young man, Dirkson, so I'm firing you before you try to take over the company.*"

One of George Bush's earliest presidential appointments was that of United States Army General Colin L. Powell to be Chairman of the Joint Chiefs of Staff. Jumping over more than thirty senior officers, he became the youngest (and the first African-American) chairman ever. The newspaper article describing his background asserts that his meteoric career started when he survived stiff competition as a City College of New York graduate and young Army Lieutenant to be selected in 1972 as one of sixteen White House Fellows where he met his future mentors.[1] In the White House he worked for the Office of Management and Budget, the director of which was Caspar W. Weinberger and his deputy Frank C. Carlucci. Years later in the Reagan administration, Weinberger became Secretary of Defense and chose by then Colonel Powell as his executive assistant. Then when Carlucci replaced Admiral Poindexter as National Security Adviser in the wake of the Iran-Contra scandal, he brought Powell in as his deputy. And when Carlucci replaced Weinberger as Defense Secretary, Powell became National Security Adviser.

Most of us will not have quite as golden an opportunity to impress potential powerful mentors as Colin Powell, but we will confront some promising possibilities. How well you perform and relate to potential sponsors will affect your career success. In this chapter we examine mentor-protégé relations, particularly what protégés can do to meet their mentors' needs. We begin with a particularly impressive woman who is moving up the ladder in a large regional bank.

JUDITH GREENE AND MARSHALL WILDE

Judith Greene is the newly appointed vice president of administration of the International Division of Trustworthy Trust Company. She joined the division as a junior analyst twelve years ago right after she graduated from Eastern College with a Bachelor of Science in Economics. She was subsequently promoted to senior analyst and area supervisor.

Judith has mixed feelings about her early years as an analyst. A lot of the work was boring because the tasks were routine and feedback inadequate. At times she felt like a nameless, faceless automaton, but she enjoyed the bank as an institution and sought opportunities both inside and outside the division to talk about investments. She was very active in several professional banking and investment societies. She got along well with most of the staff including support personnel, apparently because she did much of her own typing. She saw this not as a status issue but as a pragmatic opportunity: Her reports would already have been submitted while her peers were still awaiting theirs from the typing pool.

Judith feels that she did a better job than most analysts, but she frankly states that her break occurred rather fortuitously. Judith's husband, a manager for a local industrial firm, had graduated from a prestigious Old Ivy University. At an alumni dance he introduced her to fellow alumnus Marshall Wilde, then senior vice president in the Corporate Loan Division of Trustworthy Trust with which Tom Greene had done business. Shortly thereafter, Wilde had been named executive vice president and head of the International Division. Wilde was a dynamic and committed man interested in improving minority and female opportunities. Since Judith clearly had the requisite skills and performance record, she was subsequently promoted to area supervisor where she did a fine job (while benefitting from a number of informal conversations with Wilde).

Trustworthy Trust Company is a large, multiservice regional bank headquartered in a metropolitan downtown. Its assets rank it in the top fifty banks in the United States. Its main office is an imposing granite edifice at the center of the financial district. It fairly reeks of stability and conservatism. Exhibit 8–1 is a simplified organizational chart.

The International Division illustrated in Exhibit 8–2 is the smallest of the bank's five major units, but like the others is headed by an executive vice president. The division is charged with maintaining correspondent relations with foreign banks, exchanging currencies, and assisting its corporate customers in raising funds and conducting business in foreign countries. The division annually hires four or five MBAs with special skills and experience (usually a foreign language and knowledge of a particular country). Because of their turnover, however, Marshall Wilde is considering whether to hire more people right out of college rather than after graduate school.

New professional employees are assigned to the analyst pool where they gather data and write reports requested by various officers. Much of their information is gathered from the bank's extensive library, and some from a local university. Frequently they write or call foreign embassies and governments. The analysts are located in a common work area not affectionately termed the "bullpen." It is crowded, warm, and a bit shabby. Exhibit 8–3 gives the layout of the division.

After eighteen to twenty-four months, a junior analyst normally is promoted to senior analyst. Theoretically, this means that he or she handles more difficult assignments, but work location and process are un-

EXHIBIT 8–1: SIMPLIFIED ORGANIZATION OF TRUSTWORTHY TRUST

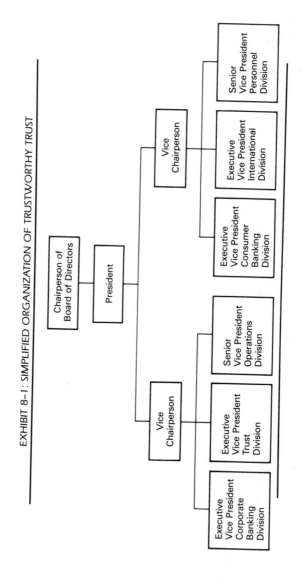

EXHIBIT 8–2: ORGANIZATION OF INTERNATIONAL DIVISION

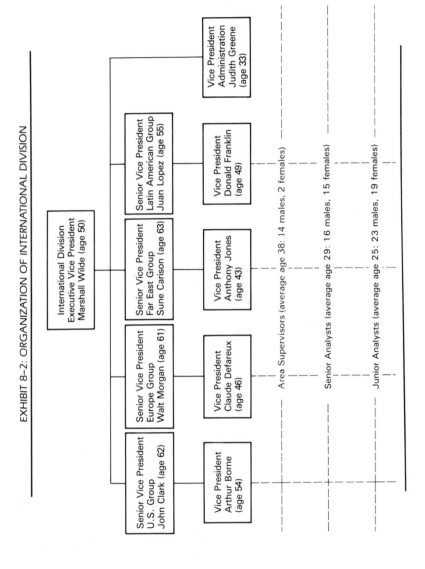

International Division
Executive Vice President
Marshall Wilde (age 50)

Senior Vice President
U.S. Group
John Clark (age 62)

Senior Vice President
Europe Group
Walt Morgan (age 61)

Senior Vice President
Far East Group
Sune Carlson (age 63)

Senior Vice President
Latin American Group
Juan Lopez (age 55)

Vice President
Arthur Borne
(age 54)

Vice President
Claude Defareux
(age 46)

Vice President
Anthony Jones
(age 43)

Vice President
Donald Franklin
(age 49)

Vice President
Administration
Judith Greene
(age 33)

Area Supervisors (average age 38: 14 males, 2 females)

Senior Analysts (average age 29: 16 males, 15 females)

Junior Analysts (average age 25: 23 males, 19 females)

EXHIBIT 8-3: LAYOUT OF INTERNATIONAL DIVISION

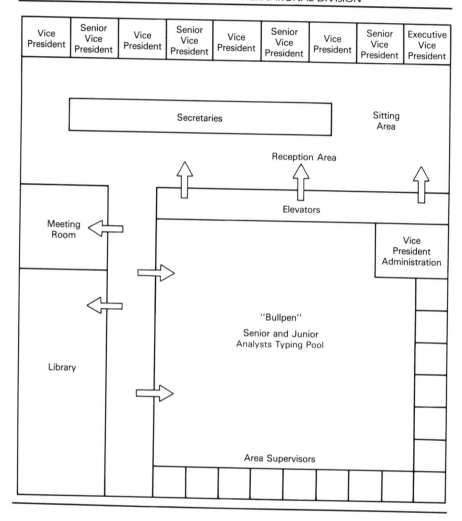

changed. The first substantial promotion comes after three to four years when a senior analyst could become an area supervisor (and is considered a junior officer). An area supervisor directs four or five analysts specializing in a specific country (such as France) or a region (such as Central America). The area supervisor makes decisions on small transactions and consults with appropriate senior officers on major matters. Once or twice a year, supervisors make three- to five-day business trips to their regions of specialization. These trips are keenly anticipated. The area supervisors' offices are located around the outside walls of the bullpen.

The division's senior vice presidents and vice presidents are the critical decision makers. Their offices are located in another area of the floor opening to the elevators. The reception space and offices are impressive and luxurious, all in colonial decor and Williamsburg green, with wall-to-wall carpeting in the hall and oriental rugs in each office. Each officer has a spacious private office with a secretary just outside the door.

These senior officers specialize by geography and travel frequently. Either the senior vice president or the vice president for each area is expected to be at headquarters, but actually both are often away on trips. About half of their time is spent traveling. They frequently complain about the onerous burden of these trips but their gripes appear to be more joking than real.

Trustworthy Trust Company is a successful institution and the International Division enjoys a good reputation. Nonetheless, Marshall Wilde has been concerned about the younger staff. Over half of them leave the bank after eighteen to thirty months. Most join smaller banks; some get married and have children; and some just drop out, throw away their watches and go skiing. Exit interviews elicit complaints about being bored, the poor working conditions, the crisis atmosphere, and not knowing what's going on or what happens to their reports. Analysts (particularly the women) are bitter about lack of cooperation and respect from clerical personnel. No one seems to be in charge of them. When a consultant was called in, he administered a questionnaire to all divisional professionals and managers. Exhibit 8-4 summarizes the analysts' descriptions of the most dissatisfying aspects of their jobs.

EXHIBIT 8-4: SAMPLE OF ANALYSTS' RESPONSES TO QUESTION:
"WHAT IS THE MOST DISSATISFYING ASPECT OF YOUR JOB?"

---

1. The detail work involved and the constant phone calls from branches for foreign exchange rates. These jobs could be done by a clerk.
2. Being involved with clerical work, such as typing and being taken for granted.
3. Lack of knowledge as to where my job will lead.
4. The closed-minded narrowness of most of senior management that leads to pettiness, lack of communication, and the lack of a more democratic environment.
5. Lack of contact with people outside the bank. Lack of physical activity.
6. Lack of experience causes me to waste too much time.
7. Lack of sufficient time for free thinking.
8. The physical working conditions are intolerable in that there is too little space, no privacy, and a very high noise level.
9. The remuneration—the salary structure is such that it presents an unoptimistic future. If one would desire to stay, one would be passing up a great deal of financial reward. In order to financially succeed in banking, one must transfer to another bank to receive financial remuneration.

In addition, the consultant conducted management training sessions for the senior officers which covered topics such as human needs, the meaning of work, motivation, and change. Unfortunately, several of the senior vice presidents and vice presidents did not attend all the meetings. Some of them expressed exception with the consultant's views on people's needs for autonomy, competence, and power. And a couple of senior officers seemed to sleep through the sessions.

Wilde has now promoted Judith to the newly created position of vice president of administration. He has not given her an explicit job description, but he sees it as dealing with the low morale among analysts and the poor administration of bullpen activities. Judith is very enthusiastic and optimistic about her opportunities in the new post.

WHAT IS JUDITH TO DO?

When Judith Greene visited my class of MBA students, she was asked if she felt guilty that she came to the executive vice president's attention only because Marshall Wilde and her husband had been college classmates. Judith replied absolutely not because she had always been an outstanding performer and chance contacts play a role in everyone's career. The key is to take advantage of them.

In taking advantage of her opportunity, however, Judith faces a paradox in that her greatest asset, Marshall Wilde's support, is also her main vulnerability. Most people interpret her new position as vice president of administration as inherently weak. The post has no history of success, with only two direct subordinates (a secretary and an assistant), and no significant budget. And her office location just off the bullpen appears to signal her distance from the "real" senior officers arrayed in their Williamsburg luxury.

Indeed, location looms particularly large to professional women sensitive to symbolic power slights. In discussing this case with a group of female human resource managers, I found them sharply divided on whether Judith should even accept the position. Half felt she should decline if Marshall were unwilling to locate her office in the line of vice presidential offices.

The other half, however, argued that there was an advantage to being contiguous to the bullpen because this is where she must have an impact if she is to meet Marshall's somewhat vague objective of improving morale among the analysts and thus reducing turnover. Minimum status symbols and physical proximity could facilitate her uncovering fundamental problems and establishing herself as a resource for solving them.

Location symbolism, whether it is more important to be closer to the ultimate power figure (especially if that person is also your primary mentor) or closer to the people you must ultimately influence, is tricky for anyone, but perhaps especially so for a woman. On the one hand, she can worry that her high sounding title without substantial human or financial resources with an office distant from the power center will be seen as tokenism. On the other hand, if she is seen as "too close" organizationally and physically to a senior male mentor, she may fear other's suspicion about her competence and "real" relation to the boss.

Regardless of location, Judith Greene is heavily dependent on support from the executive vice president, Marshall Wilde. Since she controls no significant resources, she must either get his preaction approval or postaction ratification for her initiatives. Therefore, keeping him pleased with her progress is critical. And ultimately, her future at the bank depends on Wilde's success with top management.

Before looking at Judith's specific steps, let's examine current theory and practice in mentoring and being an effective protégé.

MENTORS, SPONSORS, AND PROTÉGÉS

Mentoring in recent years has been a hot topic in popular and academic management literature. But of course the issue is an old one. The cynic's complaint has long been, "It's not what you know, but who you know." So it has been argued that rather than rewarding performance, managers promote people whom they like. Certainly, such affiliative favoritism bordering on family nepotism has occurred and still occurs too frequently. Nonetheless, most mentor-protégé relations are more benign—and if anything, the causative flow is the reverse of the cynic's. Reliably good performance captures a senior's eye and a mutually rewarding relationship develops. Perhaps two thirds of senior executives have benefitted from mentors earlier in their careers, and they seem happier with their careers than those who made it entirely on their own.[2]

Early Mentor-Protégé Relations. Biographical career descriptions frequently highlight the importance of a "special other" (usually older) who plays a crucial role in one's maturation.[3] It is rarely a parent because we discount their admiration as being unconditional. But the ninth grade science teacher who recognizes a boy's hitherto undisplayed analytical skill or the high school field hockey coach who rewards a girl's until then discouraged competitive fire can become a reference mentor never to be forgotten. In such adolescent experiences, we are not talking about role models because it is not that the boy or girl wants to be *like* the science teacher or coach. Rather, it is that the mentor has encouraged the protégé to act upon his or her potential—or as the U.S. Army television commercials put it, "To be all that you can be."

Such youngster protégé-sponsor relationships tend to be fleeting. In most cases, the protégé is too immature and self-centered to return much to the mentor. By college, graduate school, and first career job, however, the relationship potential increases. The history of academic stars is replete with stories of intense sponsor-protégé relationships where the senior professor took on an almost godlike role to the ambitious junior.[4] The senior is flattered that a bright young person admires his or her theories and the young scholar is thrilled to have the legend's guidance in reducing the threatening ambiguity of what is necessary for success.

Note the mixture of rationality and emotion. The mentor and protégé exchange skills and tasks: The student gathers data and crunches numbers while the professor conveys theory and experience. But also being exchanged is emotional reassurance—to the student who feels that someone important has confidence in him or her; to the professor, that in middle and older age, he or she is still admired and valued.

These dual task and emotional components are inherent in most mentoring relationships, but one or the other can be emphasized and at least partially separated. Thus, one person may primarily teach you about the organization and how to perform your tasks, while another provides comfort and support when you feel discouraged.

In looking back on the mentors in my life from the distance of many years, I think they took special interest in me because I reminded them of themselves. They correctly or incorrectly saw in me characteristics that they valued in themselves, be they looks, perseverance, intelligence, or commitment. By helping me to succeed, they validated the very attributes that for them explained their own success.

Mentoring Relations in Business. Surveys of middle and senior managers suggest that anywhere from 30 to 75 percent feel they have benefitted from mentorlike support from a senior colleague.[5] The great majority of protégé-mentor relations start when we are in our twenties and thirties. By the time we reach our forties, we appear to have outgrown our readiness to be the protégé of an older person, and hopefully, we have reached a level of influence and success that will allow us to begin mentoring others. The range of responses reflects the subjectivity of such relationships since most are informal and simply emerge. Although no data exist, it is possible that many mentors are not aware of the role they are playing for a protégé and that some protégés even may be insensitive to what their sponsor is attempting to do for them.

Regardless of awareness, however, the mentor's role falls on a commitment continuum: (1) passing on technical skills, (2) providing helpful "public" knowledge about career opportunities in the firm, (3) taking an emotional interest in the protégé, (4) helping the protégé understand the "ins and outs" of the organization by sharing "private" knowledge, (5) providing the protégé with high visibility opportunities to perform well, and (6) formally and informally pushing the protégé for promotions.

Teaching	Personal Support	Organizational Intervention	Promoting the Protege

Least ⊂===================COMMITMENT==================⟩ Most

Most mentoring is restricted to teaching and personal support, but the happy recipients of such support, in comparison with nonmentored peers seem to know more about their organizations, express greater job satisfaction, have better defined career plans, and greater commitment to their organizations.[6] Thus, we can have a circular chicken-egg situation: Having a mentor leads to better attitudes and performance which brings greater visibility and new opportunities to attach to high-flying star mentors.

Superupwardly mobile managers especially benefit from this ability to attach themselves to stars just a bit older and senior to them. They make it to senior executive level in approximately twelve years in comparison with most successful others who require sixteen to eighteen years.[7] As illustrated in the case of Judith Greene, it is not clear what is intentional or accidental in forming such vertical coalitions. The ambitious subordinate who is too blatantly political in seeking the sponsorship of a senior star is likely to offend his or her peers, immediate superior, and even the intended mentor. Nonetheless, effective young professionals simply don't wait for lightning to strike or their good performance to attract sponsors. They seek out information about their boss's goals, problems, and pressures.[8] They are more active in reaching out to senior others, at least to the extent of finding out what they do and investigating whose values and organizational dreams are most compatible with theirs.[9] As we saw in Chapter 5 on long-term time management, they don't allow their narrow job tasks to totally determine with whom they communicate. Former Senator Barry Goldwater recently advised new senators to find a mentor:[10]

"As soon as I got to the Senate, I had already picked out the man I admired and made it a point to get very close to him (e.g., Senator Robert A. Taft of Ohio) . . . I pretty much let him guide me. Every new senator needs a man like that, someone he feels free to go to for advice. You need somebody who's been around, who knows how to do things, knows the ins and outs, all the intricate maneuvers you don't learn overnight."

What is involved here is more reliability and trust than machiavellian politicking (although of course some of the latter is often present). An upwardly mobile star wants subordinates who are competent, reliable, and loyal, but whose loyalties are based on a shared vision rather than merely sycophancy for personal rewards. The senior wants upwardly mobile subordinates whom he or she can trust just as the would-be protégé wants a senior who can be followed with minimal compromise of personal integrity. As Goldwater puts it, "The greatest lesson that Washington teaches is no matter what you do, be honest. That sticks out in Washington" (and most every place else). His greatest presidential hero was Harry Truman because, "When he said something in the evening, he felt the same way the next morning."

Phases in Mentor-Protégé Relations. Many of us enjoy several mentors in our lives so any one is not usually permanent—at least not to the extent that we continue forever to interact with him or her.

Therefore, phases including a beginning and ending occur in most mentor-protégé relations.[11]

1. *Initiation.* A period of six months to a year when the relationship gets started and achieves importance for mentor and protégé. The protégé's dreams become concrete expectations. The senior manager provides coaching, challenging work, and visibility. The junior manager provides technical assistance, respect, and a desire to be coached. Communications occur around work tasks.
2. *Cultivation.* A period of two to five years during which career, social, and psychological support expands to a maximum. Both individuals continue to benefit from the relationship while interaction opportunities increase.
3. *Separation.* At some point, tension enters most mentor-protégé relations leading to change in feelings and behavior. Often the junior manager no longer wants guidance, but rather greater opportunity to work autonomously. Or the senior manager faces a career or midlife crisis and is less available to help. Or more simply, corporate transfers separate the individuals so social and psychological support can't be provided. However caused, the blocked opportunity can create resentment and hostility.
4. *Redefinition.* At some indefinite period after separation, the relationship may be reestablished but more like peer friendship. The mentor relationship is no longer needed and in time resentment and anger diminish. Gratitude and appreciation for past assistance may be acknowledged, but the protégé has established equal adult status.

To illustrate the evolution of these mentoring phases, I can review my own relationship over seventeen years with a mentor.

1964–1967: Initiation and cultivation. On leaving graduate school, I was hired as a lecturer by the management department head at the Wharton School of the University of Pennsylvania. He was an extremely strong leader who pushed hard for productivity while also acting as benevolent father (as leadership theory describes it, he exhibited high-task *and* high-consideration orientations). He assigned me to be a teaching assistant in his industrial relations course where he greatly valued my ability to teach the course on short (even no) notice if he was unable to make class because of his active outside affairs. He was extremely helpful in personal matters even providing a loan for moving expenses, inviting me to share in his consulting, and exercising his clout to get a prestigious university physician to travel out of state to treat my infant son when he became seriously ill. As a reward for my helpfulness and loyalty, he saw that I was promoted from Lecturer to Assistant Professor.

1968: Failure of mentorship. To the surprise of both my mentor and myself, however, my promotion to associate professor with tenure was rejected by our departmental faculty. The department head announced his immediate resignation because, in his view, his senior colleagues had blocked his protégé's promotion in retaliation for their disagreement with him about department policy. (Actually, it was probably resentment of what they viewed as his excessively authoritarian leadership.) He remained as a professor but resigned his administrative post.

1968–1969: Establishing a new relationship. My vulnerability as a protégé to a disliked senior was manifest in my being rejected as a political tactic to undermine the department head. Of course it was not "fair" that I was judged by my association rather than the merits of my work, but there was nothing I could do to change the past. I could work on the future, however.

I approached the full professor who seemed most opposed to the former department head to open a dialogue, not about the unfairness of my rejection, but around our mutual work. I asked for copies of his papers and sent him copies of mine with requests for his advice. I tried to have lunch with him or at least sit at the same luncheon table a couple of times a week. It all sounds quite manipulative in the retelling, but I discovered that our interests and values were actually much more similar than mine had ever been to those of the former department head. I came to admire this senior colleague very much. Although I had matured to the point where I no longer needed the parentlike social assistance that my first mentor had provided, I much appreciated my new mentor's intellectual guidance.

The replacement of my first mentor as department head and undoubtedly the now active support of my new sponsor resulted in my promotion sailing through after a transition year.

1970: Conflict with first mentor. During the first few years after his departure as department head, my former mentor and I maintained cordial relations, albeit sharply curtailed because I had moved on to my own courses and was no longer involved in his. However, at this time our relationship sharply deteriorated, virtually ending in anger and threats. Three incidents were involved: (1) I served on a faculty curriculum committee that voted to eliminate his course as a core requirement in the graduate program (although I voted against the change, his anger was directed to all committee members); (2) I wrote an article critical of the assertive, antiunion corporate policies which he favored; and (3) I grew a mustache which, trivial as it was, seemed to verify for him that I had joined the antiestablishment, countercultural forces then so threatening to campus conservatives.

1979–1981: Reestablishment. After being promoted to full professor in 1975, appointment as assistant to the president in 1979, and promotion to vice president of the university in 1981, my former mentor and I began to communicate infrequently but respectfully around money for his research center. Since I was responsible for university fundraising, he wanted my opinion on some proposals. By now, the heat of anger had faded, my reputation had been established in an area entirely separate from his, and I had achieved high status so that in his eyes I had become a peer (and I suppose I had finally escaped seeing him as a surrogate for my dead father).

1985–1986: Retirement and death. My former department head and mentor retired from the faculty during the same year that my second mentor and friend passed away. I remember with gratitude the fatherly assistance that my first mentor gave when I had just arrived still poor and concerned about my son's health. Yet, I realize that a break was inevitable even if his nomination of me for promotion hadn't been rejected. His domineering authoritarian style would have grated on me as I gained experience and confidence. I was probably lucky in that my initial promotion rejection forced me to be more assertive in reaching out to other older colleagues.

However self-seeking my intention in reaching out to the senior colleague who became my second mentor, it led to a long-lasting relationship greatly valued by us both. His widow told me after his death that when he went into the hospital for his final losing battle with leukemia he took with him a note I had sent him expressing my gratitude for what he had taught me about academic and human values. I still miss him.

My tale illustrates that mentor-protégé relationships are clearly not just emotionless instrumental exchanges. Sentiments and indeed passions can become involved that inflate the risk in things going sour, rather like a spoiled marriage. In academia, sexual relationships between mentoring professors and graduate students unfortunately have been quite common. And of course such affairs are not unknown in business. They are extremely dangerous to one's psychological well-being and career success—not to mention spiritual state.[12] Personally, I feel a professor bedding a student or a manager becoming involved with a subordinate is a most heinous act because of the coercion potential in their power difference. And of course, some unscrupulous students and ambitious subordinates have used their attractiveness and the older person's loneliness to manipulate them for personal gain.

Even if sex is not involved, mentor-protégé relations can involve strong emotions, especially when parent-child imagery is evoked. Escaping from sponsor domination or a protégé declaring his or her own identity can be difficult if both experience it as symbolic rejection of father or mother. Hence, like all human connections, being a mentor or a protégé involves risk of the senior being disappointed in the behavior and performance of a junior in whom time and political capital has been invested. Emotional insulation may be easier, but a manager's willingness to incur risks in committing to younger people is crucial to developing leaders.

Mentors for Minorities. Many people have suggested that women and minority professionals and managers experience special difficulty in finding mentors.[13] Since the mentor-protégé relationship is a mix of instrumentality and emotionality, people seem more comfortable identifying with someone more "like" them in gender and ethnicity. Cross-gender mentoring may be avoided because of the sexual innuendoes associated with it, although most successful female executives have benefitted from male mentors.[14] Ethnic and racial minorities may find it even more difficult to find mentors of the same backgrounds because of the underrepresentation of such minorities in middle and senior management. Even where senior minority executives are present, they may be so pressured with other minority representation pressures or so uncertain about their status that they don't have sufficient surplus energy to sponsor minority subordinates. And white male seniors may be reluctant to sponsor minorities in whom they have less confidence about their competence or ambition. They may fear losing points with their boss if a sponsored protégé subsequently fails or quits.

For some minority managers, however, social and psychological support are derived from two mentors—a majority senior who lends educational and political support and a minority senior who understands the special psychological challenges for a fellow minority professional.[15]

Peers as Mentors. Lacking satisfactory mentoring by an experienced superior manager, peers may serve as alternatives.[16] That is, a more experienced professional colleague may assist you in learning your tasks and understanding the organization's informal rules. Such people may even lend psychological support when you are confused or discouraged. This of course can be very helpful. Nonetheless, hierarchical peers are poor substitutes for a more knowledgeable and politically influential superior as mentor. Peers are likely to be somewhat competitive with only the most altruistic being unthreatened if you were to become exceptionally successful. Therefore, they might lend a hand when you are in obvious difficulty, but be less supportive if you are performing well.

Even more limiting, a peer as mentor is not able immediately to represent your interests upward in the organization by proposing you for challenging projects and promotions. Sometime in the future, however, such a person may move upward and be in a position to promote your career, so it is a wise effort on your part to develop and maintain good relations with those of your peers whom you most respect and find most congenial with your personal values and organizational aspirations. Note that your main criterion for identification should be congenial values and aspirations, not merely the peer's success. The art of forming viable vertical coalitions revolves around mentors with whom you can maintain your integrity because their values and dreams are consistent with yours. Thus, you are able to communicate candidly because you trust each other; you do not continually have to put on an act to maintain your status as valued protégé.

Assigned Mentors. To assist young graduates in adjusting to their first jobs, some firms have instituted formal mentoring programs.[17] A higher-level manager, usually not your immediate superior, is assigned as your mentor with specific responsibility for serving as a "wise godfather" to whom you can go for guidance. The intent is to ensure that a promising young professional is not hidden under a nonsponsoring first-line supervisor.

Although laudible in intent, such formal mentoring programs suffer from the handicap of formalizing the informal, rationalizing what is more a nonrational relationship. Mentor-protégé relations have a fragile chemistry that reflects mutual attraction based on shared styles or values. This could arise in a planned association, but it is certainly not automatic.

In addition, planning mentor-protégé relations implies that they are not occurring naturally. And if they are not, it probably reflects either vertical competition or narrowly focused interests of high achievers. As indicated, trust is critical to effective mentoring and managers are not likely to extend this downward if they perceive limited career advancement for themselves and fear being bypassed by ambitious juniors. Thus, a firm actively pruning middle management while still recruiting new graduates will have a hard time promoting mentorship among the uneasy middle.

Even in an expanding business, upwardly mobile managers may be just too busy and self-oriented to expend time on mentoring their juniors. It is a role that would seem to have no immediate payback. Unless top management builds feedback on mentoring performance into the performance evaluation and reward system, attention won't be paid.

One of the simplest reinforcements for formal or informal mentoring is for top management to insist that assigned protégés submit confidential evaluations of their mentor's helpfulness.[18] Confidence in confidentiality is critical, of course, for most of us would be reluctant to be candid if we thought that specific criticism of a hierarchical superior could be traced back to us.

WHAT JUDITH DID

Judith Greene accepted the position as vice president of administration, choosing to have her office located within the bullpen area containing the area supervisors, analysts, and support staff. She initially focused on improving conditions among the junior staff with minimal threat to the vice presidents and senior vice presidents. Some of her steps in the first couple of years were:

1. *Crackdown on inadequate clerical and support services.* Remember that analysts, especially the women, were particularly angry with their poor service and lack of respect from the predominantly female support staff. No one seemed to have either the interest or authority to impose discipline. Judith attacked this area first by dismissing the poorest performers, issuing threats to others, and instituting a more equitable work-order system. She chose a hard line because she wanted rapid improvement to demonstrate her potential to help analysts and supervisors. Of course she warned Marshall Wilde that there might be some complaints from the bank's human resources department, but it was easy for him to fend off such flack.

   The risk in this initial step was quite modest because it benefitted junior staff immediately while not affecting the senior officers.

She just moved into a power vacuum with the executive vice president's acquiescence. Judith did, however, run the risk of appearing to validate a token stereotype that she was really just a glorified office manager responsible for the typing pool.

2. *Redesign of the common room.* Judith implemented a total redesign of the common room moving to an open office landscape with modular furniture grouping of interdependent people based on geographic responsibilities. Although the regional supervisors' private cubicles were eliminated, the overall climate of the room was significantly improved with everyone now able to see the windows and the potted palms. More important, noise level was reduced while work communications were facilitated. Plus the expenditure of funds to improve the office was a symbolic communication to the junior officers of their importance (and of her clout).

If one were starting from scratch to design the layout of the international department at Trustworthy, one would probably take the whole floor as one's canvas, moving the senior officers out of their isolated luxury into regional configurations among their supervisors and analysts. Judith, however, concluded that such precipitent action would be too threatening to the senior officers and might strain Marshall Wilde's support. Therefore, rather than drawing on her mentor's political capital, she merely asked for the money to improve the common room, again an action which did not directly affect the senior officers.

3. *Representation and leadership of area supervisors.* As we saw, the vice presidents and senior vice presidents were too busy with their banking functions to devote time and energy to managing the area supervisors. Traveling, negotiating, and swinging deals were simply more interesting to the senior officers. Judith was able to move into this vacuum and develop power *vis-à-vis* the area supervisors by representing their interests upward to the executive vice president.

4. *Balancing analyst assignments.* Working with the area supervisors, Judith was able to develop a more equitable system for allocating tasks to the analysts. Thus, the most favored or most promising were no longer unfairly overloaded and assignment turnaround improved. Again, for the most part this was at a level of detail below the senior officers' attention, although it eventually improved the service they received.

5. *Coordinating recruiting, training, and performance reviews.* These activities were additional neglected areas into which Judith was able to move by simply initiating action with her mentor's approval. Using her developing political capital with the area supervisors, she was able to assist them in providing more timely performance feedback to the analysts.

6. *Job enrichment for area supervisors and senior analysts.* This was the first initiative which directly threatened senior officers. We've seen that they tended to be loners so that the junior professionals had little sense of how their work assisted senior officers in their duties. Judith got Marshall Wilde to mandate that senior officers will take one supervisor or senior analyst with them on all their visits with clients. The positive impact on junior officer morale was dramatic because this brought them closer to the action. To be sure, some of the senior officers complained about "babysitting" and how angry their wives would be if they traveled with a female subordinate (the illusions that middle-aged men have about their attractiveness to young professional women are quite extraordinary!), but they really had no legitimate counter to Marshall's implementation of Judith's job enrichment policy.

What is striking about Judith Greene's approach was her clever movement into the power vacuum, picking up tasks that were not formally assigned, but which no senior officer was performing. And her approach was incremental, minimizing drawing on her mentor's political capital while utilizing his financial resources to promote their shared vision of offering greater challenges to analysts and supervisors.

Marshall Wilde was certainly pleased with her contributions to the department. After two years, he made Judith president of a wholy-owned Trustworthy subsidiary (located in another city) of which he as the parent's international executive vice president was chairman. In assessing whether this was a career enhancing position, Judith had to judge whether it was a trip away from Trustworthy's power axis or whether it was a stage in an upward climb. Since six of the ten regional senior vice presidents and vice presidents had served as the subsidiary president, the appointment suggested that she was being groomed for a line banking post which was her ambition.

At the end of eighteen months as subsidiary president, she was prepared to return to any of the eight senior officer slots. And note that in moving to what is clearly the power axis, it would not be a demotion to return as the junior partner in a regional senior vice president-vice president pair (that is, her title would drop from president to vice president).

However, by this time Marshall Wilde had taken on the additional title of vice chairman of the bank with added responsibility for human resources and consumer banking, while still serving as international executive vice president. Judith was appointed senior vice president of administration with her office located next to the executive vice president (which was usually empty since Marshall worked out of his new vice chairman office). So it appeared that she might just bypass the regional vice presidency and move directly into the executive vice president position.

Judith's rapid movement was clearly fostered by her being Marshall Wilde's protégé. She was vulnerable, however, because of her identification with her sponsor. As fortune would have it, a leadership change at the top occurred and Marshall was forced out by a new chairman and president. The new leaders, however, recognized Judith's administrative skill and promoted her to international executive vice president. Still, Judith never felt quite comfortable with them and she rather quickly accepted the presidency of a smaller, regional competitor bank where she has done well.

Judith Greene was an effective protégé who was sensitive to her mentor's needs but still courageous in initiating positive actions based on his support.

ADVICE ON BEING A PROTÉGÉ

- Reach out to prospective mentors by expressing interest in their activities and drawing attention to your work. It is of course dangerous to appear too "obvious," but you can strive to be in their presence, to send them written ideas for their comment, or to join off-work service and charitable organizations in which you can demonstrate your leadership capability.
- Do not look to one mentor to carry you through a whole career; be active in reaching out to other seniors so as not to be invisible in the light from your primary mentor-star. Recognize that no relationship is permanent and that some stress is normal as you mature and move toward greater independence.
- Don't be afraid (or ashamed) to reach out to senior others who might have been rivals or enemies of your initial mentor. Express an interest in their work and invite them to give you advice.
- In cross-gender relationships, recognize the risks of sexual and romantic involvement (and avoid it!), but don't be so wary and defensive that you are unwilling to accept their support. However, keep the relationship professional by avoiding pet names, physical contact, and excessive private meetings—especially outside the office.
- Even with a same-sex mentor, don't romanticize the relationship. You may admire the person greatly, but don't be blind to his or her faults. No matter how successful, your mentor is not perfect. You might want to keep personal notes on their strengths and weaknesses.
- Recognize that all mentor-protégé relationships involve some "using" of the other person for personal gain. A mentor is never totally altruistic. He or she expects benefits from expressing an in-

terest in your career, so your critical task is finding ways to help, perhaps even becoming indispensable.

Of course you would like your mentor to be an upwardly mobile star who carries clout that can promote your career. More important, however, is that your basic ethical values and managerial philosophies be compatible. The relationship will probably backfire if you must continually compromise your own integrity in order to remain in his or her good standing. You would come to hate your mentor and he or she to see you as disloyal.

9

Loyalty and Whistle Blowing

TO ERR IS HUMAN
TO FORGIVE IS
NOT COMPANY POLICY

From *The Wall Street Journal,* with permission of Cartoon Feature Syndicate.

Loyalty is one of humankind's most admired virtues. From childhood we are taught to be loyal to one's family by not "airing its dirty linen" in public. And to "rat" or "fink" on your buddies' transgressions is *the* most heinous of sins to schoolmate groups. So it is not surprising that executives cite loyalty as a subordinate's most valued attribute. Yet, increasingly, firms express concern about employee loyalty. *The Wall Street Journal* poll of executives indicates that 55 percent agree that managers now are less willing to make sacrifices for their company and 70 percent feel that sagging loyalty has worsened the problem of declining productivity.[1]

I don't disagree with the importance attached to loyalty. It is after all the correlate of commitment to an institution which I advocate. Yet, if loyalty is blind, if loyalty is expressed in silence or in being a "yes man," the firm is likely to eventually fail and its loyal members to have compromised their integrity for naught. At times, therefore, you will be faced with a dilemma whether or not to blow the whistle on illegitimate policies and practices.

After examining a fast-track young manager facing just such a situation, we analyze various loyalty concepts and tactics for handling whistle blowing.

BILL AND J.P.'s DECISIONS AT SOUTHERN TEXTILE COMPANY

Southern Textile Company is a medium-sized, locally-owned single plant company located in a pleasant Carolina town. It manufactures several kinds of fabrics mainly for men's clothing. Most are blends of wool or cotton and synthetics. Its largest line is a wool and Dacron fabric for men's suits. Southern Textile does not manufacture the suits and it does no consumer advertising. It promotes and sells to clothing manufacturers.

Scene 1: President's office.
(present are J.P. the President; Bob, Vice President of Manufacturing; and Mike, Vice President of Marketing)

J.P.: Gentlemen, we have two subjects to discuss today. First, the shortage of Dacron for our suit fabric manufacturing operation; and second, developing the next generation of executives. Bob, what's the story on Dacron?

Bob: Well, as you know, we sell fabric containing Dacron and wool to various clothing manufacturers. Dacron is widely accepted and in great demand. It seems like everyone wants it, but Du Pont who owns the trade name, doesn't seem able to keep up with production. We just can't get enough, so we checked with a foreign manufacturing concern and they can supply synthetic fiber similar to Dacron at a 30 percent lower price.

J.P.: Then, what's the problem?

Mike: We can't sell anything but Dacron and wool. If we use another name we just won't sell anything. And I don't have the advertising budget to develop public awareness of a new fiber. I think we better just sell the stuff as Dacron. We've got to meet our obligations to good customers or we'll lose them to someone else who will be selling them Lord knows what.

J.P.: But suppose this substitute is not as good as Dacron?

Bob: But it is; we've run every test. It meets them all. It's really just as good as Dacron.

J.P.: But won't Du Pont find out that we're selling this stuff as Dacron?

Bob: I really doubt that they'd notice. We're small potatoes to them. Besides, it's their fault that they underestimated demand and didn't get their plants built.

Mike: Plus I don't think it would be in Du Pont's interest to make a stink about this. Why should they encourage someone to promote a competitive product and brand name when they know we'll all go back to them just as soon as they have the capacity to meet our needs? I think we should sell it as Dacron and wool. Bob, you can keep making tests to see if its quality holds up. I'll keep our purchasing manager trying to get Dacron from Du Pont. This could be only a temporary policy in order to maintain employment and meet our responsibilities to our customers and stockholders. What do you think, J.P.?

J.P.: I'll think about it and let you know. Okay, let's talk about the second issue. All of us are close to sixty-five and tough as it is to think about, we've got to plan for replacements in the next five years. We've got to develop our younger men; find promising young fellows among our people and give extra attention to bringing them along. It's important that we identify some strong and loyal younger managers. Jim Kuhn in Personnel has told me about the Executive MBA program up at Eastern University. They really give a person training in top management policy making. It would take someone away from us a couple of days every two weeks and for a month in the summer for a couple of years, but John Chappel over at Stevens Textile has sent two of his people up there and he thinks very highly of the result. One of his graduates is only forty but is now executive vice president.

Mike: I think it sounds like a good idea . . . and the guy to send is Bill Murphy. He's just the man—a State graduate, young, but knowledgeable, and hard working. Married to old man Simpson's daughter so she understands what it takes to succeed here at Southern. Bill's the best choice.

J.P.: That's a good suggestion, Mike. I had thought of Bill also. Send him around next week and I'll talk to him.

Scene 2: A week later. President's office. (present are the President, J.P., and William Murphy)

J.P.: Bill, I've called you to discuss your career and Southern's future. We all are aware that senior management is aging, and some are aching to spend more time trying to break ninety at Pinehurst. Since we hired few managers back in the 1960s and 1970s, I am concerned about training future replacements. We think you have the ability to move up in this firm. What do you think about Southern?

Bill: I like it very much here, sir. We have a good business and a nice group of people. Perhaps most important, we have a reputation for quality and integrity. It means a lot to me. My wife and I look forward to many years here.

J.P.: Fine, Bill. Because we think we can offer a lot. I want to move you into some jobs where you will get good, broad experience.

Bill: I'd like to move into positions of greater authority, sir, and be able to learn more.

J.P.: Good, Bill. We'd also like to send you up to Eastern University to their Executive MBA program. We'll pay your tuition and expenses and maintain your full salary while we reduce your duties here so you can keep up with your studies. You'll have an unrivaled opportunity to develop your ability for top management decision making.

Bill: It sounds like a terrific opportunity, sir.

J.P.: It is, Bill, and since the program will cost us about $60,000, making this offer reflects our confidence that you'll eventually be able to move into one of the senior jobs around here.

Bill: I'll have to talk to my wife about this, but I'm sure she will be as excited about the chance as I am. I look forward to going.

(Bill leaves)

J.P. (alone, to himself): Well, that's taken care of. Now, what do I do about that damned Dacron matter? If I don't move ahead, we're going to lose some customers for sure. And that means some people will be out of work around here.

Scene 3: Two years later at Eastern University.
(present: Bill Murphy and Frank, a classmate)

Bill: Frank, I can't believe this program is ending already. At times when the work piled up, it seemed endless, but I guess time flies when you're suffering.

Frank: Well, I'm glad it's over! I guess I didn't take to the academics as easily as you. I thought some of the profs were hopelessly idealistic and naive. But you really impressed them. Your grades must rank at the top of the class.

Bill: I was really helped by my understanding company. They gave me the time and resources to do the work.

Frank: I've told my boss at B.I.G. Electronics about you, Bill. He says he'd like to meet you. I should have kept my big mouth shut. You'll probably get my job.

Bill: You're nuts. I'm happy with Southern Textile. I've got a great opportunity there and it's a fine company. My wife especially likes the fact that it's a stable business in a nice small city. No traveling and great opportunities for hiking and fishing with the kids. The pay is not earthshaking, but it should get better now.

Frank: Well, I'm glad to hear that. But my boss will be down here next month, and he made me promise to line up a meeting with you. I'd be indebted if you'd talk to him.

Bill: Okay, but it'll be a waste of time.

Scene 4: A week later at Eastern University.
(present: Bill and Henry Riggs, President of B.I.G. Electronics Co.)

Henry: Bill, Frank has told me so much about you that I feel I know you already. I've been asking around and you've made quite an impression on the faculty and other students here.

Bill: Well, that's very nice of you to say, Mr. Riggs.

Henry: Call me Hank, Bill. I'll put my case right on the table. I can offer you a terrific opportunity in a dynamic company in one of the fastest growing industries in the world. We need drivers, go-getters who can keep up with our tremendous expanding market. We want you in our New York headquarters to help direct our multinational operations.

Bill: But, I'm happy at Southern Textile.

Henry: I know, Bill, but we offer growth, challenge, and innovation. Our potential profits are enormous—which means that we can offer some financial advantages. I know that money isn't your primary concern in all this, but I could probably double your present salary right away. And our top management salaries are probably four times what they are at your firm. It'll mean moving but also exciting travel and a chance to join the most innovative management team in America. You would be one of my right-hand men and I'd push your career

hard. You can think about it for a couple of days of course, but I want
to get this train moving.

Bill: Well . . . Okay, I'll consider it.

♫·♫·♫·♫

WHAT IS BILL MURPHY'S DILEMMA?

J.P., the President of Southern Textile Company, has made a laud-
able commitment to developing future executive strength internally by
sending Bill Murphy to graduate school. But this admirable commitment
to the "family" nature of the firm is also encouraging him to consider
substituting an off-brand fiber for the trademarked Dacron without informing his textile customers. J.P. might initiate this deception on a
"temporary" basis in the interest of "protecting" the firm's integrity and
the security of its employees—and of course holding onto current customers and profits.

Rejecting the president's specious reasoning is easy: Substituting
the fiber and selling it mislabeled is against the law. If discovered, it is
likely that Du Pont would have to press charges so the illegal behavior
would become public and Southern's customer reputation severely damaged with possible adverse consequences on employees and owners—
perhaps even bankruptcy. We can't assess the probability of detection
and punishment, but such damage should weigh heavily against illegal
activity even if the chances were that Southern would not be caught.

More profoundly, such deceptive behavior constitutes lying to customers and stealing of Du Pont's property. The negative impact on morale and loyalty of such immoral behavior could damage Southern's internal climate. Even if only a small number of people were supposed to
know, leaks would occur and knowledge of the decision would be known
more widely. Indeed, Bill Murphy has already heard some rumors.

Murphy's personal dilemma is actually a bit more complex than the
president's. His decisions fall into two general issues: (1) Does he stay or
leave? (2) Does he act or not act on his knowledge of the unidentified
fiber substitute? And neither of these is a simple yes or no matter.

Before considering Bill's decisions, let's examine various criteria for
assessing loyalty and then consider the question of whistle blowing.

CONCEPTS OF LOYALTY

Loyalty is a popular but vague concept subject to both praise and
scorn. Most managers highly value subordinates' loyalty. But what they
mean by the term varies widely. Expectations for subordinate loyalty in-

clude: (1) stay here, (2) obey me, (3) work hard, (4) sacrifice, (5) be successful, whatever it takes, (6) protect me and don't let me look bad, and (7) tell me the truth. All of these concepts are partially valid and can contribute to organizational effectiveness. Unfortunately, all can also be distorted, to the detriment of the individual and the organization.

Loyalty as Staying. The classic notion of corporate loyalty implied the following series of actions. A company gave a would-be manager a job, for which he should feel grateful.[2] As long as he put up with unilateral moves, time away from family and dictatorial bosses, he had a place—a strong attraction to depression era children. The firm, in turn, expected him to stand by it, almost right or wrong, against all outsiders.

Unfortunately, this version of loyalty rewarded unimaginative and risk-adverse employees as well as its more productive ones. In time, many firms became top or middle heavy with staff professionals and managerial employees of marginal contributions. And it was precisely these people who were targeted for pruning in the competitive-inspired downsizings of the 1980s.[3] Unfortunately, outstanding contributors were also caught in staff reductions with the result that many (perhaps most) employees today see corporate loyalty to them as essentially dead (a point doubly made by senior executives who desert in the face of an outside takeover). In turn, this reduces everyone's inclination to stay if things aren't working out. Those with the best credentials and most in demand, naturally, are most likely to leave.

Loyalty as Obedience. A superior may equate a subordinate's loyalty with doing what he or she is told. All managers have a right to expect obedience, but excessive emphasis on it enshrines the "yes man" stereotype as organizational principle. Understandably, a subordinate's willful disobedience could be construed as disloyalty, but equating loyalty and obedience assumes that authoritarian management is the only valid style, while it ignores the possibility that loyalty may sometimes reside in *not* doing what the boss has ordered because disaster could follow. Newton Minow, who was President Kennedy's Chairman of the Federal Communications Commission, is quoted as saying that in April 1962, after a story that was highly critical of Kennedy was broadcast on NBC's evening news, Kennedy called Minow. As Minow recalled the conversation:[4]

J.F.K.:	Did you see that goddamn thing on Huntley-Brinkley?
Minow:	Yes.
J.F.K.:	I thought they were supposed to be our friends. I want you to do something about that.

Implied was that the FCC chairman might explore putting pressure on NBC by stalling license renewal or imposing stricter regulation. Minow said that he did not do anything, but called a Kennedy aide the next morning and asked him to tell the president that he was lucky to have an FCC chairman who "does not do what the president tells him to." Kennedy reportedly understood (after he cooled off) and later called Minow to thank him.

More common than the boss losing his temper and issuing a poorly thought-out directive is when high-level executives are too distant in time and space from the action to really know what is going on. The classic military example is the horrible casualties suffered in France by British Army forces in World War I when supreme commanders well behind the lines ordered repeated infantry attacks across hip-deep mud fields of which they knew nothing. Hundreds of thousands of men died because there was no legitimate way to disobey what were ludicrous orders.[5] After the 1973 Yom Kippur War, the Israel Defense Forces changed its war doctrine to allow a field commander to disobey the orders of superior officers in the rear if it was clear that they had no grasp of the tactical situation.[6]

Loyalty as Effort. Young managers and professionals rightly are expected to work hard in their firm's interest. Superiors are skeptical of young employees who make minimal commitment to their work. Yet, when effort and hours worked are equated with loyalty, people tend to put in excessive hours without real contribution.

> A young insurance manager complains: "Contribution tends to be judged in terms of time spent in the office, not things accomplished. If you want to get ahead, you come in on Saturdays regardless of whether it is necessary or not. The cafeteria and offices are sometimes filled with people who just feel they can't afford not to come in on Saturday."

Thus, behavior can become a game of "face time" to convince others of your loyalty, even when it contributes little to organizational performance. One of the central scenes in Abe Burrows's play and movie, "How to Succeed in Business Without Really Trying," portrays the young Machiavellian hero coming into his World Wide Wicket Corporation office early Saturday morning to decorate his desk with empty coffee cups and cigarette butts so that he would appear to have worked all night when the president came in to pick up his golf clubs.

Unfortunately, the face-time ethic still applies in too many corporate cultures. A *Fortune* article quotes a consultant who was talking with the managing partner of a Big Eight accounting firm.[7] He commented on a junior associate who seemed to him to be on the firm's fast track:

I said, "that fellow looks like partner material."
"Nope," the senior partner replied. "He'll never make it. He leaves at 5:30 and doesn't come in on Saturdays. At this firm, you're expected to work till 7:30 every night. Half days on Saturdays."
"But how necessary is all that extra time?" I asked.
"It's not that," the partner said. "It's the discipline."

One result of such expectations is the average executive's work week during 1979 to 1985 increased from 53 to 56 hours per week—and vacation days taken declined from 16 days per year to 14.[8]

A prominent management consultant has suggested that employers and employees need to come to a new kind of understanding whereby "each can trust the other, recognizing that each side has appropriate self-interest." Thus, the employee manager says in effect, "I will give the organization intensity of effort, providing the organization in return is fair to me—in particular, that it doesn't con me about opportunity when there no longer is opportunity[9]."

Loyalty as Sacrifice. The test of ultimate effort is to require significant sacrifice as a test of faithfulness—hence, its centrality in most religious traditions. In family and tribal maturation rituals, such sacrifice has taken the form of self-denial or mutilation. It is less dramatic in business, of course, but "being the good soldier" without complaint, or even "taking a dive" for the boss is not unknown. As Gordon Gekko, the fictional villainous tycoon in the film "Wall Street" in effect puts it to his young protégé: You are either with me or against me, either willing to sacrifice your integrity with illegal inside activity or you are disloyal and not worthy of the goodies I can dispense.

Such extreme examples are not confined to the cinema. Three years ago, one of my neighbors was courted by a firm to become its vice president of marketing. Part of the deal included granting him the right to bring three associates from his past company (one of the three being his sister). After six months in the new firm, the chairman required him to show his commitment by dismissing all three. Since the vice president didn't want to be seen as a job hopper, he didn't immediately resign, but complied—which certainly soured his feeling for the company. But then, the chairman hired as one of the replacements reporting to the vice president, the (somewhat ne'er-do-well) son of the firm's executive vice president. Having no say in hiring a subordinate manager is particularly grating for almost everyone and in this case provoked my neighbor's immediate resignation.

What prompted the chairman to give such a counterproductive demand? During the original negotiation, he was probably so anxious to hire my neighbor that he promised anything. Either he was deceitful in hiding his intention to force the three out, or he only later concluded to test the loyalty of his new executive.

Sacrifice as loyalty usually involves less extreme demands than Gekko's or my neighbor's former employer; usually it is to put the company ahead of family expectations or personal recreation. This may take the form of working late regularly or during crises, postponing or canceling vacations, and accepting corporate transfers without complaint. In growth periods particularly, the so-called "IBM" syndrome ("I've been moved") is a near universal among managers on the fast track. (During its period of most rapid expansion, upwardly mobile managers at General Electric on the average moved every eighteen to twenty-four months.) Refusing a promotion requiring a move has probably been *the* most detrimental career decision because of its being seen as an act of disloyalty.

The growth in dual-career marriages and a supposedly stronger desire to balance vocational and personal life may be reducing the willingness of young managers to sacrifice for the firm. And 1980s retrenchment has led to reduced promotion and transfer rates. Nonetheless, sacrifice as a test of career seriousness and corporate loyalty is by no means extinct.

Loyalty as Success. Superiors can see loyalty as synonymous with successful performance whatever it takes. (And don't bother them if it entails shady activities they shouldn't know about, thus preserving "plausible deniability.") Honest effort is a reasonable expectation, but this version of loyalty adds a moral criterion to competence judgment. Not all young managers who miss deadlines are disloyal; the task may simply be impossible within legal or ethical limits. A superior who judges people and performance from such a loyalty perspective will discourage honest communication and encourage illicit managerial practice to achieve the success he or she demands. Hitler and Stalin at various times both suffered from making decisions based on unrealistically optimistic information from field commanders. Knowing that their paranoic leaders judged all failure (and even just unpleasant communications) as a mark of disloyalty to be punished, local officers would at best refrain from sending any messages and at worst would issue wildly optimistic reports. Thus, based on messages he received for three days, Stalin seemed to think that the Soviet Army was rebelling Nazi forces after their 1941 invasion.[10] In fact, the

Russians were in full flight, but everyone was afraid to communicate the truth. The current Soviet leader Mikhail Gorbachev is still dealing with the administrative deficiencies of a system that has treated failure as disloyalty.

Loyalty as Protection. Most superiors expect subordinates to protect them and the organization from ridicule. Subordinates who follow their superior's instructions to the exact letter *are* disloyal if they do not exercise common sense to fill in obvious gaps—particularly if the subordinates are specialists with more expertise in their areas than their manager. In return for subordinate concern such as Newton Minow expressed to President Kennedy, the superior implicitly promises to promote the subordinate's progress.

This loyalty concept sometimes includes an injunction to subordinates never to disagree with the superior in public, especially when the boss's boss or outsiders are present. This expectation is fair, but it can become dangerously distorted when a sharp distinction is made between "us" to whom loyalty is due and "them" to whom it is not. Group effort to conceal their mistakes reflects this view of loyalty. Thus, leaks of truth to outsiders is one of the most heinous antiorganization crimes because it threatens the hierarchy's security. Insecure executives especially fear that some subordinates will try to make them look bad in order to get their positions. Sometimes this motivation is attributed to a young manager even when it doesn't exist.

An especially destructive version of equating loyalty with protection is the expectation that loyal members will believe any top management lie no matter how preposterous. Fascist and Communist dictatorships have been particularly prone to escalating lies to cover up past failures and crimes, so the ultimate loyalty test becomes your willingness to at least accept the lie and better, repeat it to others. Unfortunately, this corruption can also infect democratic government and private enterprise.

Former Secretary of Defense Robert MacNamara argued that he had a right and obligation to disagree with President Lyndon Johnson about the Vietnam War, *but only in private.*[11] And if he was unsuccessful in convincing his boss to change his policy (as he apparently was), his obligation was to resign *and forever withhold public criticism.* In this view, even if one retains a private sense of integrity, loyalty demands sacrifice of one's public reputation.

Executives have a right to expect loyalty from you against competitors and detractors, but not loyalty against the law, against common morality, or against society itself. As a former IBM executive put it:[12]

Managers must warn employees that a disservice to customers, and especially to innocent bystanders, cannot be a service to the company. Finally, and most important of all, managers must stress that excuses of company loyalty will not be accepted for acts that place its good name in jeopardy.

Loyalty as Good Citizenship. A positive form of sacrifice is to view loyalty as being a "good soldier," that is, behavior that goes beyond the letter of the law, or going beyond the book in using one's common sense to do what is appropriate even if your boss neglects to give you specific orders. In the military, one form of retaliation to a disliked superior is to do exactly but *only* what he tells you to do. So if he neglects to tell you to turn off the jeep's engine and remove the keys, you might just leave it running until it is out of gas or stolen. Such impertinence might cost you something, but in a more serious situation the superior would probably bear the brunt of blame.

Four elements characterize being a good citizen: (1) the time and effort consumed in going beyond your assigned duties might lessen your performance on your official task; (2) your specific assistance is spontaneous rather than planned; (3) it is unlikely that your immediate action would be recognized by the organization's formal reward system; and (4) your action contributes to the performance of the group or organization.[13]

Why do such a thing? The strongest predictor of such behavior appears to be commitment growing out of job satisfaction. Employees who feel good about themselves and their jobs are more likely to perform acts of citizenship. Although specific acts are not usually rewarded, superiors tend to evaluate good citizens more highly. A kind of halo effect makes average performers appear more valuable to the firm.

Loyalty as Honesty. Where loyalty is seen as honesty, truth is valued over harmony.[14] Superiors expect subordinates to warn them of impending failure before the control system detects it. Openness and trust in vertical communications is particularly critical in firms with serious commitment to ethical standards.[15] Young managers may feel threatened by this standard because it tells them to report their own mistakes. As we've seen, their experience may warn against such exposure. A Turkish proverb advises, "He who delivers bad news should have one foot in the stirrup."

Most people prefer not to report impending failure in the hope that it will go away or that no news will be interpreted as good news. To the former chief executive officer of ITT, Harold Geneen, this omission of bad news was a serious managerial crime.[16] In effect he warned, "Don't let me be surprised by unpleasant news; not to report failure *before* it produces adverse results is worse than the failure itself."

One of the most distasteful inversions of a subordinate's obligation to his or her superior of communicating truth occurred in the U.S. Housing Department under Samuel R. Pierce during the Reagan administration. Secretary Pierce instructed his executive assistant Deborah Gore Dean to shelter him from bad news. By memo he "instructed" her "to omit any 'negative' news articles from those related to the department that she prepared for his perusal every morning[17]." The subsequent financial scandals of which former Secretary Pierce claims he had no knowledge testify to the folly of an executive cutting himself off from bad news. *Nothing* is so destructive to long-term performance—and little else so distorts a boss's concept of loyalty than to impel a subordinate to *not* communicate the truth upward.

The Dilemma. You may not always know what version of loyalty is expected by your organization. You may even discover that your boss entertains several contradictory views, expecting strict obedience but becoming angry if this leads to poor performance, or interpreting mistakes as disloyalty but still expecting advance warning of impending failure. Loyalty expectations may violate your personal values when no excuse for failure is acceptable and the hierarchy must be protected at all costs. Under such unhappy circumstances, the only viable solution may well be departure.

More creative subordinates, however, find ways to precipitate a superior's reexamination of what is really intended so that loyalty is perceived primarily as effective contribution to objectives. Consider an incident that Simon Ramo, the founder of an enormously successful defense electronics firm, tells about how General Bernard Schriever, the first director of the ICBM program, handled his boss Harold Talbott, the Secretary of the Air Force at the time.[18]

> At one point early in the program, a rocket-engine contractor who had lost out in the competition succeeded in gaining Talbott's support to reopen the decision and elbow his way into the project. Talbott came to Los Angeles for the purpose of changing the contractors which the Project Office has chosen.
>
> We were absolutely certain that the contractor Talbott was pushing, who had been properly evaluated against competition, was of marginal competence. It was critical to Schriever and me not to toler-

ate pressure to include unacceptable contractors who had used political influence to gain what management wouldn't give them.

Each of us was reluctant to challenge the Secretary and we sat there speechless at first, each gauging the effect of bucking a high-level presidential appointee. Schriever was an outstanding young general whose career might be ruined if he chose not to cooperate with the Secretary of the Air Force. . . .

It was General Schriever, the one with the most to lose, who beat (me) to the draw in replying. He told the Secretary that complying with the directive would impair the program and coolly explained why . . .

Talbott, glowered, then lost his temper. He was a handsome, well-built man, elegant in attire and seemingly always poised, so it was scary to see him come apart, get red in the face, and with an ugly expression yell at Schriever: "Before this meeting is over, General, there's going to be one more colonel in the Air Force!" He had given Schriever an order, he ended his tirade by saying, and expected to be obeyed.

"I can't accept the directive, Mr. Secretary," General Schriever said calmly, quietly, but with a very clear enunciation, "because I have a prior and overriding order. On being handed this assignment, I was directed to run this program so as to obtain an operational ICBM capability in the shortest possible time." His manner displayed no challenge or disrespect. He added, after a pause, that perhaps Talbott might wish to put in writing an order specifically naming his choice of contractor to replace the one already selected, and at the same time lower the priority of General Schriever's assignment.

The redness left Talbott's face and he turned pale. He made no comment and began to stare at the table, vigorously tapping a pencil on it and trying to pull himself together. He undoubtedly was thinking that if he put his directive in writing, he might have to cite more of his reasons for it than he would like . . .

In a few moments, his face returned to normal. With the fewest of words, he said to leave the contractor decision as it was and left. . . . (Later) he went about singing the praises of the ICBM program's management team.

WHISTLE BLOWING

Disclosing an employer's illegal or unethical activities to insiders *or* outsiders is the most common definition of whistle blowing. Some would extend the concept to an employee's refusal to perform such an activity even if he or she doesn't report it to anyone.

The Risk in Whistle Blowing. Blowing the whistle is not a step to be taken without thought. The consequences can be severe for the employee and his or her family because so many managers and colleagues view such behavior as disloyal, usually expressed in earthier terms like "ratting" and "finking." James Roche, a former chairman of General Motors, once said:[19]

> Some critics are now busy eroding support of free enterprise—the loyalty of the management team, with its unifying value of cooperative work. Some of the enemies of business now encourage an employee to be disloyal to the enterprise. They want to create suspicion and disharmony, and pry into the proprietary interests of the business. However this is labeled—whistle blowing, industrial espionage or professional responsibility—it is another tactic for spreading disunity and creating conflict.

Roche's blunt comments were made during the height of the anti-business climate of the early 1970s and today's business leaders would probably be more temperate in their words. Nonetheless, most managers still harbor deep skepticism about whistle blowers. Deeply disturbing are the lengths some corporations have gone to discredit a whistle-blowing employee through blatantly false accusations, unfair dismissals, and industry blackballs.[20] Employee economic hardship, family stress, divorce, and even suicide have been all too frequent.[21]

The strength of organizational rejection reflects the unhappy fact that some whistle blowing stems from employee manipulation of the firm to cover up the complainer's incompetent or dishonest behavior, or even to seek revenge on a disliked superior. Although not common, such cynical whistle blowing occurs with sufficient frequency to exacerbate management response to more valid initiatives.

So one should think carefully about one's motivation and about the credibility of one's tale before acting. The whistle blower must balance a variety of loyalties, obligations, and values: (1) an employee's obligation to the firm, (2) obligations to colleagues, (3) ethical obligations to one's profession, (4) responsibility to customers and the general public, (5) family vulnerability, and (6) sense of personal integrity.

Increase in Whistle Blowing. Most Americans believe in theory that whistle blowing is legitimate and most of us have a desire to do the right thing when we observe unethical or illegal behavior at work. Nonetheless, several organizational factors may block us from acting:

- Strong role models such as senior officers who are involved in unethical (even if unrelated) behavior. One fears that such people would not be sympathetic to your disclosures.
- Strict adherence to a chain of command principle. Firms that stress top-down authoritarian decision making and discourage upward open-door communications do succeed in holding the lid on internal complaints.
- A great number of hierarchical levels. Distance and invisibility tend to discourage internal dissenters from acting on their complaints.
- Rigid division of work. Sharply defined, separated, and narrowly specialized position assignments hinder awareness of and disclosure of unsatisfactory situations.
- Ambiguous organizational priorities. Where top leadership is not visibly active in articulating organizational missions and values, even loyal subordinates have difficulty in judging whether local behavior is desired or not desired.

Whistle blowing for what the individual perceives as positive reasons does seem to be increasing for reasons that reflect well on American society: the civil rights movement, the consumer movement, environmental protectionism, and greater sensitivity to the impact of private actions on public rights. And perhaps the courage required to blow a whistle is now a bit less. Economic expansion and relatively full employment, particularly among professional and technical employees, make it is less difficult to find another position.

Protection for Whistle Blowers. Greater willingness to go public with complaints also reflects an expansion of legal protection for such employees. Most federal laws in the last twenty years have contained specific provisions protecting whistle blowers, but the application is usually only to the specific issues in that law such as racial, gender, or age discrimination, mine safety, or water pollution, clean air, and so on. The typical phrase is, "An employer may not discriminate against any employee because such person has opposed any practice made unlawful by the (Age Discrimination in Employment Act) or has made a charge, testified, assisted or participated in any manner in an investigation, proceeding or litigation under the ADEA."[22]

This federal protection is of limited usefulness to most employees in private industry, however, and Congress will undoubtedly be considering broader measures. In the meantime, some states have passed legislation protecting whistle blowers. The Conscientious Employee Protection Act of New Jersey, for example, prohibits retaliation against employees who disclose illegal corporate activity or testify about such matters. Nonetheless, the predominant legal precedent in this country has been "employment at will," a common law principle that permitted an employer to fire an employee "for good cause, for no cause, or even for a morally wrong cause." Although under pressure in some states, this is still the traditional attitude of most jurists and legislators toward dismissal (especially of managerial staff).

Firms also need protection from self-serving employees and false accusations. In particular, whistle-blower protection laws should not be used to promote employee disagreement with company policies that are sanctioned by society—for example, to oppose activities such as legally accepted animal experimentation or to manufacture nuclear weapons for the Defense Department. Protesting such corporate activity may be desirable in a democratic society, but essentially as an off-the-job activity, not as resource consuming, time demanding, and internally disruptive whistle blowing. Therefore, legislation in this area must be carefully drawn to minimize court clogging and organizational inefficiencies from trivial and malevolent appeals.

As with most matters of human relationships, governmental legislation is never sufficient. No law can protect a whistle blower from the heartache of being rejected by former friends. Some corporations and a few independent assistance groups have tried to deal with the dilemma by offering psychological support and sometimes anonymity to whistle blowers. Within corporations, the introduction of ombudsmen is probably the most common response.[23] A senior executive operating outside the formal chain of command is permanently available at the end of a hot line to deal with employee complaints on a confidential basis. The Corporate Ombudsman Association founded in 1982 has enrolled numerous *Fortune 500* companies.

The "Whistleblower Assistance Fund" was founded in 1985 to help support those who have become "psychologically or economically devastated" because they challenged abuses at work. Another organization, the Project on Military Procurement, deals with what it calls "closet patriots"—people employed in the military or by defense contractors who see flagrant abuses and come forward as an act of conscience. Fearful of losing their jobs if they go public, employees are promised anonymity by the project which investigates and makes its conclusions available to the public.

WHAT BILL MURPHY MIGHT DO

Assessing the difficulty of Murphy's situation depends on our assumptions about the Southern Textile Company's decision concerning substituting an unlabeled foreign fiber for Dacron.

If Murphy Does Not Know of the President's Decision. If the president had decided not to use or sell the foreign substitute fiber as Dacron, or if Bill knew nothing about the firm's duplicity, his decision whether or not to return to Southern would depend solely on his own judgment of self-interest and loyalty. Self-interest in this case would have to include family concerns because they have been so central to his life. He would have to compare opportunities for self-growth, economic benefits, and quality of life. What career path would provide greater challenge to grow now and in the future? Southern is more predictable and secure, but would he become bored? B.I.G. Electronics sounds exciting, but would he really be able to handle the pace that is implied? And would Henry Riggs be as reliable a mentor as J.P.?

The dollar income now and in the future would appear substantially greater at B.I.G., but that must be weighed against the higher cost of living (and probably higher expectations and aspirations) of living in New York City or its expensive suburbs. Riggs says he could "double" Murphy's present salary, but this would not be 100 percent greater than the salary Murphy might receive shortly after his return to Southern. And I doubt that B.I.G.'s salary would allow him to duplicate the quality of housing he presently enjoys.

In assessing quality of life, beauty is clearly in the eye of the beholder because measurement is so subjective. Listening to his words about life in the small-city South and its opportunities for time with his children, hiking and fishing, suggests that Bill and his wife would feel more at home in staying with Southern. Nonetheless, others find it stultifying when job and social life are so integrated that personal privacy becomes difficult. Working in the big city facilitates divorcing one's personal life from the job and allows a more diverse cultural mix—even as leisure time is reduced.

Bill Murphy has no legal obligation to stay with Southern. The courts long ago threw out contracts obligating employees to stay with employers as compensation for their investment in the employee's training. Such a requirement would be involuntary servitude. Bill, however, may have a loyalty issue depending on his vision of loyalty. He appears to have four choices: (1) simply return to Southern with faith in the firm's salary and position assignment; (2) attempt to bargain with Southern for an acceptable salary increase and/or clarity about immediate and future promotions (being willing to leave if response is not adequate); (3) accept B.I.G.'s offer (perhaps with some effort to clarify immediate duties and future potential); and (4) expand his search by exploring other opportunities.

Clearly, Southern Textile has invested in his future and demonstrated a commitment to developing him as an individual. They did not test him against the labor market in deciding to make that investment. Nonetheless, the firm's motivation rests on its own economic interest and it would be likely to pursue that interest even if, for some unforeseen reason, to do so would mean getting rid of Murphy.

I have put Murphy's dilemma before many of my executive program, graduate, and undergraduate students: 60 percent say they would basically stay and 40 percent say they would accept B.I.G.'s or another offer. Approximately, a quarter of those leaving (10 percent of all students) say they would try to get their new employer to reimburse Southern for the expense of the Executive MBA program. It appears that a majority of the respondents would interpret loyalty in this case to include making some sacrifice of greater income and opportunity in return for the benefits of returning to Southern Textile.

If Murphy Knows of Mislabeled Substitute. Bill's decision to stay or leave is probably easier because Southern's reputation for integrity has loomed large in his evaluation of the firm. Leaving now would undoubtedly provoke much less anxiety and guilt than if the illicit substitute had not been used. Nonetheless, he still has several choices: (1) leave without saying anything inside or outside the firm; (2) attempt to bargain with Southern that he would stay if this illegal activity stops (and not say anything outside the firm); (3) blow the whistle externally, either publicly or anonymously, through communication to customers or legal authorities.[24]

The vast majority of my managerial and student respondents, under this condition of knowledge about the mislabeled fiber, indicate that they would quietly fold their tents and leave, without giving anyone inside or outside of Southern the reason for their departure. This appears to be the simplest path to balance loyalty and personal integrity. Reticence to report the illegal activity to anyone is rationalized on grounds similar to the firm's management—that the fiber is almost as good as Dacron, that manufacturers and consumers are not really being hurt, and that Du Pont will soon be able to reclaim the market. What is not stated of course is their desire to avoid the hassle of being a whistle blower.

ADVICE FOR BEING LOYAL AND WHISTLE BLOWING

- Don't obey orders that you know to be illegal or against the best interests of the firm, your superior's performance, or your reputation. The ability to say "no" (which doesn't come easily) is the highest demonstration of loyalty.[25]
- Strive to find an organization that believes loyalty is reflected in hard work, but not useless "face time"; in trying to please your superior, but not in blind obedience; in protecting your firm's reputation, but not in false communications. Most of all, try to work for a firm that believes that communicating upward truthfully and candidly is the mark of a loyal employee.
- Don't be naive in blowing the whistle. And don't expect to be a hero in your organization. Be very analytic and careful in assessing the facts on which your case would be based. Can you document company wrongdoing in a way that would persuade a skeptical reporter or a dispassionate judge that the actions and motives of management are what you say they are?
- Consult your family. Explain why you feel it is necessary to act and try to win their support. Be frank in acknowledging that they may be hurt.
- If you decide to go ahead, determine just what kind of company conduct you are protesting. If it is clearly illegal or unsafe conduct, you can hope to be vindicated and still work in the same job or industry. But if it is the lawful business or social policies that you feel you must protest, be aware that you will probably be dismissed.
- Inform yourself fully of company procedures for appealing up through the chain of command to the highest available management level. Get a written copy of such complaint procedures and follow them rigorously.
- Decide whether you want to act anonymously or publicly. If you want to keep your identity secret, consider consulting a whistle-blower group or an investigative reporter.
- Before and while moving through internal channels, document your position at every step of the way. Keep a log of everything that happens.
- If the problem is one that is regulated by law, learn what the procedures are for lodging a complaint with the relevant government agency. Look out for the time limits and whether complaints must be made first to company officials before the government.

- Stay on your best behavior with superiors and peers. You don't want to create any additional problems for yourself.
- If you are fired or forced to resign because of your protest, be aware that your right to discuss the case in public is strong but not unlimited. There could be some "gag-ruling" limitations while litigation is pending or if confidential proprietary information is involved.
- If you cannot win damages or reinstatement through an appeal to a government regulatory agency (if any) with jurisdiction over the issue you have raised, be ready to consider a lawsuit alleging that your discharge or punitive treatment violates public policy.
- Recognize that you will face ethical dilemmas no matter how moral you try to be. No evidence exists that unethical managers are more successful than ethical ones, but those who are less socially conscious may be promoted a bit faster. Therefore, periodically you should examine your personal values and question how much you will sacrifice for the firm. Try to define what is your personal line of compromise beyond which you will not retreat.
- Courage is usually required to depart from unethical situations, but it can be even tougher to stay. Staying implies you either acquiece at the expense of your integrity or that you will strive to change what is being done.[26] And this means accepting responsibility and a measure of guilt while things are cleaned up. But this is what leadership is all about.
- Do not automatically accept all the tales of managerial perversity that you hear. Attributing others' success to unethical behavior is sometimes an excuse for one's own personal inadequacies. Most of all, don't commit a wrongful act in the hope that your superior will see it as loyalty and reward you for it. Some will of course, but they may also sacrifice you when the firm is criticized.
- Above all, strive to find a firm that generally shares your personal values. Ask prospective colleagues what principles you would be fired for violating. If they can't think of anything beyond stealing, the firm is not likely to value much else (or if it does, it hasn't communicated what). If, on the other hand, they can cite behavior which you also find unacceptable, you may have an employer with which you will feel compatible.

10

Being Different in the Organization

"No, I'm not a career girl. Are you a career boy?"

From *The Wall Street Journal,* with permission of Cartoon Feature Syndicate.

White females and African-American, Asian-American, and Hispanic men and women face all the career problems discussed in this book: transitions from school to career, early frustration and disillusionment, role overload and life stress, time management difficulties, ill-defined delegation, impatience on how their advice is accepted, the ambiguity of being a protégé, and uncertainty about loyalty and whistle blowing. Indeed, they suffer an increased burden from these common problems because to even reach professional status, they are probably more intensely motivated and hence at greater risk of slighting the human and political aspects of organizational life.

In addition, however, they confront other difficulties unique to their minority status as marking them "different" from the white males that predominate the senior management of most American firms. In this chapter we examine some of these special problems starting with two bankers, a black man and white woman, who are uncertain about what are the *real* criteria being used to evaluate their performance.

UNHAPPY MANAGERS AT RELIABLE BANK

Grover Lestin, thirty-four years old, is a black banker with an amazing background of experience and jobs. Work has taken on several meanings for him as he has moved from a southern farm to assistant vice president in a northeastern bank.

Grover's parents were poor but independent farmers, owning a small piece of land in Virginia. It was a life of hard work but with much love and joy. His mother was a vivacious woman who was a perfectionist in everything she did: cooking, sewing, and attending church. She repeatedly told her five children that they could do better, that they shouldn't just settle for "getting by." Grover's father was a giant of a man whose physical strength and psychological stability conveyed to his young son a fundamental sense of security and an abiding optimism that you could fight the world on even terms. In those early years, the family was never starving and even enjoyed substantial status in the local black community. Mr. Lestin would say to his son that the world was changing and that Grover would be able to fulfill his dreams to a greater extent than he had.

Mr. Lestin died when Grover was fourteen. His mother had to give up the farm and become a housekeeper for a wealthy white family in town. Grover became the all-purpose handyman for the household. Although he loved being in town, he hated being treated as if he were stupid. Grover did attend school more regularly, but the work was so boring that his grades were poor. The teachers seemed to expect him to make trouble so he obliged them. No one was interested in his ideas.

At seventeen Grover left home and joined the Army where he spent three years in a variety of posts, including almost two years in Vietnam where he won several commendations. He liked the military and was nominated for staff sergeant shortly before he was discharged. Upon leaving the Army, Grover attended Tidewater State College, a predominantly black college where he majored in business administration. He worked hard, performed well, and graduated in the top 5 percent of his class. Unfortunately, job opportunities weren't very good at the time and Grover decided to apply for an Army commission. He subsequently became a second lieutenant and embarked on a successful military career of eight years, leading to promotions up to captain.

Six years ago, Grover decided to leave the military and try the civilian world again. He enjoyed the Army but felt that job opportunities for educated African-Americans had significantly improved. Besides, he had three young children to support and he wanted to earn more money.

Grover resigned his commission and accepted a position with the Reliable Bank in Northeastern City. He was the first black professional ever hired by this medium-sized bank and he was to initiate a new bank activity—loans to minority enterprises which in the past had not qualified for loans through the regular corporate and small business units.

After a two-month training program, Grover was appointed an assistant treasurer (AT) and given the title of manager of minority enterprise credit. Exhibit 10–1 shows where he was located on the organization chart. He was assigned a modest office and a secretary whom he shared with a regular loan officer. Grover was a little older than the others at his level, but his salary seemed fair at $32,000 and he was enthusiastic.

Grover's immediate superior, Frank Swain, Assistant Vice President for Credit, was opposed to lower credit standards for minority applicants, but President Alfred Robbins put his weight behind the effort and Grover was given substantial autonomy in making loans below $50,000. The bank's advertising soon emphasized its awareness of its social responsibilities and featured Grover in many print ads and television commercials.

During the past four years, Grover has enjoyed good relations with the bank's president. Several times Robbins has directly called him about specific problems with minority issues and even solicited advice on personnel policies affecting black employees. Grover was invited to accom-

EXHIBIT 10–1: SIMPLIFIED ORGANIZATION CHART OF RELIABLE BANK

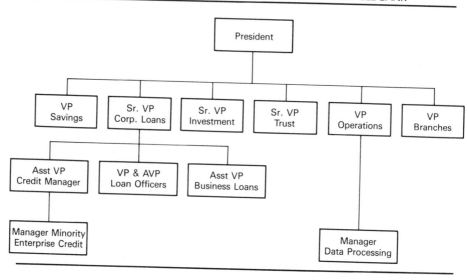

pany the president on numerous speaking engagements. In total, Grover has probably spent more time with the president than anyone except the senior vice presidents. And last year his title was upgraded to assistant vice president with a salary of $51,000.

All of this has been heady stuff to Grover and he feels a great sense of satisfaction (and some anxiety) when he considers how far he has come from the Virginia farm. He and his family live happily in a lovely historic suburb where his kids walk to the same school at which his wife teaches third grade.

Nonetheless, Grover has become increasingly distressed about his job situation. He enjoys the work and his autonomy but feels that his limited responsibility curtails his ability to contribute. Last year when his title was upgraded, he requested an increase in his loan authorization authority to the same level of equally experienced regular corporate loan officers. Frank Swain said he would look into it, but then Swain was transferred. His replacement, Andrew Widder, has put off Grover's request because, as he put it, "changes are necessary in this operation—we're losing too much money."

Grover feels that he has spent enough time in minority loans. He would like to transfer into the regular corporate department or into trust or investments where he can learn more about the banking business and prepare himself for future promotions. Grover has been especially upset that he has not been invited to the weekly informal training conferences conducted by the senior vice president of loans where large and complex financings are discussed. Grover has requested a transfer through Widder, but so far nothing has happened.

Maureen Daly is manager of data processing at Reliable. She manages a department consisting of two group supervisors, six computer operators, and six programmers. All but two programmers and one operator are men. Maureen has filled all of these positions since she came to work at the bank nine years ago as a programmer. She had always been interested in numbers since she learned early from her mother who taught mathematics in junior high school. Her father was also a teacher. Maureen grew up with high aspirations and confidence in her abilities. She majored in mathematics in college and then earned an M.S. in information systems. She has also completed all of her course work for a Ph.D., but hasn't started a dissertation.

After attending a two-day management development program and listening to Professor William Eastman talk about managerial leadership, she requested a private meeting with Eastman.

Daly: Professor Eastman, I enjoyed your session on leadership last week, although I didn't like your bias in favor of autocratic management. It seems old-fashioned and insensitive.

Eastman: I didn't mean to be biased. I thought I used the term *authoritarian*, not autocratic, and I hoped to suggest that strong leadership is sometimes appropriate and perhaps even essential in certain circumstances.

Daly: Well, maybe, but I think most young managers today know that they can't just make unilateral decisions and order subordinates around. People don't like to be dictated to; they want to feel that they are involved—and this means they must participate in departmental decisions.

Eastman: Is that the way you run your department?

Daly: Yes. Every morning I have a meeting with my two supervisors and the three senior operators and programmers to discuss what has to be done that day and what problems exist. We strive to reach concensus on each issue before going on. In addition, once a week I hold a meeting with the junior programmers and operators to discuss how things are going. I encourage them to contact me directly if they have any personal problems. I call all of them by their first names and insist they call me Maureen. I think we all get along very well.

Eastman: Well, what's your problem?

Daly: Two weeks ago I had an annual merit review and I am still distressed by what the vice president told me.

Eastman: What did he say?

Daly: He said that I didn't have control of my department; that things are "drifting"; that one of the supervisors and a senior programmer had complained to him about the time "wasted" in meetings "deciding where to locate the coffee machine" and about my supposed "inability to make decisions." He also told me that there had been complaints about horseplay on the evening shift involving a water-pistol fight I never heard anything about. Worst of all, he said I had limited promotion potential because I'm not a "strong" manager.

Eastman:	What do you think about all this?
Daly:	That's what I wanted to ask you! I don't know what to think. I try to treat my people as adults, respect their opinions, invite their participation, and motivate them to set their own performance standards, but behind my back they seem to behave like children—and my senior people bypass me to complain. Perhaps you're right after all.
Eastman:	About what?
Daly:	That managers really should be autocrats.
Eastman:	That's not what I said!

┉┉┉┉

WHY ARE GROVER AND MAUREEN UNHAPPY?

Grover Lestin and Maureen Daly are experiencing some of the most common and disturbing problems stemming from being "different" from the majority of managerial colleagues at Reliable Bank. Grover enjoys his duties as manager of minority enterprise credit and feels that he is making a valuable contribution to the African-American community as well as to the bank. He is happy with his family life, on good terms with his suburban neighbors, pleased with his children's success in school, and proud of what he has been able to provide for his family. But he is concerned about his future at Reliable, especially now that his new boss Andrew Widder is expressing doubts about the economic viability of such loans.

Grover would not describe his position as a "token" one since he does have real (although limited) loan authority and he has seen the positive impact of his work among minority entrepreneurs. Nonetheless, he recognizes that the status of minority enterprise credit is uncertain. When he was hired, the bank's motivation seemed to be social responsibility and public relations. He was to be a visible black to whom the bank could point in many public statements and advertisements. Grover's performance was based more on his activity and visibility than the economic performance of his loan portfolio. Now, however, either the social responsibility fad has passed or overall financial pressures have increased so that his performance criteria are shifting to profits generated.[1]

Aside from his belief that what he is doing in the minority community is still valid, Grover is understandably concerned about his personal future in the bank. Because of his unique status and his frequent absences from his headquarters office, Grover had not been involved much in the office social network among his peers and immediate superiors. To be sure, he knows the president well, but he has not had much opportunity to learn about Reliable's main business of corporate banking. His not being invited to the weekly loan review conferences is a disturbing symptom of his marginal status at Reliable.

Most fundamentally, Grover feels powerless. Decisions are being made that will affect his career on which he is not being consulted. He has applied for a transfer to a corporate loan area, but nothing has happened and he has been told virtually nothing. He recognizes that he might be at a competitive disadvantage in corporate loans where his peers would be markedly younger graduates of prestigious private colleges and business schools, but he feels that he could make the transition with some support from the bank. Right now, he is hearing nothing.

Maureen Daly is clearly not in a token position. Data processing is well established as a department and her predecessor as manager had been a majority male. Maureen was promoted because she was technically the most knowledgeable person in the department. She has always had great confidence in her technical skill and ability to work with anyone in solving complex problems. And until her annual merit review two weeks ago, she felt that she was an effective manager of people. Now, however, she is confused because her superior sees her as too weak a leader.

Whether Maureen is actually a weak or laissez-faire leader is uncertain. Perhaps her superior perceives her as weak because she is not a male and doesn't fit his preconceived notion of how a manager should behave. As the organization chart in Exhibit 10–1 indicates, Maureen reports directly to the senior vice president for operations, who is a much older male. The greater the difference in demographic characteristics between a superior and subordinate, in general, the lower the superior's judgment of a subordinate's effectiveness.[2] Or perhaps there is a generational difference. Maureen expresses a philosophy about youthful rejection of autocratic leadership and desire for self-determination and participation. Her refusal to see any difference between autocratic and authoritarian is indicative of her ideological commitment. Whether valid or invalid, her participative ethos may simply be incompatible with Reliable's historically more authoritarian culture.[3]

Finally, Maureen simply may be naive. She wants to treat her subordinates as "professionals," but even college graduates are often self-centered, irrational, and childish. Their horsing around appears to be out of hand and Maureen is too aloof to even notice. She expects participation in the most trivial decisions that her people see as time-wasting nonsense. So Maureen's problem is finding a leadership style with which she can be comfortable while earning her subordinates' acceptance and superior's praise.

Clearly, both Maureen Daly and Grover Lestin are experiencing difficulties because they are "different" in race, gender, values, or behavior than the majority tradition in their organization. Let's examine this issue more generally.

PROBLEMS OF MINORITY PROFESSIONALS AND MANAGERS

In the past, difficulty in gaining entry has been the overwhelming problem for minority candidates. Although certainly still an issue, thankfully opportunities have broadened enormously in recent years. But getting a job on the career ladder doesn't guarantee that all the rungs above you are solid. Minority professionals and managers particularly encounter discouragement about entering management, dead-end positions, overdependence on a sponsor, rejection by subordinates, being alone, hitting a "glass ceiling," and the burden of being a symbol.

Discouragement About Entering Management. Minorities with the appropriate educational credentials today have relatively little difficulty in getting entry into firms. More fundamental is a lack of earlier encouragement to prepare for managerial careers. Women are now flocking to undergraduate and graduate management programs, but it is a relatively recent development. In the past, women seeking anything more than "jobs" were usually oriented to traditional female careers such as teaching and nursing. Today, female management graduates are still largely at the technical and middle management levels either because most have not been with their firms long enough to make it to the top (remember this takes over twenty years for most men) or because they are blocked by a sort of "glass ceiling." (More about this later.) In 1988, women held almost 40 percent of the jobs that the Labor Department classifies as executive, managerial, and administrative, up from 32 percent only five years earlier. But women hold only 3 percent of top management positions at publicly-traded corporations.[4] This could rise to as much as 16 percent by the year 2000, however.

Black participation has apparently not greatly increased in business and management programs. Less than 9 percent of all managers are African Americans and their enrollment in higher education in general has stagnated and even declined in the 1980s.[5] This is probably because of escalating costs and continued deterioration of many urban public schools. Even bright young blacks with the financial resources to attend college are skeptical about business careers and see more promise in other professions like law and medicine. African-Americans comprise only 3 to 7 percent of the students at prestigious MBA schools, unchanged or slightly down since 1977. Nonetheless, MBA admissions officers are still recruiting talented black graduates, and recent black MBAs are among the most sought-after people in America. Only time will tell how high and far they will go.

Dead-End Positions. All too often an effective young minority manager is rewarded with a "promotion" away from the firm's power axis into a post directly related to his or her minority status. Thus, the majority of black managers (approximately 4 percent of all managers) do not have control over budgets, final hiring authority, or profit-loss responsibility, regardless of their level in the hierarchy.[6] And too often minorities in effect participate in their own subordination through acceptance of such non-line, dead-end jobs.[7] Hence, a good female market analyst may be appointed supervisor of the support staff (mainly clericals) with a nice salary increase—but not as great as her male colleague promoted to supervisor of an analyst group. Or a young African-American sales representative is appointed manager of minority community merchandising. This could be a central position depending on the firm's products or services, but often the company sees marketing to the minority community as peripheral. Once in an auxiliary or low-status position, moving back to more central and powerful activities can be very difficult. One can become dead-ended. In commenting on his firm's efforts to integrate women into the hierarchy, one corporate manager observed that it went well while the central human resources department was watching. But after five years or so, the human resources department became more concerned with newer entrants and earlier women began to get sidetracked.

Note that these dead-end positions are not strictly token jobs without content.[8] They are necessary activities that may well provide intrinsic rewards along with a nice income allowing a satisfying life off the job. A survey of executives from vice president and up at *Fortune 1000* companies indicates that the women average $124,632 per year. Nice, but men at the same levels (but mostly closer to their firms' power axes) average $213,000 per year.[9] It appears that women actually receive *more* early promotions than men and that they are happier in middle management than men.[10] The problem is that these more frequent small promotions are not traditionally on the route to the top, and they may be more vulnerable to managerial fad changes or economic downturns.

Many executives still seem to believe that most women work for fun or pin money so that underpaying them doesn't "hurt" them. Women who are seen as "breadwinners" in their families, however, feel more satisfied with their pay and perceive greater promotion opportunities.[11]

Overdependence on Sponsors. Sponsors are important and, as we've seen, sometimes difficult for minority managers to find. For this reason, some minority managers (and of course some majority ones as well) become overly dependent on a single senior person.[12] To avoid endangering the relationship, they may become too uncritically accepting. Some superiors complain about female protégés who are reluctant to ask questions or to point out their superiors' mistakes, and that women make "too much" of the simple routine action of going to see their boss about problems.[13] They think the boss is busy with other more important matters or feel they lack the ability to cope competently with a superior. Specific topics reportedly avoided include asking for a pay raise, requesting a promotion, correcting a superior who is wrong, challenging a decision, and selling a new idea (of course many young men also suffer from similar reluctance). As a result of their passivity, some female subordinates may work diligently on mis-understood problems.

Rejection by Subordinates. Although (hopefully) this attitude is declining, some white males still feel uncomfortable working for a minority superior. Males may feel threatened by a female boss because of unresolved childhood conflicts with Mom and her authority. And even "liberal" whites may be surprised by their resentment of a black superior who is necessarily tough in saying "no."

Remember that upwardly mobile managers are a little surprised to confront increased dependence as they move upward. This stress can be even greater for minority managers who recognize how easily disloyal subordinates can wreck their careers. They may try to reduce this tension by identifying downward and striving to be one of the gang with dirty jokes and hard drinks. This may ease personal strain but can be a recipe for managerial and personal disaster. You can lose credibility downward and influence upward because your own boss sees you as overidentifying with your troops.

Being Alone. The women who pioneered in management often found themselves alone in predominantly male settings where the majority didn't accept them as equal colleagues.[14] To be a "solo" minority can be very difficult.[15] Majority pressure on a lone minority person to conform is difficult to resist. This is especially true when the minority individual is alone in his or her nonconformity but still wants to be accepted as a group member.[16]

A persistent problem for minority persons is that the majority perceives them according to a stereotype. The individual's unique attributes tend to be submerged in the majority's premature categorization and blindness to how *this* particular minority individual differs from the stereotype. Peering over cultural boundaries, we tend to exaggerate differences between ourselves and others while perceiving others as being homogeneous.[17] Thus, an individual woman manager is more likely to be seen as a *female*-manager than as an individual female-*manager*.[18] And an African-American might be seen by fifty-year-old white senior executives erroneously as a member of a group that on average they don't consider as bright as whites. This perceptual bias is greater when perceiving a single "foreigner" than a group and greater with cultures less familiar to the perceiver.[19]

Some years ago, I explored perception and behavior in cross-cultural, graduate student groups where the majority was composed of American white males and the single minority members were American white females, or African-American, British, Japanese, French and Latin-American males.[20] In general:

- American white males rejected group leadership aspirations of lone minority members (with the sole exception of British males whom the American majority tended to perceive as having stronger communication skills).
- Japanese males and American white females responded to their exclusion from power by not contending for leadership, accepting marginal status, and scrupulously adhering to majority norms of timely attendance, preparation, and effort.
- African-American, French, and Latin-American males tended to respond to their exclusion by rejecting the group and violating group norms by not showing up or sharing in the work.
- Minority males generally perceived much conflict on their teams and were unhappy with the experience.
- In spite of their exclusion by the majority males, lone white American females generally perceived little conflict and were happy with the team experience. Their token status seemed to render them deaf to the conflict occurring around them.[21]

These results were generally consistent with stereotypic gender perceptions that women are more selfless and concerned with others and less self-motivated or driven to dominate others than men.[22]

I later added situations where a white American male was in the minority on a team of white American females.[23] The results:

- Women are much more likely to strive for leadership when in the majority than when alone among a group of males.
- More conflict was perceived on all-female and predominantly female teams than in all-male or predominantly male teams.

- Lone males absolutely hated being in the minority in a predominantly female team.
- Surprisingly, in general, women preferred being in a minority rather than majority status.

I recently replicated this research in the 1980s to see if relations between males and females had improved.[24] Thankfully, they have—and dramatically so. Young males and females today are much more effective in working together. Lone women on predominantly male teams are much more likely to strive for leadership and to be successful. The male members are less inclined to reject her out of hand. They are more able to tap the resources of an assertive woman than in the past. And recent research suggests that male students today may even work better in a mixed gender team than when it is all men.[25] Andrew Jackson once claimed that "One man with courage makes a majority." I would add: "One woman too." And thankfully, it takes a bit less courage than it used to.

In addition, lone males on predominantly female teams are much less unhappy about their plight; it is no longer the devastating experience that it was in the 1960s and early 1970s (although men still are clearly less adept than women when in this lonely situation). Although men still act differently toward female team members than toward other males (they interrupt women more and accept less interruption from them), their urge to dominate the females is much reduced.[26] Contemporary young women appear much less subject to the general male attribution that to be female in itself conveys less capability to exercise power.[27]

Perhaps even more important, young women seem to trust each other and work together more effectively than in the past. The perceived conflict level on all-female and predominantly female teams is markedly lower in the more recent sample. And their satisfaction level when among other women has sharply increased. A fundamental objective of the feminist movement appears closer to realization: that women must learn to trust each other and to work together more effectively if they are to compete successfully with men.[28]

The cost for contemporary women in predominantly male settings, however, appears to be a certain loss of innocence. They are clearly involved in more conflict with males than in the past when the male majority tended to reject female leadership claims and insulate them from male jockeying for power. As a result, although more successful in exercising influence, female happiness today with being in a predominantly male group is significantly *lower* than their earlier sisters. Now they perceive the conflict because through contending for leadership they are involved in it. Thus, greater involvement in conflict seems to be inevitable for the progress of women and all minorities.[29]

Hitting a "Glass Ceiling." Although women and minorities constitute up to 30 percent of the professionals and managers in many U.S. firms (and over 50 percent in banking), few have made it to the highest executive levels. Only one company on *Fortune's* list of the 500 largest U.S. industrial corporations has a woman chief executive.[30] And the situation is no better in other countries.[31]

As suggested earlier, this can reflect the length of time to make such a climb and the recency of minorities beginning to climb the ladder. In 1970, women constituted less than 5 percent of MBA students at the top graduate schools of business and management. It is over 30 percent today. Still, it has been almost twenty years since women began to attend business schools in significant numbers, so their underrepresentation at the top may also reflect other factors.

Many women today question whether their opportunities are really improving.[32] A recent Gallup poll indicates that women's feelings of being discriminated against at work have increased over the past twelve years.[33] And numerous observers comment on the discrepancy between firms earnestly courting young women for entry-level professional positions followed by either less significant promotions or slower mid-career progress.[34] Women appear to be 20 percent less likely to be promoted in any given year than male colleagues.[35] And even though they start at quite similar salaries, within ten years women may be from $3,000 to $18,000 per year behind the men they started with. Perhaps reflecting disappointment with this reality, applications from women to MBA programs have declined from their peak in 1986 (at my school from 32 percent to 25 percent).

As women approach top executive ranks, many seemed blocked by a "glass ceiling" imposed by a difficult double-bind test: "Show us that you can be tough *and* also that you have the excellent interpersonal skills that are needed at the top".[36] Thus, women are only allowed a narrow range of acceptable behavior. They must be tough, but not *too* tough; behave like a man, but *still* be feminine.[37] If a woman is too tough, she makes too many enemies and is excluded from promotions to the highest level. Aggressive behavior that might be accepted in a man (even if disliked) is rejected in an ambitious woman, as it was for Ann Hopkins who was rejected for a partnership at Price Waterhouse for lacking "interpersonal skills." But she was told that her chances for promotion would improve if she would wear makeup and jewelry and walk, talk, and dress more femininely.[38] But, stereotypic female caring and leadership that is *too* participative (perhaps seen as a bit idealistic in a man, but acceptable) also can exlude women from the ultimate promotions. The art of the successful woman executive is staying within that acceptable behavior range.[39]

Burden of Being a Symbol. Minority managers who have fought the good fight and performed better than their white male contemporaries in order to stay even may weary of their role as minority symbol. They grow tired of having to represent a minority point of view on every committee and project team. They understand but lose patience with the self-restraint that they should demonstrate lest other fellow minorities be hurt by white reaction to their losing their temper. The feeling of always being on stage, or the defendant in a never-ending trial is stressful to successful minority executives, even to the point of their experiencing greater career burnout.[40] Corning Glass Works, for example, estimates that women and minority managers drop out of the company at roughly twice the rate of white males.[41] The tension of seemingly having to operate in a bicultural world of black and white particularly exacts a heavy price, since white institutions are oblivious to their black professionals' daily transitions.[42] Greater incidence among African-Americans to high blood pressure appears to be one cost.[43]

The United States has seen a revolution in opportunity since World War II. Men from an extraordinary variety of white ethnic groups have made enormous progress in climbing corporate ladders displacing earlier establishment types. Most of these Italian, Irish, Polish, and other ethnic Americans made it by learning to behave like the traditional white, Anglo-Saxon, Protestant culture with controlled emotions, cool communications, and prudent rationality. A recent poll of male executives commissioned by the National Association of Female Executives found that men still believe that most women view their jobs too emotionally.[44] Thus, history suggests that aspiring black and female managers should learn this culture even as WASPs should learn to live with diversity. Nonetheless, some black and female reformers decry a loss of distinction. They criticize the African-American who becomes an "Oreo" (black appearance around white values, so called because of the cookie with chocolate pastry exterior and white sugar interior) or the "iron maiden" woman who behaves as coldly and unfeelingly as stereotypic males. Some feminists want us to reform corporate society and make it more "feminine" (that is, more caring and supportive). It is even suggested that women can "feminize" managerial jobs, thereby making them even more effective than a male.[45]

The weight of experience would suggest, however, that promotional success is more likely to go to those who act more in accord with traditional executive culture. As a *Fortune* survey of executive women put it:[46]

The managerial women now in line for top executive jobs are the first sizable group to compete head to head with men. Though feminists had once hoped women would "feminize" the corporation by making it more cognizant of family concerns, the opposite has in fact occurred. Successful female managers have taken on many of the values and life patterns of careerist men, who long have fixed an unblinking eye on the price. . . . Rather than try to change the corporation, they learn its rules and play by them. . . . The issue for women today is not whether the world is fair. This is the way the world is. If you wish to be a part of it, live with it.

Two African-American businessmen in 1989 purchased the Denver Nuggets of the National Basketball Association, thus becoming the first to own a major sports franchise. On being interviewed, the new owners Bertram Lee and Peter Bynoe said:[47]

I don't think the color of our skin will be the standard against which we will be principally measured. I think this is a positive. The diversity in this country is something we should celebrate. It's something that has made this country great.

(It is) clear to us when we look in the mirror each morning who we are. But we've never used it as an excuse or carried a chip on our shoulder. If we become role models—if we manage to set a standard for performance—we'll be very satisfied.

Mature minority managers may come to thoughtful decisions that the sacrifice isn't worth the reward; that they *really* don't want to be a vice president or head the finance department; perhaps staying in human resources or external affairs is more satisfying even if less central. In making such judgments, all of us experience difficulty in judging whether we are truthful to ourselves or just rationalizing failure. It is even harder for minority managers who worry whether or not they are copping out or being coopted by accepting a well-paying fringe role.

WHAT CAN GROVER AND MAUREEN DO?

Grover could exercise initiative on both a formal and informal basis. He is concerned that he is not learning about the bank's regular corporate loan area. He feels he has been excluded from the loan review sessions. But perhaps he has just not been formally invited because a secretary who sends out the announcements simply didn't find his name on the corporate loan department roster. He could just show up for the meetings. It is doubtful that anyone would complain or even that his presence would be resented. In addition, to supplement his formal education, he might request that the bank support his application (and if accepted, pay the tuition) to a local Friday-Saturday Executive MBA program. This would demonstrate his ambition and increase Reliable's investment in him.

Grover could simply remain in his minority enterprise position until completing the two-year MBA program, but he would demonstrate greater assertiveness by using his link to the president to express his desire to move into traditional corporate loan work. Sure he runs a risk of alienating Andrew Widder, but just drifting will only make his situation worse. Simply staying in minority enterprise credit could well lead to a sense of failure and even economic insecurity if Reliable decides to eliminate the activity.

At present Grover is a bit paralyzed, afraid to do anything to rock the boat, because he deeply enjoys his family and what he has been able to provide for them. He doesn't want to risk anything. This is understandable in someone who has already climbed such a long socioeconomic ladder. Still, perhaps he exaggerates the risk in drawing on his potential presidential sponsor, for now appears to be the time to do so.

Although less serious perhaps, Maureen's predicament is more ambiguous. No one questions her technical competence, but she is being criticized for behavior that reflects her deeply felt antiauthority values. She believes subordinates should be treated as "adults" and to her this means everything is decided after extensive participative discussion. But perhaps she has carried a good thing too far. Her people resent the time wasted on minor matters and they fool around on the job so that higher management perceives Maureen as a weak leader.

If Maureen continues with her present style, she at best will plateau in her current position, but more likely will be asked to return to a nonmanagerial role. This might make sense given her technical orientation, but she might forever regret foregone opportunity. To change behavior is not simple, however. She might ask the company to send her to a longer management development program, or she might seek personal counseling about her reluctance to exercise authority. My guess is that a successful woman executive or consultant might be better able to convince Maureen of the desirability of being somewhat stronger as a manager.

ADVICE ON BEING DIFFERENT

Prepare for and seek positions in knowledge-based organizations where competence is judged by technical skills or measurable performance results rather than more subjective factors like appearance, style, or judgment. The most promising situations are likely to be rapid growth and even chaotic businesses.[48]

Advice on Being Different

- Fight for high-visibility, power-axis positions, especially in midcareer. Don't accept lateral transfers or diagonal "promotions" away from the power axis unless you truly would prefer the content of the offered position and understand that getting back to the power axis is probably impossible.
- Don't accept positions where your particular sex or race would be your strongest asset. Such positions tend to be either token or peripheral to the firm's main business. Look for posts that have been filled by majority managers.
- Conform to the majority cultural style in appropriate ways: control your language, wear conservative (but feminine if you are a woman) clothes, learn to play golf or tennis, talk about stock prices or sports, or whatever is necessary to encourage the group to feel comfortable around you. This may appear to be sacrificing one's personal style, but such superficial conformity will make you less threatening, thus freeing you to maintain your integrity by being independent on more important issues.
- Do not handle your minority isolation, however, by slavishly conforming to *all* formal rules and informal traditions. Some hope to be accepted by being a super "organization man." Such passive behavior may bring you acceptance and security, but will only validate higher prejudice that minority persons are unsuited to more responsible positions.
- Remember that mentor-sponsors may be flattered by obedience and faithfulness, but that the good ones even more desire assistance and protection. Therefore, be active in initiating reports, advice, warnings, and even constructive criticism. This is best done confidentially in writing or orally on a one-on-one basis.
- Use your token visibility as an opportunity to impress your superiors that you have the ability to do other things. And don't feel apologetic or guilty about whatever extra vertical links your race or gender gives you. It is just one compensating factor against other handicaps.
- Move beyond technical expertise. Minority professionals probably have moved ahead fastest in areas where their technical competence could be clearly demonstrated. Engineering, science, and computers have been areas in which the relatively few females experience less difficulty in managing men. (This is in contrast to advertising and public relations where over half the professionals are women but they are sharply under-represented at the top.) But managerial success eventually brings you to levels where technical skill must be supplemented by interpersonal competence and general business knowledge. Early broadening training can be helpful but fundamental is an awareness that one's abilities must be expanded.

- If a woman, strive to avoid implications of sexual innuendo with male colleagues. Unfortunately, the onus for reducing sexual implications still rests primarily on women.
- However important your career, recognize that you must protect some separation between your professional and personal selves. Losing an argument or backing down on the job usually *does not* compromise your integrity as a person. And recognize that some criticism of you is often ideological, not factual. It reflects not your true worth as a person but the obsolete and biased perceptions of some who evaluate you.
- Accept that you can't carry the weight of your minority group on your shoulders. Fear of making a mistake will block you from taking the risks necessary for personal success. Don't feel that you have let your group down if you feel the cost of high office is too great and that you want better balance in your life.

11

Leading Change in Spite
of Ambiguous Authority

Years ago some academic management departments and even business schools changed their name to "administrative science." Somehow they thought that including "science" in their name would give them more prestige. It was a silly move because although management can draw on science, it is not a science itself. The artistic or skill component will always remain high. And in no area is this better illustrated than using ambiguous authority to initiate change.[1] So much depends on the sensitivity and *performing* skill of the manager/leader.[2]

In this chapter we examine this difficult issue of leading a change effort when your formal power is not clear. After looking at one of the most impressive executives I've ever had the pleasure of working with, we analyze various power forms and phases of change.

CHUCK PARDEE'S APPOINTMENT

Indefatigable Mutual Insurance is a large national company with more than 10,000 employees in the fifty states. The firm was founded ninety-nine years ago by a group of northeastern manufacturers to insure their property and employees. Over the years its insurance lines and customers expanded to selling a fairly complete package to the general public, although sales policy attempted to restrict policyholders to those considered "preferred risks." Indefatigable's basic organization has been as shown in Exhibit 11–1. Each divisional vice president had access to the president Thomas Achison if so desired, but most communications between the field and home office were with the functional vice presidents who set policy and monitor performance in their respective functional areas. The two senior vice presidents acted as staff to the president in their areas of expertise with one in actuarial and statistical matters, and the other in investments and finance. Neither had extensive staffs reporting to them. They were approximately the same age as Achison. In general, Indefatigable Mutual Insurance has been a highly centralized, regionally dispersed organization with primary power vested in the home office functional vice presidents for underwriting, sales, claims, legal, and operations.

Charles Pardee has had exceptional success at Indefatigable. After experience primarily in sales, Chuck was appointed vice president of the Middle Division at age thirty-five, the youngest such appointment in the company's history. An annual report contained an individual picture of

EXHIBIT 11–1: SIMPLIFIED ORGANIZATION CHART OF INDEFATIGABLE

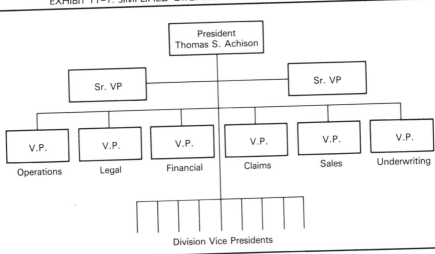

Chuck (the only divisional vice president so honored) with a caption describing him as an example of what young people could accomplish at Indefatigable. In general, however, most division vice presidents were substantially older.

After eight years as division vice president, Chuck was recently promoted to a newly created third senior vice president position and transferred to the home office. The president sent the notification shown in Exhibit 11–2.

At first, Chuck thought he had no problem. After all, he had been given a significant promotion. Nonetheless, he was concerned because he feared resentment from others and was unclear what the president wanted. Chuck had recently attended a university executive program where they had discussed a case entitled "The Dashman Company" which described a new vice president who utterly failed to exert any influence on his firm. Accordingly, Chuck decided to see Professor Eagleson who had conducted various management training programs for Indefatigable.

EXHIBIT 11–2: ORGANIZATION BULLETIN

> HOME OFFICE ADMINISTRATION
> June 29: Organization Bulletin No. 349
>
> Effective August 1, Mr. Charles Pardee, Vice President and Division Manager, Middle Division, will transfer to the President's staff at the home office as Senior Vice President.
>
> Pardee will be responsible to the President for achieving performance in accordance with company policies and objectives.
>
> Mr. Pardee will assist Division Managers in obtaining well-coordinated efforts by all departments and will establish and use measurement of results for each Division.
>
> Division Vice Presidents will report to and be responsible to Mr. Pardee.
>
> Thomas Achison
> President

During the conversation, Eagleson pointed out that there was wide disparity in the managerial styles of the various division vice presidents. For example, when conducting a training program for managers in the Northern Division, he had the divisional functional managers from memory draw an organization chart. This chart is illustrated in Exhibit 11–3. When sitting in the Northern Division vice president's office one day, a division claims manager had come in with a problem about how to treat a certain policyholder. The vice president had asked the manager to read the relevant home office regulation and then suggested that the functional manager adhere exactly to the home office rule (even though it didn't seem to fit).

By chance, Professor Eagleson had once been sitting in Pardee's office when a similar event occurred. After listening to the divisional manager and reading the home office regulation, Pardee had advised the manager that the regulation didn't exactly apply, so they were free to handle the matter as they deemed best. If headquarters would later complain to the manager, Pardee promised to say the action was his responsibility. Middle Division managers had drawn the organization chart in their training session as in Exhibit 11–4. In general, Eagleson felt that the Northern Division vice president's behavior was more typical of division vice presidents than Pardee's.

When Pardee asked Eagleson what he thought the president expected of the new position, the professor said he wasn't sure, but when he had recently seen the president about company training programs, Achison had expressed concern about his age, next year's 100th anniver-

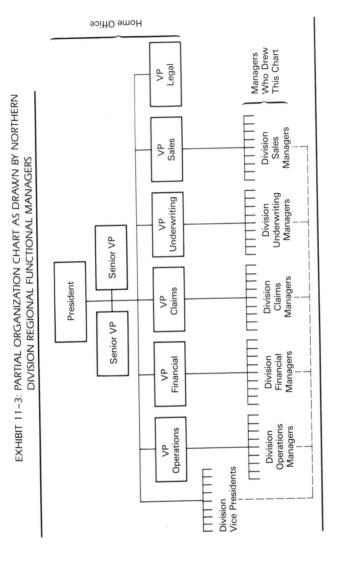

EXHIBIT 11-3: PARTIAL ORGANIZATION CHART AS DRAWN BY NORTHERN DIVISION REGIONAL FUNCTIONAL MANAGERS

Home Office

President

Senior VP

Senior VP

VP Operations

VP Financial

VP Claims

VP Underwriting

VP Sales

VP Legal

Division Operations Managers

Division Financial Managers

Division Claims Managers

Division Underwriting Managers

Division Sales Managers

Division Vice Presidents

Managers Who Drew This Chart

231

EXHIBIT 11-4: PARTIAL ORGANIZATION CHART AS DRAWN BY MIDDLE DIVISION
REGIONAL FUNCTIONAL MANAGERS

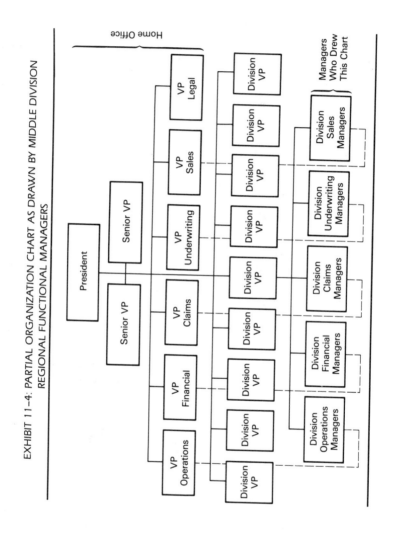

sary celebration of the firm's founding, and the company's automobile insurance losses. He had remarked during luncheon that the only thing wrong with the company was that field personnel "just didn't follow home office rules." As a result, he argued that Indefatigable was losing money on automobile insurance policies because field sales staff were selling to undesirable risks. This was contrary to the company's traditional strategy of only "preferred" risks. The president said he had decided that the sales staff had to be reduced by some 600 people.

Pondering these points, Pardee wondered if he should resist the president to protect the field staff or whether he should pick a fight with one of the home office functional vice presidents in order to impress the division vice presidents with his willingness to battle on their behalf. "In the long run," Chuck said, "my objective must be to change the mind set of the division vice presidents so they exercise more initiative in encouraging the best business decisions for their regions. I remember reading in my naval history course that back in World War I, the head of the Royal Navy, Lord Fisher, chewed out one of his overly cautious admirals by saying something like, 'In war, the first principle is to disobey orders. Any fool can obey orders.' That's the initiating spirit I would like to develop at Indefatigable—and it may well mean shifting a bit of the power out of headquarters to the field."

ᓚᓚ·ᓚ·ᓚ·ᓚ

WHY IS PARDEE WORRIED?

Success in middle management can propel you to a potential breakthrough promotion into a position with ambiguous authority. The ability to tolerate this ambiguity and to create viable power is critical.

At first reading it appears that Chuck has no problem. He is a winner whose success has brought him early recognition and now a promotion to a newly created senior vice presidency. President Thomas Achison is aging and is probably no longer capable personally of controlling the wide span of control over the fifteen people who (according to Exhibit 11–1) report to him. Some even see Chuck as the heir designate to Achison.

Nonetheless, Chuck is concerned about ambiguity in the message announcing his appointment and fears that if he tries to exercise power he might discover it lacking. The appointment notice in Exhibit 11–2 is confusing (and be assured, this is exactly how the firm sent it out; no words except individuals' names have been changed). The first sentence is very weak. Chuck's "transfer" to the "President's staff" sounds like at best a lateral move, not a promotion suggesting that he will be an adviser to the president and not a line executive.

The second sentence seems to verify that he is to be another set of eyes and ears for the president policing adherence to home office rules. "Pardee will be responsible to the President for achieving division performance in accordance with company policies and objectives." Unfortunately, this role runs counter to Chuck's opinion that home office rules excessively constrain field personnel initiative.

The third sentence, "Mr. Pardee will assist Division Managers in obtaining well-coordinated efforts by all departments and will establish and use measurements of results for each division," is a bit stronger but would cast him in a monitoring and advisory role to the divisions.

The fourth sentence, however, is most powerful: "Division Vice Presidents will report to and be responsible to Mr. Pardee." Legitimate power, the authority of a position in a chain of command, is clearly defined here, at least over the division vice presidents. Unfortunately, nothing is said about the home office functional vice presidents (claims, underwriting, sales, and so on), so it appears that he doesn't possess formal authority over them, in spite of his title as senior vice president.

Immediately talking to President Achison to get a clearer position description would be a logical recommendation to offer Pardee. But Chuck doesn't want to do this; he fears that the president's response would prematurely limit the new position's potential by overly focusing on a police and hatchetman role of cracking a whip to reduce automobile insurance losses by firing field staff. As his own division manager experience had verified, he feels the company should loosen home office ties and encourage greater autonomy, flexibility, and initiative in the field—a course of action not likely to please Achison.

Before considering what Chuck might do, we need to examine the various forms of power on which he might draw when attempting to change behavior at Indefatigable.

POWER AND INFLUENCE

Americans are often a bit skeptical about those who desire to wield power.[3] It is as if Lord Acton's famous warning "Power corrupts" has been turned on its head to "Anyone who strives for power *is* corrupt." I once served on a university search committee seeking a new dean. Faculty, alumni, and students shared in the deliberations at our first meeting when one member observed, "We don't want anyone who *enjoys* exercising power!" We all nodded sagely, visions of Lyndon Johnson and Richard

Nixon dancing in our heads. But what nonsense to appoint someone who *dislikes* influencing others to a leadership position that demands the exercise of power (no wonder academia was in such poor shape back in the 1970s). Even senior corporate executives are said to "too often shrink from the exercise of power or display ambivalence about it".[4]

Forms of Power. Power is essential to influence others for evil *or* good. When someone successfully influences another, we infer that the influencer possesses power. Thus, influence implies power and power is necessary for influence. Power, however, takes several forms.[5]

- *Coercive power* is based on a potential follower's perception that the influencer has the ability to punish with some action that will be unpleasant or frustrating to some need.
- *Reward power* is based on a follower's perception that the influencer has the capacity to reward with some action that will be pleasant or satisfying to some need. Both coercive and reward power depend on the potential influencer controlling resources such as money, equipment, or knowledge that is valued by the potential followers.
- *Legitimate power* (sometimes called authority) is based on the follower's internalized values which convince him or her the influencer has a legitimate right to influence, which he or she has an obligation to accept. This is at the core of a traditional bureaucratic influence system in which leadership positions are endowed with formal authority.
- *Referent power* is based on the follower's identification with a charismatic leader who is followed out of blind faith. The identification and influence can be maintained as long as the influencer manifests behavior and attributes esteemed by the followers.
- *Expert power* is based on the follower's perception that the influencer controls information or has personal knowledge or skills that can be useful in satisfying follower needs.
- *Representative power* is delegated upward to a leader by a group which implicitly agrees to follow as long as the leader consults the followers and generally leads in a direction that satisfies their needs.

In each of these power forms, the follower is crucial.[6] In order to influence anyone and be a leader, you must appeal to their needs. If you are holding a loaded gun to my head and you communicate a willingness to fire, the chances are that I will do what you ask. The odds are stacked in your favor. But certainly, history demonstrates similar situations in which people have chosen *not* to obey. So influence depends on the potential follower as much as on the leader-manager. The follower must make a decision to respond. Perhaps he or she doesn't have much choice, but a decision must be made.[7] Although traditional power forms like coercive, reward and legitimate authority are still used, modern management increasingly draws on expert and representative power. For example, although legitimate power may be historically the most used form of power within business, today in the United States it appears to be the *least* used (and least effective) form.[8] American managers and their subordinates seem to feel that using positional power as one's primary influence is a sign of weakness.[9] This reluctance about using formal authority is consistent with American skepticism about authority figures that dates back to our colonial era.[10] Early and late immigrants to the New World were fleeing disrespected authority in their old countries. And however much they tried to maintain authority within their families, the new society's pressures tended to undermine even parental power. Young men particularly could simply leave their father's homestead and move to empty land or, better yet, go to the labor-short cities that characterized the United States until well into the nineteenth century. This was probably the first country where a son could tell his father to "go to hell" with relative impunity. For daughters it took a bit longer.

Using Referent Power. Influence through referent power involves blind faith, a kind of Alexander the Great or Joan of Arc syndrome. We respond to the great leader who has "charisma".[11] To the ancients, charisma was God's gift of heavenly grace or magical powers to a few favored humans. Only fools would not respond to such a charismatic leader. Today of course we have a bit less faith and substantially more skepticism about charisma, but we still tend to respond to the leader who has characteristics we admire—the person who is a super model of what we would like to be.[12] We respond out of strong emotional attachment, even love, for a leader with whom we identify.[13] The relationship is personal rather than general, for charisma is not simply an attribute of the leader but the fit between his or her characteristics and our values.[14] Betty Friedan and Gloria Steinem were both charismatic leaders in the early women's liberation movement, but they tended to appeal to different groups—the older Friedan to more traditional homemakers, the more glamorous Steinem to independent career women. Further back in history, T. E. Lawrence possessed charisma for the Arabs in World War I, but his dramatic, stylistic behavior offered no appeal to postwar Britons who did not support his political bid.[15] Winston Churchill's brand of charisma was not felt until his country faced extinction in 1940 and his personal attributes matched the people's concerns.[16] Yet, these characteristics became less relevant to voters with the end of the European war in 1945 when his government was quickly voted out of power as public concern shifted from survival to jobs.

Eighty years ago much management literature stated that one was born either a leader or follower.[17] Either one had natural leadership qualities or one did not. We have less belief in this argument today because charismatic natural leaders seem all too rare. They do exist in business, but we cannot depend on their being in abundant supply. We now believe that many people can develop into effective managers through education and experience. Nonetheless, business still seems to want some attributes associated with "natural leadership" and "command presence." Witness a finding at one university that corporations hired men over six feet tall for $1,000 per year more than graduates under that magic height!

Since charismatic leaders influence people through personality not position, they often bring themselves in direct interaction with many people throughout their organizations. They bypass management levels because they want to tie people to themselves. President Franklin D. Roosevelt was often criticized as being a poor administrator because his delegation was sloppy and he evidenced little respect for government structure. He would personally contact people throughout the system and give them projects unknown to their peers or superiors.[18] He cultivated individual, personalized relationships. Similarly, Robert Johnson as head of Johnson & Johnson would descend by helicopter on his plants unannounced, bypass the senior manager and move directly to individuals whom he cultivated. Both Roosevelt and Johnson were striving to get candid information unfiltered by management hierarchy. Such behavior can be upsetting to bureaucratic managers, but it can promote identification with the top and willingness to sacrifice that can be very powerful.

The most charismatic business manager whom I ever met was Joseph Wilson who transformed an old family company called Haloid-Anderson into the modern Xerox Corporation. At the time I was a young engineer at Eastman Kodak Company enrolled in the evening MBA program at the University of Rochester. Wilson was chairman of the board of trustees of the university (as well as president of Xerox) and he talked about a revolution in American society that his new technology would initiate. Organizations of all kinds would become much more democratic and decisions stronger because xerography would allow much more information to be shared and more people could participate. And (not incidentally) if you hitched your career wagon to his company's star, you would experience great excitement and perhaps make a lot of money. He had a neat knack of combining the sacred and the profane in his motivational pitch. And it induced many bright young 1960s professionals to leave the predictable security of Kodak to join the chaos that was the fledgling Xerox.

Using Expert Power. The last active United States Marine from World War II recently retired with the observation:[19] ". . . the young men and women of today, when you give them an order, they want to know why. There is no more of this dumb order: go charge. But as long as you give them a legitimate reason, they'll charge all day long."

If as a fly on the wall we could observe all of the influence incidents in modern organizations, the most frequent would draw on expert power reflected in the follower's agreement or rational faith.[20] Expert power is the most used power form and more managers identify with using persuasion as their primary mode of influence, even with subordinates. Followers respond because they believe the leader knows what he or she is talking about, based on evidence of knowledge and ability. Under rational agreement, the followers understand and agree with the proposed action. Under rational faith, the followers may not totally understand *this* particular proposal, but they agree because of the leader's successful track record.[21]

Most managers spend more time communicating with people outside their chain of command than they spend supervising their subordinates. In influencing peers and diagonal superiors, possessing valued information is key. Based on his analysis of political parties many years ago, Roberto Michels formulated his famous "Iron Law of Oligarchy" (the "law" that Joseph Wilson felt xerography might repeal) which states that hierarchies emerge in the most democratic organizations because it is impossible to keep everyone equally informed.[22] Only a few can monitor the necessary information flows and know enough about what is going on to participate in organizational decisions. Those who occupy critical communication points accumulate expert power and emerge as leaders who make decisions that affect others.[23]

Since access to information leads to power, the formal organization chart is not a sufficient indicator of where real power rests. Influence diagrams describing the decision sequence (whose decisions precede others) would be a better indicator of power.[24] Lower-level personnel often have greater power than what is formally assigned to them because they are closer to the action and have information not readily available to higher officials.

People located at the boundary between an organization's inside and outside can be especially influential without formal authority.[25] Their ability to monitor the external world gives them access to critical information before those more internal are aware of it. And ignorance is not bliss; it is a source of stressful uncertainty. People who have privileged information that allows them to reduce ambiguity tend to amass power.[26]

The widespread use of persuasion even at the ultimate executive level is well illustrated by the words of President Harry S. Truman:[27]

And people talk about the powers of a President, all the powers that a Chief Executive has, and what he can do. Let me tell you something—from experience!

The President may have a great many powers given to him in the Constitution and may have certain powers under certain laws which are given to him by the Congress of the United States; but the principal power that the President has is to bring people in and try to persuade them to do what they ought to do without persuasion. That's what I spend most of my time doing. That's what the powers of the President amount to.

Using Representative Power. Most influence is reciprocal. To control, one must be controlled to some extent; the influencer must be influenceable.[28] The fear-dispensing dictator must punish insubordination or lose credibility. Charismatic leaders expecting blind faith must give of themselves by allowing followers to see, hear, and even touch them. Thus, every form of power implies a two-way interdependence.[29]

This mutuality means that influence can be expanded and that power can be created out of nothing. Power is not a fixed pie that can only be divided; it is not a zero-sum game requiring a manager to lose influence when a subordinate gains. Both may acquire increased influence as they mutually benefit from a relationship. Influence downward may be enhanced rather than reduced by upward influence. Both managers and workers in more effective organizations perceive themselves as possessing greater influence.[30]

In a three-tiered hierarchy, A down to B and then to C, B's effective power to influence those at C level is increased by his or her willingness to represent C's needs upward to A. The greater B's upward clout in winning resources or concessions from A that are valued by C, the greater C's willingness to respond to B's influence.[31] To the extent B successfully goes to bat for C upward to A, the C level *creates* power which is delegated upward to B.

Using representative power has a certain poker-game aspect.[32] By successfully representing subordinates upward, a manager amasses chips that can then be expended on extraordinary demands on subordinates. When I was a young ensign on a U.S. Navy destroyer, my primary assignment was as antisubmarine warfare and torpedo officer. My collateral duty was as ship's morale and recreation officer. Once when we were in port in Massawa, Eritrea on the Red Sea, at my commanding officer's direction, I had arranged for a softball game and beer party for the ship's company. Since no alcohol is allowed on U.S. Navy ships and we were in the Middle East, obtaining the beer (and ice) required some ingenuity. I was much lauded. Unfortunately, I couldn't allow my six-man torpedo gang to partake in the party because we had to prepare weapons for possible firing the next day when we were to go to sea.

Listening to the beer-inspired shouts of fun from the beach, we sweated in 100-degree heat over our torpedoes. At sundown, however, when the crew returned to the ship (and we had finished preparing the torpedoes), I felt it essential that I request special permission for my gang to leave the ship and enjoy some beer for a couple of hours to compensate them for missing the party. The captain agreed with the proviso that I allow them only half a case of beer. Silly as it sounds in retrospect, I knew that this limit would disappoint the torpedomen so I ran a risk and provided two cases without clearing it with the commanding officer. This action restored my credibility with the men and earned me some chips. Luckily, the captain never found out.

Spending the chips, however, tends to be faster than earning them. Thus, using representative power is limited in duration and frequency. It should be restricted to important issues because a middle manager like B faces some risk in picking a battle or going to bat for subordinates. He or she can lose and be rejected by A. This tends to undermine his or her credibility with subordinates who may see him or her as a friend, but no longer as a viable avenue for upward influence.[33] And if the middle manager takes subordinates' side *too* frequently or argues *too* strongly, his or her boss may see this as one having sold out, of becoming just a mouthpiece for the troops—a problem often confronting the young junior military officer. It is imperative, therefore, that a manager carefully select the limited issues which he or she will represent upward and present them rationally rather than as ultimatums (what has been called "tactician" style as opposed to being a "Shogun" attempting to usurp the Emperor's power).[34]

MANAGING CHANGE

Chuck Pardee's core challenge will be using power to change Indefatigable Mutual Insurance Company's culture and modify the behavior of key managers. He will inevitably encounter some resistance. The most profound cause of change resistance is past success because it seduces us into being satisfied with what exists.[35] Therefore, attitudinal and behavioral change begins with the premise that dissatisfaction must precede change.[36]

Creating Dissatisfaction. To achieve dissatisfaction, a change agent/manager could do nothing—just wait until people become dissatisfied with the consequences of their behavior. Aware of impending trouble, one might still decide not to warn the organization because you feel it would be too much of a shock, or that you simply would not be believed. After the outbreak of World War II, President Franklin D. Roosevelt was accused of not warning the American people about a possible Japanese attack, but he may have thought he wouldn't have been believed anyway, that the country was so committed to isolationism that only an actual attack would generate disenchantment with existing policy.[37] So, he waited until Pearl Harbor. (He actually thought an attack on Manila or Singapore was more likely.) If war was inevitable, the United States was fortunate that the attack was on Hawaii because it was so much closer to the American psyche, producing near unanimous attitude change toward the war. We were also fortunate that our aircraft carriers missed being attacked while our battleships were effectively removed from the war. This forced the United States Navy to recast its strategy toward airplanes and carriers.[38]

Thus, change classically is precipitated by a catalytic (and often cataclysmic) external event that produces crisis.[39] Unfortunately, simply waiting for such an event could lead to total disaster such as losing the war, business bankruptcy, or product loss. In the early 1960s I was working on the construction of a new paper mill for Eastman Kodak's Verifax process office document reproduction equipment. Verifax dominated the market and the new mill represented a multimillion dollar investment in continued growth. Unfortunately for Kodak, at just this time its upstart Rochester neighbor Xerox announced the first commercial application of xerography, the dry-process duplication system developed at the Battelle Institute. Almost instantly, Kodak management realized that the technological advantages of this new machine were so dramatic that Verifax would quickly die. And Kodak had no replacement under development. Work on the paper mill ceased and it essentially became an extremely expensive warehouse. It took Kodak almost twenty years to get back into the office duplication business. A smaller less diversified company might not have survived.

Because of its risks, therefore, most leaders avoid such passivity as their approach to fostering dissatisfaction. Rather, they try to generate fear. Arguing that the past is irrelevant, they define looming external threats that will cause everyone to suffer unless comfortable habits are changed. Such a Cassandra-like approach puts a premium on leader articulateness and credibility. In the 1930s when he was out of office, Churchill warned Great Britain about the growing menace of Nazi Germany, but few listened because most did not want to give up the appeasement behavior they mistakenly thought would guarantee "peace in our times." Even his oratorial and literary powers were not enough to change opinion.[40]

Timing is very important in generating fear of unchanged behavior.

Some environmental symptoms must verify the leader's warning. They must be *real.*[41] In 1977 President Jimmy Carter gave what his aids referred to as "the sky is falling speech." Sitting before a roaring fire in the Oval Office, clad in a thick cardigan sweater to communicate informality, the president described the energy crisis confronting the country. He defined the Arab petroleum suppliers and the multinational oil companies as the enemies and called for conservation and sacrifice from the American public. But he was not believed. The public did not buy his problem analysis nor his recommendations because he lacked credibility and, most of all, the "crisis" was believed to be phony (as in the "Tale of Chicken Little," he is the only one who believes the sky is falling).

The power of an enemy to unite a group (and the problem of lost cohesion when the enemy withdraws) is well illustrated in Fidel Castro's lament about lost ardor in the Cuban revolution:[42]

> Is it because we have let down our guard? Is it because the absence of an enemy has caused us to lose our faculties? Perhaps in a certain way we have been needing an enemy. When we have a clearly defined enemy, engaged in hard-fought combat, we are more united, energetic, stimulated . . .

Among American business executives, General Electric's Chairman Jack Welch particularly has drawn on this enemy metaphor to spur his firm.[43] He has argued that the United States in general is in an "economic war" with Japan and other newly emerging nations, but that G.E. has a special opportunity to show that Americans can compete and win.

As another method of initiating stress, the creative change agent/manager could create hope by articulating the possibilities of a better tomorrow if behavior were changed.[44] Even if people are satisfied with existing behavior, performance, and rewards, the leader might be able to generate hope for an even more rewarding state. Such a change agent would produce a sense of opportunity cost from the gap between what exists and what might be. To his admirers, Martin Luther King, Jr. espoused a dream for black *and* white America; attempting to make us all feel dissatisfied with the present in comparison with the more humane society that might be. *Transformational* leaders manifest this talent to redirect followers away from personal concerns to unifying objectives.[45]

These examples of Churchill, Carter, and King are all testimony to the difficulty of creating a precondition for change when free people are not dissatisfied. Unfortunately, most people are more sensitive to threats than to opportunities.[46] It is a bit easier where organizational members are not free to leave or have voluntarily committed themselves to staying as, for example, military recruits.

Unfreezing. Unfreezing involves removal of support for old attitudes, saturation with new values to be acquired, minimization of threats against change and strong encouragement of change in the desired direction.[47] The change agent/leader strives to manipulate and control the data about the world that potential followers must draw on in making a decision to change.[48]

Consider the young recruit undergoing basic military training. The recruit has little choice because leaving is difficult. His or her sergeants exert pressure. The recruit is isolated from families, friends, and indeed the outside world for a time. Even their civilian clothing may be forbidden and they are restricted to the base. The instructors drill into the recruits that their self-centered, civilian habits are bad; that individually they are weak and only through adopting military behavior can they succeed and be rewarded.[49] It can be a powerful message to young eighteen-year-olds, many of whom are away from home for the first time in their lives.

If changes can be physically isolated and communications to them monopolized by the change agent, unfreezing is difficult to resist. Debate has raged over just how difficult. In the 1950s, many were upset with the apparent "brainwashing" of American prisoners by the Chinese during the Korean War.[50] Some captured American prisoners appeared to collaborate with their captors by talking more than allowed in our uniform code of military justice. Critics argued that Americans had gone soft, lost patriotism and moral courage. The problem was less dramatic, however. Captured as isolated individuals in the rout of American forces after the Chinese unexpectedly crossed the Yalu River and entered the war, young American soldiers had no informal buddy groups to guide them on what was acceptable or not acceptable in response to interrogation.[51] And the Chinese played on this isolation by randomly transferring prisoners so cohesive groups could not develop.

Another version of this debate was played out in the trial of Patty Hearst. Kidnapped by a radical group called the Symbionese Liberation Army in the 1970s, a University of California student, Hearst was supposedly brainwashed into joining her captors' cause. She was seen participating in robberies. At her subsequent trial, her defense included a psychiatrist who argued that the unfreezing process was so powerful because the kidnappers controlled all communications to her. She could receive no messages counter to what they suggested. His conclusion was that very few people could withstand such pressure. The prosecution also produced expert testimony, however, which argued that internal communications with oneself cannot be eliminated and so a prisoner with a strong sense of personal values can withstand unfreezing pressures.

Life in business thankfully is less dramatic, but even modest isolation in a resort or university training location where daily job communications are eliminated can be quite conducive to unfreezing.

Overthrowing a central organizational cultural symbol can be a particularly powerful unfreezing tactic. Such action generates stress and dramatically communicates the need for new symbols and beliefs. A former colleague of mine recently became president of a large midwestern university renowned for its basketball prowess. The coach was the state's most famous citizen and a campus icon. However, he was also a source of controversy because of his violent temper and intemperate language. The new president sought to change the institution's culture to make academic achievement more central than athletic success. Firing the coach outright would have been a dramatic message, but the political cost to the president undoubtedly would have been too high (he might not have survived the backlash). Fortuitously (or unhappily depending on one's point of view), the coach provoked a crisis by making crudely chauvinistic statements about women so the president was given an opportunity to make a change. His approach was more creative, however. Rather than firing the coach, he issued a quiet ultimatum that he would be willing to protect the coach from those crying for his head if the coach would publicly support the president's campaign to upgrade university academics. The coach did so, apparently enthusiastically. Nothing could have had a more powerful symbolic impact. And if the coach lapses into his old injudicious mode, it will be much easier for the president to dismiss him than upon first arrival.

At General Electric in the 1980s, Jack Welch also attacked central cultural symbols of the old G.E. in order to communicate dramatically that a new set of competitive attitudes and behaviors was required. Drastically reducing the size of corporate staff (so renowned a company asset under Welch's predecessor Reginald Jones) produced much empty headquarters floor space and saved salary expense, but more fundamentally said to the far-flung decentralized operating divisions that they too were overstaffed. His staff personnel reductions earned him the nickname of "Neutron Jack" (after the neutron bomb that destroys people, but not buildings). But whether said in bitterness or jest, the name itself reinforces the cultural change message Welch was trying to convey.

Change through Modeling. Your second-grade teacher, angry with undesired "childish" behavior, might have pointed to polite little Homer and asked why you couldn't be like him, sitting quietly at his desk with pencils neatly in place and folded hands.[52] It was implied that you would be happier if you were like Homer, and the teacher would see that you'd be miserable if you weren't. In the military recruit training example, actual change begins with the introduction of a model to be emulated—usually a noncommissioned officer whose appearance and behavior are the epitome of what the recruits are to become.

To the harried young military recruit, an impressive example can be powerful. I well remember my United States Marines platoon sergeant, even after thirty-five years. He was not the stupid or sadist stereotype of some war movies. Rather he was a gray-haired sergeant-major who had won the Navy Cross and was twice selected as enlisted man of the year. He was immaculate in appearance, wise in judgment, and gracious in demeanor. His toughness was cushioned by compassion. He appeared to live a stable and moral life. (I never even heard him utter an oath!) To my group of confused teen-aged midshipmen, he was an admirable model who obviously knew how to behave and was rewarded by the system. Most of us tried to be like him.

It is not farfetched to similarly understand the substantial pressures on the young graduate who enters a New York law firm, Big Six accounting company, or prestigious consulting partnership. Working hours and professional demands are so great that the young professional essentially becomes isolated in an all-enveloping environment that generates enormous stress. Anxious recruits seek models of successful partners who appear to represent the attitude and behavior that work.

Change through Internalizing. Emulating a model is helpful, but change is not likely to persist unless it is internalized. A change agent could design a learning experience, so through trial and error a person learns needed behavior. For example, if the sergeant wants to teach the recruits to keep their heads down while advancing, he can set up machine guns that fire live (if plastic) bullets at a height of 36 inches above the path. After showing the recruits how to cradle their weapons and crawl on knees and elbows, he has them traverse the path so they understand why they should keep their heads down. More complexly, the military training group can design a mock battle problem in which soldiers who persist in self-seeking behavior are captured (symbolically by having a bag of flour broken over their heads). If the exercise is properly executed, the trainee will internalize the lesson through improvisation: to survive, one must be part of a team whose members look out for one another.[53] Some insurance firms put their new recruits through a similar exercise (albeit in a boring airport hotel) sometimes titled "hell week" at which they are to experience intensely the need to coordinate various insurance functions in servicing a policyholder.

To persist for very long, any new behavior must become personally satisfying, not on an intellectual level as much as on a gut basis. Consider a program I attended which was designed to change the behavior of middle-aged executives in order to reduce their incidence of heart attacks. At the first session, a trainer showed a film depicting an overweight fortyish man playing tennis on a hot summer afternoon. He walks off the tennis court, inhales deeply on a cigarette, gets into his Continental and drives about a mile to his home where he proceeds to have two beers, a rare steak, and a gooey fudge dessert. The screen fades to black. The next scene shows his shrouded form being loaded into an ambulance.

The change agent was striving to generate fear based on identification with the unfortunate film hero. Nonetheless, many in the audience laughed at the final scene—partly to put emotional distance between themselves and the sad events, and partly because the film's attempted manipulation was too blatant.

At the second meeting of the executive group, a physician in a white jacket gave a lecture complete with slides that summarized data on the causes of cardiovascular disease including the benefits that could be derived from exercise. The emphasis was on facts and rational persuasion. At the end of the session, a therapist distributed little movement meters called pedometers that he asked the executives to attach to their clothing and to carry at all times as they went about their normal activities in the subsequent week.

When the participants returned for the third week, the therapist had listed all their names on a blackboard where he recorded the readings from their pedometers. He then singled out the person with the least movement during the week to explain (for example, why he drove a mile to the train station every day rather than walking, why he took the elevator to his third floor office rather than climbing the stairs, and so on). Similarly, the change agent asked the person with the greatest pedometer reading what he did to integrate exercise into his normal routine. Thus, negative and positive models were defined along with modest ridicule and praise.

But not having a heart attack is insufficient feedback for newly learned exercise behavior to persist. It must work on another level. The therapist observed:[54]

> If people say they're doing it for their health, I know they won't stick with it more than a week. The only thing that will make a person succeed is pure narcissism. If you can get someone to admit that, he or she is hooked for life. People will do anything to get in shape if they feel it's going to make them look good and be sexy.

In my executive group, this took the form of a stout participant who along around the sixth week exclaimed his happiness with the program because "for the first time in fifteen years I feel in touch with my stomach!" Before, rather like Mount Everest, it was just *there*. But now he was beginning to develop sufficient muscle tone to gain a sense of control over his abdomen—a portion of the anatomy linked to a mature male's sense of virility and attractiveness.

Refreezing. Once a conversion process has occurred and the training has concluded, a change agent/manager faces another difficult task: refreezing the new attitudes and behavior. The changee must be supported and rewarded for continuing the new behavior.[55] After leaving the intensive and isolated recruit training, the soldier moves to an assignment where he is less separated from civilian life. He can leave the base in street clothes and may even live elsewhere. Old friends and family may not appreciate his new military attitudes. Indeed, they may even ridicule the soldier's hair style and polished shoes. This presents the service with the problem of continuing to support the values inculcated at basic training. If it does not, and especially if even military colleagues criticize the military way, attitudes and behavior that have been painfully learned will fade.

Refreezing is particularly difficult following treatment programs for alcohol or drug abuse. After an intensive insulated change experience at an isolated treatment center, reentry into the world can present irresistible cues to revert to old self-abusive behavior. In business, however, refreezing newly learned attitudes and behaviors is more likely if they immediately and reliably contribute to greater individual effectiveness and organizational performance.[56]

WHAT CHUCK PARDEE DID

In assessing the power that Chuck Pardee could draw on to implement change, he clearly possesses legitimate power over the division managers. He has the authority to issue directives to them and they would have an organizational obligation to obey. Chuck probably also has some reward and coercive power over the terms of the division manager's employment. He could issue a directive calling for changed behavior on their part. And such approaches do sometimes work when the desired behavior is explicit and narrow so that compliance can be measured. If closer adherence to home office rules (as the president wants) were his objective, this approach might work.

But Pardee's ambition is different—and greater. He seeks a broadening of division behavior, a more creative exercise of leadership in the regions so that functions are integrated and actions taken in the best interests of the firm under the local conditions. He wants division vice presidents to feel "empowered".[57] For managers who have been trained mainly to follow instructions, such a vision could be threatening.

Chuck undoubtedly also benefits from his successful track record and the aura of expertise and personal charisma associated with a winner. He considered picking a fight with one of the functional vice presidents to demonstrate his power and gain loyalty from the division vice presidents. If he could find a home office rule that bugged all of the field staff, perhaps he could order them to ignore it in return for his promise to protect them from home office retaliation. Many field people felt that the home office rules were obsolete or not applicable to the special conditions in the different regions. Chuck even found an especially silly home office rule forbidding sales of home, fire, and casualty insurance to "any household that has empty beer cans on the front porch." Perhaps an old analysis in the home office region had indicated a link between such empty cans, careless smoking, and house fires. But many field personnel maintained that it didn't apply in their area, that New England is not the United States, and perhaps the best families in Milwaukee have empty beer cans laying about.

If Pardee and the division vice presidents had succeeded in such a hopefully more substantive challenge, it could have been a dramatic and symbolic event building his representative power. In the actual situation, however, Pardee concluded that discretion was the better part of valor. He did not provoke such an open challenge to a functional vice president because he feared that the offended vice president would have appealed the matter directly to the president who, given his orientation toward control, would probably have sided with the home office executive, thus undermining Pardee's standing.

Rather than issuing an edict or provoking confrontation, Chuck Pardee pursued a more gradual course of expanding awareness and lifting aspirations. Here are some of the steps he initiated:

- Upon accepting the new position, he immediately called all of the division vice presidents to express his excitement about the new position and its possibilities for helping the field perform more effectively. He invited each of them to a week-long planning retreat which he was scheduling at a resort in New Hampshire (their families were invited to join them on Friday afternoon for the weekend at Chuck's expense). In the meantime, he asked the division vice presidents to talk to a consultant who would be coming to interview them to gather information for discussion at the retreat.
- Chuck wanted to avoid having the interviews simply be an occasion for griping so the questions followed a sequence: (1) What are your dreams for your division? How would you like to see it *vis-à-vis* your regional competitors in five years? (2) What resources, particularly from headquarters, are required to fulfill this aspiration? (3) What existing home office policies and procedures might hinder fulfillment of your plan?
- Chuck ran a small risk in inviting such speculation by division vice presidents. He implied that he would listen and try to change some home office conditions. Inability to show enough progress on this

front would undermine his position. More subtly, there is some risk in asking the bureaucratically minded division vice presidents to think about ambiguous possibilities. Some might well become anxious and want out.

- At the retreat Chuck led a discussion of the interview results, encouraging everyone to participate in a nonthreatening climate. He tried to present himself as a model not afraid to deal with unpleasant facts or uncertain opportunities. Because the division vice presidents had never really talked as a group (and they certainly had never been treated in such a first-class manner by the firm), a sense of shared destiny and group spirit began to emerge.

- Chuck invited each of the home office functional vice presidents to talk individually to the group of division vice presidents. This provided the first opportunity in memory for the field managers collectively to exchange views on the organization with the functional executives.

- Chuck asked the president to come on Friday and be the featured speaker at the evening dinner dance that would include all division vice presidents, functional vice presidents, and spouses. He asked Achison to talk about the upcoming centennial, the glorious history of the firm, and its buoyant future. Chuck specifically asked the president to refrain from talking about the problems in automobile insurance or the plan to prune the field staff. He assured Achison that he would have taken care of the matter prior to Friday evening.

- Chuck could have fought the president on the firing issue, perhaps by asking for time in which to develop an alternative solution. He chose not to do this. Rather, during the retreat he presented a series of speakers to the division vice presidents: an attorney commenting on the rise in jury damage awards in automobile accidents, a repair shop owner describing his increasing parts and labor costs, a major car company executive analyzing the increased production costs from government-mandated safety features, and a former state insurance commissioner explaining why company proposed rate increases were no longer automatically ratified (partially because some state commissioners were running for governor). All this testimony demonstrated that the losses in automobile coverage stemmed *not* from field personnel disobeying home office rules, but rather from changes in the essential business. Therefore, temporarily reducing car insurance sales and reducing the sales staff emerged as a prudent answer to a business problem, not as punitive punishment. Those unhappy people dismissed were not mollified, of course, but the climate of those remaining was affected less adversely.

- Other than entertaining them at the retreat, toward the home office functional vice presidents, Chuck took a slower approach. He did not provoke early confrontation over obsolete rules. He chose to patiently and persistently try to educate them on the field perspective. "Accidentally on purpose" he tried to be in the vicinity of each functional vice president two or three times a week to simply pass on something he had heard from the southwest or southeast vice president about what the "crazy" competitors in that region were doing. More formally, he had lunch with each functional vice president at least twice a month to chat about regional developments. This gentle upward representation of the field in time encouraged a more flexible posture among home office executives.

- With respect to the division vice presidents, Pardee's essential objective was to convert them from a kind of surface-of-the-cone role to power-axis functional integrators within their regions. Not all of the managers he inherited were able to make this transition even with Chuck's support and encouragement. Consequently, where necessary, Chuck began to "encourage" some early retirements and to replace these division vice presidents with people more in his own image—those who were comfortable with ambiguity and who saw opportunity in the inadequacies of the home office rules.

Clearly, Pardee was a master in utilizing multiple power forms including reward, legitimate, referent, expert, and representative. He well represented the definition of power attributed to Harry Hopkins, President Franklin D. Roosevelt's extraordinary aide: "Power is the ability to do a job, not the ability to dominate." Coordination skills loomed larger than hierarchical authority.[58] Just as impressively, Pardee drew on the phases of change to lift executive aspirations, generate fear if practice was not changed, present himself as a model of modern flexible management unafraid of ambiguity, but most fundamentally orchestrating an experience where initially the division vice presidents and eventually the home office functional vice presidents learned how to work together more effectively.

Pardee's subtle style of dealing with ambiguous power paid off for him personally. Within two years, his title was changed to executive vice president which confirmed his seniority over the functional vice presidents and senior vice presidents (even though his job description was not modified). And not long after, he became president of Indefatigable.

ADVICE ON LEADING CHANGE IN SPITE OF AMBIGUOUS AUTHORITY

- Recognize that a clear position description is not always a virtue if it would limit your power and responsibility below what is necessary to improve your organization's performance. The key is to focus on what is necessary for organizational improvement, not on simply expanding your own empire.

- Remember that limited formal legitimate power is not always a debilitating handicap in your capacity to influence behavior and exercise leadership. Explore the other power bases on which you can draw: What resources or information do you control? What personal friendships can you draw on? What potential follower values can you manifest in your behavior? What expertise do you possess that others might recognize? What follower wants might you represent upward?

- Recognize the imbalance in upward representation: that you run a risk of losing so that battles should be limited to high-win or extremely important issues; that you will probably lose more often than you win on the important matters; and that expenditure of political capital occurs faster than amassing it.

- In a new position, unless the situation is a crisis, begin by spending considerable time gathering information and developing relationships. Take on any low-cost/high-payoff tasks first—that is, tasks that require little power to implement, but have the possibility of yielding high returns in power.

- Be aware that most organizations are a bit hypocritical in that managers who violate rules but are unsuccessful in performance are often punished, but that good performance usually leads to rule violations being ignored.

- Fight the illusion of painless change by recognizing that all change begins with stress that you may sometimes have to create. But be honest in your threats and promises. Nothing will undermine your credibility more than lack of personal consistency or verification by external events.

- Recognize that to lead change, you must be willing to change your own behavior. Power to lead implies interdependency with those you are trying to change. You should be willing to serve as a personal model of the attitudes, behavior, and performance you are trying to create.

- Remember that for changed behavior to persist, it must *work*. Changees must experience it as meeting their personal and organizational needs after the intensive phase of the change process has ended. Therefore, as a manager you must recognize, support, and reward those who adopt the new.

12

Becoming a Middle-Aged Manager

"I'll never make it . . . I suffer from acrophobia."

Recently I was having dinner with five of my closest friends, all successful and over fifty years of age. Someone asked how you know when you are entering middle age at work. He was told, "When the firm no longer sees you as 'young and promising.'" A poll was then taken as to what age this occurs and the mean response was forty-three to forty-five. At this, another (and wiser) guest observed, "Well, I'd rather be 'mature and accomplished' anyway." Then, a third (and wisest of all) friend said, "make that mature and accomplish*ing!*"

Difficult as it may be for most readers of this book to believe, middle age comes awfully quickly in management. We have been such a youth-oriented society that the peak promotion years traditionally have been forty to forty-five and after that, unless one is poised to make it to the very top, promotions tend to come more slowly if at all. Over fifty, your resume depreciates quickly.[1] And I am not talking about "failures" or "losers." Many very effective and successful executives just below the top levels were casualties forced out in the staff prunings that accompanied mergers and corporate restructurings in the 1980s. Indeed, one of success's ironies is that it can make you more vulnerable to the inflexibility and obsolescence that in middle age can undermine personal effectiveness and happiness.[2] As *The Wall Street Journal* survey of the "shattered" expectations of mid-life executives put it:[3]

> By 45, most managers have weathered a failure or two, made peace with authority figures and, ideally, fully guided and inspired some younger managers. By then, too, most know whether or not they have a shot at top management jobs. The majority won't make it and must accept for them that the race is over.

In this chapter we examine how successful achievement oriented managers can confront mid-life problems and strive to keep mentally alive. We begin with the dangers confronting successful middle aged executives from the perspective of a loving child. Here are the words of a twenty-seven year old MBA student about her father.

A DAUGHTER TALKS ABOUT HER FATHER

My father's friends from high school and college paint a portrait of an intensely achievement-oriented, ultra-serious young man. Graduating from high school with straight A's at the age of 16, he briefly entered a seminary. After deciding that this wasn't what he wanted from life, he went to college as an engineering major. One of his friends describes him as the kind of student who would stay up all night to figure out a tough problem, even when he knew that he would be the only one to come up with a solution (perhaps because he would be the *only* one). No matter what the task, no matter how difficult the assignment, he was driven to do the best job he could do.

After graduating he began work at Westinghouse as an electrical engineer. Soon afterwards he married my mother. He sat down every year and outlined his goals for the year. He projected his salary increases for the next fifteen years. Each year, he plotted a new point on his graph and compared his actual progress with the goal he had set. Every year he exceeded his expectations.

My parents had five children in seven years. My mother stayed home with us; my father worked and traveled. He told my mother that he had to pay his dues. He had to work hard now to prove himself so that he could keep moving up the ladder. Later, he said, he could slow down, stay home more and spend more time with the kids. His career progressed quickly.

Becoming an Entrepreneur. At Westinghouse, my father learned about computers. And after working his way up through the ranks, he and some colleagues decided to go off on their own. They were among the brightest minds working on semiconductors and they believed they could achieve more working for themselves.

They formed a small company called Higher Technology, Inc. My father served as vice president for engineering. The technology they were working with was becoming increasingly critical to the computer industry and therefore to the American economy. The company grew and prospered because the demand for the product was high.

However, to sustain the company's growth, my father and his colleagues had to devote their lives and energies to the work. There were many late nights and long weekends with no vacations to relieve the stress.

My brother, sisters and I were young children at this point. I was seven when the company was founded. We didn't see much of my father for many years. I still remember a car ride I once took with him when I was about ten. He had agreed to drop me off at my friend's house. It struck me during that ride that this was the first time I had ever been in a car alone with my father.

The years passed quickly; we were all growing up and the company was struggling onward. Competition was beginning to take its toll. The semiconductor market was booming, but there was no room for small firms. National Semiconductor, Texas Instruments and IBM were entering the battlefield. My father's company didn't have the firepower to survive the shakeout. Eventually the inevitable happened: the company was bought by a bigger player.

After years of working hard, inventing chips that hadn't yet been imagined, and controlling a company, my father was unemployed. To be sure, he had made a lot of money, but he had nothing to do. He had no hobbies; his family had moved on without him; and he was having trouble convincing anyone to hire a senior executive in his mid-forties.

He felt useless. He tried to get involved with a hobby. He built radio-controlled airplanes for awhile. He learned about the stock market so he could manage the money he had earned from the sale of the company. He went on vacation. He tried to get to know his children.

Universe Electronics. Eventually, my father found another job. Paging through the *Wall Street Journal,* he saw an advertisement for a vice president of engineering at Universe Company's electronics division. A few weeks later, after almost a year of unemployment, my father started working again. He had accepted the job because it was offered to him and he wanted so much to run something.

Although he worked hard, he hated his new position. He didn't like answering to a boss whom he didn't respect and he didn't like the corporate culture at Universe. Most of all, he didn't like the loss of control he felt working for someone else.

Nonetheless, my father spent almost ten years at Universe becoming a nationally recognized expert in laser-scanning technology. But he was never happy in this position and he became increasingly tired and disinterested in life. He would come home from work, eat a short silent dinner, and then settle into his chair where he would nod off over a book. One by one we all left home, relieved in a way to escape from my father's oppressive unhappiness.

He wouldn't leave his job because he needed to work. And as he moved into his fifties, he became convinced that he could never start a new job. Who would hire a tired, beaten executive who was set in his ways? He didn't have the energy to start a new life, so he got old before his time. Eventually when he approached age 55, he decided to retire early. He had enough money to support himself and my mother. And he thought he could keep himself busy with his investments. He even decided to get a certificate in financial planning and start helping other people manage their money.

The Last Job. My father was retired for only eight months. He drove my mother crazy around the house, "moping" as she said. He had thought he was ready to start living a new kind of life—a life that didn't involve a fifty-hour work week and a staff of 200 engineers. But he wasn't.

When my father's friend Sid approached him with a job offer, my father told him no. Sid had worked under my father at Universe and had now formed his own company. He knew my father had enough experience and wisdom to advise his new firm and help it stay afloat. So Sid persisted. No one knows what Sid said to convince him, but my father decided to return to work.

His last career ended in less than a year. He had signed a three-year contract and was determined to honor it. But he was tired and sick. He kept working relentlessly, traveling to the west coast, returning home exhausted and interested in nothing.

When he found out he had cancer, my father wasn't surprised. He had known for a long time that something was wrong. He had ignored the signs hoping it would go away, determined to keep working. He had major surgery twice in four weeks. And as he lay recuperating, he talked about how soon he could return to work. He wanted to stay until January so he could get his bonus.

He never did return. He got sicker and sicker and he had little energy left to live or fight. He knew he would never survive to old age and he just didn't seem interested in prolonging the life he had left. Eight months after his initial diagnosis, at age 56 he died of pneumonia following surgery.

I often wonder what my father thought about during all those long, quiet months of sickness. He had made a lot of decisions along the way that plotted his life's course. He had decided to devote himself to his career when his children were babies, leaving my mother with five children and little help. He had decided to form his own company, forcing him to spend even more time working and less time with his family. He had accepted a job he probably knew he would hate because he had to satisfy his intense desire to work and be valuable, and he decided to cut short his retirement because he couldn't resist the temptation of money, power and work.

꒰ꜟꜟꜟ꒱

WHAT MADE FATHER RUN?

Like taxes and to do lists, death eventually comes to us all. My student's father certainly died young and we have no knowledge of a possible link between his fatal illness and his later career and personal difficulties. But we can see themes that warn us all of the dangers of career success.

His focus on his job was so intense that outside interests and family enjoyment were postponed. His intensity brought financial and professional success, but also such personal inflexibility that his high activity eventually was transformed into inertia. His daughter observes:

> Once my father had defined a goal, he pursued it doggedly until he reached it. He never wavered from his course once it was set. This intensity carried him far in life. It helped him to develop great technical expertise and to rise quickly through his company. More importantly, it gained him the respect of everyone who knew him.
>
> But I believe that my father's stubborn intensity caused him to make mistakes. Once a decision was made, it was never questioned. When he determined that he would remain at his position at Universe until he was ready to retire, he could not leave, even though he was unhappy. Later he made a commitment to Sid and would not break that promise until he was physically incapable of returning to work.

In addition, our reporter's father became so used to controlling people and events that later ambiguity was very threatening to him.

> My father had an intense desire to control. Any time we played a game in my family, he read the rules and told us how to play. He opened up the little bags and counted the pieces. And he usually won the game.
>
> I can understand that as a boss he must have been both a comfort and a torment. In crises it must have been nice to have someone who remains calm under fire, ready to solve any problem. But in quieter times the control must have been overwhelming. I know I felt the frustration of having my father take control of every situation that I wanted to manage myself.
>
> He was so organized! His days like his years were planned in advance. He attacked every problem in a systematic, analytical way. These skills enabled him to become a successful executive. However, when these skills failed him, when problems were too ambiguous to be analyzed step by step, he felt out of control.

Let's look at some of some concepts that may be useful in understanding the dangers accompaning success and middle age in management.

LATER CAREER STAGES

In Chapters 1 and 2, we discussed personal maturation and early career stages. After the difficulties of making the transition from school to work and exploring various jobs until commitment to a career is made, most of us in our thirties experience *the* most rapid self-actualizing expansion in our lives.[4] Most of us accept our growing interdependence with family and work associates in return for dramatic growth in use of our potential that is matched (hopefully) with greater autonomy, authority, and income. For career-oriented, ambitious men and women, this period from thirty to forty years of age is marked by enormous concentration on work and family. As a consequence, social contacts tend to be reduced, many friendships lapse, and time for hobbies and play are very limited. All of this sets the stage for some of the common mid-life problems.

Changing Managerial Skill Demands. As we saw in Chapter 2, modern corporations can be visualized as a smaller managerial and professional pyramid sitting atop a truncated larger operating pyramid. Blue-collar, white-coverall and most clerical and support personnel are in the lower portion, substantially blocked by educational limitations from entry into the upper pyramid. As illustrated in Exhibit 12-1, that upper managerial/professional arena can be divided into three layers which define the primary personal skills needed to succeed there.[5]

EXHIBIT 12-1: PRIMARY MANAGERIAL SKILLS

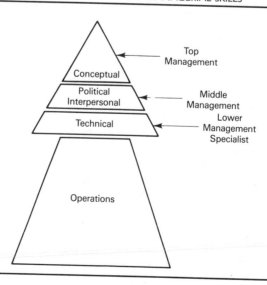

The primary skill requirements in the upper pyramid's lower section are technical: understanding equipment, procedures, processes, and analytical techniques. Entry depends on the firm's judgment (usually based on educational credentials) that you can perform or quickly learn the tasks. Rewards and promotions are based on a combination of performance and senority at this primarily technical level. Some people will be satisfied with remaining here, but most graduates probably aspire to advance upward.

The primary skills in the middle of the upper pyramid are different. They are more oriented toward interpersonal, communicational, human relations, and political abilities. To be effective as one moves into middle management you need to influence people, to build coalitions, and to function as a team member. Of course, technical skills do not suddenly become irrelevant. They are still important, but there is generally a shift in relative weight from the technical to the political as one moves upward.

This can be a difficult transition for many capable young professionals. They may feel overwhelmed with the unfamiliarity of the new challenges.[6] They find themselves promoted to first-line management precisely because they are the most technically competent, but they soon become anxious about the interpersonal dimension. The worst course for such people is to ignore leadership and attempt to do all the technical work alone. Unless they are superhuman, however, the load will be just too great to handle. Failure would be inevitable and higher executives would conclude that the young specialist-now-manager does not have promotion potential.

The transition from the middle to the upper sector is even more difficult. Emphasis shifts from interpersonal to conceptual skills: ability to think strategically, to understand how the parts and functions can be integrated, to perceive the "big picture." Of course political skills (and even technical knowledge to some extent) are still important, but an additional and rarer attribute is needed to move successfully to top-policy levels. A president of the Koppers Company has commented on what it was like years ago as a young engineer without an MBA making the transition to management.[7]

> As an engineer, I was suddenly in a whole new world. In those days, an engineer got exposed to very little. I had had a survey course in business law and economics, but all I remembered about economics was that there is decreasing utility in adding more fertilizer to land. I didn't know how to read a profit and loss statement or a balance sheet and here I was 33 years old. I had never done any significant philosophizing.

These skill transitions suggest a lengthening of time perspective as one matures and climbs. The early, short-run anxieties of immediate task accomplishment become tempered by longer-run interpersonal or political perspectives. Time must be carved out of the present to invest in relationships. Further along, successful conceptual people seem able to project their visions well into the future, to spend time now on activities on which they may receive little or no personal feedback. Thus, greater personal patience, longer-time perspectives, expanded ambiguity tolerance, and faith in the future become essential in managing at the top.

Plateauing. The geometric reality of organizational pyramids is that a squeeze occurs as one moves closer to the top. Unless a firm is rapidly expanding, insufficient openings exist to maintain an early career promotion rate. In recent years, this rate of upward mobility has probably sharply declined. Staff pruning and reorganization to eliminate excessive management levels in order to speed up decisions is reducing the number of possible hierarchical promotions.[8] A beneficial aspect of this trend is better visibility for junior managers and longer tenures in positions, thus offering greater opportunity to really learn their tasks. But, measuring career progress by promotion frequency is so ingrained in American culture that the slowdown also will cause frustration and uncertainty.

In a less competitive past, large American corporations often handled loyal of burned-out managers by transferring them away from critical operating positions on the power axis to peripheral staff positions with apparent high status but little power.[9] Thus, social prestige was protected, but the way upward opened up for younger stars. Of course, insiders usually saw through the facade and the "losers'" egos were bruised a bit, but they could reduce the pain by enjoying their secure salaries until retirement. In recent years, however, it is precisely these upper middle managers from forty-five to fifty-five years old who have been most hurt by the corporate restructurings and staff eliminations. More than any other age group, the career expectations of many of these executives have been shattered.[10]

Of course, moving away from the power axis to the organizational cone's surface is not necessarily a sign of "losing." It is a mature and wise move if a manager truly prefers the actual content and behavior of the new role. In many corporations (unfortunately) personnel or human resource management is seen as peripheral and is populated by people who didn't make it up the power axis functions. Nonetheless, human resources management clearly offers attractive career challenges, particularly if you can make senior line management understand how increasingly critical it is to firm performance.

But in making such a move outward, you should be aware of the near impossibility of ever moving back to the power axis. The new role should be what you *want* to do, probably until departure or retirement.[11]

Small firms offer a special problem as you move upward. Remember in Chapter 2 we argued that beginning professionals and managers in small companies tend to be more challenged and satisfied with their autonomy than similar young graduates starting in large firms. Fifteen or so years later, however, as such people approach senior management the satisfaction reverses. The more experienced managers in large firms report more challenge and autonomy, whereas senior managers in small companies complain about lack of authority and autonomy.[12]

The problem in the small organization is that one can start bumping into the top—and discover that you were born to the wrong parents because your firm is still family dominated. Or if not family controlled, the small firm may be run more authoritarianly because the chairperson is the founder-genius who invented the critical product and owns most of the stock (not rare in entrepreneurial firms). He or she may simply reserve all important decisions to him or herself. This can be particularly frustrating because it is much easier to move from a senior executive position in the large to the small than the reverse.

Generativity versus Stagnation.

The so-called "mid-life crisis" has become a cliche with its images of buying a sports car, chasing younger sex partners, job failure, and divorce.[13] The cliche is of course an exaggeration of what is a normal challenge for most people. But it is still a challenge.

Sometime in the mid to late forties, most of us become aware that the illusionary optional doors of our life have closed—that we really can no longer consider doing what mother wanted by going to medical school or fulfill father's wish for us to get a law degree in order to enter politics and make it to the U.S. Senate. We may not *really* have wanted to do these things but the distant possibility was in itself a comfort when our real career was going poorly. Age and responsibility (and enjoyment of what our income provides) gradually dissolve these comforting illusions.

Indeed, mid-life problems can be even greater if our career has gone smashingly and we have fulfilled our youthful dreams. Easy, early success can be particularly burdensome because later accomplishments may pale in comparison.[14] For some, the question can mirror the popular song, "Is that all there is?" Or less pessimistically, "Is the dream from my 20's still valid for the last quarter of my life?" For many (perhaps most), it may well be, but even the happiest people must at least reexamine the dream and make a new commitment.

People who encounter stress from their very success often have skewed their values in the service of their careers. The pain they feel is from a life out of tune with their deepest beliefs.[15] A psychoanalyst with many such patients comments:[16]

More and more successful people are becoming troubled, conflicted, or emotionally damaged by their work and career climb. . . . In these people, the drive for career success exists alongside a parallel, but less visible, drive for meaning and fulfillment from work which becomes subordinated to career striving. One of the people studied was a public relations executive for a television network who was becoming addicted to cocaine. She and her boyfriend had a relationship based mainly on the enjoyment of their possessions. They had a beautiful house in an exclusive section of Georgetown, a BMW and a Volvo, expensive video and stereo equipment, trips to Europe, safaris in Kenya. But she complained it was all hollow. . . . Such people are trying to find a way to feel more alive, or to protect themselves against the sense of emptiness.

Most are not neurotic, but are the "working wounded." Unfortunately, many of these people continue to suffer. It's the lucky ones who have developed a life of balance, in keeping with their full values.

Following the maturation issues described in Chapter 1 (trust–mistrust, autonomy–shame, initiative–guilt, industry–inferiority, identity–confusion, and intimacy–isolation), the problem of mid-life is generativity versus stagnation.[17] People with high needs for achievement and power (characteristic of many executives) have found excitement in confronting new tasks, using their analytical, creative, and political skills to accomplish valuable results. The question becomes whether repetition of this pattern will continue to satisfy, or whether new behavior is necessary to avoid stagnation. Five general options exist: repetition, shifting focus off the job, finding new challenges within your career, shifting satisfaction to nurturing, and changing careers.

Repetition. Some of us (probably a minority) are simply able to continue what we've been doing, still finding exciting risk and achievement satisfaction from our tasks right up until retirement age and even beyond. Whether this works or not depends on the fit between our needs and the job's possibilities. For example, research on MIT graduates suggests that virtually *no* engineering graduates were happy simply practicing engineering until retirement.[18] Indeed, it is not an exaggeration to say that *there is no such thing a as a viable life-long career in engineering.* The tasks become too repetitious and boring (perhaps because management shifts the more challenging work to younger engineers skilled in newer analytical techniques). In contrast, Ph.D. scientist graduates seemed to find continuing stimulation in their research and development activity. They encountered no mid-life decline in career satisfaction, probably because they enjoyed more autonomy and opportunity to stay at the cutting edge of their fields. Most of us would probably find simple repetition very stifling, leading to frustration and stagnation.

Shift focus off the job. If life at work becomes sour at mid-life, some of us attempt to maintain a sense of generativity by focusing more on family or avocation. We continue to do our jobs until a probably early retirement but make this less central to who we are.[19] Something like 25 percent of all men over fifty-five appear to be retired either because of illness, forced departure, or voluntary retirement! Rediscovering family and pursuing hobbies can indeed be satisfying. People who retire successfully generally seriously pursued an avocation long *before* actual retirement so the shift in focus occurred gradually rather than traumatically.

This graceful shift is attractive, but unfortunately it probably wouldn't work for most of us. Career-centered, ambitious men in the United States (we know little about the retirement transition with women, but it appears to be much less traumatic than for men) tend to so define their personal self-worth in terms of job success that we don't believe ourselves when we say we are making a mature decision to shift our life focus away from work toward home and family. In a perverse way, men often "blame" their spouses and children for imagined lack of support that supposedly handicapped them in achieving greater career success.[20] Given the popular notion that excessive career commitment undermines family happiness, it is ironic that higher income and feelings of success are both associated with *greater* family involvement.[21]

Find new challenges within your career. An exciting life includes numerous repetitions of engagement and letting go:[22]

- We confront a task about which we know little.
- We experience the stomach butterflies that entice us to flee.
- We begin to master the new task and enjoy an exhilarating sense of personal growth as we improve and repeat the task with a sense of accomplishment.
- But then the learned task becomes a bit too easy so we begin to seek a new challenge.

Thus, at the very time when we are at peak performance, we let go of the known and embrace another unknown repeating the cycle of anxiety, growth, and mastery. By "losing" the past, we confront the future and stay vital.[23]

Some years ago the Museum of Modern Art in New York City mounted a comprehensive retrospective of the art of Pablo Picasso. The paintings and sculptures were arranged in chronological order from the top down a circular walkway so viewers could observe seventy years of output without changing floors. What struck me was the periodic dramatic style changes—from the artist's youthful realism to his imitation of the late nineteenth century impressionists to his twentieth century co-invention of cubism to his personalized neoclassicism and onto the grotesque comic structures of post-World War II. I didn't like all the styles (and I doubt that Picasso did either), but that is not the point. What he did was remain alive by letting go of what he already did well in order to embrace/invent something that he didn't know.

In effect, we deny death and remain *alive* to the extent that we have sufficient physical energy and moral courage to repeat this cycle by letting go of what we know in order to confront that which we don't.[24] The most creative of us seem able to unceasingly explore new aspects of our jobs, even without later career promotions or position changes.

Shift satisfaction to nurturing. Repeatedly inventing new tasks and styles is a difficult road, perhaps suited only to the geniuses among us. More feasible for most of us is shifting our career focus away from personal accomplishment toward creating an environment in which others can achieve. "Those who can, do; those who can't, teach" is a bit harsh, but shifting to the role of mentor and teacher can be very effective for emphasizing generativity in later career. Effective nurturing that takes joy in seeing a subordinate surpass you reflects the most attractive aspect of the "good face of power" we discussed earlier.[25] The great Renaissance Italian artist Leonardo da Vinci is supposed to have said, "The master whose student doesn't surpass him has failed."

This change of self-image from being a personal dominator-achiever to orchestrator of an environment in which others can achieve is particularly appropriate in modern firms employing well-educated professionals. With the pace of technical innovation and competitive transformation, senior management's personal experience is less relevant to centralized decision making and less popular among young managers and professionals seeking autonomy and responsibility. Thus, the "gamesman" or "innovator" type executive who enjoys creating an environment that challenges and gives freedom within limits to subordinates is the most successful.[26] Of course, it can be a fine and difficult line between such innovative leadership and laissez-faire abdication.

Such innovator-type mentoring is certainly an attractive answer to the generativity versus stagnation issue, but intensely achievement-oriented careerists often find it impossible to subordinate their personal accomplishment to that of protégés. Some even see their juniors as threats so that they are eliminated as soon as their abilities begin to approach their superiors'. Such fearful executives can even self-destruct as they reject juniors making themselves less accessible, while their leadership style becomes increasingly autocratic.[27]

Changing careers. The old saying is that "you can't go home again." What is implied is that no one can turn back the clock and start over (however attractive such a notion is in numerous movies and daydreams). Perhaps, however, one can revitalize one's life by starting a new career, thus sort of recycling back to the exciting establishment phase of career growth as illustrated in Exhibit 12–2. In the 1970s much enthusiasm was voiced for corporate efforts to facilitate such recycling by providing educational benefits and sabbaticals enabling employees to retrain for new careers elsewhere.[28] Many of these benefits have been victims of the harsher economic realities of the competitive 1980s, but some large firms like IBM and Xerox still tout their support for such career renewal.

I once helped conduct a program to train middle-aged business executives to become Health Maintainence Organization administrators. Most of the executives had been quite successful (average income was close to $200,000 per year), but they had either plateaued, were bored

EXHIBIT 12–2: CAREER AND GROWTH STAGES

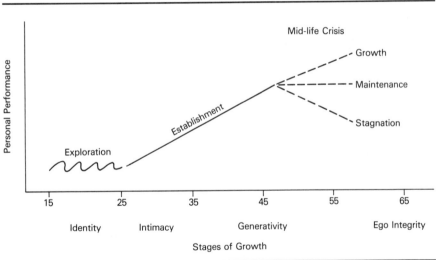

with their jobs, or hoped to make another contribution. Because physicians tend to be poor managers, Penn's Leonard Davis Institute for Health Economics developed a program to help them prepare for new careers as managers of HMOs. It was exciting to feel the enthusiasm of these middle-aged "students" as they embarked on a new career in a new institution.

Such career changes and the preparation for them, unfortunately, is very expensive. Someone has to foot the bill for education and living while in training. A few firms like IBM supplement the salary of an early retiree if they enter teaching or community services, but for most people starting a new career will usually mean a significant income reduction (for the business executives becoming HMO administrators, the average starting salaries were about $80,000—not bad, but a far cry from their earlier $200,000). Most successful career changes seem to occur where merger or pruning has forced out executives with a nice early retirement package of a year's salary plus a pension to ease the transition. But even here, it helps greatly if the exiled executives already had strong volunteer or avocational interests that they were able to build into new careers.[29]

Predictions of the decline of the "linear life" have been voiced.[30] That is, the predominant future pattern will not be the past's education–work–families–retirement. Pictured, rather, are more flexible, cyclical lives alternating work, education, and leisure through several repetitions. And even that retirement will be postponed or eliminated for most because of more demand for employees than people available. For some it may be an attractive image, but the reality today is still tending toward earlier retirement (a third of all males retire while still in their fifties; the average age is sixty-two).

Tactics for Staying Vital.

Habit and preoccupation are the ultimate threats of success.[31] As we master our jobs and grow older, we tend to behave without thinking, sort of sleepwalking through our lives allowing our perceptive skills to atrophy. Fiftyish men particularly demonstrate a propensity to insulate themselves, to draw back from the competitive fray, to lose touch with customers and markets.[32] One study of 2,000 executives concluded that the single most important attribute of those who handled success well (and were able to maintain it) was their ability to embrace change.[33] To stay so vital requires maintaining the ability to perceive uniquely, to see *differences.*

Experience can be a great source of learning of course. It can certainly save a lot of time as we fit current problems into the learned categories from the past. Unfortunately, it can also waste time and cause disaster if we categorize prematurely and erroneously.[34] Richard Nixon was regarded as one of the most effective managers (if not leader) among modern U.S. presidents. Friends and enemies alike, however, wondered at the bungling of the Watergate episode that led to his resignation in 1973.

He seemed so cool and rational with respect to foreign policy, but he was inept and emotional in dealing with his biggest domestic crisis.[35] Perhaps Nixon simply categorized it improperly. He seemed to perceive Watergate as a political matter, not as an important national moral issue. He believed that after some temporary flack the hubbub would die down as people lost interest. The "political" cue mentally filed the problem into a slot that activated an inappropriate and inadequate response. Nixon was incapable of seeing Watergate deeply and uniquely until it was too late.

You have heard of people who have worked for twenty years, but don't have twenty years' experience; they merely repeated the first year twenty times. Such people may treat a new problem as if it were like past ones, but in fact it is new and unique. Keeping alive this ability to perceive deeply requires frequent exercise. This means building into our daily life regular repetition of the process of letting go of the known and confronting the unknown—change for the hell of it. This doesn't require quitting your job, divorcing your spouse, and moving to Hawaii. Rather it means frequent small encounters with threatening changes. Here are some tactics.

After-action memos. The police and military generally require formal reports after significant actions. Since these reports become part of a permanent record, all too often they become somewhat fanciful or sanitized versions of reality. Nonetheless, writing a short "for my eyes only" memo after major projects or annual cycles like budget preparation or performance reviews can be a helpful device for avoiding making the same mistakes over and over. This is not a "cover-your-ass" memo but simply a note to yourself that can be filed with its predecessors.

Filed away, but not forgotten. Perhaps annually (I found the first couple of summer vacation days particularly appropriate), peruse your memo file for patterns. Is there some communication habit you could change? Some routine but major task that you could handle differently? For example, as I described in Chapter 6, while in process on major projects, I often undercommunicate upward. I simply haven't kept superiors adequately informed so they had to deal with their own anxieties while awaiting my results (as good as they should have known they would be).

This kind of behavioral pattern might emerge from your after-action files and be a candidate for the following innovation objective.

Innovation objectives. Every three to six months you might focus on one major aspect of your job and put it on trial for its life. Could it be eliminated? Could it simply be ignored until someone complains? Or could you experiment with changing it? In applying this tactic to my own work, for example, the task that jumped out at me was grading. After fifteen years as a teacher, I was experiencing increasing difficulty in evaluating student papers. I found myself giving no Fs or Ds and almost no Cs. Everyone was getting a B or an A. Had I become too lax? Had I been corrupted by the grading inflation that has affected schools everywhere? Did I court student popularity so avidly that I wanted everyone to be happy? Or was I such an outstanding teacher that all my students were able to master the material?

I would have liked to answer the last question in the affirmative, but I needed to probe deeper. What could I change? Perhaps I could give no tests or require no papers (sure to be popular with students, but a cop-out of a teacher's responsibility). Or perhaps I could delegate all grading to a graduate student assistant who could deal with unhappy students (tempting, but likewise irresponsible in my opinion). Or, perhaps I could change my testing format. Because I believe that life is an open book rather than a closed-book examination, I give only take-home cases and essay questions which require students to write fairly lengthy reports (which are of course easier to read than scribbled in-class quizzes). But grading such reports is quite subjective. It is often difficult to defend my judgment when an ambitious student complains. Perhaps I could change my method. Other professors use a more objective true-false or multiple-choice format. Such tests are easier to grade and seem to provide more defensible numbers as grades.

This specific example of my personal grading problem is obviously not important to most readers (and will not elicit your sympathy I'm sure), but the point is that we all have central aspects of our jobs in which we experience difficulty. I once asked a group of managers at one of the world's best-managed firms, Johnson and Johnson, what activity they found most difficult, so much so that it was the number one thing on which they procrastinated. Their most common reply was giving a negative performance evaluation, particularly to a subordinate older in age than the evaluating manager. They want to avoid an unpleasant confrontation, or they don't believe the older person will change anyway, or they are not confident of their performance criteria. What they might do is focus on one or two older, unsatisfactory subordinates for a few months, experimenting with changing the mode of performance feedback. Perhaps they could write a memo to themselves *every* time they observe the subordinate in action. Then they could schedule time *every* week to discuss these observations while they are fresh rather than letting unrecorded impressions pile up until a fruitless annual interview ritual. The new approach may or may not work, but the very action of confronting a difficult new behavior will help preserve your vitality.

Growth objectives. Most creative ideas don't spring fully defined from the creator's mind like Botticelli's Venus springing from the sea. Rather, most creativity is borrowing something from one context and applying it to another. So more creative people tend to have wider and more random interests outside their specialization.[36] Quarterly, semi-annual, or annual personal growth objectives are intended to encourage you to focus on a new field or activity—learning how to play the piano at age thirty-five; studying Spanish at age forty; starting to paint at fifty. All can be vehicles for keeping alive your ability to perceive uniquely.

I had been painting pictures with oil paints for many years when I decided to try watercolors. What to the uninitiated appears as a trivial shift, however, turned out to require very different observational skills. Oil painting for me is a spontaneous medium in which errors are easy to correct by simply painting over the offending portion. The smell and feel of the semi-solid paint is very *physical.* Waterpainting turned out to be entirely different. It is so planned and intellectual. What is key is where on the paper you *don't* paint—the whites are much of the finished picture. And errors cannot be covered up! The paint is too transparent. Consequently, the entire painting must be planned in advance in great detail so the scene being painted must be studied much more deeply than when oil painting. It is precisely this intense study that is the purpose of periodic personal growth objectives that involve modest but repeated confrontations with the unknown. In these encounters it is less important that you actually master the new than that you give it a good effort.

Maintenance objectives. The final periodic target is what improvement you might make in your diet, physical activity, or recreation. What can you do at the most personal level to improve your well-being? As the founder of my university, Benjamin Franklin, told us long ago, mastering your own eating, exercise, and play habits can provide a tonic to your total life situation. Being in control of yourself in mid-life will spill over onto the job and improve your task mastery and flexibility.

My own first application of this maintenance objective led to the virtual elimination of soft drinks from my diet. Long a cola freak (since I didn't drink coffee, I had to find something containing caffeine to keep me awake in college and the Navy), I consumed more than six cans a day. Since I hated the taste of sugar substitutes, that is a lot of refined sugar. The reduced sugar intake was desirable and the twenty-pound weight loss rewarding, but even more beneficial was the verification that I could do it.

The major purpose of all these tactics is to help maturing managers to perceive situations as unique, to retain their ability to see how the present is different from the past, and how the future will be different still. As you grow older, you need to retain a tolerance for ambiguity.

Transcending Your Career. Numerous senior executives have said to me that they never really felt comfortable in their careers until they sort of "transcended" their ambitions. It is not that they gave up the race, but they became less concerned with the winning and happier with merely running. The key to this turning point lies in accepting oneself, in giving up the tyranny of external evaluations.[37] Many come to recognize that if in old age they are lying on a bed somewhere dying, what they will be happy or sad about is not what they accomplished in their careers. Rather at the final critical moments, most of us will bear regret or pride about what we did for those we loved, particularly our children. Paradoxically, this very lessening of career centrality can often promote personal success as you become less fearful of making mistakes and more willing to run with intuition.

No one of course can truly "transcend" time, but ultimately the most effective senior executives seem to lift their time horizons. Most achievement-oriented managers are dominated by a Newtonian view of time as constant, unvarying motion in which each interval is unique but equal. As we saw in Chapter 5, the activist ethic associated with this perspective encourages constant, short-range activity. It discourages speculation and fosters guilt feelings when one is not busy. The paradox for managers is that they need to relax a little in order to work more effectively—relax the intensity of their work on present problems and address themselves more to future possibilities. They need to value today less and tomorrow more.

Managers tend to avoid thought about the future because it is ambiguous. Clear-cut, programmed, short-run problems are difficult but satisfying to solve. In contrast, formulating wishes about the future, conceiving what we want the future to be, and perceiving the future as history is difficult and threatening.

The threat is twofold. First, we tend to fear the kind of time necessary for such thought. It must be unstructured, open, and seemingly undirected—all attributes counter to time-haunted, efficiency-minded people. Wide-open time, like space, can be frightening. Second, incorporating concern about the future into the present necessitates clarifying what we really want, and this means defining fundamental values of management, organizations, and society. As we wrestle with problems of U.S. competitiveness, government debt, and environmental pollution, such clarification is critical for all of our futures.

An old American Indian proverb states, "All that is seen is temporary." The present is not unimportant nor is the world an illusion, but future-oriented, time-transcending executives should have the kind of detachment often found in people who accomplish great things while refusing to be devoured by current events and present time.

Now let's return to the daughter's description of her father's career and see what she feels she has learned from him.

WHAT DAUGHTER LEARNED FROM HER FATHER

I am my father's daughter in many ways. From him I inherited a love of power and a need to control, an intensity in pursuing my goals, a strong sense of organization, and an identity based on a need to succeed at work. In the future, I hope to be able to use my legacy in a positive way, while avoiding some of the mistakes my father made.

I have a photograph of myself in high school. I'm seated behind my father's imposing wooden desk, sitting in his huge leather chair. And I'm smiling. I used to tell my father that my ultimate goal was to be in that chair for real. I wanted to sit behind a big desk and have people deferentially pop their heads in and ask for a minute of my time. And I wanted them to be nervous.

I've learned some things about power since that time. Although I still want to be in a powerful position, I think about it in a different way. I want to use power as a means of transferring my knowledge to others and guiding a group of people to success. Obviously, I'm not ready for that yet. I learned from my father that power is something you need to grow into, and that needs to be given to you willingly rather than demanded.

More importantly, I've learned that power must be moderated. A manager's job is not only to get the job done well, but also to develop his or her subordinates. Any manager who insists on controlling every situation will most likely stifle her subordinates' development.

I have the same stubborn intensity my father possessed. At work I often set goals and deadlines for competing projects. Once I had committed to finishing a project by a certain date, I did everything to get it done on time. Even when no one else seemed to care if it got done, I would stay up all night finishing it. Often my pursuit of goals and my commitment were not useful to myself or my company, and may even have distracted me from starting new, more important projects.

I believe now that goals should be flexible. What seems like a valuable goal when a project begins doesn't always make sense a few months later. I can't say I'm ready to change my ways yet, but I've realized that stubborn persistence toward the wrong goal can be more of a liability than a strength.

I also learned my father's time management and organizational skills. I manage work overload on the job and at school by staying one step ahead of the game. I write prioritized to-do lists; I finish papers or projects a day early; and I schedule my days tightly so there's no room for decisions because I always know what I need to do next. I keep panic at bay by convincing myself that I control my work, rather than it controlling me.

Nonetheless, like my father, when my system falls apart, I get very anxious. I can't tolerate uncertainty or unexpected schedule changes and I'm resentful of people who interfere with my sense of order. I'm inflexible because I'm overscheduled.

Life in an organization is often uncertain. Managing time well is important of course, but so is flexibility and adapting to change. Managers are interdependent, and the people I will have to depend on won't be as organized as I am. I've already realized this on group projects. My group members often procrastinate. As a result, I drive them crazy with my incessant hounding, and they drive me crazy with their inability to buckle down and get the job done before the last minute.

What's the solution? I'm not sure. I wouldn't trade my ability to manage time for anything. But I do think I need to develop more flexibility and let others get the job done in their own way, without becoming resentful.

I've been working since I formed my own bakery at the age of twelve. I babysat, ran a day care center, worked in department stores, waitressed and worked as a writer. I worked throughout college even though my parents would have provided me with money. I never took the trip to Europe I had planned when I graduated because I wanted to work. Why? Because I need to earn money. I feel lost without a job; without a paycheck; without a title.

What's the result of all this diligent working? When I'm old, will I look back and fondly remember the days of delivering pizza to hungry teenagers? If I look at my father's example, probably not. If I listen to anyone who's finished their career, probably not. But will that stop me from working? Probably not.

However, there are still important lessons to be learned from my father's experiences and the reflections of senior executives. I can try to look forward and imagine how I will feel about my life in thirty years. Will I be proud of the things I've done, or regretful about the things I've sacrificed?

The two most important lessons I've learned from my father is the need to find your own way in your career and strike a balance between work and outside life. Finding your own way can be difficult, especially at lower levels. I've often found it hard to resist the temptation to conform to my employers' expectations. I watched my father resist the culture of Universe Electronics. He didn't change the organization, but he didn't change himself either. And from that I learned that it is possible to survive in an environment very different from yourself and still maintain your identity. But I also learned that you probably won't be very happy so you should strive to find a compatible firm.

In addition, I've learned the importance of balance. Work and career success are important. To succeed and be happy, managers need to set career goals and commit to reaching them. But work is not enough. You can't define yourself solely in terms of success at work, or every setback will be devastating.

My hope is that I will remember some of the messages I took from my father's life as I travel along my way. And while I might not always do the right thing, I hope that I will always feel that I've made the best decision I could. Someday, when I'm older and I'm looking back on my career, I hope that I can say that I've been true to myself and that I've focused my energy on the things that are really important.

ADVICE ON HANDLING MIDDLE AGE IN MANAGEMENT

- Recognize that technical and interpersonal skills are necessary for management success but insufficient to suit you for senior management. Expose yourself to broadening experiences that will help you develop a conceptual and integrating perspective.
- Don't put all your eggs in your career basket. In addition to family concerns, cultivate outside service and advocation activities as you approach mid-life.
- Examine what is the most viable path for you to maintain personal generativity. Can you infuse your existing duties with sufficient novelty? Can you find serious off-job pursuits that will provide new reinvigorating challenges? Can you find new enjoyment from mentoring your juniors to perform better, perhaps even surpassing you?
- Most ambitiously, perhaps, is there a dramatically new career which you could prepare for and eventually move into?
- If and when you experience mid-life uneasiness with your career, share these feelings with your spouse and children. They initially may not like or understand what you are saying but necessary later changes, if any, will be much easier if they don't come as a surprise.
- Learn from the tragedies of others that leaving your family and living a middle-aged bachelor's life is seldom a viable answer to the pain of losing career momentum and being plateaued on the job.
- Learn from your major experiences by writing private after-action memos to yourself. Periodically review them to detect unhelpful behavior patterns that you might try to modify.
- Conscientiously work on confronting novelty by building change into your job and personal life. Periodically experiment with changing one major activity in your job—eliminate it, ignore it, delegate it, or change it.
- Similarly, periodically define personal growth and maintenance objectives that will force you to confront a new task in a way that will exercise your ability to perceive deeply and to master yourself.

Conclusion

Advice on Handling Career Problems

When after fifteen years as a management professor I moved full time into university administration as a vice president, I was worried that my new subordinates would read my textbooks and expect me to practice what I had preached. Therefore, at my first departmental meeting I told my assembled staff of 120 that I encouraged them all to buy my books, *but under no circumstances should they read them!*

The gap between normative theory and management practice is wide. No one can be as good as the books suggest. Things are just too uncontrollable. Thankfully for you and your firms, most of this book's readers will not be entering management after fifteen years in academia. You should be less spoiled than I was. Nonetheless, life at work will be a bit different than you expect: less structured and more ambiguous, less rational and more emotional, less controllable and more insistent, less unethical but more demanding of courage. Each chapter in this book has ended with a set of explicit advisements about the issues raised. Let me, therefore, draw out what I think are the most important axioms to keep in mind as you begin your career.

- Your career is important. You may accept the likelihood of some early dissatisfaction, but don't think that you can successfully treat your job as merely a vehicle to find life's satisfactions elsewhere. Unhappiness on the job will spill over into your personal life, even corrupting a happy family. So don't be afraid to change jobs and don't feel guilty about it.
- But it is better to move earlier and later rather than in the middle. The period from your late twenties to early forties should include a solid eight to twelve years with one organization, demonstrating your ability to make a valuable contribution in a measurable way.
- Your career may be important, but it is not your whole being. No career failure should be allowed to touch the inner self that defines your basic integrity. *You* are more important than your career. Always maintain some distance between yourself and whatever you do to make a living.
- Involve your family in your job and career. Balancing career and home needs is essential in the long run, and it will be easier to main-

tain to the extent that family members understand the realities of your duties.

- Be honest with yourself. All people experience career setbacks. Those who bounce back and those who don't are equally ambitious and hard working. What distinguishes those who are defeated by failure is defensiveness, trying to conceal their mistakes or blaming them on others. Those who recover admit publicly and to themselves that they erred and then try to correct the causes.
- To do good requires you to exercise power. Don't shrink from acquiring and using power because you don't want to "hurt" people. Yes, you will undoubtedly hurt someone while leading any significant change, but accepting responsibility (and some "guilt" feelings) is essential to even the most idealistic and altruistic leadership.
- You can't be all things to all people. Effective time managers try to overcome role overload and stress by experimenting with their environment—projecting themselves ahead in time, ignoring certain demands, downplaying more urgent trivia, focusing on more important objectives, and attempting to renegotiate with their demanders.
- Long-term time management means defining what objectives are less and more deferrable, and fighting for more time to invest in those more deferrable, less explicitly cued, and more important but ambiguous objectives like adaptation and revitalization.
- Your courage will be especially tested in situations where your superior has assigned you a task which holds promise of making you a star, but on which he or she has only ambiguously defined your authority. You must find clever ways to precipitate a clarification of the delegation terms.
- Don't be overly concerned with prestige or status symbols like title, office size, and furnishings. What counts is that you are performing interesting tasks that provide opportunities for you to demonstrate a contribution to the organization's central objectives—and that you find and commit to such a situation by your late twenties/early thirties.
- Remember that you are not likely to influence others effectively if you rely primarily on "pulling rank" using your positional authority. Effective power grows out of your expertise, your personal relationships, and your judicious willingness to represent your subordinates' interests upward.
- Recognize that "knowledge" may be "power" but that overly analytical, achievement-oriented staff professionals often neglect investing sufficient time in developing the interpersonal skills necessary to be an effective manager.
- Finding a star mentor is terrific, but being a protégé also carries

certain responsibilities. Don't be seduced by the mentor who wants to be a "father" dominating all aspects of your career in return for your loyal passivity. On the other hand, don't be afraid to make commitments to those whose values and organizational dreams you share.

- Loyalty is dead only if you define it as blind acceptance of whatever the organization hands you. But loyalty is alive and essential in other forms—especially giving honest effort, protecting your superior, and communicating upward truthfully.

- In no area is naivete more dangerous than in blowing the whistle on an organizational activity with which you disagree. Most of all, it should not be an emotional outburst, but a conscience-driven, deeply thought-out plan of action.

- Courage is required to dissent from unethical but popular behavior. Resignation is sometimes the proper course. Nonetheless, staying and changing group or organizational behavior usually requires even more courage—and is to be even more admired.

- "Being different" in race, gender, or ethnicity can be tough in any group or organization, but effective minority managers find ways to minimize the threat that they present to the majority. Sure it is unfair to burden additionally such minority managers with adjusting their own behavior, but until all of us become more skilled at valuing differences, the onus will be on the minority person to present himself or herself as in the mainstream.

- The acid test of managerial competence is the ability to lead an unpopular change effort even when your authority to do so is unclear. Waiting until you are certain you have all the necessary power is a recipe for paralysis. Such change agent-managers are particularly courageous in recognizing that real change is impossible without causing some stress among the people effected—"no pain, no gain."

- Management and leadership are not mutually exclusive, but most of the time being a manager involves less heroic initiatives than being a leader manifests. Yet, I doubt that one can be an effective leader without being an effective manager, at least not in the corporate world. Becoming a leader, however, particularly requires great clarity of purpose, a focus on a relatively short list of initiatives, and courage to push for an outcome you think is needed even if unpopular.

- Effective leader-managers in the long run are "friendly" with their work colleagues and subordinates but don't depend on them for "friendship" or verification of self-worth. Look for affirmation of your inherent value from yourself and from families and nonjob friends, not from those who might be adversely affected by your valid but necessary tough decisions.

- "Time happeneth to us all." All too soon, we start being viewed as middle-aged by our organizations. Those who handle this mid-life transition well are those who ensure that they are performing activities that they truly value and enjoy, while in small ways they demonstrate the discipline and courage to give up things which they do well in order to confront unknown demands and develop new skills, especially in nurturing the performance of creative juniors.

Optimism and a lack of cynicism are great allies in handling all of these career and life challenges. Of course one can't be a naive, Pollyanna type oblivious to the world's meanness and unethicalness. Nonetheless, believing that you have a good shot at handling your affairs sensitively and ethically will go a long way toward assisting your managerial success.

Good luck—And have courage!

Endnotes

INTRODUCTION

May Sarton quoted in J. LeCarre, *The Russia House* (New York: Knopf, 1989), foreword. The quote is from M. Sarton, *Journal of a Solitude*, (New York: W. W. Norton & Co., 1973).

[1]R. Baumhart, *Ethics in Business*, (New York: Holt, Rinehart and Winston, 1968).

[2]*Business and Society Review;* "Symposium: Do Good Ethics Ensure Good Profits," no. 70 (Summer 1989), pp. 4–10.

[3]A. Etzioni, "Good Ethics is Good Business—Really," *The New York Times*, February 2, 1989, op. ed., p. A34.

[4]J. B. McGuire, A. Sundgren, and T. Schneeweis, "Corporate Social Responsibility and Firm Financial Performance," *Academy of Management Journal*, 31, no. 4 (1988), 854–872.

[5]D. L. Kanter and P. H. Mirvis, *The Cynical Americans: Living and Working in an Age of Discontent and Disillusion* (San Francisco: Jossey-Bass Publishers, 1989).

[6]*The Wall Street Journal*, September 8, 1987, p. A1.

[7]C. Peterson, M. E. Seligman, and G. E. Vaillant, "Pessimistic Explanatory Style Is a Risk Factor for Physical Illness: A Thirty-Five Year Longitudinal Study," *Journal of Personality and Social Psychology*, 55, no. 1 (1988), 23–27. See also J. Scott, "Cynical, Angry People Run More Risk of Heart Ills, Study Says," *Philadelphia Inquirer*, January 17, 1989.

[8]J. L. Badaracco and R. L. Ellsworth, *Leadership and the Quest for Integrity* (Boston: Harvard Business School Press, 1988).

[9]S. Jeffers, *Feel the Fear and Do It Anyway* (New York: Harcourt Brace Jovanovich, 1987).

[10]On President Truman, see: D. Acheson, *Present at the Creation*, (New York: Norton, 1969), pp. 731–733; and H. S. Truman, *Year of Decisions* (Garden City, N.Y.: Doubleday, 1955).

[11]M. Meyer, *The Alexander Complex: The Dreams that Drive Great Businessmen* (New York: Time Books, 1989), p. 2.

[12]G. Keillor, "Toasting the Flag," *New York Times,* July 2, 1989, section 4, p. E13 (N).

[13]J. B. Miner, "The Real Crunch in Managerial Manpower," *Harvard Business Review* (November-December, 1973), pp. 146–158.

[14]M. Maccoby, *The Gamesman* (New York: Simon & Schuster, 1976). See also A. Bennett, *The Death of the Organization Man* (New York: William Morrow, 1990).

[15]M. Maccoby, *Why Work: Leading the New Generation* (New York: Simon and Schuster, 1988).

[16]E. Erikson, *Childhood and Society* (New York: Norton, 1964).

[17]Dwight Waldo quoted in E. E. Williams, Jr., "Democracy and Organizations—Are They Compatible," *The Wharton Account,* 5, no. 2 (December, 1965), p. 4.

[18]D. J. Levinson, *The Seasons of a Man's Life* (New York: Knopf, 1978).

[19]M. Maccoby, *Why Work: Leading the New Generation.*

[20]P. Tillich, *The Courage To Be* (New Haven: Yale University Press, 1950).

[21]J. I. Klein, "Science and Subterfuge," *Academy of Management EXECUTIVE,* 3, no. 1 (1989), 59–62.

[22]W. G. Bennis and B. Nanus, *Leaders: The Strategies for Taking Charge* (New York: Harper & Row, 1985).

CHAPTER 1: GROWING UP AT WORK

[1]The Ted Kennedy story is told in I. Berg, *The Business of America* (New York: Harcourt, Brace & World, 1968), p. 336.

[2]J. Main, "B-Schools Get a Global Vision," *Fortune,* July 17, 1989, pp. 78–86. Quotation is of William Daniels, p. 85.

[3]P. B. Bates and K. W. Schaie, *Life-Span Development Psychology* (New York: Academic Press, 1973).

[4]On maturation and "other-direction," see D. Riesman, et al, *The Lonely Crowd* (New Haven: Yale University, 1950) and J. S. Coleman, *The Adolescent Society: The Social Life of the Teenager and its Impact on Education* (New York: Free Press, 1971).

[5]A. Montague, "Sociogenic Brain Damage," *American Anthropologist,* 74, no. 5 (1972), 1045–1061.

[6]E. Erikson, *Childhood and Society* (New York: Norton, 1964).

[7]C. C. Manz, D. Adsit, S. Campbell, and M. Mathison-Hance, "Managerial Thought Patterns and Performance," *Human Relations,* 41, no. 6 (1988), 447–465.

Endnotes

[8]D. C. McClelland, *The Achieving Society* (New York: Van Nostrand Reinhold, 1961).

[9]M. Hennig and A. Jardim, *The Managerial Woman* (Garden City, N.Y.: Anchor/Doubleday, 1977).

[10]E. P. Hollander, and R. H. Willis, "Some Current Issues in the Psychology of Conformity and Nonconformity," *Psychological Bulletin* 68 (1967), 62–76.

[11]T. J. Scheff, "Shame and Conformity: The Deference-Emotion System," *American Sociological Review,* 53 (June, 1988), 395–406.

[12]D. Goleman, "Therapists Find Last Outpost of Adolescence in Adulthood," *The New York Times,* November 8, 1988, p. 15 (N).

[13]J. B. Miner, "Decline and Stabilization of Managerial Motivation Over 20 Year Period," *Journal of Applied Psychology,* 67, no. 3 (June, 1982), 297–305.

[14]R. May, *Power and Innocence* (New York: W.W. Norton, 1972).

[15]M. B. Arthur and B. S. Lawrence, "Perspectives on Environment and Career: An Introduction," 5, no. 1 (1984), 1–8. See also M. B. Arthur, D. T. Hall, and B. S. Lawrence, *Handbook of Career Theory* (New York: Cambridge University Press, 1990).

[16]H. Gunz, "The Dual Meaning of Managerial Careers: Organizational and Individual Levels of Analysis," *Journal of Management Studies,* 26, no. 3, (May 1989), 225–250.

[17]M. W. McCall and E. E. Lawler, III, "High School Students' Perception of Work," *Academy of Management Journal,* 19, no. 1 (March 1976), 17–24.

[18]E. H. Schein, "Culture as an Environmental Context for Careers," *Journal of Occupational Behavior,* 5, no. 1 (1984), 71–81.

[19]M. London, *Developing Managers: A Guide to Motivating and Preparing People for Successful Managerial Careers* (San Francisco: Jossey-Bass Publishers, 1985).

[20]E. Siegel, "Decision Processes Leading to Career Choice and Resulting Career Dedication: A Study of the Fields of Medicine and Accounting," Working Paper, The Wharton School, University of Pennsylvania (Philadelphia, 1978).

[21]S. Gould, "Characteristics of Career Planners in Upwardly Mobile Occupations," *Academy of Management Journal,* 22, no. 3 (1979), 539–550.

[22]M. D. Fottler and T. Bain, "Sex Differences in Occupational Aspirations," *Academy of Management Journal,* 23, No. 1 (1980), 144–149.

[23]Unhappy careerists quoted in D. Sifford, "Second Thoughts on Choos-

ing a Life's Work in College," *Philadelphia Inquirer,* February 27, 1989.

[24]W. L. Mihal, P. A. Sorce, and T. E. Comte, "A Process Model of Individual Career Decision Making," *Academy of Management Review,* 9, no. 1 (1984), 93–103.

[25]P. T. Costa, R. R. McCrae, and J. L. Holland, "Personality and Vocational Interests in an Adult Sample," *Journal of Applied Psychology,* 69, no. 3 (1984), 390–400.

[26]P. Nulty, "The Hot Demand for New Scientists," *Fortune,* July 31, 1989, pp. 155–163.

[27]R. A. Bhagat and M. B. Chassie, "Determinants of Organizational Commitment in Working Women," *Journal of Occupational Behavior,* 2, no. 1 (1981), 17–30.

[28]D. J. Levinson, *The Seasons of a Man's Life* (New York: Knopf, 1978).

[29]See D. T. Hall, "A Theoretical Model of Career Subidentity Development in Organizational Settings," *Organizational Behavior and Human Performance,* 6 (January, 1971), 50–76 and J. F. Veiga, "The Mobile Manager at Mid-Career," *Harvard Business Review* (January-February, 1973), p. 115ff.

[30]A. Zalesnik et al., *Orientation and Conflict in Career* (Boston: Graduate School of Business Administration, Harvard University, 1970).

[31]E. Fromm, *Escape From Freedom* (New York: Farrar Rinehart, 1941).

[32]J. Steiner, "What Price Success?" *Harvard Business Review,* (March-April 1972), pp. 69–74.

[33]Soren Kierkegaard, the Danish philosopher, is quoted in R. May, *The Meaning of Anxiety* (New York: W. W. Norton, 1977), p. 392.

CHAPTER 2: DEALING WITH EARLY DISAPPOINTMENT

[1]S. Kleinman, *Real Life 101: Almost Surviving Your First Year Out of College* (Master Media Ltd., 1989).

[2]Quoted in A. Bennett, "The Baby Busters: New Generation Asks More Than Its Elders of Corporate World," *The Wall Street Journal,* October 26, 1988, p. A1.

[3]D. Goleman, "Feeling Sleepy? An Urge to Nap is Built In," *The New York Times,* September 12, 1989 p. B5 (N).

[4]A. Gonzalez, and P. G. Zimbardo, "Time in Perspective," *Psychology Today,* (March, 1985), pp. 21–26.

[5]"Work, Work, Work," *Philadelphia Inquirer,* January 23, 1989, p. B1.

Endnotes

[6]F. S. Worthy, "You're Probably Working too Hard," *Fortune,* April 27, 1987, pp. 133–140.

[7]A. Bernstein, "Why More Mothers Are Not Getting Married," *Business Week,* May 22, 1989, pp. 74–75.

[8]A. L. Otten, "Portrait of Young Consumer as Wastrel," *The Wall Street Journal,* October 3, 1989 p. A1.

[9]L. Reibstein, "The Not-So-Fast Track: Firms Try Promoting Hotshots More Slowly," *The Wall Street Journal,* March 24, 1986 p. B1.

[10]R. E. Kelley, *The Gold Collar Worker* (Reading, Ma.: Addison-Wesley, 1985).

[11]L. W. Porter, "Where is the Organization Man?" *Harvard Business Review,* (November-December, 1963), pp. 53–61.

[12]M. McComas, "Atop the Fortune 500: A Survey of the C. E. O.'s," *Fortune,* April 28, 1966, pp. 26–31.

[13]M. Newcomer, *The Big Business Executive* (New York: Columbia University Press, 1955).

[14]P. Nulty, "The Hot Demand for New Scientists," *Fortune,* July 31, 1989, pp. 155–163.

[15]M. McComas, "Atop the Fortune 500: A Survey of the C. E. O.'s."

[16]F. J. Staszak and N. J. Mathys, "Organization Gap: Implications for Manpower Planning," *California Management Review,* 17, no. 3 (Spring, 1975), pp. 32–38.

[17]I. Berg, *Education and Jobs: The Great Training Robbery* (New York: Praeger, 1970).

[18]J. Livingston, "Pygmalion in Management," *Harvard Business Review* (July-August, 1969), pp. 81–89.

[19]D. E. Berlew and D. T. Hall, "The Socialization of Managers: Effects of Expectation on Performance," *Administrative Science Quarterly,* 11, no. 2 (1969), p. 208.

[20]Quoted in A. Bennett, "The Baby Busters: New Generation Asks More Than Its Elders of Corporate World."

[21]D. B. Greenberger, S. Strasser, L. L. Cummings, and R. B. Dunham, "The Impact of Personal Control on Performance and Satisfaction," *Organizational Behavior and Human Decision Processes,* 43 (1989), pp. 29–51.

[22]W. Kiechel, "The Importance of Being Visible," *Fortune,* June 24, 1985, pp. 14–15.

[23]D. C. McClelland and D. Burnham, "Power is the Great Motivator," *Harvard Business Review* (March-April, 1976), pp. 100–110.

[24]C. M. Kelly, *The Destructive Achiever: Power and Ethics in the American Corporation* (Reading, Ma.: Addison-Wesley, 1988).

[25]J. P. Siegel, "Machiavellianism, MBA's and Managers," *Academy of Management Journal,* 16, no. 3 (1973), 404–411.

[26]C. Hymowitz, "Five Main Reasons Why Managers Fail," *The Wall Street Journal,* May 2, 1988, p. B1.

[27]A. Murray and P. Truell, "Capital Offence," *The Wall Street Journal,* January 16, 1990, p. A1.

[28]Executive quoted in C. W. Tarr, "How To Humanize MBA's." *Fortune,* March 31, 1986, p. 153.

[29]P. H. Weaver, "Life Among Motown's Machiavelli's," *The New York Times,* October 2, 1988, section 3, p. F3 (N).

[30]M. Maccoby, *Why Work: Leading the New Generation* (New York: Simon & Schuster, 1988).

[31]W. Kiechel, "The Workaholic Generation," *Fortune,* April 10, 1989, pp. 50–62.

[32]E. E. Jennings, *The Mobile Manager* (New York: McGraw-Hill, 1971).

[33]J. Main, "B-Schools Get a Global Vision," *Fortune,* July 17, 1989, pp. 78–86. Quotation is of William Daniels, p. 85.

[34]J. P. Siegel, "Machiavellianism, MBA's and Managers."

[35]D. Moment and D. Fisher, *Autonomy in Organizational Life* (Cambridge, Ma.: Schenkman, 1975).

[36]M. McComas, "Atop the Fortune 500: A Survey of the C. E. O.'s."

[37]H. Levinson, "On Being a Middle-aged Manager," *Harvard Business Review,* (July-August, 1969), pp. 51–60.

[38]L. Baird and K. Kram, "Career Dynamics: Managing the Superior/Subordinate Relationship," *Organizational Dynamics,* (Spring, 1983), pp. 46–63.

CHAPTER 3: OVERCOMING OVERLOAD AND STRESS

[1]J. C. Quick, R. E. Hess, J. Hermalin, and J. Q. Quick, *Career Stress in Changing Times* (Binghamton, N.Y.: The Haworth Press, 1989).

[2]"Treading Time," *The Wall Street Journal,* August 1, 1988, p. A1.

[3]B. J. Hunnicut, "Are We Working Too Hard?" *The Wall Street Journal,* January 4, 1990, p. A18.

[4]R. K. Merton, *Social Theory and Social Structure,* rev. ed, (New York: Free Press, 1957).

[5]On conflict between role desire and demands, see: C. N. Greene, "Relationships among Role Accuracy, Compliance, Performance Evaluation, and Satisfaction Within Managerial Dyads," *Academy of Management Journal,* 15, no. 2 (1972), 164–175; D. J. Levinson, "Role,

Personality and Social Structure in the Organizational Setting," *Journal of Abnormal and Social Psychology,* 58 (1959), 170–180; and L. G. Hrebiniak and J. A. Alutto, "Personal and Role-Related Factors in the Development of Organizational Commitment," *Administrative Science Quarterly,* 17, no. 4 (1972), 555–569.

[6]B. L. Ashforth, "The Experience of Powerlessness in Organizations," *Organizational Behavior and Human Decision Processes,* 43, (1989), 207–242.

[7]K. Heller, "A Job With Hang-Ups," *Philadelphia Inquirer,* January 15, 1989, p. 1F.

[8]R. M. Kanter, "Power Failure in Management Circuits," *Harvard Business Review,* (July-August, 1979), pp. 65–75.

[9]R. Ritti, *The Engineer in the Industrial Corporation* (New York: Columbia University Press, 1971).

[10]L. Gordon, "Survey: College Students Feel More Stress," *Philadelphia Inquirer,* January 9, 1989.

[11]L. J. Peter and R. Hull, *The Peter Principle* (New York: Morrow, 1969).

[12]C. Rossiter, *The American Presidency,* rev. ed., (New York: Harcourt Brace Jovanovich, 1960).

[13]R. A. Webber, "Innovation and Conflict in Industrial Engineering," *The Journal of Industrial Engineering,* (May, 1967), p. 13.

[14]R. L. Kahn, et al., *Organizational Stress* (New York: John Wiley & Sons, 1964).

[15]H. O. Pruden and R. M. Reese, "Inter-organization Role Set Relations and the Performance and Satisfaction of Industrial Salesmen," *Administrative Science Quarterly,* 17, no. 4 (1972), 601–618.

[16]H. E. R. Unterhoeven, "General Managers in the Middle," *Harvard Business Review,* (March-April, 1972), pp. 75–85.

[17]On role stress problems of women, see: D. T. Hall and F. E. Gordon, "Career Choices of Married Women: Effects on Conflict, Role Behavior and Satisfaction," *Journal of Applied Psychology,* 58, no. 1 (1973), 42–48; U. Sekaran, "Understanding the Dynamics of Self-concept of Members in Dual Career Families," *Human Relations,* 42, no. 2, (1989), 97–116.

[18]A. Hochschild, with A. Machung, *The Second Shift: Working Parents and the Revolution at Home* (New York: Viking Press, 1989). Hochschild quoted in G. Kolata, "Mothers with Dark Circles," *The New York Times Book Review,* June 25, 1989, p. 3.

[19]M. Seeman, "Role Conflict and Ambivalence in Leadership," *American Sociological Review,* (August 1953), pp. 373–380.

[20]T. J. Peters and R. H. Waterman, *In Search of Excellence* (New York: Harper & Row, 1982).

[21]S. Hamilton, and B. I. Fagot, "Chronic Stress and Coping Styles: A Comparison of Male and Female Undergraduates," *Journal of Personality and Social Psychology*, 55, no. 5, (1988), 819–823.

[22]A. Quindlen, "What Makes A Workaholic Keep Working?" *The New York Times*, July 21, 1988, p. 15 (N).

[23]B. A. Gutek, "Understanding Failure to Perceive Work-Family Conflict," *Academy of Management Annual Meeting*, August 15, 1989.

[24]A. L. Cowan, "Women's Gains on the Job: Not Without a Heavy Toll," *The New York Times*, August 21, 1989, p. A1.

[25]N. Lin and W. M. Emsel, "Life Stress and Health: Stressors and Resources," *American Sociological Review*, 54, (June 1989), pp. 382–399.

[26]H. B. Braiker, *The Type E Woman: How to Overcome the Stress of Being Everything to Everyone* (New York: Dodd Mead, 1987).

[27]C. Cherniss, *Professional Burnout in Human Service Organizations* (New York: Praeger, 1980).

[28]M. D. Glicken, and K. Janka, "Executives Under Fire: The Burnout Syndrome," *California Management Review*, 24, no. 3 (1982), 67–72.

[29]T. W. Johnson, and G. Graen, "Organizational Assimilation and Role Rejection," *Organizational Behavior and Human Performance*, 10 (1973), 72–87.

[30]P. D. Moen, Dempster-McLain, and R. M. Williams, Jr., "Social Integration and Longevity," *American Sociological Review*, 54, (August 1989), 635–647.

[31]L. Hirschhorn, *The Workplace Within: Psychodynamics of Organizational Life* (Cambridge, Ma.: MIT Press, 1988).

[32]F. N. Schwartz, "Management Women and the New Facts of Life," *Harvard Business Review*, (January-February, 1989), pp. 65–76.

[33]*Philadelphia Inquirer*, March 4, 1989, p. 1B; see J. A. Speller, *Executives in Crisis* (San Francisco: Jossey-Bass, 1989).

[34]M. J. McCarthy, "Women's Salaries Reflect Disparities in Executive Suites," *The Wall Street Journal*, December 1, 1986, p. A1.

[35]P. F. Drucker, *The Effective Manager* (New York: Harper & Row, 1967).

[36]N. Gross, A. W. McEachern and W. S. Mason, "Role Conflict and Its Resolutions," in E. E. Maccoby et al., ed., *Readings in Social Psychology* (New York: Holt, Rinehart & Winston, 1958).

[37]A. L. Cowan, "Women's Gains on the Job: Not Without a Heavy Toll."

Endnotes

[38]W. Kiechel, "The Guilt-Edged Executive," *Fortune*, May 28, 1984, p. 219.

[39]W. Kiechel, "When Executives Crack," *Fortune*, July 23, 1984, p. 133.

[40]On compartmentalization, see: O. G. Brim and S. Wheeler, *Socialization After Childhood* (New Work: John Wiley, 1966) and Hall, D. T., "A Model of Coping With Role Conflict: The Role Behavior of College Educated Women," *Administrative Science Quarterly*, 17, no. 4 (1972), 471–486.

[41]On the so-called "Mommy track," see F. N. Schwartz, "Management Women and the New Facts of Life," *Harvard Business Review*, (January-February, 1989), pp. 65–76 and E. Ehrlich, "The Mommy Track," *Business Week*, March 20, 1989, pp. 126–129.

[42]D. S. Holmes, and B. Kent Houston, "Effectiveness of Situation Redefinition and Affective Isolation in Coping with Stress," *Journal of Personality and Social Psychology*, 29, no. 2 (1974), 212–218.

[43]L. Festinger, *A Theory of Cognitive Dissonance*, (Palo Alto: Stanford University Press, 1957).

[44]W. J. Zerbe and D. L. Paulhus, "Socially Desirable Responding in Organizational Behavior: A Reconception," *Academy of Management Review*, 12, no. 2 (1987), 250–264.

[45]Quoted in D. Sifford, "What To Do When Marriage Partners Change Radically," *Philadelphia Inquirer*, July 27, 1989.

[46]F. E. Hall and D. T. Hall, *The Two Career Couple* (Reading, Ma.: Addison-Wesley, 1979).

[47]D. Sifford, "Spouse As A Key Factor in Career Success or Failure," *Philadelphia Inquirer*, February 2, 1989.

[48]B. A. Gutek, "Understanding Failure to Perceive Work-Family Conflict."

[49]W. Kiechel, "The Workaholic Generation," *Fortune*, April 10, 1989, pp. 50–62.

[50]R. Samuelson, "Temps Take Over and It's Not All Good," *Philadelphia Inquirer*, August 30, 1989.

[51]*Working Mother*, April, 1988.

[52]J. Greber, *The Silent Partner* (New York: Ballantine, 1985).

[53]W. Kiechel, "The Workaholic Generation."

[54]R. Kutter, "She Minds the Child, He Minds the Dog," *The New York Times Book Review*, June 25, 1989, p. 3. The book reviewed was A. Hochschild, with A. Machung, *The Second Shift: Working Parents and the Revolution at Home* (New York: Viking Press, 1989).

[55]F. Rhodewalt and J. B. Zone, "Appraisal of Life Change, Depression and Illness in Hardy and Nonhardy Women," *Journal of Personality and Social Psychology*, 56, no. 1 (1989), pp. 81–88.

[56]L. M. Crary, A. Pazy, and D. M. Wolfe, "Patterns of Life Structure and Variability in Self," *Human Relations*, 41, no. 11 (1988), 783–804.

CHAPTER 4: MANAGING SHORT-TERM TIME

[1]W. Engstrom and R. A. Mackenzie, *Managing Your Time* (Grand Rapids, Michigan: Zondervan, 1967).

[2]H. Kissinger, *White House Years* (Boston: Little, Brown, 1979).

[3]A. Uris, "How to Have Time for Everything," *Dun's Review,* August, 1957, p. 53.

[4]P. F. Drucker, "How to Manage Your Time," *Harper's Magazine,* December 1966, pp. 56ff.

[5]A. M. Schlesinger, Jr., *The Coming of the New Deal* (New York: Houghton Mifflin, 1959).

[6]G. Reedy, *The Twilight of the Presidency* (New York: Norton, 1970).

[7]C. Clifford, quoted in *Time,* June 8, 1970.

[8]R. M. Nixon, *Memoirs* (New York: Grosset & Dunlap, 1978).

[9]E. C. Bliss, *Getting Things Done: The ABC's of Time Management* (New York: Scribners, 1976).

[10]G. E. Vaillant, *Adaptation to Life* (Boston: Little, Brown, 1977).

[11]J. B. Rotter, "Generalized Expectancies for Internal Versus External Control of Reinforcement," *Psychological Monograph,* 609, vol. 80. no. 1 (1966).

[12]J. Trickett, "A More Effective Use of Time," *California Management Review,* 4, no. 4 (Summer, 1962), pp. 21–30.

[13]C. Rossiter, *The American Presidency,* rev. ed., (New York: Harcourt Brace Jovanovich, 1960). On more recent presidential styles, see R. E. Neustadt, *Presidential Power and the Modern Presidents* (New York: The Free Press, 1990).

[14]R. E. Kennedy, *Thirteen Days: A Memoir of the Cuban Missile Crisis* (New York: W.W. Norton & Co., 1969).

[15]P. F. Drucker, *The Effective Manager* (New York: Harper & Row, 1967).

[16]M. Dowd, "Kindness is Foundation as Bush Builds Bridges," *The New York Times,* February 6, 1989, p. 33 (N).

CHAPTER 5: MANAGING LONGER-TERM TIME

[1]A. Morita (President of Sony), "Something is Wrong in America," *The New York Times,* October 1, 1989, section 3, p. F2(N). But see also

Endnotes

R. F. Yates, "Working Themselves to Death: Japanese Find the Daily Grind Can be Lethal," *Philadelphia Inquirer,* April 26, 1990, p. 1A.

[2]R. A. Webber, *Time is Money* (New York: Free Press, 1980).

[3]R. Stewart, R., "Studies of Managerial Jobs and Behaviour: The Ways Forward," *Journal of Management Studies,* 26, no. 1, (January 1989), 1–10.

[4]A. Taylor III, "How a Top Boss Manages His Day," *Fortune,* June 19, 1989, pp. 95–97.

[5]R. A. Webber, *Time and Management* (New York: Van Nostrand Reinhold, 1972).

[6]F. Allen, "Chief Executives Typically Work 60-Hour Weeks, Put Careers First," *The Wall Street Journal,* August 19, 1980, p. B1.

[7]M. Moran, "Executives Waste Time Talking on the Telephone, Survey Says," *Philadelphia Inquirer,* August 2, 1989.

[8]R. A. Webber, "U.S. Senators: See How They Run," *The Wharton Magazine,* 5, no. 2, (Winter 1980–1981), 36–43.

[9]E. E. Jennings, *The Mobile Manager* (New York: McGraw-Hill, 1971).

[10]C. B. Randall, *The Folklore of Management* (Boston: Little, Brown, 1961).

[11]J. Pfeffer and G. R. Salancik, *The External Control of Organizations* (New York: Harper & Row, 1978).

[12]L. F. McCollum, of Continental Oil Company, quoted by the editors of *Nation's Business* in *Lessons of Leadership* (Washington, D.C.: Chamber of Commerce, 1966), p. 168.

[13]D. C. McClelland, J. W. Clark, and E. L. Lowell, *The Achievement Motive* (New York: Appleton-Century-Crofts, 1953).

[14]G. A. Steiner, *Strategic Planning: What Every Manager Must Know* (New York: Free Press, 1979).

[15]R. Heilbroner, *The Future as History* (New York: Harper & Row, 1960).

[16]Discussion of planning from R. A. Webber, *Management: Basic Elements of Managing Organizations,* third edition, (Homewood, Ill: Richard D. Irwin, 1979).

[17]P. F. Drucker, *The Practice of Management* (New York: Harper, 1954).

[18]W. G. Bennis, *Organizational Development* (Reading, Ma.: Addison-Wesley, 1969).

[19]A. P. Sloan, Jr., *My Years with General Motors,* edited by J. McDonald with C. Stevens, (Garden City, N.Y.: Doubleday, 1964).

[20]J. B. Quinn, "Strategic Goals: Process and Politics," *Sloan Management Review,* (Fall, 1977), pp. 21–37.

[21]D. Kearns, *Lyndon Johnson and the American Dream* (New York: Harper & Row, 1976).

[22]W. R. Dill, T. L. Hilton and W. R. Reitman, *The New Manager: Patterns of Behavior and Development* (Englewood Cliffs, N.J.: Prentice-Hall, 1962).

[23]L. Bruce, "Winning Webs," *International Management,* (July-August, 1988), pp. 26–28.

[24]J. Trickett, "A More Effective Use of Time," *California Management Review,* 4, no. 4 (Summer, 1962) pp. 21–30.

[25]A. Lakein, *How to Get Control of Your Life and Time* (New York: Peter H. Wyden, 1973).

[26]F. S. Worthy, "How CEO's Manage Their Time, *Fortune,* January 18, 1988, pp. 88–98.

[27]E. Jones, *Essays in Applied Psychoanalysis* (London: Hogarth, 1951).

[28]Survey of executives from *Business Management,* "How 179 Chief Executives Waste Their Time," (March, 1968), pp. 12–14.

[29]M. Moran, "Executives Waste Time Talking on the Telephone, Survey Says."

[30]*The Wall Street Journal,* "Time at the Top," August 13, 1968.

[31]K. P. O'Donnell and D. Powers, *Johnny, We Hardly Knew Ye,* (Boston: Little, Brown, 1983).

[32]R. A. Webber, *Time and Management.*

[33]R. A. Mackenzie, *The Time Trap* (New York: Amacom, 1972).

CHAPTER 6: CLARIFYING DELEGATION

[1]B. B. Boyd and J. M. Jensen, "Perceptions of the First-Line Supervisor's Authority," *Academy of Management Journal,* 15, no. 3 (1972), 331–342.

[2]K. Hall and L. K. Savery, "Tight Rein, More Stress," *Harvard Business Review,* (January-February, 1986), pp. 4–7.

[3]J. P. Kotter, "Power, Dependence and Effective Management," *Harvard Business Review,* (July-August, 1979), pp. 125–136.

[4]N. R. F. Maier, "The Subordinate's Role in the Delegation Process," *Personnel Psychology,* 21 (1968), pp. 179–191.

[5]H. Sherman, *It All Depends: A Pragmatic Approach To Organization* (Tuscaloosa, Alabama: University of Alabama Press, 1966).

[6]S. E. Ambrose, *Eisenhower: The President* (New York: Simon & Schuster, 1984).

[7]On the Bay of Pigs Invasion, see A. M. Schlesinger, Jr., *A Thousand Days* (New York: Houghton Mifflin, 1965) and P. Wyden, *Bay of Pigs* (New York: Simon & Schuster, 1979).

[8]John McCloy is quoted in his obituary, *The New York Times,* March 12, 1989, p. 23(N).

[9]A. R. Dowd, "What Managers Can Learn From Manager Reagan," *Fortune,* September 15, 1986, p. 32.

[10]G. M. Boyd, "The Bush Style of Management: After Reagan, It's Back to Details," *The New York Times,* March 19, 1989, p. A-2.

[11]C. Barnard, *The Functions of the Executive* (Cambridge, Ma.: Harvard University Press, 1938).

[12.]W. Oncken, Jr. and D. L. Wass, "Management Time: Who's Got the Monkey?" *Harvard Business Review,* 52, no. 6 (November-December, 1974), 75–80.

[13]T. Taylor, *Nuremberg and Vietnam: An American Tragedy* (Chicago: Quadrangle Books, 1970).

[14]A. F. Reel, *The Case of General Yamashita* (Chicago: University of Chicago Press, 1949).

[15]C. C. Walton and F. W. Cleveland, Jr., *Corporations on Trial: The Electrical Cases* (Belmont, Ca.: Wadsworth, 1967).

[16]*The Wall Street Journal,* "Lee Iaccoca Calls Odometer Policy 'Dumb,'" July 2, 1987, p. A1.

[17]Lincoln's letter quoted in H. J. Maihafer, "The Rewards and Dangers of Overdelegating Authority," *The Wall Street Journal,* September 24, 1987, p. A1.

[18]C. C. Vance, *Boss Psychology: Help Your Boss Make You a Success* (New York: McGraw-Hill, 1976).

CHAPTER 7: GIVING ADVICE

[1]J. D. Hittle, *The Military Staff: Its History and Development* (Harrisburg, Pa.: Stackpole, Books, 1961).

[2]E. Dale and L. R. Urwick, *Staff in Organization* (New York: McGraw-Hill, 1960).

[3]R. A. Webber, *Time and Management* (New York: Van Nostrand Reinhold, 1972).

[4]L. Greiner and V. Schein, *Power and Organization Development: Mobilizing Power to Implement Change* (Reading, Ma.: Addison-Wesley, 1988).

[5]M. J. Prietula and H. A. Simon, "The Experts in Your Midst," *Harvard Business Review,* (January-February, 1989), pp. 120–124.

[6]V. Thompson, *Modern Organization* (New York: Alfred A. Knopf, 1963).

[7]P. Levinthal and M. Fichman, "Dynamics of Interorganizational Attachments: Auditor-Client Relationships," *Administrative Science Quarterly*, 33, (1988), pp. 345–369.

[8]L. B. Johnson, *The Vantage Point: Perspective of the Presidency* (New York: Holt, Rinehart & Winston, 1971).

[9]D. Kearns, *Lyndon Johnson and the American Dream* (New York: Harper & Row, 1976).

[10]D. Dalton, "Conflicts Between Staff and Line Managerial Officers," *American Sociological Review*, (June, 1950), pp. 342–351.

[11]R. H. Doktor, "Some Cognitive Implications of Academic and Professional Training," *Experimental Publication System of the American Psychological Association*, Issue No. 7, Manuscript 255, 1970.

[12]L. W. Porter, "Where is the Organization Man?" *Harvard Business Review*, (November-December, 1963), pp. 53–61.

[13]P. R. Lawrence and J. W. Lorsch, *Organization and Environment* (Boston: Harvard Graduate School of Business Administration, Harvard University, 1967).

[14]R. C. Sampson, *The Staff Role in Management* (New York: Harper & Row, 1955).

[15]G. C. Fisch, "Line-Staff is Obsolete," *Harvard Business Review*, (September-October 1961), pp. 67–79.

[16]W. French and D. Henning, "The Authority-Influence Role of the Functional Specialist in Management," *Academy of Management Journal*, 9, no. 3 (1966), 187–203.

[17]M. Maccoby, *The Gamesman* (New York: Simon & Schuster, 1976).

[18]D. A. Kolb and R. E. Boyatzis, "On the Dynamics of the Helping Relationship," in Kolb, Rubin and McIntre, eds., *Organizational Psychology: A Book of Readings* (Englewood Cliffs, N.J.: Prentice-Hall, 1974).

[19]Consultant quoted in W. Pasmore, book review, *Academy of Management EXECUTIVE*, (May 1889), p. 159.

[20]E. E. Hamilton, "The Facilitation of Organizational Change: An Empirical Study of Factors Predicting Change Agents' Effectiveness," *The Journal of Applied Behavioral Science*, 24, no. 1, (1988), 37–59.

[21]J. B. Miner, "Success in Management Consulting and the Concept of Eliteness Motivation," *Academy of Management Journal*, (September, 1971), pp. 367–378.

[22]N. J. Perry, "A Consulting Firm Too Hot To Handle?" *Fortune*, April 27, 1987, pp. 91–100.

CHAPTER 8: BEING A PROTEGE

[1] R. Halloran, "Bush Plan to Name Colin Powell to Head Joint Chiefs," *The New York Times,* August 10, 1989, p. A1(N).

[2] G. R. Roche, "Much Ado About Mentors," *Harvard Business Review (January-February, 1979), pp. 1–8.*

[3] D. J. Levinson, *The Seasons of a Man's Life* (New York: Knopf, 1978).

[4] G. Sheehy, "The Mentor Connection: The Secret Link in the Successful Woman's Life," *New York Magazine,* April 5, 1976, pp. 33–39.

[5] M. G. Zey, *The Mentor Connection* (Homewood, Ill.: Dow Jones Irwin, 1984).

[6] G. R. Roche, "Much Ado About Mentors."

[7] E. E. Jennings, *The Mobile Manager* (New York: McGraw-Hill, 1971).

[8] J. J. Gabarro and J. P. Kotter, "Managing Your Boss," *Harvard Business Review,* (January-February 1980) pp. 63–71.

[9] S. C. Bushardt, R. N. Moore and S. C. Denath, "Picking the Right Person for Your Mentor," *SAM Advanced Management Journal,* 47, no. 3 (1982), 46–51.

[10] Former Senator Barry Goldwater quoted in M. Tochin, "From Barry Goldwater Without Soft Soap, To," *The New York Times,* October 4, 1988, p. 12(N).

[11] K. E. Kram, "Phases of the Mentor Relationship," *Academy of Management Journal,* 26, no. 4 (1983), 608–625.

[12] L. Westoff, "Mentor or Lover," *Working Woman,* October, 1986, pp. 38–42. See also, J. Hearn, et al., eds., *The Sexuality of Organization* (Newbury Park, Ca.: Sage Publications, 1990).

[13] See S. Feinstein, "Women and Minority Workers in Business Find a Mentor Can Be a Rare Commodity," *The Wall Street Journal,* November 10, 1987, p. A1; B. R. Ragins, "Barriers to Mentoring: The Female Manager's Dilemma," *Human Relations,* 42, no. 1, (1989), pp. 1–22.

[14] M. Hennig and A. Jardim, *The Managerial Woman* (Garden City, N.Y.: Anchor/Doubleday, 1977).

[15] D. Thomas, "Mentoring and Irrationality: The Role of Racial Taboos," *Human Resource Management,* 28, no. 2 (1988), 279–290.

[16] K. E. Kram and L. A. Isabella, "Mentoring Alternatives: The Role of Peer Relationships in Career Development," *Academy of Management Journal,* 28, no. 1 (1985), 110–132.

[17] L. Phillips-Jones, "Establishing a Formalized Mentoring Program," *Training and Development Journal,* 37, no. 2 (February, 1983), 38–40.

[18]K. E. Kram, *Mentoring at Work* (Lanham, Maryland: University Press of America, 1988).

CHAPTER 9: LOYALTY AND WHISTLE BLOWING

[1]*The Wall Street Journal,* September 8, 1987, p. A1.

[2]W. Kiechel, "Resurrecting Corporate Loyalty, *Fortune,* December 9, 1985., pp. 207–208.

[3]P. Hirsch, *Pack Your Own Parachute - How to Survive Mergers, Takeovers and Other Corporate Disasters* (Reading, Ma.: Addison-Wesley Publishing Co., 1989).

[4]D. Wise, *The Politics of Lying* (New York: Random House, 1973).

[5]L. MacDonald, *Somme,* (New York: Atheneum, 1983).

[6]G. Melloan, "Ariel Sharon: An Israeli General's Own Story," *The Wall Street Journal,* September 7, 1989, p. A12(N).

[7]Consultant quoted in F. S. Worthy, "You're Probably Working too Hard," *Fortune,* April 27, 1987, pp. 133–140.

[8]F. S. Worthy, "You're Probably Working too Hard."

[9]Harry Levinson quoted in W. Kiechel, "Resurrecting Corporate Loyalty."

[10]H. E. Salisbury, *The 900 Days: The Siege of Leningrad* (New York: Harper and Row, 1969).

[11]H. L. Trewhitt, *McNamara: His Ordeal in the Pentagon* (New York: Harper & Row, 1971).

[12]IBM executive quoted in S. W. Gellerman, "Why 'Good' Managers Make Bad Ethical Choices," *Harvard Business Review,* (July-August, 1986), pp. 85–90.

[13]D. W. Organ, *Organizational Citizenship Behavior* (Lexington, Ma.: Lexington Books, 1988).

[14]J. Kouzes, "When Leadership Collides with Loyalty," *The New York Times,* January 24, 1988, section 3, p. 3.

[15]Business Roundtable, *Corporate Ethics: A Prime Business Asset,* (Washington, D.C.: Business Roundtable Corporate Ethics Project, February, 1988).

[16]H. Geneen and A. Moscow, *Managing* (New York: Avon, 1985).

[17]L. Maitland, "The Dean Files: Flattery in the Quest for Power," *The New York Times,* July 23, 1989, p. 16(N).

[18]S. Ramo, *The Business of Science: Winning and Losing in the High-Tech Age* (Farrar, Strauss & Girous/Hill & Wang, 1988). Quoted in *Fortune,* April 25, 1988, pp. 315–318.

[19]James Roche quoted in K. Walters, "Your Employees' Right to Blow the Whistle," *Harvard Business Review,* 53, No. 4 (1975), pp. 26–34.

[20]N. R. Kleinfield, "The Whistle Blowers' Morning After," *The New York Times,* November 9, 1986; section 3, p. 3.

[21]J. R. Emshwiller, "For Ford Engineer, Life Became Unbearable Ordeal of Inquisitions," *The Wall Street Journal,* April 14, 1988, p. B1.

[22]Age discrimination clause from 29 United States Code, 623(d) 1982.

[23]M. Brody, "Listen to Your Whistleblower," *Fortune,* November 24, 1986, pp. 77–79.

[24]R. P. Nielsen, "Changing Unethical Organizational Behavior," *The Academy of Management EXECUTIVE,* 3, no. 2, (1989), 123–130.

[25]For unfortunate political example of someone who couldn't seem to say "no," see S. Gillers, "No More Meeses," *The New York Times,* May 1, 1988, section 4, p. E27(N).

[26]A. O. Hirschman, *Exit, Voice and Loyalty: Responses to Decline in Firms, Organizations and States* (Cambridge, Ma.: Harvard University Press, 1970).

CHAPTER 10: BEING DIFFERENT IN THE ORGANIZATION

[1]E. D. Irons and G. Gilbert, *Black Managers* (New York: Praeger, 1985).

[2]A. S. Tsui and C. A. O'Reilly, III, "Beyond Simple Demographic Effects: The Importance of Relational Demography in Superior-Subordinate Dyads," *Academy of Management Journal,* 32, no. 2 (1989), 402–423.

[3]A. Jacobson, *Women in Charge* (New York: Van Nostrand Reinhold, 1985).

[4]A. L. Cowan, "Women's Gains on the Job: Not Without a Heavy Toll," *The New York Times,* August 21, 1989, p. A1.

[5]C. Leinster, "Black Executives: How They're Doing," *Fortune,* January 18, 1988, pp. 109–120.

[6]C. Leinster, "Black Executives: How They're Doing."

[7]P. V. Martin, D. Harrison and D. DiNitto, "Advancement for Women in Hierarchical Organizations: A Multilevel Analysis of Problems and Prospects," *Journal of Applied Behavioral Science,* 19, no. 1 (1983), 19–33.

[8]R. M. Kanter, "Tokenism: Opportunity or Trap?" *MBA,* January, 1978, pp. 15–21.

[9]M. J. McCarthy, "Women's Salaries Reflect Disparities in Executive Suites," *The Wall Street Journal,* December 1, 1986, p. A1.

[10]On promotions for women see L. P. Stewart and W. B. Gudykunst, "Dif-

ferential Factors Influencing the Hierarchical Level and Number of Promotions of Males and Females Within an Organization," *Academy of Management Journal,* 25, No. 3 (1982), 586–597; and A. S. Tsui and B. A. Gutek, "A Role Set Analysis of Gender Differences in Performance, Affective Relationships and Career Success in Middle Managers," *Academy of Management Journal,* 27, no. 3 (1984), 619–635.

[11]L. A. Witt, "Breadwinner vs. Non-Breadwinner Differences in Married Women's Job Satisfaction and Perceptions of Organizational Climate," *Human Relations,* 41, No. 6, (1988), 483–491.

[12]G. Sheehy, "The Mentor Connection: The Secret Link in the Successful Woman's Life," *New York Magazine,* April 5, 1976, pp. 33–39.

[13]C. C. Vance, *Boss Psychology: Help Your Boss Make You a Success* (New York: McGraw-Hill, 1976).

[14]For early reports on professional woman alone, see: C. F. Epstein, *Woman's Place: Options and Limits in Professional Careers* (Berkeley, Ca.: University of California, 1970); A. Theodore, ed., *The Professional Women* (New York: Schenkman, 1971); and B. Rosen and T. H. Jerdee, "Sex Stereotyping in the Executive Suite," *Harvard Business Review,* 52 (March-April, 1974), 45–58.

[15]C. Woman and H. Frank, "The Solo Woman in a Professional Peer Group," *American Journal of Orthopsychiatry,* 45 (January, 1975), 164–171.

[16]On conformity pressures, see: M. Sherif, "Group Influences Upon the Formation of Norms and Attitudes," in G. E. Swanson, *et al.,* eds., *Readings in Social Psychology* (New York: Holt, Rinehart, and Winston, 1952); L. Festinger, S. Schacter, and K. Back, *Social Pressures in Informal Groups* (New York: Harper and Row, 1950).

[17]D. T. Campbell, "Stereotypes and the Perception of Group Differences," *American Psychologist,* 22 (October, 1967), 818–829.

[18]K. M. Bartol, "Female Managers and Quality of Working Life: The Impact of Sex-role Stereotypes," *Journal of Occupational Behaviour,* 1, (1980), 205–221.

[19]J. S. Bruner and H. V. Perlmutter, "Compatriot and Foreigner: A Study of Impression Formation in Three Countries," *Journal of Abnormal and Social Psychology,* 55, (September, 1957), 253–260.

[20]R. A. Webber, "Majority and Minority Perceptions and Behaviors in Cross-Cultural Teams," *Human Relations,* 27, (December 1974), 873–889.

[21]D. S. Saenz, and C. G. Lord, "Reversing Roles: A Cognitive Strategy for Undoing Memory Deficits Associated with Token Status," *Journal of Personality and Social Psychology,* 56, no. 5, (1980), 698–708.

Endnotes

[22]See: M. S. Horner, "Fail: Bright Woman," *Psychology Today,* 3, (November, 1969), 36–38; and A. H. Eagley and V. J. Steffen, "Gender Stereotypes Stem From the Distribution of Women and Men into Social Roles," *Journal of Personality and Social Psychology,* 46, (1984), 735–754.

[23]R. A. Webber, "Perceptions and Behaviors in Mixed Sex Teams," *Industrial Relations,* 15, no. 2 (May, 1976), 121–129.

[24]R. A. Webber, "Changes in Perceptions and Behavior in Mixed Gender Teams," *Human Resource Management,* 26, no. 4, (Winter, 1987), 455–467.

[25]L. L. Carli, "Gender Differences in Interaction Style and Influence," *Journal of Personality and Social Psychology,* 56, no. 4, (1989), 565–576.

[26]L. Smith-Lovin and C. Brody, "Interruptions in Group Discussions: The Effects of Gender and Group Composition," *American Sociological Review,* 54, (June 1989), pp. 424–435.

[27]A. H. Eagley and W. Wood, "Inferred Sex Differences in Status as a Determinant of Gender Stereotypes About Social Influence," *Journal of Personality and Social Psychology,* 43 (1982), 915–928.

[28]G. N. Powell, *Women and Men in Management* (Newbury Park, Ca.: Sage Publications, 1988).

[29]C. K. Barnett, "Prologue: Special Issue on Women in Management, *Human Resource Management,* 26 (1987), p. 148.

[30]S. Fraker, "Why Women Aren't Getting To The Top," *Fortune,* April 16, 1984, pp. 40–45.

[31]N. J. Adler and D. Izraeli, *Women in Management Worldwide* (Armonk: M. E. Sharpe, 1987).

[32]L. L. Moore, *Not as Far as You Think,* (Lexington, Ma.: Lexington Books, 1986).

[33]Gallup poll March 1987.

[34]L. P. Stewart and W. B. Gudykunst, "Differential Factors Influencing the Hierarchical Level and Number of Promotions of Males and Females Within an Organization."

[35]K. Cannings, "Managerial Promotion: The Effects of Socialization, Specialization and Gender," *Industrial and Labor Relations Review,* 42, no. 1 (October, 1988), 77–88.

[36]E. H. Raynolds, "Management Women in the Corporate Workplace: Possibilities for the Year 2000," *Human Resource Management* 26, (1987), 265–276.

[37]A. M. Morrison, R. P. White, and E. V. Velsor, "Executive Women: Substance Plus Style," *Psychology Today,* August 1987, pp. 18–26.

[38]M. J. McCarthy, "Supreme Court to Rule on Sex-Bias Case," *The Wall*

Street Journal, June 14, 1988, p. B–1. See also, "Promoting 'Femi-nity,'" editorial, *The New York Times,* May 6, 1989, p. 34.

[39]A. M. Morrison, R. P. White, and E. V. Velsor, "Executive Women: Sub-stance Plus Style."

[40]F. E. James, "More Blacks Quitting White-Run Firms," *The Wall Street Journal,* June 7, 1988, p. A1.

[41]M. J. Williams, "Women Beat The Corporate Game," *Fortune,* Septem-ber 12, 1988, pp. 128–138.

[42]D. A. Thomas and C. P. Alderfer, "The Influence of Race on Career Dy-namics," Working Paper no, 712, Department of Management, The Wharton School, University of Pennsylvania, Philadelphia, 1987.

[43]L. Williams, "Stress of Adapting to White Society Cited as Major Cause of Hypertension in Blacks," *The Wall Street Journal,* May 5, 1986, p. B1.

[44]Poll reported in *The Wall Street Journal,* June 21, 1988, p. A1.

[45]C. Bird, *Everything a Woman Needs to Know to Get Paid What She's Worth* (New York: McKay, 1973).

[46]M. J. Williams, "Women Beat The Corporate Game," p. 138.

[47]Quoted in "Blacks Acquire Nuggets," *Philadelphia Inquirer,* July 11, 1989, p. 1D.

[48]A. B. Fisher, "Where Women Are Succeeding," *Fortune,* August 3, 1987, pp. 78–85.

CHAPTER 11: LEADING CHANGE IN SPITE OF AMBIGUOUS AUTHORITY

[1]L. R. Pondy, R. J. Boland, Jr., and H. Thomas, *Managing Ambiguity and Change* (New York: John Wiley & Sons, 1988).

[2]P. B. Vaill, *Managing as a Performing Art* (San Francisco: Jossey-Bass Publishers, 1989).

[3]J. Pfeffer, *Power in Organizations,* (Boston: Pitman, 1982).

[4]Abraham Zalesnik quoted in P. Binzen, "A New Commandment for Man-agers," *Philadelphia Inquirer,* April 9, 1984, p. 3D.

[5]J. R. P. French and B. H. Raven, "The Bases of Social Power," in D. Cart-wright, ed., *Studies in Social Power* (Ann Arbor, Mi: University of Michigan Press, 1959).

[6]H. A. Simon, *Administrative Behavior* (Glencoe, Ill: Free Press, 1957).

[7]N. W. Biggart and G. G. Hamilton, "The Power of Obedience." *Adminis-trative Science Quarterly,* 29, no. 4 (1984), 540–549.

[8]K. R. Student, "Supervisory Influence and Work-Group Performance," *Journal of Applied Psychology,* 52 (1968), 188–194.

[9]M. Maccoby, *Why Work: Leading the New Generation* (New York: Simon & Schuster, 1988).

[10]A. M. Schlesinger, Jr., *The Imperial Presidency* (New York: Houghton Mifflin, 1973).

[11]M. Weber, *The Theory of Social and Economic Organization* (Glencoe, Ill.: The Free Press, 1964).

[12]T. L. Hudson, ed., *Perspectives on Interpersonal Attraction* (New York: Academic Press, 1973).

[13]D. Bryne, *The Attraction Paradigm* (New York: Academic Press, 1971).

[14]J. MacGinnis, *Heroes* (New York: Viking Press, 1976).

[15]J. E. Mack, *A Prince of our Disorder: The Life of T. E. Lawrence* (Boston: Little, Brown, 1976).

[16]W. Manchester, *The Last Lion - Winston Spencer Churchill: Alone 1932–1949* (Boston: Little, Brown & Company, 1988).

[17]R. Bendix, *Work and Authority in Modern Industry* (New York: Wiley, 1956).

[18]J. M. Burns, *Roosevelt: The Lion and the Fox* (New York: Harcourt Brace and World, 1956).

[19]Quoted in A. Perry, "Last Active Marine From World War II Will Retire From the Corps at 62," *Los Angeles Times,* September 30, 1987, p. 1.

[20]D. Kipnis, S. M. Schmidt, C. Swaffin-Smith and I. Wilkinson, "Patterns of Managerial Influence," *Organizational Dynamics,* 12, no. 3 (1984), 58–67.

[21]R. Albanese, "Criteria for Evaluating Authority Patterns," *Academy of Management Journal,* 16, no. 1 (March 1973), 102–111.

[22]R. Michels, R., *Political Parties* (Dover Publications, 1959). Originally published in 1915.

[23]H. Guetzkow and H. Simon, "The Impact of Certain Communication Nets Upon Organization and Performance in Task-Oriented Groups," *Management Science,* 1, nos. 3 and 4 (April–July, 1955), 233–250.

[24]L. L. Roos, and R. I. Hall, "Influence Diagrams and Organizational Power," *Administrative Science Quarterly,* 25, no. 1 (1980), 57–71.

[25]D. J. Brass, "Being in the Right Place: A Structural Analysis of Individual Influence in an Organization," *Administrative Science Quarterly,* 29, no. 4 (1984), 518–539.

[26]J. Pfeffer and G. R. Salancik, *The External Control of Organizations* (New York: Harper & Row, 1978).

[27]Harry Truman quoted in C. Rossiter, *The American Presidency*, rev. ed., (New York: Harcourt Brace Jovanovich, 1960).

[28]P. Blau, *Exchange and Power in Social Life* (New York: Wiley, 1964).

[29]J. P. Kotter, *Power in Management* (New York: Amacom, 1979).

[30]V. Ries, "Influence Structure in Yugoslav Enterprise," *Industrial Relations*, 9 (1970), 148–166.

[31]M. Patchen, "Supervisory Methods and Group Performance Norms," *Administrative Science Quarterly*, (December 1962), pp. 275–293.

[32]D. M. Herold, "Two-Way Influence Processes in Leader-Follower Dyads," *Academy of Management Journal*, 20, no. 2 (1977), 224–237.

[33]R. T. Mowday, "Leader Characteristics, Self-Confidence, and Methods of Upward Influence in Organizational Decision Situations," *Academy of Management Journal*, 22, no. 4 (1980), 709–725.

[34]D. Kipnis and S. M. Schmidt, "Upward-Influence Styles: Relationship with Performance Evaluation, Salary and Stress," *Administrative Science Quarterly*, 33 (1988), 528–542.

[35]A. Sagle and D. Elizur, "Job Experience, Persuasion Strategy and Resistance to Change," *Journal of Occupational Behavior*, 6, no. 2 (1985), 157–162.

[36]L. E. Greiner, "Antecedents of Planned Change," *Journal of Applied Behavioral Science*, 3, no. 1 (1967), 51–86.

[37]J. Lash, *Roosevelt and Churchill* (New York: W. W. Norton, 1976).

[38]G. W. Prange, *At Dawn We Slept* (New York: McGraw-Hill, 1981).

[39]L. E. Greiner, "Patterns of Organization Change," *Harvard Business Review*, May-June, 1967, pp. 119–130.

[40]W. Manchester, *The Last Lion - Winston Spencer Churchill: Alone 1932–1949*.

[41]B. A. Spector, "From Bogged Down to Fired Up: Inspiring Organizational Change," *Sloan Management Review*, (Summer, 1988), pp. 29–34.

[42]Fidel Castro quoted in "Castro Says 'Traitors' Hurt Cuban Revolution," *The New York Times*, July 28, 1987, p. A3.

[43]S. Sackmann, "The Role of Metaphors in Organization Transformation," *Human Relations*, 42, no. 6, (1989), 463–485.

[44]J. M. Bartunek, "Changing Interpretive Schemes and Organizational Restructuring: The Example of a Religious Order." *Administrative Science Quarterly*, 29, no. 3 (1984), 355–372.

[45]N. M. Tichy and D. O. Urich, "A Call for the Transformational Leader," *Sloan Management Review*, 26, (Fall 1984), 59–68.

[46]S. E. Jackson and J. E. Dutton, "Discerning Threats and Opportunities," *Academy of Management Quarterly,* 33, (1988), 370–387.

[47]On unfreezing, see: K. Lewin, "Group Decision and Social Change," In T. M. Newcomb and E. L. Hartley, eds., *Readings in Social Psychology* (New York: Holt, Rinehart and Winston, 1958) and N. M. Tichy, "Agents of Planned Social Change," *Administrative Science Quarterly,* 19, no. 2 (1974), 164–182.

[48]H. Tanaka, "Power as Maximizing Behavior," *Behavioral Science,* 34, (July 1989), 199–206.

[49]I. Garfinkel, "Conditions of Successful Degradation Ceremonies," *American Journal of Sociology,* 61 (1956), 420–424.

[50]J. E. Kinkead, *In Every War But One* (New York: W.W. Norton, 1959).

[51]E. I. Schein, "The Chinese Indoctrination Program for Prisoners of War," *Psychiatry,* 19 (1956), 149–172.

[52]J. I. Porras, K. Hargis, K. J. Patterson, D. G. Maxfield, N. Roberts, and R. J. Bies, "Modeling Based Organizational Development: A Longitudinal Assessment," *Journal of Applied Behavioral Science,* 18, no. 4 (1982), 433–446.

[53]J. Zacker and M. Bard, "Effects of Conflict Management Training on Police Performance." *Journal of Applied Psychology,* 58, no. 2 (1973), 202–208.

[54]S. Wallace, "How Does Your Exercise Rate?" *The MBA,* July-August, 1977, p. 52.

[55]J. R. White, and G. Steinbeck, "Motivating Executives to Keep Physically Fit," *Harvard Business Review,* (March-April 1978), p. 16ff.

[56]W. W. Burke, *Organizational Development: Principles and Practices* (New York: Columbia University Press, 1982).

[57]P. Block, *The Empowered Manager: Positive Political Skills at Work* (San Francisco: Jossey-Bass Publishers, 1987).

[58]E. H. Schein, "Reassessing the 'Divine Rights' of Managers," *Sloan Management Review,* Winter 1989, pp. 63–68.

CHAPTER 12: BECOMING MIDDLE-AGED IN MANAGEMENT

[1]J. Solomon, "Early Retirees Fall Into Career Oblivion," *The Wall Street Journal,* March 24, 1989, p. B1.

[2]A. Howard and D. W. Bray, *Managerial Lives in Transition: Advancing Age and Changing Times* (New York: Guilford Press, 1988). For men who do well through middle age, see R. S. Weiss, *Staying the Course* (New York: The Free Press, 1990).

[3]Quote from C. Hymowitz, "Stable Cycles of Executive Careers Shattered by Upheaval in Business," *The Wall Street Journal,* May 26, 1987, p. B1.

[4]D. J. Levinson, *The Seasons of a Man's Life* (New York: Knopf, 1978).

[5]R. L. Katz, "Skills of An Effective Administrator," *Harvard Business Review,* (September-October, 1974), pp. 90–102.

[6]M. R. Louis, "Managing Career Transition: A Missing Link in Career Development," *Organizational Dynamics,* 10, no. 4 (1982), 68–77.

[7]F. Byrom, quoted in *Fortune,* July 1976, p. 184.

[8]L. Reibstein, "The Not-So-Fast Track: Firms Try Promoting Hotshots More Slowly," *The Wall Street Journal,* March 24, 1986, p. B1.

[9]J. W. Lorsch and H. Takagi, "Keeping Managers Off The Shelf," *Harvard Business Review,* (July-August, 1986), pp. 60–65.

[10]C. Hymowitz, "Stable Cycles of Executive Careers Shattered by Upheaval in Business."

[11]T. P. Ference, "The Career Plateau: Facing Up to Life at the Middle," *The MBA,* July-August 1977, pp. 21–22.

[12]L. W. Porter, "Where is the Organization Man?" *Harvard Business Review,* (November-December, 1963), pp. 53–61.

[13]P. C. Chew, *The Inner World of the Middle-Aged Man* (New York: Macmillan, 1976).

[14]S. Berglass, *The Success Syndrome* (New York: Plenum, 1986).

[15]D. LaBier, *Modern Madness: The Emotional Fallout of Success,* (Reading, Ma.: Addison-Wesley, 1986).

[16]Douglas LaBier quoted in D. Goleman, "The Stange Agony of Success," *The New York Times,* August 24, 1986, section 3, p. 1.

[17]E. Erikson, "Identity and the Life Cycle," *Psychological Issues,* 1, no. 1, (1959).

[18]See J. M. Bardwick, "Plateauing and Productivity," *Sloan Management Review,* 24, no. 3 (1980), pp. 67–73; and P. M. Connolly, *Promotional Practices and Policies: Career Building in the 80's* (New York: Pergamon, 1988).

[19]P. Thome, "The Causes and Effects of Middle-Aged Blues," *International Management,* June 1989, p. 66.

[20]G. E. Vaillant, *Adaptation to Life* (Boston: Little, Brown, 1977).

[21]U. E. Gattiker and L. Larwood, "Predictors for Managers' Career Mobility, Success and Satisfaction, *Human Relations,* 41, no. 8, (1988), 569–591.

[22]O. Rank, *Art and Artist: Creative Urge and Personality Development,* (New York: Knopf, 1932).

[23]J. Viorst, *Necessary Losses* (New York: Simon & Schuster, 1986).

[24]E. Becker, *The Denial of Death* (New York: The Free Press, 1973).

[25]D. G. Winter, *The Power Motive,* (New York: The Free Press, 1973).

[26]M. Maccoby, *Why Work: Leading the New Generation* (New York: Simon & Schuster, 1988).

[27]M. F. R. Kets de Vries, "Prisoners of Leadership," *Human Relations,* 41, no. 3 (1988), 261–280.

[28]S. R. Connor and J. S. Fielden, "Rx for Managerial 'Shelf Sitters'," *Harvard Business Review,* (November-December 1973), pp. 113–120.

[29]J. Sonnenfeld, *The Hero's Farewell: What Happens When CEO's Retire* (New York: Oxford University Press, 1988).

[30]K. Dychtwald, *Age Wave: The Challenges and Opportunities of an Aging America* (Jeremy P. Tarcher, 1989).

[31]J. T. McCay, *The Management of Time* (Englewood Cliffs, N.J.: Prentice-Hall, 1959).

[32]W. Kiechel, "The Ages of a Manager," *Fortune,* May 11, 1987, pp. 170–171.

[33]F. Bartolome and P. A. L. Evans, "Must Success Cost So Much?" *Harvard Business Review,* (March-April 1980), pp. 137–148.

[34]B. F. Blake, et al., "The Effect of Ambiguity Upon Product Perceptions," *Journal of Applied Psychology,* 58, No. 2 (1973), 239–243.

[35]T. H. White, *Breach of Faith: The Fall of Richard Nixon* (New York: Atheneum Press, 1975).

[36]On creativity see: H. Anderson, ed., *Creativity and Its Cultivation* (New York: Harper, 1959); and C. W. Taylor, *Climate for Creativity* (New York: Pergamon, 1973).

[37]R. E. Hill and E. L. Miller, "Job Change and the Middle Seasons of a Man's Life," *Academy of Management Journal,* 24, no. 1 (1981), 114–127.